Transnational Celebrity
Activism in Global Politics

Transnational Celebrity Activism in Global Politics

Changing the World?

Edited by Liza Tsaliki, Christos A. Frangonikolopoulos and Asteris Huliaras

intellect Bristol, UK / Chicago, USA

First published in the UK in 2011 by
Intellect, The Mill, Parnall Road, Fishponds, Bristol, BS16 3JG, UK

First published in the USA in 2011 by
Intellect, The University of Chicago Press, 1427 E. 60th Street,
Chicago, IL 60637, USA

A catalogue record for this book is available from the
British Library.

Cover designer: Holly Rose
Copy-editor: Integra Software Services
Typesetting: Mac Style, Beverley, E. Yorkshire

ISBN 978-1-84150-349-3

Printed and bound by Gutenberg Press, Malta.

Contents

Introduction

The Challenge of Transnational Celebrity Activism: Background, Aim and Scope of the Book

Liza Tsaliki, Christos Frangonikolopoulos and Asteris Huliaras

The development of a new cultural vocabulary, wherein 'celebrityhood' holds a preeminent position, indicates the pervasiveness of celebrity culture in our everyday lives and popular culture. Celebrities, pretty much like stars, can be seen as persons who, in the eyes of other members of the society, are especially remarkable and attract universal attention despite the fact that they usually hold limited or non-existent institutional power; in fact, as we shall argue in this volume, we have entered a new era where celebrities increasingly occupy institutional positions of power – in this case through activist, diplomatic and charity initiatives.

In this context then, and taking a cue from Alberoni (2007), perhaps in present day society, which is marked by a high level of interdependence, celebrities can provide a common point of reference for all without the institutional barriers that would separate, for example, the king or nobles from their lay public. Celebrities attract unconditional admiration and interest and are usually credited with capacities superior to those of other people, as a result of which they are invested with a Weberian (1968: 241) charisma. It is this notion of charisma, in conjunction with a number of converging factors, such as the recent rise of philanthrocapitalism, a climate of political correctness, a strong civil society among many western states where volunteering is firmly grounded, as well as the West's collective guilt over its accumulated wealth compared to Third World suffering, which make celebrities amenable to becoming advocates of activist causes on human poverty.

The economy of celebrity culture, says Graham Turner (2004), dictates that celebrities develop a strategy for building and maintaining consumer (i.e. audience) loyalty by forging and safeguarding a symbiotic relationship with the media; taking this further, we suggest that celebrity activism and charity may be interpreted as part and parcel of this symbiosis, whereby the celebrity persona is this all-round individual who, apart from feeding publicity events to the media upon mundane matters such as their latest show, film, album, romance, vacation and the like, also takes active interest in 'heavy artillery' matters such as Third World debt, world famine, child soldiers or the vaccination of children in Africa. Then, when the publicity frenzy focuses on the individual celebrity, the good cause gets maximum media coverage and exposure as well.

Perhaps, this is one way for the celebrity industry to develop a facet of social corporate responsibility – when it capitalizes heavily on the likes of the Brangelina couple (active in Congo, Ethiopia and Sudan among other countries), Coldplay's Chris Martin (in Ghana where the singer works on fair trade on behalf of Oxfam), Jay-Z (in Nigeria, where the rap idol and spouse of Beyonce is also renowned for supporting a United Nations' project for drinkable water), actress Natalie Portman (in Uganda, following a documentary on gorillas in Rwanda, where she supports FINCA, a charity providing funding to remote communities around the globe), football legend Pele (in Egypt, where he supports the Littlest Lamb charity, which has recently set up an orphanage), and many others, including Prince Harry, His Highness Albert of Monaco and Carla Bruni-Sarkozy, to put the message across continents. As a result, drawing from a previous era when film stars operated as a means to promote consumer capitalism (Turner 2004) – a process initiated in the 1930s and 1940s and continued to this date – celebrity activism can be seen, we suggest, as a way to negotiate the promotion of philanthrocapitalism and environmentalism across the globe.

Although a system for celebrity creation has been in place firmly since the birth of mass commercial culture, public visibility of celebrities has grown considerably as a result of new mechanisms for garnering attention – i.e. SNSs, microblogging.[1] Changes in the organization of publicity and in technology have had a profound impact on the operation of celebrity, already since the mid-nineteenth century, where celebrity was established as a mass phenomenon through newspapers and the telegraph; whereas in the first half of the twentieth century, the myth that fame was a 'natural cream-rising-to the-top phenomenon' largely reigned, around 1950, changes in the celebrity-building system (i.e. breakdown of studio control, rise of television, a boom in the supply of celebrities) destabilized the prevailing celebrity discourse and the publicity enterprise invited audiences as insiders to the publicity game itself (Gamson 1992/2007: 142).

Although today the relationship between audience–celebrity is close and clearly articulated compared to earlier times (which means that audiences of today are aware of the manufactured nature of the celebrity images they consume and of the publicity machine that engulfs these images as opposed to the less media-savvy audiences of the early celebrity texts during the first half of the twentieth century), we argue that the extent to which audiences are suspicious of celebrities' interior motives (i.e. quest for self-exposure, capitalization of a noble cause for self promotion etc.) when it comes to embracing altruistic objectives is debatable, and it is to this end that targeted qualitative audience research is needed.

Taking Gamson's argument further (1992/2007), we also argue that we should, perhaps, read the emerging narrative of celebrity activism as an attempt at establishing a greater sense of connection and intimacy between the famous and their admirers, pretty much as was the case in the 1930s and 1940s when celebrity publicity was presented as containing a blown-up version of the 'typical' (i.e. 'normal', mainstream) way of life (1992/2007: 146). By viewing celebrities as part of the same civil society who, like the rest of us, do charitable work and raise awareness on sensitive and noble human causes, we essentially perceive them as 'ordinary' folks, thus collapsing the distance between us and them. In fact, the development of celebrity activism may be the latest manifestation of the revised relationship between fame and achievement,[2] whereby celebrities need to perform achievements (through activism and charity) in order to retain fame. In this context, the 'celebrity in the public interest' narrative justifies the opulence and extravagance the lives of celebrities are often associated with in the eyes of the public, where the celebrity gives something back (to the people, to the community) through various institutional initiatives of activism and charity. It is possible, then, that alongside rising skepticism and cynicism about the connection between celebrity and authenticity in the latter part of the twentieth century, and the awareness of the systematic production of celebrity images and culture for commercial purposes, we, the audience, still want to read unstaged and spontaneous good deeds into celebrity actions – as a result, celebrities, despite being artificially generated, deserve our respect and adoration. In this context, celebrities, much like stars, may be seen to serve an ideological function, articulating ideas about personhood and individualism in a capitalist society, and illustrating both the promise and perils that the notion of individuality entails for all of us as entities upon which social forces act (Dyer 1979/1998, 1986).

Arguably, then, in celebrity engagement with politics, we witness an inversion of the compensatory role of the star. Dyer's account of the stars' ability to compensate for qualities absent from people's lives (1979/1998) is based on the premise that compensation is not synonymous with the revival of a value or quality under threat, but, instead, implies that attention shifts from that particular value, to another, lesser, 'compensatory' one. Dyer sees in compensation the shift from active involvement in business, politics and the productive sphere to active involvement in leisure and consumption. In this light, celebrities perform a 'compensatory' role as they render the *consumption* of politics and activism an attractive imperative by instigating activist engagement and motivating public endorsement of their cause, while concurrently reinforcing their image as 'doers of good'.

Having said that, the ironic knowingness of the artificiality of celebrityhood is not necessarily problematic as celebrities are often caught 'simultaneously mocking and indulging their icon status' (Gitlin 1989 cited in Gamson 1992/2007: 152); on one level, the mocking of glamour by celebrities themselves serves to deconstruct them in the eyes of their public, while, on another, the constant visibility of publicity mechanisms works to offer the public the position of control. Is it possible then, we ask, that this awareness of celebrity artificiality and self-mockery may serve, in effect, to engage audiences with celebrities, making the plight of celebrity activism more pervasive and effective, as audiences, conscious of the orchestrated nature of the campaigns, may see the sincerity and gravity of the plight itself, past the artificial image?

Well, not everybody would agree with such a notion. Nick Couldry and Tim Markham (2007) argue that those who follow celebrity culture are the least engaged in politics anyway and the least likely to use their social networks to involve themselves in action or discussion about positive-type issues. More specifically, there is intense debate, the argument goes, between those who fear absolute decline in politics as a transformative force (for example, Gitlin 1998; Giroux 2001), and those who argue that politics is being renewed and further democratized by popular culture (Corner and Pels 2003; Van Zoonen 2005, among others). In this debate, celebrity culture is of particular interest since celebrities serve as role models for millions, and are increasingly involved and used by politicians to further political narratives. In effect, as Corner and Pels argue, with traditional forms of ideological or partisan allegiances being substituted by a pull towards post-ideological lifestyle choices, aesthetics and style overtake more traditional forms of political engagement. Celebrity culture, which then follows, is arguably an essential component of public debate regarding issues that require public resolution, as the proliferation of celebrity culture means that it can no longer be dismissed as external to the world of public issues (Rojek 2001; Turner 2006). This, echoing Walter Benjamin (1973), may also mean that in the current era where politics is aestheticized, political activism may merely serve as a prop to extend celebrity aura and its reproducibility.

Having said that, the extent to which celebrity culture is connected to the broader realm of public and political issues – perceived as something broader than traditional party politics – remains to be explored. Based on qualitative and quantitative research findings in the UK, Couldry and Markham take up a skeptical approach to claims that celebrity culture in the broad sense may contribute positively to political engagement and question our understanding of popular culture (of which celebrityhood is a part) and politics (of which activism is a part); they contend that we should refrain from making presumptions about the positive political resonance of celebrity narratives to the people's public connection. Indeed, if Couldry and Markham are correct and those who follow celebrity culture are also the least likely to be politically engaged, then the entire edifice regarding the sensitization and mobilization of the wider public about the issues that contemporary celebrity activism stands for is bound to crumble. Hence, as Turner has pointed out (2006), there is a problematic relationship between celebrity culture's 'demotic' turn and prospects for democratic renewal and political and social change, which means that the impact of celebrity activism may be more limited and problematic than what we would like to think.

On the other hand, what is still open to interpretation, and calls for further empirical investigation, is the pedagogic potential of celebrities within the realm of activism. One of the reasons for maintaining a celebrity culture argues David Marshall, is that celebrity has been a pedagogical aid in the discourse of the self, serving as beacon of the public world for much of the twentieth century (2010); celebrity taught generations how to engage and use consumer culture to 'make' oneself by defining the Zeitgeist of any particular moment (Marshall 2010: 36): from hairstyles and sartorial styles to celebrity gossip on the narratives of divorce, drunkenness, personal deviance, violence, affairs and many other stories, the pedagogy of the celebrity has served to articulate a public sphere different from the one constructed through the official culture, and thus heightening the affective connection of celebrities to an audience (Marshall 2010: 37). Would it be too naïve then to expect celebrities to be able to *teach* audiences about activism and charity worldwide as well as to generate a following for their charitable causes as massive as Ashton Kutcher's famous Twitter–CNN race[3]?

Aim and scope of this book

This is the contextual framework within which this volume on transnational celebrity activism is set, as celebrities have been playing an increasingly important role in the process of global politics over the past few years. Angelina Jolie, Brad Pitt, Mia Farrow and Bob Geldoff, to take just a few examples, are prominent in their humanitarian work and political activism across the globe, and, through their actions, have brought attention to a wide variety of issues and causes to an increasingly linked global audience. Having said that, it is worth clarifying that this book, although engaged with the intersection between politics and celebrity spectacle, is not concerned about celebrity politicians of the likes of Barak Obama.[4]

Celebrity activism, however, and despite the fact that it is evolving into an ever-growing internationally visible phenomenon, still remains an under-researched theme within academia. Overall, the literature on the role of individuals who are not state agents is meagre in both size and depth; while the role of statesmen has become an object of analysis within the domain of foreign policy analysis; the impact of individuals who are not agents of political authority has received scant, if any, attention, and we hope to have worked towards filling this void with the present volume on transnational celebrity activism.

So far, there is only one directly relevant work that has so far dealt with celebrities in global politics – Andrew F. Cooper's *Celebrity Diplomacy* (2008), the work of a former diplomat who examines ways in which celebrity activism is changing the *nature* of diplomatic practice. There is also work that brings together and examines:

1. **Media and celebrity culture**, with emphasis on the history and mechanisms of fame, the place of celebrity in the circulation of power and consumption, the effect of celebrity on the economy and the incursion of celebrity into politics and the academy. Among them are: Leo Braudy, *The Frenzy of Renown: Fame and Its History* (New York: Vintage Books, 1997); John Corner and Dick Pels, *Media and the Restyling of Politics: Consumerism, Celebrity and Cynicism* (London: Sage, 2003); Tyler Cowen, *What Price Fame?* (Cambridge MA: Harvard UP, 2000); Carl Freedman, 'Polemical Afterword: Some Brief Reflections on Arnold Schwarzenegger and on Science Fiction in Contemporary American Culture', *PMLA* 119.3 (2004): 539–46; Joshua Gamson, *Claims to Fame: Celebrity in Contemporary America* (London: University of California Press, 1994); David P. Marshall, *Celebrity and Power: Fame in Contemporary Culture*, (Minneapolis: University of Minnesota Press, 1997); Sharon O'Dair, 'Stars, Tenure and the Death of Ambition', *Michigan Quarterly Review* 36.4 (1997): 607–27; David Shumway, 'The Star System Revisited', *Minnesota Review: A Journal of Committed Writing* 52–54 (2001): 175–84; Graeme Turner, Frances Bonner and P. David Marshall, *Fame Games: The Production of Celebrity in Australia* (Cambridge: Cambridge University Press, 2000); Graeme Turner, *Understanding Celebrity* (London: Sage, 2004); Liesbet Van Zoonen, *Entertaining the Citizen: When Politics and Popular Culture Converge* (Lanham: Rowman & Littlefield, 2005); Darrell M. West and John Orman, *Celebrity Politics* (Upper Saddle River: Prentice Hall, 2003); Sean Redmond and Su Holmes, *Stardom and Celebrity: A Reader* (London: Sage, 2007); Su Holmes and Sean Redmond, *Framing Celebrity: New Directions in Celebrity Culture* (London: Routledge, 2006).

2. **Case studies from a political science or media studies view**. These include: Joshua William Busby, 'Bono Made Jesse Helms Cry: Jubilee 2000, Debt Relief, and Moral Action in International Politics', *International Studies Quarterly*, 51 (2007): 247–275; Geoffrey Allen Pigman and John Kotsopoulos, '"Do This One For Me, George": Blair, Brown, Bono, Bush and the "Actor-ness" of the G8', *The Hague Journal of Diplomacy*, 2 (2007): 127–145; Lisa Ann Richey and Stefano Ponte, 'Better (Red)TM than Dead? Celebrities, consumption and international aid', *Third World Quarterly*, 29.4 (2008): 711–729. Also interesting are: Jo Littler, '"I feel your pain": cosmopolitan charity and the public fashioning of the celebrity soul', *Social Semiotics*, 18.2 (2008): 237–251; Kate Nash, 'Global citizenship as show business: the cultural politics of Make Poverty History', *Media, Culture & Society*, 30.2 (2008): 167–181; Gary Armstrong, 'The global footballer and the local-war zone: George Weah and Transnational Networks in Liberia, West Africa', *Global Networks*, 7.2 (2007): 230–247; William J. Brown et al. 'Social Influence of an International Celebrity: Responses to the Death of Princess Diana', *Journal of Communication*, December 2003: 587–605; Bob Clifford, 'Merchants of Morality', *Foreign Policy*, March–April 2002: 36–45; Michael P. Marks and Zachary Fisher, 'The King's new bodies: Simulating Consent in the Age of Celebrity', *New Political Science*, 24.3 (2002): 371–394.

3. **The role of individuals in public diplomacy**: for example, Paola Grenier, 'The New Pioneers: The People Behind Global Civil Society', in Helmut Anheier, Marlies Glasius and Mary Kaldor (eds), *Global Civil Society 2004/5*, London: Sage, 2004, pp. 122–157; Philip G. Cerny, 'Political Agency in a Globalizing World: Towards a Structurational Approach', *European Journal of International Relations*, 6.4 (2000): 435–463; Kiyoteru Tsutsui and Christine Min Wotipka, 'Global Civil Society and the International Human Rights Movement: Citizen Participation in Human Rights International Nongovernmental Organizations', *Social Forces*, 83.2 (2004): 587–620; Sidney Tarrow, 'Rooted Cosmopolitans and Transnational Activists', *Rassegna Italiana di Sociologia*, No. 2 (2005).

Bearing this in mind, and taking Andrew Cooper's work on *Celebrity Diplomacy* (2008) as a starting point, this book aims at taking this line of analysis further by bringing together a number of theoretical and empirical approaches on celebrity activism and global politics.

More specifically, we endeavour to analyse and present what we know so far on the *causes*, *methods* and *consequences* of celebrity activism in contemporary global politics. By examining the different backgrounds and dynamics of celebrity activists (Hollywood, the music industry, etc.), as well as how they promote their causes, mobilize public support and media attention, the following issues have been raised and problematized:

1. Is celebrity activism emerging into a distinct influential factor in international politics, or is it merely an extension (or a new dimension) of those figures' public relations and image-making strategies? In this respect, we wish to probe the extent to which celebrities truly hold the cultural power to re-focus and direct inter/national spotlights on their causes of choice, or whether their claims are mere expressions of enormous egos.

2. Are celebrities capable of making governments review aspects of their policies, or does their activism represent little more than an ephemeral political engagement in order to constantly stay in the spotlight? Here we investigate whether celebrities are able to direct public attention to a certain political cause and sustain that attention long enough to ensure measurable lasting change.

Beyond these questions of influence and authenticity, this book also investigates whether some celebrity initiatives re-enact the very mechanisms of oppression they ostensibly seek to dismantle; for example, whether their humanitarian efforts may reify relationships of inequity between the West and the Rest, reinforcing, through a refracted lens, colonial narratives. In this context, we also discuss

3. Whether celebrity activism is principled and strategically designed towards highlighting certain issues and shaping the international agenda, or whether it merely follows headline news.
4. The role celebrities play in raising awareness of political issues (global poverty, AIDS, etc.) and
5. The way in which celebrity activists are perceived by civil society and the media, both in developing and developed countries.

Our volume takes an *interdisciplinary, crosscultural* approach, linking theoretical considerations to more empirically based case studies; our contributors themselves comprise an interesting multi-cultural, inter-disciplinary, transnational mosaic of academics and allow for an inspiring, vibrant mixture of well-established and young aspiring researchers and critics.

Book structure

Following this introductory chapter, the book is divided into four sections, each one fleshing out a different perspective of celebrity activism. **Section One** extrapolates upon the relationship between '*Transnational Celebrity Activism, Diplomacy and Global Politics*'. Huliaras and Tzifakis, in the chapter 'Bringing the individuals back in? Celebrities as transnational activists', set up a theoretical framework for considering the phenomenon of celebrity activism. The authors unpack the kinds of issues that mobilize celebrities and ponder on the extent to which celebrity activism is effective in advancing global causes. To this avail, they first discuss the international relations literature on the role of individuals and suggest general hypotheses on the factors that may turn these influential individuals into accomplished transnational activists; they then offer a second set of hypotheses that try to make sense of the growth of celebrity activism before they analyse its impact in terms of public awareness, fund-raising and political lobbying.

Mark Wheeler celebrates the success of the institution of the UN Goodwill Ambassadors and raises the issue of how celebrities can be seen as part of a new 'pseudo politics' designed to undermine civic engagement in 'Celebrity Politics and Cultural Citizenship: UN Goodwill Ambassadors and Messengers of Peace'. Wheeler discusses the extent to which celebrity endorsements affect political behaviour by focusing on how the United Nations has utilized its Goodwill Ambassadors and Messengers of Peace to draw international media attention to their activities. He demonstrates how celebrities can provide focus for their causes, thereby transcending other agencies of social authority and thus become integral in the sphere of political communication. In order to address questions regarding celebrities' effectiveness or counter-productiveness in shaping political agendas, Wheeler assesses the worth of the 'celebritization' of the political process by providing information on the origins, development and employment of UN Goodwill Ambassadors and Messengers of Peace, and considering how the UN and its agencies have developed their celebrity relations from ad-hoc to fully fledged systems of political campaigning. He argues that the celebritization of politics should not be dismissed as an erosion of culture, but must be viewed within the framework of a change in political aesthetics in which there will be both positive and negative outcomes. In fact, he continues, the UN experience counters the accusation of star passivity as celebrities have promoted new or alternative discourses, and, while their activities have been mixed, they have affected credible interventions within international policy circles.

Annika Bergman Rosamond follows in a chapter that engages with the wider research question whether celebrity activism is developing into a distinct influential factor in international politics, or whether it is it merely an extension of those figures' public relations and image-making strategies. The chapter 'The cosmopolitan–communitarian divide and celebrity anti-war activism', focuses on celebrity contestations of prevailing security cultures, discourses and practices in global politics, and the extent to which celebrities can shift the boundaries of ethical responsibility to include their fellow citizens as well as those of other nations. A key argument put forth here is that individual celebrity promotion of universal human rights, global peace projects and redistributive justice across borders is consistent with cosmopolitanism's privileging of the rights of individuals over those of sovereign states. Having presented some of the dilemmas emerging from the communitarian–cosmopolitan debate in international relations the chapter turns to the role of individuals in global politics. It takes the view that celebrities are communicative agents who raise awareness surrounding issues of global obligation and help legitimize certain courses of action. At best, celebrities evoke a sense of ethical obligation to distant others, and, at worst, they give rise to donor fatigue or public reluctance to consider the negative effects of global poverty, sexual violence, ethnic and religious repression in faraway places. The chapter then looks at the way in which three American celebrities have used their star status to communicate their anti-war message to global and national audiences and, in so doing, portrayed themselves as possible candidates for moral agency in global politics.

Section Two addresses *'Celebrity Activism and Conflict'*. The chapter 'Can Celebrity Save Diplomacy? Appropriating Wisdom through *The Elders*' by Henk Huijser and Jinna Tay, points to the blurring of the line between politician and celebrity, and contends this is a positive development, one connected to profound shifts in diplomacy. The authors explore the role of 'celebrity diplomacy' as a specific form of 'celebrity activism' through the Elders – an initiative introduced by Peter Gabriel and Richard Branson in July 2007, which aims to resurrect the function of elders in traditional societies, as modelled on the role and status of elders in African village societies, and counts among its members the likes of Desmond Tutu, Jimmy Carter, Kofi Annan, Mary Robinson and Nelson Mandela. The authors ask whether the celebrity status of the Elders, as well as that of their founders, limits them to awareness-raising alone, or whether they can effect meaningful change and a shift in the way diplomacy operates on a global level. This is based on the fact that none of the Elders holds public office, which means that they may work for the common good rather than external political interests, and as a result they may be able to overcome the considerable limitations of the current context of political diplomacy. On top of this, the Elders may avoid some of the connotations of 'celebrity activism' as something that celebrities do as an image-building exercise, since all of them are well past the need for image building. Huijser and Tay argue that while 'celebrity' has the potential to create awareness, raise much-needed funds, and drive 'political action', concurrently, it is firmly wedded to contemporary politics of entertainment and media consumption, and thus its ability to effect structural change in global politics is significantly curtailed.

Roy Krøvel's chapter, 'Fighting superior military power in Chiapas, Mexico: Celebrity activism and its limitations', provides a strong, insider's look at the relationship of celebrities and the Zapatistas, suggesting that stars have an important impact, at least temporarily in promoting political causes. He offers a critical insight of the Chiapas conflict as covered by the author himself and analyses the celebrity activism attracted by the Zapatistas. Krøvel puts the violent events in Chiapas into a historical perspective, trying to evaluate practices of celebrity activism, before returning to the debate on celebrity diplomacy in the light of the Chiapas events. Taking Huliaras and Tzifakis (2008) as his starting point, he elaborates on the dynamics of celebrity activism in order to facilitate analysis of the interaction between celebrities and the solidarity movement in Chiapas; he then uses Chandler's understanding of celebrity activists in Chiapas as 'illusory participants' (2004, 2007) and Tarrow's notion of 'rooted cosmopolitans' (2005) to enhance our understanding of celebrity advocacy in Chiapas. This is followed by extensive empirical research of media representations of the Zapatistas movement based on content analysis of newspaper articles and online reporting from various NGOs, as well as on personal interviews. The author concludes that the Zapatistas case shows that celebrity activism must be understood in close relationship to social movements, both local and global NGOs and networks of solidarity activists, and that much more investigation is needed on the interplay between celebrities and activists, especially in cases like Chiapas where the causes embraced are overtly political. He also calls for a broader understanding of celebrities, one that includes other, less famous, individuals than Hollywood stars.

A somewhat different dimension of celebrity activism is offered by Evanthis Hatzivassiliou and Georgios Kazamias in a chapter on Spiro S. Skouras in the 1940s and 1950s, providing useful historical context and presenting Skouras' transnational initiatives as having limited success. In 'Hollywood Goes to the Eastern Mediterranean: Spiro S. Skouras and 'Unorthodox Power', *1940s and 1950s*', the authors take the view that diplomacy remains a more narrowly defined function, one that requires official representation and official roles in the settlement of international problems and presents an early attempt at celebrity activism in the case study of Spiro S. Skouras, President of 20th Century Fox in the mid-twentieth century. The authors treat Skouras as an early example of transnational activism within the emerging post-war order in Greece, rather than the manifestation of an emerging 'Greek lobby' in the US or a case of informal diplomacy, and raise questions regarding the ability of celebrities to accurately understand what is at stake regardless of their commitment to a cause. His failure, as a lone rider, it is argued, is indicative of a lack of one the preconditions of success for later forms of celebrity activism, namely, an external 'enabling factor', such as UN concurrence, or the support of an important NGO, and go on to suggest that even at this early stage celebrity diplomacy was more likely to be successful in *humanitarian* crises rather than in purely political ones.

Drawing on convincing empirical data, Virgil Hawkins suggests in the chapter 'Creating a Groundswell or Getting on the Bandwagon? Celebrities, the Media and Distant Conflict', that marketing potential has a profound shape on celebrities' choices of humanitarian initiatives and that the works are not likely to bring sustained attention to a conflict or issue. Hawkins raises questions upon the impact and the reasons celebrities have for deciding to support certain conflict situations over others. In an attempt to explore whether celebrities really manage to pluck conflict-related humanitarian crises from obscurity and place them front and centre in the public agenda, Hawkins investigated the links between celebrity activism and media coverage in the USA in response to the conflict in Darfur and the Democratic Republic of Congo (DRC); his research covered critical periods of media attention and/ or celebrity involvement of US newspapers, as well as network and cable news transcripts, including both 'hard news' (the main news programmes) and 'soft news' programmes (such as ABC's *20/20*, CBS's *60 Minutes*, NBC's *Dateline*, CNN's *Showbiz Tonight*). He identified that one problem with celebrity attempts to draw attention to a conflict situation is that the attention generated generally ends up being focused on the celebrity him/herself, with the issue the celebrity is trying to draw attention to remaining at the background issue. Hawkins concludes that the impact of celebrities in drawing attention to foreign conflicts is not as powerful as is often assumed. In the short term, stories about celebrity activism in response to conflicts occasionally became news stories, and caused a very brief rise in coverage, although in the long term, it seems that even increasingly active celebrities may not be able to increase or sustain media or public interest in faraway conflicts.

Section Three ponders on '*Celebrity Activism, Global Humanitarianism and the Global South*'. Sue Tait's chapter 'Consuming ethics: conflict diamonds, the entertainment industry and celebrity activism' appears to agree with the previous argument, and looking at the example of 'blood diamonds', suggests that some initiatives elide their own complicity in exploitation, as well as that of consumer culture more generally. Tait discusses the politicization of conflict diamonds by the Hollywood and hip hop industry, by focusing on the film *Blood Diamond* and the documentary *Bling: A Planet Rock*. Set within a context of consumer capitalism, her analysis argues that the role of celebrity activists, who may have no special knowledge of a humanitarian issue, should be to provide models for public action. She proposes two axes of analysis, one guided by the work of Ngwarsungu Chiwengo regarding the way in which suffering of some victims is made to matter over the suffering of others, and how the entertainment industry has rendered the issue of conflict diamonds an issue of global public concern. The other is based on Bhikhu Parekh's concept of globally oriented citizenship in order to explore celebrity advocacy and evaluate the potential of specific media texts to enable publics to bear witness to suffering. Tait critiques popular cultural responses to the issue of conflict diamonds on the basis that they channel the ethical burden of western/northern audiences through the prism of consumption, covering over broader inequities within systems of global capitalism and calls for shifting globally oriented citizenship beyond fashion.

The role of celebrities is further politicized by Riina Yrjölä who discounts the beneficial effects of star initiatives off-hand, also seeing them as participating in the violence and oppression they ostensibly seek to alleviate. In the chapter 'The Embodied and Embedded Politics of Celebrity Humanitarianism', the author critically examines the different visual and textual representations of Bob Geldof and Bono in the British media in order to unplug the suitability and accuracy of celebrity humanitarian actions. She argues that no specific empirical research exists on celebrities' media representations on Africa, and that neither the ways in which celebrities act and represent the African poor to global citizens, nor what kind of truths celebrities create themselves have been questioned. This is happening because whereas the previous generation of celebrity activists, in the 1960s, were engaged in anti-war activism, perceived as openly political and radical, present-day celebrity activists are perceived as having undertaken an ethical action aiming at a more humane, co-operative and peaceful global world; as a result, because their campaigns are fundamentally moral, doubting the rightness of celebrity humanitarianism has become increasingly difficult, if not impossible. The chapter then proceeds to examine how Geldof and Bono – the two most visible spokespersons acting on behalf of Africa – are constituted in the British media as legitimate humanitarian actors and truth-tellers, and to analyse how 'Africa' and its place in a world system becomes produced through these discourses.

This chapter is followed by another case study in celebrity activism, this time focusing on a contemporary celebrity and popular culture icon, Madonna. Graham Finlay calls for a higher standard of celebrity activism, one motivated by respect for democratic practice, in 'Madonna's Adoptions: Celebrity Activism, Justice and Civil Society in the Global South', and touches upon the politically and ethically sensitive issue of the adoption of children from under-privileged countries by present-day celebrities. Acknowledging that it is exactly this blurring of the distinction between personal and public lives that makes celebrity activism identifiable, he addresses two issues regarding Madonna's adoptions, which reflect on the role of celebrities in the Global South and the role of 'civil society' as developed by northern NGOs and in the Global South itself: the first problem is one of justice, raising ethical questions about individual responsibility to alleviate global poverty, what kind of actions produce the best outcomes, and what distributive effects those actions have; the second is one of democracy as celebrities have been accused of undermining democracy because of their lack of democratic legitimacy and accountability and because they distract from the details of the issues involved. Finlay analyses these charges against celebrity activism from the point of view of democratic theory and international distributive justice. He argues that despite democratic concerns about the role of unelected NGOs and civil society networks, the benefits of celebrity child adoption are complicated by the need for the recipients of aid to determine the conditions under which this aid is received and by the importance of any celebrity intervention to respect the appropriate process for determining people's needs and the rule of law.

Finally, **Section Four** focuses on *'Transnational Celebrity Activism, 'Celebrityhood' and Media Representations'*. Taking a cue from Huliaras and Tzifakis, Michael, Cynthia and Rachel Stohl suggest that stars may bring baggage that are at odds with the stated aims of their humanitarian campaigns; furthermore, this takes place in a new age, marked by changes associated with globalization, of at least potentially greater public participation. More specifically, in 'Linking Small Arms, Child Soldiers, NGOs and Celebrity Activism: Nicolas Cage and the Lord Of War' the authors argue that celebrity activism is the outgrowth of the 'new diplomacy' that emerged as a result of Woodrow Wilson's 'Fourteen Points speech' and the establishment of the League of Nations. Globalization and the emergence of new communication technologies facilitated this new kind of diplomacy, though it is the fundamental communicative principles of the new diplomacy that have resulted in changes in both organizational and network factors associated today with celebrity activism. The chapter then examines the role of Nicolas Cage in Andrew Niccol's *Lord of War*, a film that seeks to explore the arms trade, and the personal dilemmas, or lack thereof, of a person who traffics weapons for a living and the experiences of government pursuers. Their analysis addresses five basic questions related to celebrity activism, and offers a discussion of the technological changes that enhance the likelihood and efficacy of celebrity activism.

Within a similar approach, Dorothy Njoroge's chapter, 'Calling a New Tune for Africa? Analysing a Celebrity-led Campaign to Redefine the Debate on Africa', celebrates the roles of celebrity activists within the media who may work against them. The author discusses celebrity involvement in international issues by examining celebrity efforts to influence the debate on African development through the Make Poverty History campaign in 2005. After contextualizing the African crisis within a narrative of hopelessness and despair, a magnet drawing philanthropists, economic innovators, industrialists, celebrities, religious leaders and others who want to craft solutions to its endemic problems, and presenting the African crisis discourse as this was defined by agencies such as the World Bank and the International Monetary Fund, Njoroge employs Critical Discourse Analysis with the *Financial Times* (FT) and *The Times* (of London) in order to examine how the media crafted each side of the debate on the African development crisis. She concludes that although celebrities may not have managed to change the debate in the media, they raised Africa's profile in the international arena and even though the press was unwilling to explore systemic causes of poverty, celebrity rhetoric forced a discussion and raised visibility and media access on this issue, thus extending the contours of the debate on Third World poverty in the global arena.

In the chapter 'Fame and Symbolic Value in Celebrity Activism', Giorgos Plios theorizes celebrity advocacy and attempts to cast a wide net of the history of fame. At first he discusses celebrity diplomacy and activism from the perspective of political economy and mass communication theory where he reads celebrity as the personification of symbolic value. Plios views the symbolic value of celebrity diplomats/activists as something that consists of shifting a certain humanitarian, political issue from a specific social, political and cultural framework to another, and in this sense, following Cooper's notion of 'entrapment'. He perceives celebrity diplomacy and activism as something similar to persuasion or public relations, since celebrities place their fame in the service of international or national institutions and organizations. Then, he distinguishes between two types of well-known or public persons (famous people and celebrities) and two types of socio-political activity exerted by them in the field of international relations (activism and diplomatic activity), before offering a further classification of celebrity diplomats and activists: those that come from the 'marriage' of spectacle and politics; the ones originating from the fields of art, entertainment and culture; representatives of various social organizations such as leaders of social movements and trade unions; and executives of economic organizations such as corporate leaders, national and international financial organizations, banks and industries.

Ana Jorge addresses the cultural and ideological power of stars by focusing her analysis of celebrity advocacy on the Portuguese UN Goodwill Ambassador Catarina Furtado. In 'Celebrity Culture and postcolonial relations within the Portuguese media landscape: The case of Catarina Furtado', she contextualizes the celebrity narrative within postcolonial relations and the country's semi-peripheral character. Hence, the chapter offers at first an insight into the Portuguese historical and geopolitical context, before it moves on to analyse Portuguese star, Catarina Furtado, as a central element in the emergence of celebrity culture within the Portuguese media landscape, and of the ways in which her personal and media narratives are interwoven with her activism. Jorge uses the campaign to help Guinea-Bissau promoted by Furtado to highlight the artist's advocacy, and concludes that in Portugal, contrary to other national contexts, celebrity activism can be seen rather as a sign of intermediate development and the state's incapacity to tackle with development issues and its colonial past. She also argues that the UN's strategy of communicating through celebrities is not universally replicable, and that the specific condition of Portugal as a semi-peripheral and postcolonial culture has particular implications on the ways in which celebrity activism is developed.

The volume wraps up with the chapter 'Big dog celebrity activists: barking up the wrong tree', where Varihi Scott suggests stars have potential that is underutilized, and that they often recreate the same inequities in their initiatives that they ostensibly seek to reduce. Scott points to the importance of the 'objects' of humanitarian initiatives having control over their own representations. To be more precise, using communication for development as his analytical perspective, Scott discusses how celebrity-founded initiatives, which enable marginalized people to represent themselves, fare in comparison to more traditional methods. By using examples such the 'Live8' and 'Live Aid' concerts that illustrate the extent to which humanitarian causes are being addressed or have been overcome, the chapter compares and contrasts between communication activities working at opposite ends of society in order to highlight some of the problems related to celebrity involvement in the humanitarian area of international politics. Scott contends that we seem as if we have come to accept such initiatives as the obvious response, which is far from being the only course of action available, and that in that respect, commercially driven activism-based concerts talk down to us, thus reinforcing the status quo and shrinking our imagination. Other types of initiatives, such as the Red Nose Day telethon in Britain, may engender public awareness and participation; however, the problem here, the chapter argues, is that the images and messages they create about the people they want to help are much more widely available compared to audio-visual material from poor countries, and in this sense, these telethon initiatives are not concerned with communication for development; not only that, but the methods used and the power wielded by the concert and telethon organizers, form a wall that prevents people in actual need of help from communicating directly with those who are keen to help them.

In 'Making sense of transnational celebrity activism: causes, methods and consequences' by Liza Tsaliki, Christos Frangonikolopoulos and Asteris Houliaras, all different perspectives and arguments are brought together in the conclusions. This is an analysis that raises and discusses the causes that lead and work towards the increasing influence of celebrity activism; the methods employed by translational activism in order to draw attention to globally affecting problems; and the consequences this kind of activism has on our making sense of these global issues and on bringing them closer to resolution.

References

Alberoni, F. (2007), 'The Powerless "Elite": Theory and Sociological Research on the Phenomenon of the Stars', in S. Redmond and S. Holmes (eds), *Stardom and Celebrity: A Reader*, London: Sage.

Benjamin, W. (1973), 'The Work of Art in the Age of Mechanical Reproduction', in W. Benjamin, *Illuminations*, London: Fontana.

Braudy, L. (1986), *The Frenzy of the Renown: Fame and its History*, Oxford: Oxford University Press.

Chandler, D. (2004), 'Building Global Civil Society "From Below?"', *Millennium – Journal of International Studies*, 33: 2, pp. 313–339.

—— (2007), 'The possibilities of post-territorial political community', *Area*, 39: 1, pp. 116–119.

Chiwengo, N. (2008), 'When wounds and corpses fail to speak: Narratives of violence and rape in Congo (DRC)', *Comparative Studies of South Asia, Africa and the Middle East*, 28: 1, pp. 78–92.

Cooper, A. F. (2008), *Celebrity Diplomacy*, Boulder: Paradigm Publishers.

Corner, J. and Pels, D. (2003), Media and the Restyling of Politics, London: Sage.

Couldry, N. and Markham, T. (2007), 'Celebrity Culture and Public Connection: Bridge or Chasm', *International Journal of Cultural Studies*, 10: 4, pp. 403–421.

Dyer, R. (1979/1998), Stars, 2nd edn, London: BFI.

—— (1986), Heavenly Bodies: Film Stars and Society, London: BFI.

Gamson, J. (1992/2007), 'The Assembly Line of Greatness: Celebrity in Twentieth-Century America', in S. Redmond and S. Holmes (eds), *Stardom and Celebrity: A Reader*, London: Sage.

—— (2002), 'The Web of Celebrity', *The American Prospect*, 30 November 2002, Available at http://www.prospect.org/cs/articles?article=the_web_of_celebrity. Accessed 10 November 2010.

Giroux, H. (2001), *Public Spaces, Private Lives*, Lanham, MD: Rowman & Littlefield.

Gitlin, T. (1998), 'Public Sphere or Public Sphericues?', in T. Liebes and J. Curran (eds), *Media Ritual and Identity*, London: Routledge.

Huliaras, A. and Tzifakis, N. (2008), 'The Dynamics of Celebrity Activism: Mia Farrow and the "Genocide Olympics" Campaign', *Karamanlis Working Papers in Hellenic and European Studies* (No 7/July), 26.

Kellner, D. (2009a), 'Barak Obama and Celebrity Spectacle', in T. Luke and J. Hunsinger (eds), *Putting Knowledge to Work & Letting Information Play: The Center for Digital Discourse and Culture*, Center for Digital Discourse and Culture: Virginia Tech.

—— (2009b), 'Barack Obama and celebrity spectacle', *International Journal of Communication*, 3: 1, pp. 1–20.

—— (2010), 'Celebrity diplomacy, spectacle and Barak Obama', *Celebrity Studies*, 1: 1, pp. 121–123.

Marshall, D. (2010), 'The promotion and presentation of the self: celebrity as marker of presentational media', *Celebrity Studies*, 1: 1, pp. 35–48.

Parekh, Bhikhu (2003), 'Cosmopolitanism and global citizenship', *Review of International Studies*, 29: 1, pp. 3–17.

Petersen, A. H. (2009), '"We're making our own paparazzi": Twitter and the construction of star authenticity', *Flow – A Critical Forum on Television and Media Culture*, 9: 14, [on-line]. Available from: http://flowtv.org/?p=3960. Accessed May 2009.

Rojek, C. (2001), *Celebrity*, London: Reaktion.

Tarrow, S. G. (2005), *The New Transnational Activism*, New York: Cambridge University Press.

Turner, G. (2004), *Understanding Culture*, London: Sage.

—— (2006), 'The Mass Production of Celebrity: "Celetoids", Reality TV and the "Demotic" Turn', *International Journal of Cultural Studies*, 9: 2, pp. 153–65.

Van Zoonen, E. (2005), *Entertaining the Citizen: When Politics and Popular Culture Converge*, Lanham, MD: Rowman & Littlefield.

Weber, M. (1968), *Economy and Society*, New Jersey: Bedminster Press.

Notes

1. It is not just that the Internet drastically widens the pool of potential celebrities by lowering the entry barriers and bypassing the tightly controlled publicity system of Hollywood, speeding the process of claims to fame by celebrity-wannabes; it is being used by the existing entertainment industry as just another marketing outlet for old-style celebrity (Gamson 2002): we can chat with Britney Spears or George Clooney on AOL!, get romance tips from Melanie Griffith on MelanieGriffith.com, and tweet with Ashton Kutcher. For an interesting insight into the way in which celebrities are using social media to present themselves in an era of 'presentational' culture, see Marshall (2010).
2. For a contextual analysis of the relationship between fame and achievement, see Braudy (1986).
3. In 2009, actor Ashton Kutcher challenged CNN to match his number of followers and passed the one million followers mark on Twitter before CNN did (Petersen 2009).
4. For more background analysis, see Kellner (2009a, 2009b, 2010).

Part I

Transnational Celebrity Activism, Diplomacy and Global Politics

Chapter 1

Bringing the Individuals Back in? Celebrities as Transnational Activists

Asteris Huliaras and Nikolaos Tzifakis

Introduction

Bob Dylan, Neil Young and John Lennon made, with their songs, pop protest fashionable in the 1960s. George Harrison and Ravi Shankar organized a concert for Bangladesh in 1971 and Bob Geldof raised tens of millions of dollars for Ethiopian famine victims with the 1984 Band Aid. Yet the current scale of celebrity involvement in international politics, with particular emphasis on the less developed world, has no historical precedent. Nowadays, many celebrities have become well-recognized global activists: for instance, Mia Farrow has campaigned against the government of China for its policy towards Darfur (Huliaras and Tzifakis 2010); Sir Roger Moore has launched the 'Schools for Africa' campaign in order to raise funds for the construction of schools in Malawi; Danny Glover has visited vulnerable children in critically affected countries by HIV/AIDS and has participated in several fund-raising and advocacy events for UNICEF. Movie stars and pop singers are increasingly active in campaigns against hunger, disease and inequality; in June 2010, the 'Look to the Stars' website, counted 2,194 celebrities supporting 1,559 charity causes. In the exaggerated words of a journalist: 'With so many Hollywood actors, British rock stars, and American talk show hosts beating a path to [Africa] – building schools, visiting refugee children, raising awareness on AIDS and the fighting in Darfur – it's a wonder the entertainment industry can still function' (Baldauf 2006).

Notwithstanding that celebrity activism has evolved into an ever-growing internationally visible phenomenon, very little has been written on its causes and, even less, on its impact.[1] Why do celebrities increasingly turn their attention to global problems? For what types of issues do celebrities usually mobilize? Which factors seem to enable them to assume key roles, or 'special missions' in transnational advocacy networks?[2] Overall, how effective is celebrity activism in the advancement of global causes?

This chapter aims at investigating this type of transnational activism. The first part briefly reviews the international relations literature on the individual as a level (or unit) of analysis. It claims that the relevant literature on the role of individuals who are not state agents is meager in both size and depth and attempts to formulate general hypotheses on the factors that may facilitate the emergence of influential individuals as transnational activists. The second part of the chapter systematically organizes and presents in testable hypotheses additional factors that account for the specific growth of celebrity activism. Finally, the third part analyses the impact of celebrity activism in terms of public awareness, fund-raising and political lobbying.

The Role of Individuals in Global Politics: Transnational Activists, Social Entrepreneurs and Pioneers

In international relations, the lack of theoretical work on the level of analysis of the individual is stunning. This state of affairs without doubt reflects the state-centric nature of the discipline (Lipschutz 1992). Not only is the state considered as the dominant actor in international politics, it is additionally approximated by the mainstream theoretical approach as a unitary rational actor and accordingly, most contemporary work is 'actor-general' (i.e., it disregards the difference that human beings and groups make) (Hudson 2005). Yet, as Byman and Pollack (2001: 108) remarked, 'How can we explain twentieth-century history without reference to Adolph Hitler, Joseph Stalin, Vladimir Lenin, Franklin Roosevelt, Winston Churchill, Mahatma Gandhi or Mao Zedong?'

The discussion of the impact of individuals on the process of international politics seems to be exhausted with the study of agents of state authority.[3] Relevant literature is indeed almost exclusively confined within the realm of foreign policy analysis; several analyses focus on how personality traits and personal characteristics of leaders impact on their political attitude.[4] However, the impact of individuals who are not agents of state authority has received scant, if any, attention in the discipline. To the extent that global civil society and its activities have increasingly emerged in the post-Cold War era as a distinct research field of international studies,[5] the absence of interest in the role of individual members of transnational actors should not be entirely attributed to the mainstream state-centric view of international politics. Indeed, as Helmut K. Anheier (2007: 3) remarked, the problem with the global civil society literature lies in the fact that the debate 'has become very conceptual and overly focused on the issue of definitions relative to empirical research findings'. Moreover, most empirical work focusing on the role of specific categories of global civil society actors (e.g., philanthropic foundations or women movements)[6] is system-oriented in the sense that it attempts to highlight the overall impact of these types of actors. In addition, many of these studies are predominantly concerned with the influence of transnational activists upon governments, neglecting to analyse the impact those people have working within and across societies (Wapner 1995). Furthermore, these idiosyncratic approaches to issue-specific global civil society actors have not contributed as such to the formulation of theoretical propositions.[7] Above all, as Doug McAdam suggested, the theoretical literature on social movements, which has been developed in the fields of political science and sociology is 'myopically domestic' (cited in Khagram et al. 2002: 6). In addition, this literature utilizes different concepts from the international relations scholarship to refer to similar phenomena and, thus, a theoretical dialogue among scholars from these disciplines requires both 'translation' and 'grappling with each other's empirical frames of reference' (Khagram et al. 2002: 5).

The meager literature, in both volume and depth, on the role of individuals who are not state agents in international politics can be analytically divided into two categories. The first concerns attempts to examine the enabling (contextual or external) conditions for individuals to adopt a more active international role. The second category includes studies of the personal traits of individuals.

In relation to the first category, Philip G. Cerny (2000) widened the agent-structure debate to allow for a more consistent account of the role of 'social agents'. Although Cerny made no explicit reference to individuals, he also did not exclude them from his conceptualization of 'social agents' in which he assembled transnational-cause groups and social movements. Cerny argued that while the structure may constrain or enable the activities of such actors, the latter may, under certain conditions, in turn contribute to the preservation or the transformation of the structure. Cerny's assertion that the current conditions of globalization are permissive for such a structural change is worth noting. Indeed, technological advances and the growth of interdependence among nations have given a new impetus to a concern for distant and different others (Sack 1977: 257). The development of transnational television networks and the capacity for 'real-time' coverage of international crises have unleashed an 'electronic internationalism' (Ignatieff 1997: 10). Barriers of citizenship, religion, race and geography, which had once divided moral space are breaking down, creating an emergent 'global conscience' (Ignatieff 1997: 11). The rapid expansion of the Web provides not only an important means for information but also a critical networking and organizing tool (Deibert 2000). The regular organization of an increasing number of international conferences (such as the UN Human Rights Commission's annual meeting in Geneva) provides the opportunity to networkers from different counties 'to converge, share information, and strategize future campaigns' (Burgerman 1998: 909). Global activist networks are constantly growing out of altruistic solidarity and sympathy as much as out of reciprocity and some sense of sharing a common identity (Reitan 2007: 20–21). Altogether, the globalization of all types of flows and the complex internationalization of the links, networks and relations among different (e.g. state and non-state) actors have allowed several organizations and people with a sense of a mission to find ways to co-operate and coordinate their actions (Tarrow 2005: 7–9).

From a different perspective, Kiyoteru Tsutsui and Christine Min Wotipka (2004) examined patterns of citizen participation in global human rights movements through membership in human rights non-governmental organizations (NGOs). Their survey demonstrated that there is a correlation between citizens' decision to participate in such NGOs, on the one hand, and the extent of domestic and global opportunities as well as the level of education and development of their country, on the other.

Hypothesis 1: *External (contextual) conditions such as globalization and the level of human development of the country of origin may facilitate the emergence of influential individuals who are not state agents.*

In relation to the second category of the relevant literature, Lord Beveridge introduced in 1946 the term 'pioneer' in order to describe those people who had crafted the UK voluntary sector in the nineteenth century. Beveridge identified three factors that seemed to enable the emergence and success of pioneers. These were (1) middle class origin, (2) strong motivation, and (3) access to material resources (Grenier 2004: 122–5).

Pamela E. Oliver and Gerald Marwell (1992) studied the work of highly motivated activists who have tried to mobilize collective action by larger groups of people. The two authors defined as activists those 'people who care enough about some issue that they are prepared to incur significant costs and act to achieve their goals'. As far as the motivations of activists are concerned, Oliver and Marwell claimed that these are 'complex and often involve self-identity and expressiveness as well as instrumental goal-attainment'.

Sydney Tarrow attempted to identify the common features and characteristics of transnational activists. These encompass

> individuals and groups who mobilize domestic and international resources and opportunities to advance claims on behalf of external actors, against external opponents, or in favor of goals they hold in common with transnational allies. (2005: 29)

Tarrow supported that these people usually have three common features: (1) they emerge from domestic political or social activities (they do not usually begin at the international level); (2) they are better educated and connected and more frequent travellers than most of their compatriots and (3) they soon return to their domestic activities. Their main difference from national activists is their ability to move between domestic and international levels and take advantage of opportunities for the advancement of their causes (2005: 43). Owing to their constant connection with the domestic level, Tarrow argued that transnational activists are what Mitchell Cohen (1992) has termed as 'rooted cosmopolitans'. Moreover, Tarrow (2005: 29) made a preliminary attempt to classify transnational activists in relation either to their role (e.g. norms entrepreneurs, on behalf of NGOs or of social categories), or their disposition towards international institutions (i.e. insiders versus outsiders).

Another corpus of our knowledge concerning the impact of individual change-makers revolves around the concept of 'social entrepreneur'. According to the Ashoka organization,

> Social entrepreneurs are individuals with innovative solutions to society's most pressing social problems. They are ambitious and persistent, tackling major social issues and offering new ideas for wide-scale change. Rather than leaving societal needs to the government or business sectors, social entrepreneurs find what is not working and solve the problem by changing the system, spreading the solution, and persuading entire societies to take new leaps.

Several attempts to define the characteristics of the typical social entrepreneur tend to portray a social hero with entrepreneurial talent (Seelos and Mair 2005: 244); for instance, apart from being entrepreneurial, innovative and transformative, the most successful social entrepreneurs have additionally the traits of leaders, storytellers, people managers, visionary opportunists and alliance builders (Leadbeater 1997). Paola Grenier researched the motives of social entrepreneurs who received support by organizations such as Ashoka and the Schwab Foundation for Social Entrepreurship. She found out that among their principal motivations are factors such as originating from a family in which values and ethics are central, a certain type of professional background and training (mainly teachers, doctors, nurses and lawyers) and personal suffering and/or deprivation or contact with people in such living conditions (2006: 130–131).

Another study suggested that we may distinguish between three different types of social entrepreneurs depending on how they define opportunities, view their missions, acquire resources, and address social problems (Zahra et al. 2009: 520). The first type is the social bricoleur who generally has noble motives and acts at the local level with modest resources. The second type is the social constructivist who has complex and multifaceted ambitions to introduce social change and reform through planning and development of formalized or systemized scalable solutions. Lastly, the third type is the social engineer who is usually driven by 'missionary zeal and unbounded belief in the rightness' of their causes and attempts to address systemic problems through the introduction of revolutionary change that might even upset the equilibrium within their social environment.

David Chandler offered a different view of two seemingly divergent sets of actors, i.e. radical anti-globalization activists and radical Muslim activists. The author suggested that these categories of activists have the following three common traits (1) non-instrumentality of actions, (2) low emphasis on arguments and ideas, and (3) highlighting of differences and divergence of identities (2007: 116). These types of radical activists, he argued, represent expressions of a 'post-territorial' form of political community. Protest takes the form of individuated acts of symbolism that allegedly aim at raising awareness. Nonetheless, Chandler suggested that the actions of these activists are designed to elaborate upon their individual identity and 'make us aware of their "awareness" rather than engage us in an instrumental project of changing or engaging with the outside world' (2007: 117–118).

Finally, Paola Grenier (2004) revisited the work of Lord Beveridge and employed the term 'pioneer' in order to study the profile of 27 leading global civil society figures. Her research led to three main findings. The first was an endorsement of Cohen's concept of 'rooted cosmopolitans' denoting the pioneers' ability to connect local and global opportunity structures. Grenier attributed this ability to the international exposure and experience that many pioneers witnessed during childhood and upbringing. The second proposition is that the pioneers become involved as a result of their perception of the existence of 'systemic paradoxes' and 'disharmonies or anomalies between different institutions and practices'. It is their feeling of injustice that makes them take action. Finally, the third proposition is a confirmation of Beveridge's argument that there are certain enabling conditions facilitating the emergence of a pioneer. More precisely, Grenier used the term 'transformational capacities' to describe a pioneer's leadership capacities, education level, access to financial resources and personal motivation (2004: 144–50).

Hypothesis 2: *Personal characteristics of individuals such as middle or upper class origin, access to material resources, higher education level, frequent travelling and strong motivations may enable their transformation into pioneers, social entrepreneurs, or transnational activists.*

To sum up, mainstream literature highlights two types of enabling factors that facilitate the emergence of influential individuals who are not state agents, namely external conditions and the personal traits of individuals. The next section attempts to elaborate further enabling conditions (i.e. external and individually related traits) in respect of celebrity activism.

The Causes of Celebrity activism

In recent years, celebrities have taken an active interest in world politics. Movie stars represent UN agencies in disaster areas and lobby the Capitol Hill for peacekeeping missions. Celebrities generate hundreds of millions of dollars in donations and engage the media in global issues more than at any time in recorded history. In 2006, *Time* magazine put Bono on its cover, declaring him – along with billionaire Bill Gates – 'person of the year' for having 'persuaded the world's leaders to take on global poverty'. What really drives celebrity activism for global issues, then, one might ask.

There are at least three more external factors that explicate the growth of this phenomenon.

- First, the United Nations. Especially since 1997, the organization has made an extensive effort to mobilize movie stars, singers and athletes for global causes. The concept of 'goodwill ambassadors' was first introduced by UNICEF several decades ago. According to the UN agency:

  > Fame has some clear benefits in certain roles [...]. Celebrities attract attention, so they are in a position to focus the world's eyes on the needs of children, both in their own countries and by visiting field projects and emergency programmes abroad. They can make direct representations to those with the power to effect change. They can use their talents and fame to fundraise and advocate for children and support UNICEF's mission to ensure every child's right to health, education, equality and protection. (UNICEF website)

Danny Kaye, the comic movie star, was the first in a long list of UNICEF ambassadors. Indeed, the idea has not always worked smoothly. For instance, when Harry Belafonte declared President George W. Bush 'the greatest terrorist in the world', many UN officials felt extremely uneasy. Nevertheless, the number of UNICEF ambassadors continued to rise unabatedly as successful appointments clearly dominated the scene.

The UN courtship of celebrity was particularly boosted by Kofi Annan, who viewed all criticism directed against the United Nations as a public relations problem. In 1997, the then Secretary-General decided to use writers, actors, singers and sportsmen extensively in order to persuade reluctant governments to honour their pledges made in UN forums and to inspire international public opinion to support UN causes (Alleyne 2008). His vision led to a spectacular growth in the number of goodwill ambassadors – by June 2010, the United Nations had 175 such ambassadors. Among the UN agencies, UNICEF had 33 international ambassadors (encompassing celebrities such as Jackie Chan, Whoopi Goldberg and Susan Sarandon), UNESCO 42, FAO 32, UNAIDS 9 (among them Annie Lennox), UNFPA 11, UNDP 6, UNHCR 9, UNIFEM 4 (including Nicole Kidman), UNODC 6 (among them Nicholas Cage), WHO 5 and UNIDO 4.[8] In addition to these, the United Nations created in 1997 an elite group of celebrities called Messengers of Peace in order to 'help focus global attention on the noble aims of the UN'. By June 2010 there were twelve Messengers of Peace, including Charlize Theron, George Clooney and Michael Douglas.[9] The use of celebrities by the United Nations has proved particularly effective both in raising public awareness and in fund-raising for the organization's agencies. As a result, other international organizations adopted similar communication policies. For instance, the Council of Europe has also proceeded to nominate its own goodwill ambassadors since 2000. Among them feature Bianca Jagger for the fight against the death penalty,[10] and Fanny Ardant for the DOSTA campaign aiming at bringing closer Roma and non-Roma citizens in European countries.[11]

• A second factor that explains the growth of celebrity activists has been their use by NGOs.

Like the United Nations, the latter understood that global celebrities can direct media attention on certain issues, raise public awareness and provide access to the highest levels of government. Celebrities are particularly capable of reaching out to the lay people and solicit the support of many of them to the advancement of global causes (Traub 2008). As a result, many NGOs have appointed celebrity promoters.[12] The American Red Cross has a National Celebrity Cabinet, which currently (2010) comprises 43 members including Pierce Brosnan, Jane Seymour and LL Cool J.[13] Save the Children works with several celebrities, including Gwyneth Paltrow, Ben Affleck, Julianne Moore, and Paula Abdul.[14] And Oxfam America, copying UN agencies, has nineteen 'ambassadors' including Archbishop Desmond Tutu, the rock band Coldplay and actors Kristin Davis, Colin Firth and Scarlett Johansson.

• Finally, a third particularly important external factor is that celebrities enjoy far more freedom to act than they did a few decades ago.

In the words of Daniel Drezner, the 'entertainment industry is not as authoritarian as it once was' (2007: 23). Celebrities have more freedom to move around and more space to manage their own brand. In the music industry, there is an important growth of independent labels and net labels mainly owned by the artists themselves who want to have greater control over their music as well as bigger royalty profits. While the overwhelming majority of singers would still prefer to sign with the so-called 'Big Four' music labels – Sony, EMI, Warner, and Universal – others seem to prefer to record in home studios and/or promote their music through the Internet. In the movie industry, the power in Hollywood has shifted from moguls to actors in the last decades. Now many actors are able to demand multi-million dollar fees for their appearances. Indeed corporate moguls – like Summer Redstone of Paramount Pictures or Rupert Murdoch who controls 20th Century Fox – continue to enjoy a lot of power. But to a large extent, celebrities have much autonomy and more power than ever before. Quite a few of these actors have become directors as well as producers (Hau and How 2007).

Hypothesis 3: *External (contextual) factors such as the UN media policy and the less authoritative character of the entertainment industry have recently facilitated the growth of celebrity activism.*

Celebrities have, almost by definition, all those personal characteristics (e.g., transformation capabilities, frequent travelling) that Tarrow and Grenier identify in transnational activists and pioneers. Yet, there are two additional individual-level factors that explain celebrity activism.

- The first and probably the most important factor is that celebrities embrace global causes or take political initiatives in order to remain celebrities.

We live in a world where fame cannot be retained without continuous publicity. Celebrities need to differentiate themselves from lesser stars of stage and screen. And the image of a star in a war-torn African country, surrounded by undernourished black children and thus making a nice contrast for photographers, attracts immediate attention. Celebrity interest in Africa or in global poverty offers excellent branding opportunities. Moreover, the positions of goodwill ambassadors provide international clout and offer to their beholders 'clear advantages of both credibility and ability to expand personal networks' Cooper 2007: 127). Also, celebrity activism can reflect other self-interests like the effort to change a tarnished image or to distract public attention from past scandals. Clearly, personal interests drive celebrity involvement in global causes. When they visit poor countries or donate money to charities they usually do it with the maximum of publicity. When, in January 2005, Formula One world champion Michael Schumacher decided to contribute $10 million to tsunami relief, he did not act discreetly: his manager announced the gift live, in a phone call to a nationally broadcast telethon on German TV (Traub 2008). That is not an exception. Celebrity activism is done rather professionally: many stars employ 'philanthropic advisors' that prepare notes, organize meetings and develop priorities. Some celebrities are at least as much motivated by self-promotion as by philanthropy. But the commitment and quality of celebrity engagement varies widely. And there is a lot of evidence that many of their actions reflect genuine interest. For instance, Mia Farrow has worked less frequently since the 1990s in order to devote more time to raising her fourteen children (ten of which were adopted) and help people in need around the world (Huliaras and Tzifakis 2010). However, in general, it is extremely difficult to determine what people's motivations really amount to. A good example is Angelina Jolie's interest in the suffering of refugees. She has not only visited refugee camps around the world, but she has also donated more than $6 million to help them. The actress has said that she gets paid a 'ridiculous amount of money' and that she has decided to donate one third of it to charity (Harman 2007). Some, however, doubt her good intentions. According to a commentator, 'when Angelina Jolie attends the Davos Economic Forum or sponsors a Millennium Village in Cambodia, she is trying to create a brand image that lets America forget about her role in breaking up Brad Pitt and Jennifer Aniston' (Drezner 2007: 24).

- The second factor that explains celebrity activism is diffusion; celebrities mobilize celebrities.

A clear case is Bono who 'built the superhighway between Africa and Hollywood' (Traub 2008). In 2004, he was invited to Brad Pitt's home to address a group of celebrities that included Tom Hanks, Sean Penn, Julia Roberts, Justin Timberlake and the architect Frank Gehry. Pitt joined and Bono played a crucial role in mobilizing many celebrities in the One Campaign (http://www.one.org/) to push for 'an additional 1% of the U.S. budget toward providing basic needs like health, education, clean water and food' in Africa. Bono has also recruited George Clooney who has set an example for others who have then attempted to mimic the former's commitment. In other cases, celebrities have pressured other celebrities to become more active.[15] For instance, Mia Farrow has exerted pressure (with success) on Steven Spielberg to quit from the post of artistic director of the 2008 Olympics in protest to China's policy over Sudan (Huliaras and Tzifakis 2010: 269).

Hypothesis 4: *Personal characteristics such as the need for individuals to prove themselves as celebrities and their participation in social networks may increase the likelihood that celebrities may turn into activists.*

The next part of the chapter analyses the content of celebrity activism and briefly assesses its impact.

The impact of celebrity activism

Celebrities have nowadays learned to avoid highly contested political issues. Sean Penn's pre-war tour of Iraq, with its 'credulous, childish appearances with members of the peace-loving

Baath Party' (Long 2006) became a negative example. And also Madonna's adoption of a Malawian baby with procedures of dubious legality was a lesson learned for other celebrities. Some commentators sarcastically joked that Madonna, who was never particularly known for acts of philanthropy, could use part of her $850 million fortune to adopt the entire country (Patty 2006) (see also Graham Finlay, this volume).

Most celebrities carefully sign up for humanitarian causes such as the fight against global poverty instead of highly controversial issues such as US military campaigns. According to Daniel W. Drezner, this happens because celebrities care not to let political controversies endanger their careers. He recalls that when Michael Jordan was once asked to endorse a Democratic Party candidate for the Senate, he refused on the grounds that 'Republicans buy sneakers too' (2007: 27). The fight against global malnutrition and AIDS, or the call for the deployment of a peace-enforcing mission in Darfur are indeed political but, in a sense, rather 'soft' issues for western governments' foreign policies. Celebrity campaigners' real message to policy-makers is a call for 'more attention' to Africa than a demand for radically changed policies. Celebrities no longer challenge the structures of the global economic system, and their discourse is not as radical, subversive or anti-establishment as it used to be during the 1960s (Panton 2007). This fact has enabled decision-makers to sign up to their causes. Indeed, politicians – who feel the erosion of their legitimacy as fewer and fewer people turn out to vote – find in celebrities a way of reaching out to the population at large and sending the message that politics can make a difference.

The impact of celebrity activism can be discussed at three levels: in terms of public awareness, fund-raising and political lobbying. Celebrities are particularly effective in raising public interest. First of all, Hollywood movies attract a lot of attention from traditional media outlets and, if they have an underlying political message, they do influence public discussion on certain issues. Lately, several successful movies have focused on Africa, among them blockbusters such as *Tears of the Sun*, *The Constant Gardener*, *The Interpreter* and *The Last King of Scotland*. Some of these movies were heavily criticized for the way in which they portrayed Africa and the 'Let-the-Bwana-do-it-mentality' that dominated their scenarios. A commentator has argued that in each of these films, 'beleaguered black folks marooned in forlorn, blood-drenched African nations get to see justice done because of the heroic efforts of some truly fabulous white people, a glorious tradition that stretches back at least as far as the Tarzan movies' (Queenan 2007). However, all these films helped boost Africa's coverage in the major TV networks and other media outlets and raise awareness for the plight of poor nations. According to a recent study, in the week that the Hollywood film *Blood Diamond* was released in the US, the major news networks 'ABC', 'CBS' and 'NBC' mentioned the role of conflict diamonds in Sierra Leone's civil war eleven times (see also the chapter by Sue Tait, this volume). By contrast, during the longer than a decade war (from 1991 to 2003), the issue of diamonds received scant mentioning (on average, twice per year) (Harman 2007). Moreover, because all these movies were filmed on location, they changed the ways in which celebrities tended to see the world and created charitable impulses in both the cast and crew. For example, actors and staff that filmed *The Constant Gardener*, set up a charity to try to improve conditions in Kenyan slums (Associated Press, 2006).

Celebrities also influence the public, especially in the US, through so-called 'soft news' programmes (Baum 2003). Many Americans do not get their information on world politics from the *New York Times* or the NBC but, instead, from outlets ranging from talk shows like the *Oprah Winfrey Show* or Dave Letterman's *Late Show* to imitation news programmes including the *Inside Edition* and *Entertainment Tonight*. All of them are programmes where the entertainment industry enjoys traditionally constant coverage and where Hollywood celebrities usually appear (Baum 2003). These tabloid-like programmes focus on breathtaking episodes of human drama. However, in recent years they increasingly cover international events. This coverage is often the only information on global issues that their viewers receive. The result is that 'celebrities have a comparative advantage over policy wonks in raising public interest for global issues' (Drezner 2007: 25). According to one review, 'The baby born in Namibia to Angelina Jolie and Brad Pitt probably put that south African desert nation on the map for many of her parents' fans' (Associated Press 2006).

But does this raise public awareness? Some analysts argue that people who watch soft news become more 'attentive', but they do not necessarily acquire more in-depth knowledge of global issues. Matthew A. Baum supports the view that it is unclear 'whether more information necessarily makes better citizens, particularly if the quality of that information is suspect' (2003: 288).

In terms of fund-raising, celebrities have given significant sums of money to charity. Billionaire entertainer Oprah Winfrey tops the celebrity generosity league. In 2005, she donated $52 million, and in 2006 another $11 million to various charitable causes (including her own foundation) (Ejiofor 2006).[16] Many other celebrities have donated several millions of dollars to charities: Steven Spielberg, Arnold Shwarzenegger and Paul McCartney appear in the top ten. Moreover, celebrities can be particularly effective in raising money from private companies and the general public. When, after a visit to Africa, George Clooney appeared on Winfrey's show in April 2006, contributions to UNICEF rose by 20 per cent, and when Angelina Jolie gave an interview in CNN, donations to UNHCR spiked by more than half a million dollars (Boustany 2007); almost nine years following Princess Diana's death, the charitable fund set up in her name is still collecting money (it has raised almost $200 million) spent on asylum seekers and other causes (Bennett 2006).

Finally, in terms of political lobbying, celebrity activism has not had very impressive results. Although celebrities have helped put certain issues (such as poverty) higher up on the global agenda,[17] they cannot equally claim that they have persuaded rich states to do more for the poor countries of the world. Of course, celebrities have at times been successful. This has been the case when they worked within large transnational networks encompassing NGOs and other segments of civil society. A clear case is the Jubilee 2000 campaign for the reduction of Third World debt. Another well-known example is the International Campaign to Ban Landmines (ICBL) with the participation of Princess Diana and Elizabeth Dole that contributed to the acceleration of the conclusion of agreement on the Ottawa Treaty.

More recently, the 'Save Darfur' Coalition of dozens of advocacy groups and humanitarian organizations and several celebrities (such as Mia Farrow and George Clooney) seems to have strengthened a gradual shift in China's policy towards Sudan. Nevertheless, it will be fair to remark that celebrities are usually latecomers in the defence of charity causes. It is usually NGOs who solicit the support of celebrities to existing networks rather than the other way around (see also Virgil Hawkins, this volume).

Altogether, celebrity effectiveness has substantially improved during the last years. Celebrities have *learned* how to act. They have learned that they should be advised by professionals who *know* how to raise issues and mobilize supporters. Moreover, they have learned from their mistakes, avoiding simultaneous campaigns and sending strong signals on single issues.

Hypothesis 5: *Celebrities are particularly effective in raising pubic opinion interest and mobilizing resources. The success of their involvement in political lobbying seems to be dependent on the extent to which they work within networks and coalitions and elaborate pragmatic goals.*

Conclusions

This chapter has observed the lack of theoretical work on the role of individuals who are not state agents in global politics. Given the fact that there is a large diversity of roles in terms of capabilities, methods and objectives among different individuals supporting transnational causes (ranging from terrorists to anti-globalization activists and entrepreneurs), we decided to focus on a specific category of transnational political activity, that is to say, celebrity activism. In this case, some preliminary hypotheses have been formulated in need of affirmation, reformulation, or altogether rejection by subsequent case studies.

The chapter has supported the view that there are two major sources of explanation for the growth of celebrity (and altogether transnational) activism. The first refers to the domestic and international context that may encourage celebrities to sign up for transnational causes. The second refers to the personal traits of celebrities themselves.

At the international level, the main causes of the increased interest and engagement of celebrities in charities are the following: the globalization of flows of information, the internationalization of links and networks among different state and non-state actors, and the decision of the United Nations, the Council of Europe and NGOs to solicit external promoters of their policies. To the extent that celebrity activism represents mainly an Anglo-Saxon phenomenon, there seems to be some additional factors that explicate celebrity activism at the national level. This chapter has singled out two national level enabling factors: the level of human development of the country of origin and residence of celebrities, and the degree of liberalization of the entertainment industry of which they form a part.

With respect of their personal attributes, celebrity activists have access to important material resources, ample media attention and frequent travelling opportunities. Nevertheless, not all celebrities have identical motivations. Some may be genuinely concerned with humanitarian causes, while the interest of others might be part of an image-making strategy. What becomes clear, is that all of them comprehend that support for charity causes offers the possibility to prove themselves as celebrities. And once they are introduced to the struggle for a given cause, many celebrities usually turn to their colleagues to solicit more support. In other words, celebrities form social networks in which they frequently mobilize each other to undertake joint action.

The overall balance sheet of their activism is positive, particularly on such matters as raising public interest, mobilizing resources and, to a lesser extent, political lobbying. Celebrity activism has become more pragmatic recently in the sense that it avoids getting involved in controversial issues and it demonstrates greater restraint in its demands and manifestations. More importantly, celebrities have learned that they have greater political leverage when they enter into coalitions and develop activities within larger networks.

To conclude, this chapter does not pretend to have developed an uncontestable complete theoretical framework that can explain such a diverse and complex phenomenon. It has, instead, attempted to articulate some preliminary propositions that might instigate a more consistent and systematic research engagement with this category of transnational political activity.

References

Alleyne, M. D. (2008), 'The United Nations' Celebrity Diplomacy', *SAIS Review*, XXV:1, pp. 175–185.

Anheier, H. K. (2007), 'Reflections on the Concept and Measurement of Global Civil Society', *Voluntas*, 8:1, pp. 1–15.

Anheier, H. K. and Daly, S. (2004), 'Philanthropic Foundations: A New Global Force?', in H. Anheier, M. Glasius and M. Kaldor (eds), *Global Civil Society 2004/5*, London: Sage, pp. 158–176.

Baldauf, S. (2006), 'Madonna the latest pop star to shine celebrity on Africa', *The Christian Science Monitor*, 12 October 2006.

Baum, M. A. (2003), *Soft News Go to War: Public Opinion and American Foreign Policy in the New Media Age*, Princeton: Princeton University Press.

Bennett, C. (2006), 'Why have the 7/7 victims received such pitiful compensation?', *The Guardian*, 6 July 2006.

Boustany, N. (2007), 'Hollywood Stars Find an Audience for Social Causes', *The Washington Post*, 10 June 2007.

Burgerman, Susan D. (1998), 'Mobilizing Principles: The Role of Transnational Activists in Promoting Human Rights Principles', *Human Rights Quarterly*, 20:4, pp. 905–923.

Busby, J. W. (2007), 'Bono Made Jesse Helms Cry: Jubilee 2000, Debt Relief, and Moral Action in International Politics', *International Studies Quarterly*, 51:2, pp. 247–275.

Byman, D. L. and Pollack, K. M. (2001), 'Let Us Now Praise Great Men: Bringing the Statesman Back In', *International Security*, 25:4, pp. 107–146.

Cerny, P. G. (2000), 'Political Agency in a Globalizing World: Towards a Structurational Approach', *European Journal of International Relations*, 6:4, pp. 435–463.

Chandler, D. (2007), 'The Possibilities of Post-Territorial Political Community', *Area*, 39:1, pp. 116–119.

Christie, J. (2008), 'Athletes join celebrities, activists to protest against China's record in Sudan', *Globe and Mail*, 12 February 2008.

Cohen, M. (1992), 'Rooted Cosmopolitanism', *Dissent*, 39:4, pp. 478–483.

Cooper, A. F. (2007), 'Beyond Hollywood and the Boardroom', *Georgetown Journal of International Affairs*, 8:2, pp. 125–132.

—— (2008), *Celebrity Diplomacy*, Boulder: Paradigm Publishers.

Crichlow, S. (2005), 'Psychological Influences on the Policy Choices of Secretaries of State and Foreign Ministers', *Cooperation and Conflict*, 40:2, pp. 179–205.

Deibert, R. J. (2000), 'International Plug 'n Play? Citizen Activism, the Internet, and Global Public Policy', *International Studies Perspectives*, 1:3, pp. 255–272.

Drezner, D. W. (2007), 'Foreign Policy Goes Glam', *The National Interest*, 92 (November/December 2007), pp. 22–28.

Ejiofor, M. (2006), 'Generous Celebs', *Forbes*, 5 May 2006.

Etheredge, L. S. (1978), 'Personality Effects on American Foreign Policy, 1898–1968: A Test of Interpersonal Generalization Theory', *The American Political Science Review*, 72:2, pp. 434–451.

George, A. L. (1969), 'The 'Operational Code': A Neglected Approach to the Study of Political Leaders and Decision-Making', *International Studies Quarterly*, 13:2, pp. 190–222.

Grenier, P. (2004), 'The New Pioneers: The People Behind Global Civil Society', in H. Anheier, M. Glasius and M. Kaldor (eds), *Global Civil Society 2004/5*, London: Sage, pp. 122–157.

—— (2006), 'Social Entrepreneurship: Agency in a Globalizing World', in A. Nicholls (ed.), *Social Entrepreneurship: New Models of Sustainable Social Change*, Oxford: Oxford University Press, pp. 119–143.

Harman, D. (2007), 'Can Celebrities Really Get Results?', *The Christian Science Monitor*, 23 August 2007.

Hau, L. and How, P. (2007), 'The Star Economy: The Top-Earning Actors Over 35', *Forbes*, 14 November 2007.

Hermann, M. G., Preston, T., Korany, B. and Shaw, T. M. (2001), 'Who Leads Matters: The Effect of Powerful Individuals', *International Studies Review*, 3:2, pp. 83–131.

http://www.ashoka.org/social_entrepreneur. Accessed 15 July 2010.

http:www.charitywatch.org/hottopics/africa_crises.html. Accessed 15 July 2008.

http://www.coe.int/t/dc/files/Ambassadeurs/default_en.asp. Accessed 17 June 2010.

http://www.coe.int/t/dc/files/pa_session/june_2010/20100622_news_ardant_EN.asp?=. Accessed 17 June 2010.

http://www.looktothestars.org. Accessed 28 June 2010.

http://www.redcross.org/portal/site/en/menuitem.53fabf6cc033f17a2b1ecfbf43181aa0/?vgnextoid=e8beb7901438b110VgnVCM10000089f0870aRCRD&currPage=04aeb7901438b110VgnVCM10000089f0870aRCRD. Accessed 15 June 2010.

http://www.savethechildren.org/get-involved/celebrities-get-involved/. Accessed 15 June 2010.

http://www.un.org/sg/mop/. Accessed 15 June 2010.

http://www.un.org/sg/mop/gwa.shtml. Accessed 15 June 2010.

http://www.unicef.org/people/people_ambassadors.html. Accessed 15 June 2010.

Hudson, V. M. (2005), 'Foreign Policy Analysis: Actor-Specific Theory and the Grounds of International Relations', *Foreign Policy Analysis*, 1:1, pp. 1–30.

Huliaras, A. and Tzifakis, N. (2010), 'Celebrity Activism in International Relations: In search of a framework for analysis', *Global Society*, 24:2, pp. 255–274.

Ignatieff, M. (1977), *The Warrior's Honor: Ethic War and the Modern Conscience*, New York: Henry Holt.

Jones, B. R. J., Jones, P., Dark, K. and Peters, J. (2002), *Introduction to International Relations*, Manchester: Manchester University Press.

Keck, M. E. and Sikkink, K. (1998), *Activists beyond Borders: Advocacy Networks in International Politics*, New York: Cornell University Press.

—— (1999), 'Transnational Advocacy Networks in International and Regional Politics', *International Social Science Journal*, 51:159, pp. 89–101.

Khagram, S., Riker, J. V. and Sikkink, K. (eds) (2002), *Restructuring World Politics: Transnational Social Movements, Networks, and Norms*, Minneapolis: University of Minnesota Press.

Leadbeater, Charles (1997), *The Rise of the Social Entrepreneur*, London: DEMOS.

Lipschutz, R. D. (1992), 'Reconstructing World Politics: The Emergence of Global Civil Society', *Millennium: Journal of International Studies*, 21:3, pp. 389–420.

Littler, Jo (2008), '"I feel your pain": cosmopolitan charity and the public fashioning of the celebrity soul", *Social Semiotics*, 18:2, pp. 237–251.

Long, R. (2006), 'Using Your Star Power', *Foreign Policy*, 154 (May/June 2006), pp. 74–78.

Nash, K. (2008), 'Global citizenship as show business: the cultural politics of Make Poverty History', *Media, Culture & Society*, 30:2, pp. 167–181.

Oliver, P. E. and Marwell, G. (1992), 'Mobilizing Technologies for Collective Action', in A. Morris and C. Mueller (eds), *Frontiers of Social Movement Theory*, New Haven: Yale University Press. http://www.ssc.wisc.edu/~oliver/PROTESTS/ArticleCopies/MobTechOliverMarwell.pdf. Accessed 10 May 2010.

Panton, J. (2007), 'Pop Goes Politics', *The World Today*, 63:6, pp. 4–6.

Patty, D. (2006), 'Charity with strings attached', *The Guardian*, 5 October 2006.

Pigman, G. A. and Kotsopoulos, J. (2007), '"Do This One For Me, George": Blair, Brown, Bono, Bush and the "Actor-ness" of the G8', *The Hague Journal of Diplomacy*, 2:2, pp. 127–145.

Queenan, J. (2007), 'Tarzan's children: Why movies about Africa require white saviors', *Los Angeles Times*, 14 January 2007.

Reitan, R. (2007), *Global Activism*, Oxon: Routledge.

Richey, L. A. and Ponte, S. (2008), 'Better (Red) TM than Dead? Celebrities, consumption and international aid', *Third World Quarterly*, 29:4, pp. 711–729.

Risse, T. (2007), 'Transnational Actors and World Politics', in W. Ch. Zimmerli, K. Richter and M. Holzinger (eds), *Corporate Ethics and Corporate Governance*, Heidelberg: Springer, pp. 251–286.

Sack, R. D. (1997), *Homo Geographicus: A Framework for Action, Awareness and Moral Concern*, Washington: Johns Hopkins University Press.

Seckinelgin, H. (2002), 'Time to Stop and Think: HIV/AIDS, Global Civil Society, and People's Politics', in M. Glasius, M. Kaldor and H. Anheier (eds), *Global Civil Society 2002*, Oxford: Oxford University Press, pp. 109–136.

Seelos, C. and Mair, J. (2005), 'Social Entrepreneurship: Creating new Business Models to Serve the Poor', *Business Horizons*, 48:3, pp. 241–246.

Sen, P. (2003), 'Successes and Challenges: Understanding the Global Movement to End Violence Against Women', in M. Kaldor, H. Anheier and M. Glasius (eds), *Global Civil Society 2003*, Oxford: Oxford University Press, pp. 119–147.

Tarrow, S. (2005), *The New Transnational Activism*, Cambridge: Cambridge University Press.

The Associated Press (2006), 'Africa hot destination for committed celebrities', 19 June 2006.

Traub, J. (2008), 'The Celebrity Solution', *The New York Times*, 9 March 2008.

Tsutsui, K. and Min Wotipka, C. (2004), 'Global Civil Society and the International Human Rights Movement: Citizen Participation in Human Rights International Nongovernmental Organizations', *Social Forces*, 83:2, pp. 587–620.

Wapner, P. (1995), 'Politics Beyond the State: Environmental Activism and World Civic Politics', *World Politics*, 47:3, pp. 311–340.

Zahra, S. A., Gedajlovic, E., Neubaum, D. O. and Shulman, J. M. (2009), 'A Typology of Social Entrepreneurs: Motives, Search Processes and Ethical Challenges', *Journal of Business Venturing*, 24:5, pp. 519–532.

Notes

1. Some notable exceptions are Cooper (2008), Busby (2007), Pigman and Kotsopoulos (2007), Richey and Ponte (2008). Also interesting are Littler (2008), Nash (2008).
2. For the concept of transnational advocacy network, see Keck and Sikkink (1998, 1999).
3. See for instance Jones et al. (2002: 20–23).
4. See *inter alia*: Crichlow (2005), Etheredge (1978), Hermann et al. (2001), George (1969).
5. It is worth noting here that neither the emergence of transnational actors nor the development of theories about them, represent recent phenomena. For a more detailed account, see Risse (2007).
6. See for example, Anheier and Daly (2004), Sen (2003).
7. See for instance Seckinelgin's (2002) very informative work on the attempt of individuals and groups to raise awareness concerning the immediate needs for treatment of AIDS victims.
8. For more detail, see http://www.un.org/sg/mop/gwa.shtml. Accessed 15 June 2010.
9. See http://www.un.org/sg/mop/. Accessed 15 June 2010.
10. http://www.coe.int/t/dc/files/Ambassadeurs/default_en.asp. Accessed 17 June 2010.
11. See http://www.coe.int/t/dc/files/pa_session/june_2010/20100622_news_ardant_EN.asp?=. Accessed 17 June 2010.
12. See http:www.charitywatch.org/hottopics/africa_crises.html. Accessed 15 July 2008.
13. See http://www.redcross.org/portal/site/en/menuitem.53fabf6cc033f17a2b1ecfbf43181aa0/?vgnextoid= e8beb7901438b110VgnVCM10000089f0870aRCRD&currPage=04aeb7901438b110VgnVCM1000008 9f0870aRCRD. Accessed 15 June 2010.
14. See http://www.savethechildren.org/get-involved/celebrities-get-involved/. Accessed 15 June 2010.
15. A good example is provided in the case study that follows. It concerns Farrow's assailing of Steven Spielberg for working as an artistic consultant to the Beijing Olympics opening ceremony. See Christie (2008).
16. See also, *The Chronicle of Philanthropy* at http://philanthropy.com/.
17. Interview with Jonathan Watts, *The Guardian*, 26 August 2006.

Chapter 2

Celebrity Politics and Cultural Citizenship: UN Goodwill Ambassadors and Messengers of Peace

Mark Wheeler

Introduction

This chapter will examine the meaning of celebrity in political culture by considering how far celebrities influence public policy and what kind of effect they have on political efficacy. Much of the existing literature (Boorstin 1971; Louw 2005) has suggested celebrity is part of a new 'pseudo politics' designed to undermine civic engagement. To provide a less prescriptive analysis, this survey will discuss the extent to which celebrity endorsements affect political behaviour.

Therefore, to understand how celebrities provide credibility for agendas among target audiences, this analysis will concentrate on how the United Nations (UN) has utilized its Goodwill Ambassadors and Messengers of Peace to draw international media attention to their activities. These examples demonstrate how celebrities can provide focus for their causes, thereby transcending other agencies of social authority, to become integral in the sphere of political communication.

As there has been a recalibration of celebrity from the domain of Hollywood film stars to an era in which fame has become ubiquitous, there has been an evolution of celebrity engagement in political affairs. This has been viewed by some as a dilution of political engagement (Postman 1987). However, it provides a means through which to examine whether celebrity relations have provided a reconfigured form of agency in modern politics:

> The power of agency [...] is captured by the continued rise of Angelina Jolie. At the outset of her involvement with the UNHCR, it might have been expected that Jolie would have been a magnified version of the [embarrassment] of Ginger Spice. [...] Instead [...] Jolie has exhibited many of the potential strengths [...] [by developing] [...] a growing appreciation of what her role could be. [...] Agency does not mean untrammeled individual autonomy. Part of [her] narrative is about personal growth. But behind her [...] is a substantive amount of organisational backing. (Cooper 2008: 116)

Thus, with regard to celebrity politics' impact on citizenship engagement, it is necessary to consider whether celebrities encourage greater debate on a range of causes. How far is their endorsement of campaigns matched by an effective ability to shape political agendas? To what extent can they be ineffective 'loose cannons' whose involvement may be counter-productive? In effect, what is the worth of the 'celebritization' of the political process?

To respond to these concerns, this analysis will be divided into three sections. First, it will outline the academic debate concerning the celebritization of politics. The traditional paradigm has viewed the involvement of celebrities in politics as a means to mislead a culpable public. Conversely, a more holistic literature has married the interests of politics, popular culture and public engagement to investigate a new aesthetic in modern political affairs. Most especially, John Street has developed the concept of 'celebrity performance' to assess the credibility of star power within the realm of political activity (Street 2003).

While both positions discuss the merits or deficiencies of the celebritization of political affairs, there has been little detail on how celebrities may determine political outcomes. Therefore, the second section will provide information on the origins, development and employment of UN Goodwill Ambassadors and Messengers of Peace. It will consider how the UN and its agencies have developed their celebrity relations from ad-hoc to fully fledged systems of political campaigning. Street's typology of celebrity performance provides a framework through which to analyse the three main stages of celebrity activism within the UN (Street 2003, 2004). These range from an embryonic period in which celebrities understood themselves to be 'good' international citizens into a transformative era in which star power became politicized. In the most recent phase of celebrity activism, the former UN Secretary-General, Kofi Annan controversially deployed a far wider range of celebrities as a means to propagate the organization's aims.

Finally, this study will conclude about what the activities of the UN Goodwill Ambassadors and Messengers of Peace indicate about the concepts of cultural citizenship. In effect, have these developments led to new forms of diplomacy and political initiatives? And what have been the strengths and weaknesses in the UN's deployment of celebrity activists? Therefore, as there has been a range of styles within this area of celebrity performance, how do we make sense of these types of invention?

Celebrity Politics as a Form of False Consciousness

Many criticisms of celebrity politics view the production of celebrity as the product of a 'manufactured process' fabricated by media exposure (Louw 2005). Political communications have evidenced the convergence of public relations (PR) techniques with commercial pressures drawn from global media over journalism. These developments have provided the context for the further inclusion of celebrity built on the marketization of images in a more identity-driven political process. Critics such as Neil Postman 'accuse those in the political realm of internalizing a media-inspired desire to be palatable and entertaining' (Postman 1987 cited in Higgins 2005: 3). They claim that there has been a decline in rationality as televisual style dominates substantive debate (Street 2003: 91).

This has led to a literature that suggests that the 'Americanization' of politics has had a negative impact on political communication, audiences, the public sphere and civic engagement (Postman 1987). In such a pessimistic extrapolation 'politics has been subsumed within the culture industry, so that the political is now another commodity to be marketed, purchased and consumed in a cycle of false needs and unsatisfied desires' (Calcutt 2005).

Daniel Boorstin argued that celebrities are products of the image-making industries in which their fame is dictated by their 'well-knownness' (Boorstin 1971). Concurrently, as P. David Marshall claims, politicians have accorded to the needs of fame to 'sell' themselves as commodities to voters in an era of partisan de-alignment. Marshall suggests that the relationships between 'leaders' and the 'crowd' that have evolved in late capitalist societies are vital to 'the mass's support of the individual in mass society' (Marshall 1997: 43). Therefore, public interest in celebrity politicians and politicized celebrities has been manipulated through pseudo-events staged by a cynical media to construct a perceived myth of individual aspiration (Boorstin 1971: 58). In turn, the public is presented as being culpable as it cannot understand that it has been manipulated by elite marketing tactics.

This anxiety over the withering effects of celebrity on the political process may be traced back to the American sociologist, Leo Lowenthal who argued that US media coverage had replaced 'idols of production' such as politicians with 'idols of consumption' such as film stars (Lowenthal 1944). Similarly, C. Wright Mills contended that the attention placed on celebrities meant that they had become a new power elite (Mills 1956).

Following on this logic, Eric Louw has argued that the exportation of the US culture values accompanying the globalization of the mass media-branded performers have narrowed the gap between politics and entertainment (Louw 2005: 192). In his definition of 'pseudo-politics', Louw suggests there has been a public relationization of political issues 'in which celebrities are now enlisted to whip up mass public opinion' (Louw 2005: 191). By defining politics as the latest manifestation of the fame game, he views the media as a site of ideological control.

Thus, the most common analysis of celebrity-ness has referred to the ubiquitous growth of the visual media in which fame operates as a tool through which to manipulate public opinion. Invariably, the use of celebrity in political affairs has been presented as an anti-democratic phenomenon in which celebrities form a 'powerless' elite composed from stars who are 'bards of the powerful' (Monboit 2005). It is contended such a usage of performance is pitched on artifice and sells prescriptive ideas to a disengaged public.

Celebrity and Politics: Aesthetics and Popular Discourses

An alternative literature contends there are dangers in seeing the manufacture of celebrity politics as a mechanism of elitist control in which the construction of fame is a form of 'false consciousness'. The traditional paradigm may be criticized as it sees the mass media as being inherently monolithic and perceives political communication as a top-down process between political elites and a passive electorate. Such an approach ignores the effects of celebrities in forging new or alternative social formations for engagement.

Instead, it is necessary to identify the trends towards the celebritization of politics through an exploration of the how and why celebrities seek to influence politics. John Corner and Dick Pels contend the traditional forms of ideological or partisan allegiances have eroded to be replaced by a focus on post-ideological lifestyle choices, which foregrounds matters of aesthetics and style (Corner and Pels 2003). As voters float away from centrist political parties, the public have favoured 'more eclectic, fluid, issue- specific and personality-bound forms of political recognition and engagement' (Corner and Pels 2003: 7).

Therefore, celebrities command credibility through a conjunction of de-institutionalization, personalization and parasocial familiarity to transcend other agencies of social authority. Corner argues that through their 'mediated personas' – the individual's public image – film, television and music stars have created new forms of identification in which they attain public admiration, sympathy and authenticification to effect political expression (Corner 2003: 83). As Ellis Cashmore (2006: 218) comments, there has been a shift in which celebrities have assumed a moral authority for policy agendas among target audiences. Thus, within the celebrity classes, there is a conscious understanding that fame may draw public attention to a range of causes (Dreyfus 2000).

John Street contends that such a use of fame is neither an exceptional or exaggerated form of representation, but a vital characteristic of modern political culture (Street 2004: 449). He refers to Joseph Schumpeter's analogy between the worlds of commerce and politics, to demonstrate how modern political communication has been dominated by marketing as the parties 'compete' for electoral support. While this may appear to indicate the marketization of the political process, Street demonstrates how Schumpeter intended his comparison between business and politics to rescue democracy from the dangers of dictatorship. Therefore, Street suggests politics should be seen as a type of show business in which the currency is fame and the products are the stars' performances as:

> In focusing on the style in which politics is presented, we need to go beyond mere description of the gestures and images. We need to assess them, to think about them as performances and to apply critical language appropriate to this. [...] To see politics as coterminous with popular culture is not to assume that is diminished [...] The point is to use this approach to discover the appropriate critical language with which to analyse it. (Street 2003: 97)

Thus, Street's distinction within the field of Celebrity Politicians (CP) between those politicians who have used their celebrity to encourage their political worth (CP1s), and the growing significance of celebrities lending their fame to political causes (CP2s), provides a typology through which to identify how celebrity operates as a form of political capital. By establishing these definitions, Street identifies that celebrity politics is not an exceptional form of representation, but a necessary feature of modern political culture (Street 2004: 449).

Therefore, as celebrities have assumed a moral authority and provide credibility for political agendas, it is necessary to investigate their integral roles in political campaigns. While symbolism and charisma have always shaped political communications, can celebrities use their reputations and charisma to invigorate politics with new ideas? Does the modern usage of celebrity represent a broader re-configuration of economic, political and social change?

Thus, in the light of these questions, celebrity politics should be understood as a multi-faceted phenomenon. This does not mean scholars should uncritically embrace celebrity activism. Instead, it is necessary to establish the tools through which to analyse the respective impact of celebrity politics to assess its worth in modern political culture. Most especially, there should be a consideration of the conditions through which celebrities can influence initiatives and what the effect of their involvement has been.

The Mediation of Celebrity Diplomacy: United Nations (UN) and UN Agencies' Goodwill Ambassadors and Messengers of Peace

While celebrity involvement in political affairs has been identified as a recent phenomenon, an institutional analysis of the use of Goodwill Ambassadors by UN agencies such as UNICEF and UNHCR, offsets the apparent 'novelty' of celebrity politics as a short-term or recent phenomenon. Since UNICEF's appointment of Danny Kaye as its first Goodwill Ambassador in 1953, the UN has employed celebrities to raise funds, affect international policy agendas and draw attention to development causes (Annan 2003).

The UN case demonstrates how celebrities can use their guile by providing points of identification for internationally orientated organizations that are seeking to mobilize public opinion. Further, with the extensive coverage of trips made to 'southern' states by UNICEF and UNHCR Goodwill Ambassadors such as George Clooney and Angelina Jolie, it is clear that these agencies place considerable value on the impact of the publicity generated. Consequently, celebrities have assumed a level of international importance and have recognized their ability to draw media attention to their agencies' causes (Cooper Summer/Fall 2007a). Thus, we may judge their activities through the framework of celebrity performance to determine how such forms of activism have grown in their importance.

Celebrities as Good International Citizens

The initial forms of celebrity activism referred to the development of ad hoc, inter-personal relationships between film stars and UN officers. The first notable celebrity activist, Danny Kaye, became involved with UNICEF through his accidental meeting with the agency's Executive Director, Maurice Pate, on a flight between London and New York in 1953. Shortly afterwards, Kaye toured UNICEF projects in Myanmar, India, Indonesia, Korea, Thailand and Japan to publicize the agency's activities in alleviating the plight of children. He filmed his trip for a documentary feature entitled 'Assignment Children', which was shown to an audience of an estimated 100 million and whose profits entered UNICEF's coffers.

Throughout the 1950s and 1960s, Kaye focused attention on UNICEF activities through a range of trips to war-torn or blighted areas. For Kaye it meant he could use his 'celebrity [to] really [...] amount to something that mattered and changed people's lives' (Puttnam January 16, 2007). Consequently, he understood it was his responsibility to publicize UNICEF's works, and Kaye was a newsworthy presence, most especially when he performed an improvized victory ballet while accepting the Nobel Peace Prize for UNICEF in 1965.

Following on from this model of celebrity involvement, Jack Ling, UNICEF's Director of the Information Division, courted stars including Peter Ustinov, Elisabeth Taylor, Richard Burton, Eddie Albert, Muhammad Ali, Pele, Sacha Distel and Dinah Shore. While not all of them would become Goodwill Ambassadors, they hosted fund-raising European gala events and fronted television appeals. One of the most successful was the appeal for the relief of Japanese child-victims of the Osaka Earthquake in 1970 in which UNICEF raised over $200,000.

A greater linkage occurred when UNICEF combined with George Harrison, Ravi Shankar and Harrison's business manager, Allan Klein, to stage two concerts on 1 August 1971 at Madison Square Gardens to a total of 40,000 people to raise monies for Bangladeshi children who had suffered in the Bhola cyclone. This natural disaster existed in tandem with the turmoil resulting from the Bangladesh war that had left a tremendous refugee problem in West Bengal. Thus, when a range of international superstars, including Harrison, Shankar, Eric Clapton, Ringo Starr and Bob Dylan, sang a 'Song for Bangladesh' at the end of the shows, it was evidence of how their celebrity status could bring the plight of Bangladesh to the attention of the international community.

The success of the concerts and the subsequent album demonstrated to UNICEF how effective celebrity fund-raising could be, while the resulting vast sums of monies brought to attention the need to professionalize UNICEF's fund-raising activities. With these factors in mind, the Bee Gees, Robert Stigwood and David Frost organized a further fund-raising concert at the UN General Assembly called 'Music for UNICEF' in 1979, which included ABBA, Kris Kristofferson, Olivia Newton John, Donna Summa and Rod Stewart. For this concert, each star signed a parchment supporting UNICEF goals, pledged to donate their royalties from the concert, and to place monies from one of their songs into the agency's coffers.

Throughout these celebrity trips, galas and concerts, the ad-hoc relations were formalized as the extension of celebrity fund-raising meant greater institutional structuring was required. Moreover, long-standing UNICEF Goodwill Ambassadors such as Kaye and Peter Ustinov (1968–2004), conceived themselves as good international citizens who could engender a 'thick layer of goodwill for UNICEF' (Ling 5 June 1984: 9). Therefore, their activities were conformist and did not cause controversy about how the UN worked in relation to its scope.

In many respects, the celebrity who provided the template for this 'glamorous [...] conformity' (Cooper 2008: 18) was Audrey Hepburn. Although, Hepburn did not become a UNICEF Goodwill Ambassador until the 1980s, her reputation as a survivor of World War II and her elegance as a fashion icon meant that she epitomized the credible use of politicized celebrity. She made constant trips to war-torn states with little fear for her personal safety or the pampering of her ego. She developed a professional attitude to celebrity diplomacy throughout her visits to Ethiopia and Somalia, and employed her fame to meet African Leaders and to take her causes to the US Senate. She avoided taking sides and used her celebrity to drive humanitarian causes by insisting that the worst violence in Africa was widespread poverty:

> Audrey Hepburn created a model of star power expressed via the UN organisational structure that other celebrities could – and did in quite large numbers – try to follow. It was a model that allowed celebrities to go global with their enthusiasms … In this model, glamour worked to enhance the sense of commitment. (Cooper 2008: 20)

However, as international crises heightened both during and after the Cold War with the greater fragmentation of nationalisms, along with the growth of the world debt in developing states, celebrity activists started to become more politicized.

Transformative Celebrity Diplomacy

As there was an increase in celebrity activity in the 1980s and 1990s, which reflected the extension of the employment of celebrities by UNICEF and other agencies, notably UNHCR and the World Health Organization (WHO), celebrities felt they had a moral duty to become more politically engaged. A greater consciousness within the celebrity classes emerged with reference to Bob Geldof's 'Live Aid' and 'Feed the World' campaigns (Cooper September 2007b).

This more engaged form of celebrity activism may be traced back to UNICEF's decision to attempt to forge a relationship with Marlon Brando in 1966 when the star raised funds for children affected by famines in India. For UNICEF, Brando's involvement was a double-edged sword. On the one hand, he had previously shown an undoubted commitment to civil liberties and a compassion for international conceptions of justice (Wheeler 2006). On the other, Brando had used his celebrity to gain a political notoriety and was unpredictable. Therefore, when UNICEF Director of Information, Jack Ling, worked with Brando, he found that the actor's mercurial nature could be counter-productive (Ling 5 June 1984: 9). Yet, while, Brando's relationship with the agency was sporadic, it cast the die as UNICEF appointed a number of more politically conscious celebrity ambassadors.

In 1978, UNICEF asked the Swedish actress Liv Ullman to become a Goodwill Ambassador. Ullman had previously visited Thailand to add weight to a Swedish mission dealing with refugees. During this trip, she decided she should engage in the welfare of the oppressed and was approached by Ling about working for UNICEF as she had shown a commitment to international causes. He impressed upon Ullman that UNICEF's philosophy was for the celebrity activist to make trips to see the agency's work and it did not simply want to receive the publicity associated with her name.

Thereafter, Ling accompanied Ullman on her first UNICEF visit to Sri Lanka in 1978 and she became a more autonomous figure when representing Kampuchean refugees and the Vietnamese Boat people (Ling 5 June 1984: 8). Ullman demonstrated a greater political consciousness than her predecessors, and due to her status as a 'serious European' film actress, she came across as a creditable figure. She proved highly effective when representing UNICEF in US House and Senate Hearings, and led delegations to the US State Department (Ling 5 June 1984: 8)

Consequently, Ullman reconceived the role of the Goodwill Ambassador by taking a clear stance on injustice and poverty. She expressed her outrage in a manner more akin to Geldof than Kaye or Hepburn: 'We must be so outraged. We mustn't wait and talk about making resolutions; we must urgently start acting now' (Ullman 8 February 1993). Ullman reported on the plight of the Vietnamese Boat people to a Norwegian non-governmental organization (NGO) and, in 1982, participated in a demonstration marking a UN Day, which consisted of a four-mile 'human bridge of peace' stretching between the American and Soviet embassies in Stockholm.

In adapting to this sea change of attitudes, some Goodwill Ambassadors have become more critical of the moral stance of the UN. Mia Farrow is a longtime UNICEF Goodwill Ambassador, and has become a devoted advocate for preventing the continued genocide in Darfur by arguing that the small peacekeeping force deployed by the African Union (AU) is insufficient in the face of the ongoing tragedy. The AU forces have attempted to halt the bloodshed but need reinforcements, not to mention greatly increased international diplomatic support. Therefore, while the celebrity visits may draw media awareness, it remains to be seen if this attention may have the desired outcome of effecting change on the ground.

One of the more problematic cases referred to Richard Gere, who has represented the UN with reference to World Health/Aids and ecological matters, visited refugees with UNICEF in FYROM and appeared at numerous events with former UN Secretary-General Kofi Annan. While supporting the UN's position on the 2003 Gulf War, Gere's enthusiasms led him into taking controversial stances. For example, on the trip to FYROM, Gere insisted on staying overnight in the refugee camp, a request which was denied by governmental officials. Moreover, he participated in a campaign to get Palestinians out to vote in the 2005 elections and his efforts were seen to be patronizing and unwarranted.

However, as Gere has been a devotee of the exiled Tibetan leader, the Dalai Lama, he has come into greater conflict with the UN vis-à-vis its non-recognition of Tibet. In the late 1990s, Gere, as the chairman of the International Campaign for Tibet, made high-profile visits to the UN Headquarters in New York to support Tibetan hunger strikers and backed the US Resolution to the United Nations Human Rights Commission (UNHRC) to criticize China's human rights record. He accused the UNHRC, when it voted to take no action, of being shamefully manipulated by the Chinese. More recently, along with Farrow, Gere supported calls for the boycotting of the 2008 Beijing Olympics.

Thus, the UN's deployment of more politically engaged celebrities such as Farrow and Gere has proved problematic. In this transformative era of celebrity diplomacy, stars have felt they should use their fame to expose injustices. However, this deployment of celebrity diplomats has led to difficulties as politicized stars have publicly fallen out with the UN. Moreover, the positive and negative connotations of celebrity politics have been intensified in the latest phase of UN celebrity activism with the escalation of the number of Goodwill Ambassadors and the creation of Messengers of Peace.

Embracing Celebrity Culture: Kofi Annan's Public Relations Revolution

When Kofi Annan was appointed as the UN Secretary-General on 1 January 1997, the organization engaged in the ubiquitous employment of celebrities as Goodwill Ambassadors. By Annan's departure in 2007, there were over 400 UN Goodwill Ambassadors, and the Secretary-General had established a new tier of celebrity activists known as Messengers of Peace. In many respects, this demonstrated how the omnipresent creation of celebrity had permeated the political environment (Drezner 11 January 2007). Moreover, Annan's decision to escalate the number of Goodwill Ambassadors was designed to counter-balance the US's realist foreign policies and to offset a perceived sense of public cynicism by utilizing celebrity diplomacy to bring media attention to the UN's causes in a manner akin to the so-called 'CNN' effect (Cooper 2008: 28).

Annan oversaw a public relations revolution in which the UN's Department of Public Information (DPI) became more persuasive. Mark D. Alleyne comments Annan had a 'supremely American faith in publicity campaigns and [a] propensity to view of all of the criticism of the United Nations as a matter of public relations' (Alleyne 2005: 176). Therefore, he felt significant reforms were required to improve the UN's public profile. In March 1997, Annan announced the UN's communications would better serve the international news media by utilizing the most up-to-date information technologies. Subsequently, a Task Force on the Reorientation of United Nations Public Information Activities produced a 34 page report entitled 'Global Vision, Local Voice: A Strategic Communications Program for the United Nations'. This argued the DPI needed to employ a more strategic form of communication.

In 1999, a Communications Coordination Service was set up to resolve the long-standing 'Balkanization' of public information amongst the UN Departments. Further, Annan established the post of Director of Communications in the Office of the Secretary-General, and appointed Gillian Sorensen as the assistant Secretary-General for External Relations (Alleyne 2005: 178). These actions reflected the values of the modern 'Public Relations state' in which the state has become the heart of the news machine as governmental activities have been conceived as newsworthy and legitimate (Deacon and Golding 1994: 7).

The second strand of Annan's communications revolution referred to the wider deployment of celebrity diplomats. In 2002, he hosted a conference called 'Celebrity

Advocacy for the New Millennium' and declared 'he wanted celebrities to be the tools the United Nations would use to eventually get reluctant governments to take seriously the rhetorical pledges they make during every General Assembly' (Alleyne 2005: 179). Annan believed that celebrities could influence international public opinion to support the UN's goals of idealism and universalism in an era in which most states in the UN system have embraced an increasingly realist logic.

To enhance this process, Annan inaugurated the Messengers of Peace programme in 1997 to identify nine individuals who would propagate the UN across the global media. This group of 'distinguished men and women of talent and passion' are composed from those celebrities whose fame has been understood to provide a global focus to the 'noble aims of the UN Charter: a world without war, respect for human rights, international law and social and economic progress' (United Nations 2007). They are selected from the fields of art, literature, music and sports and receive the highest honour the Secretary-General can bestow upon a global citizen for an initial period of three years. Since the programme's inception, more than ten individuals have served as Messengers of Peace, and the current cohort includes Michael Douglas, Jane Goodhall, Daniel Barenboim and George Clooney.

However, this expansion has not been without controversy and the performances of celebrity advocates may be characterized as being mixed. The undoubted success d'estime has been the film actress, Angelina Jolie, whose image has been transformed from a Hollywood wild-child to a credible international figure. Her links with UNHCR were established over several years in which she 'auditioned' to become a Goodwill Ambassador. Jolie became acquainted with the plight of refugees through trips to West Africa and UNHCR's programmes. Since assuming her position as UNHCR's 'poster star', Jolie has appealed to a young and marginalized audience. Her photogenic qualities have meant that she has attracted the attention of the world press and UNHCR has sought to place similarly 'attractive' refugees in the camera frame next to her to provide an iconographic representation of displacement.

Jolie's success has been dependent on her displays of personal commitment and she has attempted to transcend her role of being a UN Goodwill Ambassador into becoming a figure who uses her international fame to affect policy agendas. Jolie's emotive response has led to her diaries being published, and in February 2007 she wrote an open editorial in *The Washington Post* about the crisis in Darfur. Subsequently, in her press junket to promote her film *A Mighty Heart*, she included interviews with 'Foreign Policy's' website and a glowing profile in *Newsweek* which was modestly titled 'Angelina Jolie Wants to Save the World' (Smith 25 June 2007).

Therefore, Jolie's activism would appear to epitomize Annan's belief that through the escalation of celebrity diplomacy, the UN's mission for universalism can be enhanced. However, her activities also indicate the extent to which the policy has proven problematic as she has intertwined her emotional rhetoric with her position as a celebrity diplomat. Invariably, her response to thorny international problems has been framed in 'terms of scenario, in which, once certain key scenes are linked [...] the plot will proceed inexorably to an upbeat fade' (Dideon 1998: 519). Thus, Jolie has accelerated the process of star power, but may be seen to have succumbed to a series of naive interventions which have been indulged by a compliant media (Cooper 2008: 34–5).

Moreover, the increased employment of celebrity diplomats has, in certain cases, been one of ever-diminishing returns. Most notably, the UN suffered from the indignities associated with the celebrity failures represented by former Princess Sarah 'Fergie' Ferguson and Geri Halliwell ('Ginger Spice'). In the case of Fergie, her financial collapse, caused by her divorce from Prince Andrew, meant that she could not afford to perform pro bono tasks for the UN. With regard to 'Ginger Spice', her inability to perform her tasks as an advocate for family planning and her marked decline in fame, meant she did not stand the test for even a comparatively short period of time.[1]

> These ill-judged choices played into a sentiment that the UN was getting out of control in its efforts to catch the celebrity wave. [...] Annan himself was reportedly shocked by meeting a celebrity who told him she was a UN Goodwill Ambassador, although he didn't know who she was. (Cooper 2008: 30)

Consequently, these difficulties have led to concerns being raised that the greater deployment of celebrity diplomats has undermined the UN's position as a serious force in world affairs. Instead of enhancing Annan's vision, it has been suggested that there was a trivialization of the UN's mission.

In 2003, the Secretary-General issued the first ever 'Guidelines for the Designation of Goodwill Ambassadors and Messengers of Peace' to specify the functions, conditions of services and termination of contracts with celebrity diplomats. This marked an institutional concern to maintain control over the escalating use of stars and was an attempt to affect guidelines across the whole of the UN (Fall and Tang 2006: 2). Subsequently, the UN's Joint Inspection unit reported back to the Secretariat that there should be a significant rationalization of the numbers of Goodwill Ambassadors, greater quality mechanisms, self-generated funds for travel and finite periods of operation (Fall and Tang 2006: 4).

Despite these problems, a more nuanced understanding of star power needs to be effected as the broader employment of film, music and sports stars. In a commercially dictated global media, the mass escalation of Goodwill Ambassadors may have been one of the few realistic responses open to Annan to promote the UN's activities. Undoubtedly, the activities of a number of celebrity ambassadors have existed beyond parody. However, in terms of celebrity performance, the ability of celebrities such as Jolie and Clooney to bring focus to international campaigns, to impact on policy agendas and to advocate the principles of the UN to the world's public, has been of significant worth in a period of greater fragmentation and heightened international conflict.

Conclusion

This analysis has sought to analyse the development of the celebritization of international politics. It has outlined the academic debates that have emerged between critical theorists and writers who argue for a more holistic approach to political aesthetics. The traditional paradigm needs to be critically evaluated as it over-simplifies passivity, both in terms of celebrity activism and public engagement. In particular, it has been noted that celebrities have become more politically conscious in an era of the global mediation of communications. The celebritization of politics has brought about new forms of political engagement, which indicate a dialectic transformation of high politics with a more populist approach to cultural citizenship.

It is necessary to affect the analytical tools through which to critically engage with these developments. Thus, the celebritization of politics should not be dismissed as an erosion of culture, but must be viewed within the framework of a change in political aesthetics in which there will be both positive and negative outcomes. Street's typology of celebrity performance has provided an effective framework to define the three main stages of celebrity activism within the UN (Street 2003, 2004).

In the early stages of UNICEF activity, celebrity activists such as Kaye and Ustinov can be defined as 'good international citizens' whose activism was conformist. Throughout these years, the UN's usage of celebrities was transformed from an ad hoc, inter-personal series of relations between the entertainment and political realms into a more sophisticated form of engagement. In tandem, certain Goodwill Ambassadors such as Hepburn, while remaining conformist, brought greater dignity to the role and transcended international public opinion.

In an era of transformative celebrity diplomacy, star activities became characterized by a greater intensity in style and a widening of their roles. These changes in the Goodwill Ambassador's behaviour were matched by their growing consciousness of their importance in making interventions within international political initiatives and their wider usage by a range of UN agencies. It should be noted that the more politicized era of celebrity diplomacy may be seen to exemplify both the strengths and difficulties of utilizing stars to active causes. Politicized celebrities have been critical of many regimes and the role of the UN itself. This may, in part, be reflective of a certain naivety in understanding the processes of political diplomacy. Further, it may be seen to indicate how a gulf exists between celebrity and political expectations in which popular political 'narratives' uncomfortably clash with the realist policies that have defined international power. It has led to criticisms that while star power may bring public attention to international affairs, it is limited in affecting real change.

These concerns came into greater focus during Annan's tenure as the UN Secretary-General from 1997 to 2007 in which a phase of ubiquitous celebrity diplomacy occurred wherein there was a significant escalation in the numbers of national, regional and international Goodwill Ambassadors and the introduction of Messengers of Peace. Annan's intensification of celebrity involvement referred to a recalibration of fame within an expanding range of global media sources, and to a public relations revolution in developing strategic communications to enhance the UN's concepts of idealism and universalism.

The success of film stars such as Jolie and Clooney may be seen to indicate that Annan's vision of politicized celebrities advancing the UN's idealist values across the world's media has been effective. Jolie, most especially, has become a credible international figure and has sought to use her star power to pressurize recalcitrant states to accord with agreements they have made in the General Assembly. Yet, it should be noted her influence may prove counter-productive as her leading role in UNHCR's campaigns may reflect an overestimation of her powers to effect lasting change. Moreover, the celebrity failures associated with Sarah Ferguson and Geri Halliwell provided the UN with a salutary lesson in widening the numbers of celebrities acting as Goodwill Ambassadors.

Therefore, in analysing the political aesthetics involved in defining the UN's experience of celebrity involvement, a mixed picture has emerged. Undoubtedly, Goodwill Ambassadors and Messengers of Peace have lent weight to the public campaigns waged by the UN in a commercially driven global news media. They have provided a definable focus for public engagement and have utilized their star power to affect pressure upon international policy-makers. Yet, as Annan's tenure indicated, while the escalation of celebrity power has its advantages, there are dangers in over-simplifying complex international policy debates and utilizing emotional responses. However, in returning to the wider debate about the respective merits of celebrity activism, this chapter has shown that the UN experience counters the accusation of star passivity. Celebrities have promoted new or alternative discourses, and while their activities have been mixed, they have affected credible interventions within international policy circles.

References

Alleyne, Mark D. (2003), *Global Lies? Propaganda, the UN and the World Order*, Basingstoke: Palgrave, Macmillan Publishers.

—— (2005), 'The United Nations' Celebrity Diplomacy', in *SAIS Review*, Baltimore: The John Hopkins University Press.

Annan, Kofi (2003), 'Secretary-General praises celebrity advocates as "new kind of star", shining light on hardship, injustice, in remarks at UNICEF gala', UN Press Release SG/SM/9049/ICEF/1863.

Boorstin, Daniel (1971), *The Image: A Guide to Pseudo-Events in America*, New York: Atheneum.

Calcutt, Andrew (9 September 2005), 'Celebrity Politics and the Politics of Celebrity', *A Paper Presented at the Annual Conference of the Association for Journalism Education*, London: University of Westminster.http://www.ajeuk.org/docs/andrew_calcutt_paper.doc

Cashmore, Ellis (2006), *Celebrity/Culture*, Abingdon, New York: Routledge.

Cooper, Andrew F. (Summer/Fall 2007a), 'Beyond Hollywood and the Boardroom: Celebrity Diplomacy', *Georgetown Journal of International Affairs*, Issue 8.1, pp. 125–32.

—— (September 2007b), 'Celebrity Diplomacy and the G8: Bono and Bob as Legitimate International Actors', *Working Paper No.29, The Centre for International Governance Innovation*, Waterloo, Ontario, Canada.

—— (2008), *Celebrity Diplomacy*, Boulder, London: Paradigm Publishers.

Corner, John (2003), 'Mediated Persona and Political Culture', in John Corner and Dick Pels (eds) *The Media and the Restyling of Politics*, London, Thousand Oaks, New Delhi: Sage Publications.

Corner, John and Pels, Dick (2003), 'Introduction: The Restyling of Politics', in John Corner and Dick Pels (eds), *The Media and the Restyling of Politics*, London, Thousand Oaks, New Delhi: Sage Publications.

Deacon, David and Golding, Peter (1994), *Taxation and Representation: The Media, Political Communication and the Poll Tax*, London: John Libbey.

Dideon, Joan (1998), 'Vacant Fervor', in Christopher Sylvester (ed.), *The Grove Book of Hollywood*, New York: Grove Press.

Drake, Philip and Higgins, Michael (2006), 'I'm a Celebrity, get me into Politics: The Political Celebrity and the Celebrity Politician', in Su Holmes and Sean Redmond (eds), *Framing Celebrity: New Directions in Celebrity Culture*, London and New York: Routledge.

Dreyfus, Richard (2000), 'Interview' quoted from Kenneth Bowser, *Hollywood DC: A Tale of Two Cities*, Freemantle Corporation (Broadcast on Bravo TV Network, November).

Drezner, Daniel W. (11 January 2007), 'Foreign Policy goes glam', *National Interest online*, downloaded from http://www.nationalinterest.org/Article.aspx?id=16012. Accessed 17 April 2008.

Fall, Papa Louis and Tang, Guangting (2006), *Goodwill Ambassadors in the United Nations System*, Geneva: UN Joint Inspection Unit.

Higgins, Michael (2005), 'The "public inquisitor" as media celebrity', *Unpublished Paper Presented at the Media and Politics Specialist Group (MPG) Panel at the Political Studies Association (PSA) Conference*, 5–7 April, University of Leeds.

Lowenthal, Leo (1944), 'The Triumph of Mass Idols', *Literature, Popular Culture and Society*, Palo Alto, California: Pacific Books, pp. 109–40.

Ling, Jack (5 June 1984), 'Interview with Mr Jack Ling conducted by Judith Spiegleman at UNICEF HQ', downloaded from www.unicef.org/thailand/UNICEF_in_Thailand_Fifty_Years.pdf. Accessed 17 April 2008.

Louw, Eric (2005), *The Media and Political Process*, London, Thousand Oaks, New Delhi: Sage Publications.

Marshall, P. David (1997), *Celebrity and Power: Fame in Contemporary Culture*, Minneapolis/London: University of Minnesota Press.

Mills, C. Wright (1956), *The Power Elite*, New York: Oxford University Press.

Monboit, George (21 June 2005), 'Bards of the Powerful: Far from challenging G8's role in African Poverty, Geldof and Bono are giving legitimacy to those responsible', *The Guardian*, downloaded from http://www.guardian.co.uk/politics/2005/jun/21/development.g8. Accessed 17 April 2008.

Postman, Neil (1987), *Amusing Ourselves to Death: Public Discourse in the Age of Show Business*, London: Methuen.

Puttnam, David (16 January, 2007), 'Look to the stars: Lord David Puttnam argues that the behind-the-scenes work of celebrities is vital to UNICEF's success', *The Guardian*, downloaded from http://www.guardian.co.uk/society/2007/jan/16/internationalaidanddevelopment.comment. Accessed 17 April 2008.

Smith, Sean (25 June 2007), 'Angelina Jolie wants to save the world', *Newsweek*, downloaded from http://www.prnewswire.com/cgi-bin/stories.pl?ACCT=104&STORY=/www/story/06-17-2007/0004609611&EDATE=. Accessed 17 April 2008.

Street, John (2003), 'The Celebrity Politician: Political Style and Popular Culture', in John Corner and Dick Pels (eds), *The Media and the Restyling of Politics*, London, Thousand Oaks, New Delhi: Sage Publications.

—— (2004), 'Celebrity Politicians: Popular Culture and Political Representation', *The British Journal of Politics and International Relations*, 6:4, pp. 435–452.

Ullman, Liv (8 February 1993), quoted in Frank Sesno 'Women and Children Make Up 80 per cent of the World's Refugees' CNN.

United Nations (2007), 'United Nations Messengers of Peace', UN Web Services, Department of Public Information, New York. downloaded from http://www.un.org/sg/mop/. Accessed 17 April 2008.

UNICEF Celebrity Relations & Special Events Section, Division of Communication (2006), *UNICEF: A Guide to Working with Goodwill Ambassadors*, New York.

Wheeler, Mark (2006), *Hollywood: Politics and Society*, London: British Film Institute.

Note

1. Halliwell took a robust approach to becoming an Ambassador based on her fame. Unfortunately, her less than diplomatic stance led to her only making one high profile trip to the Philippines concerning family planning and AIDS awareness in which she was accused by UN officials of not being 'up for the job'. For further details see Cooper (2008: 29).

Chapter 3

The Cosmopolitan-Communitarian Divide and Celebrity Anti-war Activism

Annika Bergman Rosamond

The question whether states and global institutions are morally obliged to protect distant others is a key feature in normative international relations (IR) scholarship. Most inquiries into this ethical dilemma focus on the moral agency of sovereign states and institutions and their pursuits of cosmopolitanism at the global stage, rather than the morally inspired acts of individual human beings (Erskine 2003; Brown 2003). In fact, Toni Erskine (2004: 22) has made numerous contributions to ethical debates on the possibility of assigning moral agency to states and international institutions such as the United Nations. In her words

> moral responsibility requires that those who are called on to uphold duties, and those who are held to account for evading them, must be moral agents – entities that, by definition, possess capacities to contemplate, recognise the significance of, and ultimately execute different courses of action. (Erskine 2004: 22)

A moral agent is an entity that has a pronounced self identity over time, which enables it to deliberate on moral dilemmas and make decisions accordingly (Erskine 2003, 2004). This chapter provides a critical examination of the morally inspired acts of individual celebrities in international society. The intention is not to decide whether such acts are good or bad, but to widen the debate on global ethics so as to include the other-regarding discourses and practices of individuals. In so doing, the chapter engages with the wider research question whether celebrity activism is developing into a distinct influential factor in international politics, or whether it is it merely an extension of those figures' public relations and image-making strategies (Huliaras and Tzifakis 2008: 5).

Moreover, the chapter is inspired by Andrew Cooper's research on celebrity diplomacy and his contention that there is an advantage in linking individual star power to a collective project, as well as that celebrities have 'the power to frame issues in a manner that attracts visibility and new channels of communication at the mass levels' (2008: 7). Similarly, P. David Marshall argues that 'celebrities [...] hail national and international audiences in the way only presidents, royalty and prime ministers can hope to achieve' (2006: 3). Having access to such audiences gives the individual celebrity a chance to influence foreign and security policies of their political community and, as such, help determine the boundaries of ethical inclusion and exclusion within and beyond borders. This chapter, then, focuses on celebrity contestations of prevailing security cultures, discourses and practices in global politics, and the extent to which celebrities can shift the boundaries of ethical responsibility to include their fellow citizens as well as those of other nations, for example, by highlighting the atrocities and human suffering of people living in war zones or the distinct experiences of serving soldiers and war veterans.

The discussion is situated within IR debates on the communitarian–cosmopolitan divide in global politics, and in particular, on the question whether it is possible to reconcile local ethical obligation to co-nationals and non-nationals alike. The communitarian–cosmopolitan debate can tell us something about celebrities' mixed motives for taking an interest in the welfare and security of distant others. This contention will be sustained through a case study that centres on three distinguished celebrities' objections to war and military intervention, with due emphasis on the US-led military invasion of Iraq in 2003 – Susan Sarandon, Sean Penn and George Clooney, all of who have been vocal critics of George W. Bush's decision to take the USA to war in Iraq. I make the assumption that the supposedly good deeds of celebrities are constituted within cosmopolitan, communitarian and personal conceptions of civic obligation and notions of good citizenship, some of which are self serving, helping individual celebrities to improve their image, and others aiming at improving the lives of their fellow citizens and distant others alike. As Huliaras and Tzifakis (2008: 14) have argued, 'when they visit poor countries or donate money to charities, they usually do it with the maximum of publicity'.

A key argument put forth here is that individual celebrity promotion of universal human rights, global peace projects and redistributive justice across borders is consistent with cosmopolitanism's privileging of the rights of individuals over those of sovereign states. However, the discursive power of celebrities, although being framed within a cosmopolitan-minded ethic, is not innocent since the individual entertainer cannot possibly concern themselves with every injustice in global politics and, therefore, has to make hard choices as to which projects to promote and which to leave behind. The individual celebrity can thus choose to ignore those issues that might not be all that popular with their fan base or international audience. As Marshall (2006: 3) contends, 'the texts that surround the celebrity are the source material for determining what is exhibited and what is repressed by the individual celebrity'.

Having introduced the conceptual context in the chapter, I discuss the communicative turn in contemporary IR scholarship by providing a brief investigation into the role of culture and global communications in constituting our collective understanding of global developments. I point to the significance of wedding the study of culture, broadly defined, with the insights of IR scholarship in order to better understand the acts preformed by individual celebrities in global politics. The conceptual arguments presented in the first part of the chapter are sustained through the provision of a case study that deals with a select few American celebrities' opposition to military intervention and war more broadly.

The Cosmopolitan–Communitarian Divide in IR

Cosmopolitanism gives preference to the protection of individual rights as opposed to those of sovereign states and because, the argument goes, we are all part of the same moral order, there is no 'inside' or 'outside' in international society, which renders attempts to differentiate between nationals and non-nationals meaningless (Brown 2002; Caney 2005; Beitz 1979; Erskine 2008). Key to cosmopolitan thought is the idea that all human beings have an inherent ability to engage in moral reasoning and through its application they are able to make ethical judgements that favour of universalist conceptions of duty rather than particularistic ones.

In contrast with cosmopolitans, communitarians conceptualize morality as something socially constructed within the political community rather than being shared by humanity at large. From a communitarian perspective, we are morally obliged to promote the welfare of the members of our own political community and it is only when we have done so that we might think about the well-being of distant others. In brief, 'communitarianism as a doctrine in its own right is about the moral identity of individual human beings, according to which one's own identity as a member of a particular community is far more important than membership of some notional society of all human beings' (Dower 1998:59). Furthermore, communitarians contend that what brings human beings together is their shared sense of 'particularism' (Walzer 1994: 83) rather than membership of a world community. From a strict communitarian perspective, it is morally justifiable to put the interests of the members of one's own community ahead of those of humanity, because political community is assumed to be a good thing in itself, worth defending (Walzer 1994).

Cosmopolitanism differs in this respect because it contends that it is our shared sense of humanity that protects us from human rights abuses and oppression rather than political community, and whether we reside in the affluent North or the less developed South should not matter. This way of thinking, however, is inconsistent with the erection of national borders since we have duties to 'men and citizens' alike (Linklater 1982). Having said that, very few cosmopolitan thinkers wish to do away with sovereign boundaries in their entirety, but argue for a world community composed of nation states sensitive to the needs of distant others in a thin cosmopolitan fashion. Immanuel Kant (1795), for example, made a case for an international 'federation of states' composed of republican and responsible governments in which international law and free trade would prevail. In the same vein, Andrew Linklater (1982, 1998), a contemporary international theorist, has developed an international theory that seeks to overcome the tension between communitarianism and cosmopolitanism by arguing for a new form of political community. His thin cosmopolitanism can offer insights into the analysis of global duty beyond borders by enabling us, for example, to think about the extent to which foreign and security state policies should be couched within ethical considerations rather than realist language and practice. Furthermore, Linklater's (1982: 15) theory helps us to reconcile our duties as 'men and citizen'. In his book *Transformation of the*

Political Community (1998), he explores ways in which we can reconcile our communitarian and cosmopolitan loyalties in what amounts to a thin cosmopolitan approach to global ethics. However, Linklater does not prescribe an ethical reasoning that denounces social and cultural diversity. The greatest challenge is not the lack of universal ethical principles, but the insufficient recognition of cultural difference (Linklater 1998: 75). In so doing, he advocates a new form of political community that builds upon cultural difference and a strong sense of obligation to distant others.

Drawing upon Habermas's discourse of ethics, he envisages the formation of universal communication communities in which the ethical boundaries are renegotiated in a way that allows for inclusion rather than exclusion. The idea is that all humans who are affected by a certain decision or way of reasoning should be invited to participate in political dialogue (Linklater 1998: 96), even if that ideal is hard to achieve in reality. Celebrities, nonetheless, can shed light on certain issues and stimulate dialogue across borders since 'fame culture offers "ordinary" and "extraordinary" people the chance of a heightened level of intimacy, an intimacy that potentially perhaps inevitably, destabilizes the borders and boundaries of identity' (Redmond 2006: 27).

Having presented some of the dilemmas emerging from the communitarian–cosmopolitan debate in IR, let me now turn to the role of individuals in global politics. As will be argued below, celebrities are often in the habit of depicting themselves as agents of cosmopolitanism, with a strong sense of obligation to distant others. In this context, Cooper (2008: 3) describes Bono as a 'moral entrepreneur' and suggests that what Bob Geldof 'does well is to mobilize and shame' governments into action. Their individual star quality and power ensure that celebrities have some saying in the selection of what events, developments and issues will be embraced by the international community. Mia Farrow's decision to go on hunger strike in 2009 in protest against the Sudanese government's treatment of the people living in Darfur refugee camps did not do much to transform Sudanese refugee policy, but brought home to millions of people, nonetheless, the severity of the situation in Darfur. Stars like Farrow are equipped with the power to select what global causes to promote and what developments to ignore, and this is a highly ethical choice that risks excluding some individuals while including others. What is more, such decisions are subjective and are framed within the practices and values of the celebrity's personal experiences and cultural specificities. As the brief case studies will demonstrate, celebrities are not untouched by communitarian loyalties to their own nation and the values governing that sphere. It should also be noted that celebrities might have deeply personal reasons for getting involved in the promotion of a particular cause. For instance, British actress Joanna Lumley, star of the much acclaimed TV comedy *Absolutely Fabulous*, has told the media that her decision to promote the right of British army Gurkha veterans to settle in the United Kingdom, upon retirement, was affected by her own father's wartime experience, having served alongside Gurkhas on various military missions.

Despite the role played by celebrity activists in the conduct of ethical conversations across borders, there is not all that much written on the topic in the IR literature, with the exception of people like Andrew Cooper (2008), Liza Richey and Stefano Ponte (2008). As Huliaras and Tzifakis (2008: 7) have observed 'the impact of individuals in the process of international politics seems to be exhausted with the study of agents of political authority'. However, if we align ourselves with the cosmopolitan assumption that individual rights are to be placed above those of sovereign states, then it makes sense to investigate the acts of the people working towards this goal. There is something fundamentally cosmopolitan about celebrities using their star power to spread the message of peace and a more equally distributed global income. As Cooper (2008: 91) has argued, celebrity diplomacy is a 'cosmopolitan activity' that serves to 'further the oneness of humanity'. He argues that cosmopolitan-minded celebrities promote 'a universal ethos' that is 'at odds with parochial attitudes and the tight restrictions of sovereignty' (Cooper 2008: 91). A key argument here, however, is that universalism of the kind Cooper describes, is not inherently opposed to cultural difference as has been developed above when considering Linklater's work (1998). The current chapter, nonetheless, concurs with the idea that celebrity diplomacy is perhaps not as global as it might seem, since it is dominated by 'high-profile individuals whose fame is a projection of the cultural power of the Anglo-sphere' (Cooper 2008: 91).

To sum up then, the cosmopolitan–communitarian debate can tell us something about the ethical underpinnings of celebrity activism by exploring the extent to which we have a moral duty to the welfare needs of citizens beyond borders. It also provides an excellent opportunity to place the emphasis upon the other-regarding acts of individuals in the international society by asking relevant questions about the agents who might be charged with the task of transforming the international order. Celebrities' efforts to rub off the values of their own political community as well as their privately held beliefs on global politics are not innocent since they risk including some distant others while excluding others. Furthermore, their activism is not necessarily mitigated through normal democratic processes and there are few checks and balances on their actions, but as Marsh et al. have recently argued (2010: 333), celebrity politics also has 'a unique capacity to reach out to and mobilise otherwise apathetic publics, and sometimes manage to give powerful voices to the disenfranchised in society and on the world stage'. For better or worse, celebrity is part of our contemporary global psyche and collective sense of culture, in particular, since 'people model themselves in part on the lives of those they admire' (Inglis 2010: 13), and megastars such as Madonna and Bono can provide an imaginary escape route from everyday boredom and give hope of achieving a 'better society, a decent home, a just world' (Inglis 2010: 13).

The Co-constitutive Relationship between Culture, Communications and International Relations

There is a growing interest in the co-constitution between culture and global communications in contemporary IR scholarship leading a number of scholars to critically investigate the effects that global communications and culture have on IR (Weber 2008; Lacy 2003, 2007).

Such scholarship goes beyond neorealist accounts of IR and their focus on exogenous forces as determinants of state behaviour, by allowing for non-systemic explanations that connect global politics with culture and communications. Stuart Croft's (2006) discursive investigation into the relationship between popular culture and the US-led War on Terror is of interest here. He contends that 'without understanding what has occurred in America at the level of popular culture, its meaning and impact, it is not possible to fully comprehend the American crisis discourse that is the "War on Terror"' (Croft 2006: 1). The discipline of IR has thus undergone a 'communicative turn' (Albert et al. 2008: 43). Scholars siding with this contention accept that both texts and visuals are key shapers of global audiences' understanding of international events, developments and social life (Weber 2008: 137; Hansen 2008). As Cynthia Weber (2008: 153) has argued, the 'supplementation of the linguistic turn with the visual turn should enable IR scholars to better understand how power and political responsibility function through contemporary forms of global communication'. The speedy circulation of texts and images across borders, through the various communicative channels, ensures global mass audiences. Human beings, provided they have access to global communication channels, are thus exposed to the same social world, even if their interpretations of that reality are subjective and constructed within specific domestic settings. As the editors of a special issue of the *Review of International Studies* on Global Communication argue, 'humans nowadays communicate and are being communicated with globally: they are invariably [...] connected with, mediated and remediated by what is going on elsewhere in the world as well as their locality' (Constantinou et al. 2008: 7).

Celebrities are part of this communicative turn and their presence within IR enables them to make appeals to mass audiences; in so doing, they brand themselves as moral agents with a strong sense of responsibility to distant others. They are thus 'constructed, circulated and consumed through the busy channels of media production' (Holmes and Redmond 2006: 6). Phrased differently, celebrities are communicative agents who raise awareness surrounding issues of global obligation and help legitimize certain courses of actions while negating others. They use their star power to communicate the devastating effects of famine, conflict, natural disasters, displaced people and refugees to domestic and international audiences. Cooper explains celebrities' global influence by noting that

> [...] the advantages of linking individual star power to a collective project are clear. Celebrities have the power to frame issues in a manner that attracts visibility and new channels of communication at the mass as well as the elite levels (2008: 7). [Furthermore], [...] MTV and other mechanisms – including both text messaging and a proliferation of blogs about Bono and other celebrity diplomats – provide a multitude of connections to global audiences. (2008: 10)

As much as celebrities are admired for such efforts, they are also criticized for selfishly using global media outlets to deplore poverty and war for the purpose of furthering their own careers and creating images of themselves as universal well-doers. Huliaras and Tzifakis

(2008: 13) argue that 'it is certain that interest in Africa or in global poverty offers celebrities excellent branding opportunities. Moreover the positions of goodwill ambassadors provide international clout'. Matthew Bishop and Michael Green (2008: 9) develop a similar argument by observing that celebrity philanthropists make

> some people uneasy. What does a rock star really know about the poor in Africa? Yet just as celebrities are now an integral part of capitalism, due to their ability to touch and influence the mass market, so too they are becoming a key ingredient in philanthrocapitalism, particularly on issues in which mobilizing public opinion is crucial.

At best, celebrities evoke a sense of ethical obligation to distant others, and, at worst, they give rise to donor fatigue or public reluctance to consider the negative effects of global poverty, sexual violence, ethnic and religious repression in faraway places. While leaders around the world largely agree that internationally acclaimed stars are central to the discursive condemnation of poverty and conflict, there are those who feel that celebrity and politics should be kept apart. Those who object to the involvement of celebrities in the shaping of foreign and security policy are particularly sceptical of the inconsistency between their great personal wealth and rather limited financial commitment to international justice. Bono has been criticized for his decision to transfer some of his personal wealth to the Netherlands to evade paying taxes in Ireland, which provoked similar discussions. British columnist, Marina Hyde sums up the celebrity dilemma by writing that

> once upon the time [...] the entertainment industry was an industry which made entertainment. Its workforce was required to do quaint things like show up at movie sets, or make music [...] Today, that brief has expanded and includes such things as 'attempting to negotiate with the Taliban' and 'being brought in to fix the Iraqi refugee crisis. (2009: 1)

What is more, by focusing on the trauma of certain nations and ignoring others, celebrity activists help to 'excommunicate' (Mattelart 1996) certain audiences. As such, 'the subaltern cannot effectively communicate his or her life story and predicament. S/he is constantly represented and communicated [...] through dominant structures and forms of communication that are not her own' (Constantinou et al. 2008: 10). In this sense, Richard Gere has been known to speak 'for the entire world' which he has done amongst other things in the Palestinian context (Hyde 2009: 1).

What is perhaps lacking in some of the celebrities' approaches to global poverty and conflict is irony and self-deprecation. James Brassett's work (2007, 2009) on the constitutive relationship between 'British irony' and 'global justice' is of particular interest here because it provides insight into the role of irony in evoking compassion across borders. Brassett (2007: 1) suggests that 'the growing interest in irony might be understood in terms of a long running liberal recognition of the relativity of one's own position'. In his view, irony enables us to conceptualize the limits of our ethical commitments beyond borders. His investigation centres around the British graffiti artist Banksy's ironic take on political and societal developments and the use of irony in the comedy of British actor Ricky Gervais. Brassett (2007, 2009) investigates Gervais's use of ironic self-deprecation in constituting global responsibility across borders. On a British television aid show Gervais invited Bob Geldof, Bono and celebrity chef Jamie Oliver to engage in ironic self-mockery by asking them to perform in a sketch that openly scorned their own global philanthropy, hoping that such a provocation would inspire popular generosity 'by making the viewer think about their own involvement in the fiction that global justice campaigns "actually achieve something"' (Brassett 2007: 20). Similarly, Drake and Higgins' (2006: 93–94) deconstruction of Bono's speeches, demonstrate that he too employs 'self-mocking' irony when appealing to global audiences.

The argument made so far is that celebrity culture, media and global communications help constitute international politics by exposing domestic and international audiences to moral dilemmas of a global reach, and as such inspire public dialogue and support for certain foreign and security policy actions while objecting to others. Hence, the 'star or celebrity is not just a desired object but also an intimate doorway for connecting people' (Holmes and Redmond 2006: 3). Through the projection of certain global dilemmas as being particularly pressing, celebrity activism both inspires ethical dialogue across communities and national boundaries, and hinders it by raising questions about the individual celebrity's sincerity and real commitment to the issue at hand. Below I shall look at the way in which three American celebrities have used their star status to communicate their anti-war message to global and national audiences and in so doing portrayed themselves as possible candidates for moral agency in global politics.

Celebrity Opposition to War

The United State's decision to launch the Second Gulf War attracted a great deal of opposition amongst celebrities, some of whom were more vocal than others. From the onset, it was clear that the ethical justifications for and against the military intervention were to be negotiated through media representations of the Iraqi leadership as the *radical other* that constitutes a threat to national and international security (Campbell 1992). While there was support for that media construction amongst some people, there was a great deal of scepticism as to the legality of a military intervention.

There is a long history of using texts and images in questioning the ethics of war and the inequalities within international society more broadly. War poetry, for example, tends to be critical of the brutish nature of violent conflict rather than celebrating the glory of war; Wilfred Owen's poem *Dulce et decorum est. Pro patria mori* ('Sweet and fitting it is to die for one's country'), which was written towards the end of the First World War, questioned whether war really was 'sweet and fitting' and if it was honourable 'to die for one's country'

(Owen 1988: 188–89); Pablo Picasso's legendary painting *La Guernica* depicts the brutalities of the Spanish Civil War in a notorious attempt to problematize the use of brute force and give voice to the sufferers of war; in the aftermath of September 11 and the US-led invasions into Afghanistan and Iraq, there was a surge in texts and visuals that critiqued the 'War on Terror'. A number of novels and non-fiction books have debated the tension between the Muslim and non-Muslim worlds (Buruma 2006; Updike 2006); the legendary British pop artistic duo Gilbert and George use a combination of texts and images to produce a distinct art form; the piece 'Six Bomb Pictures', which is composed of six individual images – Bomb, Bombs, Bomber, Bombers, Bombing and Terror – draws attention to the London bombing of 7 July 2005 and the threats of terror that Londoners have had to endure since then (*The Guardian* 19 December 2006).

What follows here is a brief account of the war activism pursued by American movie stars Susan Sarandon, Sean Penn and George Clooney, all of whom have articulated a strong sense of scepticism towards staging a war against Iraq as part of the 'War on Terror' exercise. The three celebrities have been chosen because they have made their motivations for opposing the military intervention vocal and very public, and more importantly, they have shaped them within a largely cosmopolitan language. The celebrities put in the limelight here are not the only artists and celebrity activists who have strongly objected to the Iraqi war – people like Mia Farrow and Jane Fonda have expressed very similar views – however, the limited length of this chapter does not allow for an extensive survey of all those efforts. Suffice is to say that over 100 celebrities signed in 2002 a letter addressed to President Bush in which they declared their objection to the Iraqi war (*Associated Press* 13 February 2003).

The objective here is not to judge the three celebrities' normative commitment to international peace and justice, nor to try to decide whether their deeds are morally right or wrong, but to sustain the argument made above – i.e. that IR scholarship needs to be more sensitive to such individual efforts to make positive contributions to humanity. This is important since there are signs of politics and celebrity culture moving closer together, which, if not taken seriously, could compromise the integrity of individual states' foreign and security policies.

Susan Sarandon – A Grand Dame of Celebrity Activism

The first celebrity activist to be examined here is Susan Sarandon, an Oscar-winning actress and UNICEF goodwill ambassador, who has gained a reputation for opposing global injustices including famine and AIDS. She is also known for her promotion of different national and international welfare projects and schemes as well as taking issue with the oppression of human rights in Central America and elsewhere. Sarandon's commitment to these causes, according to her, is an outflow of her student days and dedication to empowerment in the USA and beyond. In her own words, 'Like many people of my generation, this empowerment became part of who I am and this belief in democracy and justice for all was not just theoretical [...] I've been so fortunate in finding a profession which encourages me to do that and to follow my passion and curiosity' (*The Washington Post* 13 February 2003). Her ethical stance is that 'Everyone has a responsibility towards this larger family of man, but especially if you're privileged, that increases your responsibility' (Sheahen undated). So, people like herself are charged with the task of seeking to transform the international community in a cosmopolitan fashion.

In order to transform her words into deeds, Sarandon agreed to be one of the main speakers at an anti-Iraqi war rally in New York, attended by 100,000 people in early 2003 ('BBC News' 17 February 2003). Sarandon's opposition to the war is defined by her firm belief that pre-emptive strike is never justified and that 'there are alternatives to war. Nothing has been proved so far that warrants an invasion of Iraq' ('BBC News' 17 February 2003). She is of the view that violence can never combat violence and opposes war as an institution of international society. Rather cleverly, the actress blamed George W. Bush for having 'hijacked our losses and our fears', which could be interpreted as her way of saying that Sadam Hussein and his alleged weapons of mass destruction were never a real threat to the US society, but a social construction used by the President to justify the invasion of Iraq. Sarandon's position is that Americans '*do not want to risk their children or the children of Iraq*' (Morales 2003:1), thus expressing a sentiment that could be described as cosmopolitan because the actress does not differentiate between the children of USA and Iraq but groups them together. Sarandon's outspoken criticism of the Iraqi war made her an easy target for people who objected to her anti-war sentiments. She was labelled unpatriotic and a 'Bin-Laden lover' with some of the criticism originating within the entertainment industry itself (Klatell 2006). Seen from this perspective, her cosmopolitan-minded efforts to save the lives of 'man and citizen' alike were deemed anti-American and unpatriotic. Sarandon takes issue with this reading of her activism by contending that as much as pre-emptive warfare scares her, she is 'equally frightened by the systematic threats to our civil liberties', and strongly opposes George W. Bush's frequent use of othering disourses such as the famous phrase 'you're either with us or against us', since it reveals an objection to asking relevant questions about the war. Saradon argues that such questioning has come to be considered as 'anti-American'. To sustain this claim, she points to the war-time tendency to assume that 'a patriot is someone who follows and doesn't question' governmental policy (*The Washington Post* 13 February 2003). As her male counterpart Sean Penn, Saradon asks for more dialogue within and beyond national society, and, in so doing, arriving at other solutions than brute force to resolve disputes between states. Her cosmopolitanism thus does not centre on the use of force to spread the liberal message across the globe but on the dispersion of social, economic and political rights through other means.

While being deemed unpatriotic and anti-American by some US citizens, she has been celebrated by others, in particular for her efforts to improve the lives of homecoming American war veterans. In her own words, 'it's really important to listen to what the veterans are telling us about what they need' and 'I think we need to acknowledge the toll that it takes on them physically and psychologically and spiritually' (McCarthy 2007). Rather than being anti-patriotic and opposed to bounded community, her stance on conflict and war demonstrates a strong sense of dual obligation to Iraqi civilians and homecoming US soldiers and their families. If we were also to consider the mythical status of war veterans and citizen soldiers in constituting political community itself, then Sarandon's efforts to promote such individuals' entitlements to social justice and participation in public dialogue would seem to be far from being un-American but quite the opposite.

Sean Penn – A Man of Practical Action

Sean Penn has been just as vocal as Susan Sarandon in opposing the invasion of Iraq. Sean Penn's anti-war activism is consistent with his overarching commitment to justice within and beyond borders. What defines his activism is a strong dedication to discursive condemnations of what he sees as malpractices in American foreign and domestic policy, which he combines with practical action in places like New Orleans, Haiti and elsewhere. More recently, and since the break-up of his marriage, he has become involved in the build-up of the Haitian nation through financial donations as well as voluntary aid work, including digging trenches, delivering food and medicine to the needy, and going on fund-raising trips to Washington and the United Nations (Adams 2010).

As for the war in Iraq, he firmly believed that it was unjust and damaging to both US soldiers and civilians on the ground. In 2002, he went on a three-day trip to Iraq to see for himself what problems the Iraqi people were facing at the time. His firm belief was that a war could be avoided but that it would involve 'enormous commitment on the part of the Iraqi government as well as the United States' (Lyon 2002). When asked whether he was afraid of appearing unpatriotic by paying a visit to Iraq, he answered that it was actually his patriotism that made him go to Iraq in the first place. In his words, 'I'm here for a simple reason, which is because I'm a patriot and an American who has benefited enormously from being an American, and because I had areas of personal concern and conscience that led me to come to Iraq' (Lyon 2002). Furthermore, 'if there's going to be blood on my hands, I'm determined that it's not going to be invisible. That blood is not just Iraqi blood, it's the blood of American soldiers' (Lyon 2002). Penn's dual concern for man and citizen tells us that he is a man of cosmopolitan principles who does not believe that supporting his country's war policy at any cost is consistent with patriotism. Throughout the war, he advocated the withdrawal of troops from Iraq and the protection of innocent civilians in that country.

In 2002, in an attempt to use his celebrity status to prevent the Iraqi war from taking place, Penn paid $56,000 to have an open letter to George W. Bush published in *The Washington Post*, in which he criticized the President and his foreign policy towards Iraq:

Like you, I am a father and an American. Like you, I consider myself a patriot. Like you, I was horrified by the events of this past year [...] However, I do not believe in a simplistic and inflammatory view of good and evil. I believe this is a big world full of men, women, and children who struggle to eat, to love, to work, to protect their families, their beliefs, and their dreams. (Penn 2002)

Again the activist/actor uses language that is couched within a cosmopolitan conception of duty and rights, telling a story about a world that is joined together through our common humanity in which men, women and children all have the same bodily needs and in which their lives are based upon the same basic premises. In the same letter, he states that

My father, like yours, was decorated for service in World War II. He raised me with a deep belief in the Constitution and the Bill of Rights, as they should apply to all Americans who would sacrifice to maintain them and to all human beings as a matter of principle. (Penn 2002)

His celebration of the American Constitution and Bill of Rights, demonstrates that his world-view is constituted within the values of the American nation and that he is loyal to the liberalism of that political community, while opposing the US government demonstrating its military clout beyond the water's edge. His position is thus that human rights are universal in reach and that Americans and non-Americans alike should be granted the same entitlements. He encourages President Bush to 'support us, your fellow Americans, and indeed, mankind. Defend us from fundamentalism abroad but don't turn a blind eye to the fundamentalism of a diminished citizenry through loss of civil liberties' (Penn 2002).

As an outflow of his commitment to civil liberties and rights, Sean Penn co-led a town hall anti-Iraq war meeting in Oakland, California in March 2007, which was attended by some 800 people. The key premise of the meeting was that 'We do support our troops, but not the exploitation of them and their families' ('Fox News' 26 March 2007). Penn used very colourful language to describe his feelings with regards to Iraq:

The money that's spent on this war would be better spent on building levees in New Orleans and health care in Africa and care for our veterans. Iraq is not our toilet. It's a country of human beings whose lives that were once oppressed by Saddam are now in Dante's Inferno. ('Fox News' 26 March 2007)

Penn's language reveals a strong commitment to distributive justice at the global level by urging the regime to redirect the money spent on war to the needy at home and abroad. In other words, Penn and the other people attending the town hall meeting do not morally differentiate between Americans and Iraqis since both nations are entitled to peace and social and political justice. As we shall see below, Penn's disregard for the reactions of the Bush regime to his war protests is also a feature of George Clooney's celebrity activism.

George Clooney: A Man of Big Words

Like the other two celebrities examined here, George Clooney is a person with a strong sense of obligation to distant others. His anti-war sentiments are couched within his leftist politics and related principle of social justice. He is perhaps best known for his attempts to make a contribution to peace in Darfur, although he also strongly objected to the Iraqi invasion. His commitment to international justice and peace was rewarded when he was presented with the Bob Hope Humanitarian Award in September 2010 for being the main driving force behind the 'telethons' that took place in the aftermath of 9/11, Hurricane Katrina as well as the earthquake in Haiti.

George Clooney has, alongside Mia Farrow, been the US entertainment industry's strongest advocate of peace in Darfur. He has been lobbying the White House and was granted a private meeting with President Obama in 2009 with the goal to discuss Darfur and Africa more generally. Despite his best efforts, the actor/activist has not been able to prevent refugees from being killed in the camps of Darfur despite a ceasefire being signed by the Sudanese government and one of the most influential rebel groups in the area in February 2010. Clooney describes his failed efforts to bring peace to Sudan:

> I've been honoured to be able to lend my celebrity to help wherever I can, especially on behalf of the United Nations. But in the case of Darfur, it's been the greatest failure of my life. ('Peace FM Online 2 September 2010)

Clooney's frustration was the topic of his satirical acceptance speech at the Emmy Award ceremony in 2010, focusing on the lack of long-term commitment to trouble spots and war-torn regions in Africa and elsewhere, saying that

> When the disaster happens, everybody wants to help, everybody in this room wants to help, everybody at home wants to help. .The hard part is seven months later, five years later, when we're on to a new story. Honestly, we fail at that, most of the time. That's the facts. I fail at that. (Saunders, 2010)

George Clooney's objection to the Iraqi war is thus part of a wider self-narrative that tells a story about a person dedicated to international justice and peace and who attempts to use his star power to impact upon global events and what he saw as the misguided foreign policy choices of the Bush regime. His demeanour is that of a self-deprecating person who is very willing to admit his own shortcomings. Despite this, he takes his celebrity status very seriously and attempts to use it in a constructive way. In line with his leftist politics, George Clooney accused the Bush administration of conducting itself in a fashion similar to that of the *Sopranos* – the famous television show that portrays the New Jersey mafia in a less than flattering way – again using humour to deliver his message. He was very critical of the political discourse of the Bush regime and its use of expressions such as the 'axis of evil' as a collective term to define certain states. Clooney objected to the use of such discursive constructions urging people to

'Listen to the language!' 'Evil'. 'Nexus of evil?' 'Evil-doer' 'What's wrong with their vocabulary'? (*Discover the networks org*, undated).

He urged the US government to conduct a dialogue with Sadam Hussein before 'jumping in and killing people first?' ('BBC News' 20 January 2003). He also warned against the civilian casualties that an invasion of Iraq would result in and noted that 'I don't believe we're going to wait until the last resort to do it. That's what bothers me' ('BBC News' 20 January 2003). George Clooney's views on American foreign policy during the Bush era, have made him a target of the American Right, which depicted his activism as unpatriotic. From this brief account of Clooney's celebrity activism we can extract that he is not a person who is afraid of shaking the foundations of the US war policy and that he is not wedded to his own political community at any cost, but, if needed, is willing to critique it from within. He has even critiqued his own allies in the Democratic Party for not being sufficiently outspoken on Iraq.

From the brief outline above, I have shown that the three celebrities' objections to the Iraqi war is an outflow of their co-constitutive commitment to international and domestic justice as well as the liberal values embodied in the American constitution. Their attitude is that they – as privileged individuals and artists – have a duty to distant others as well as their fellow Americans, and that they should use their star power productively to improve the lives of others. The US administration, nonetheless, decided to launch a pre-emptive war against Iraq in 2003, despite a great deal of opposition to the intervention prior to it, throughout the operation, and in its aftermath. As argued above, a deconstruction of the discourses couching the anti-war activism of the three celebrities demonstrates that they share a commitment to a cosmopolitan notion of a shared moral order and humanity. This is particularly visible in their questioning of the treatment of Iraqi civilians. The war itself is critiqued on the basis of its illegality, the key objection being that pre-emptive war hurts civilians and American soldiers alike.

Their communitarianism lies in their belief in America as a great nation worth preserving. They agree that the war veterans and their families should be given financial support and believe that this position is consistent with their overarching commitment to a cosmopolitan international order. Sean Penn defines the American constitution and the Bill of Rights as key markers of his own character. It is clear that his strong belief in the American nation is what made him oppose the intervention to Iraq rather than a wish to destabilize the political community itself. Susan Sarandon's experience as a young radical during her student years is also telling here. George Clooney is perhaps the odd one out because he has often been depicted as a pretty boy who happens to be a very good actor, but in fact he is a deeply political individual who inherited his interest in politics from his father who was a local

TV personality in Kentucky. Clooney dedicated his film *Goodnight and Good Luck* to his father as a way of acknowledging the latter's influence on the star's interest in politics and journalism. Even if the three individual celebrities selected here are not unique in opposing war and other injustices, they stand out because they were all prepared to speak out against the political establishment with regard to Iraq, and as such they do not comply with the thesis that contemporary 'celebrity activism is [...] not extremely anti-establishment' (Huliaras and Tzifakis 2008: 15). In a climate defined by celebrities being propped up by personal advisors and preferring to act through NGOs (Cooper 2008), the three celebrities examined stand out because there is a fair amount of individualism embedded in their activism.

A Few Concluding Remarks

This chapter initially provided a brief account of the communitarian–cosmopolitan debate in IR by identifying variations in their conceptions of global obligation to distant others. Drawing upon the work of Andrew Linklater, it highlighted the significance of ethically inspired dialogue between political communities and argued that celebrities have an important role to play in bringing light to international security developments and pressing issues such as war and poverty. This was followed by a brief discussion of the co-constitutive relationship between global politics, culture and communications, which has lead IR scholars to closely examine this increasingly important nexus. It was argued that celebrity culture, media and global communications help to constitute international politics by exposing domestic and international audiences to moral dilemmas of a global reach.

In sum, the chapter made a case for moving beyond statist conceptions of global duty so as to include the other-regarding acts of individuals on the global stage, in particular celebrities, since they figure in a large way in the global peace movement and in the promotion of redistributive justice across borders. Their presence in such processes has given rise to a new and very interesting research agenda and this chapter has sought to contribute to such work. By placing the emphasis upon the cosmopolitan–communitarian debate in IR, this chapter has developed the thesis that celebrity activism is constituted within the interaction between universal and particular loyalties to nationals and non-nationals. As we have seen above, the three celebrities examined here are all prone to resort to universal language whilst celebrating the liberal and constitutional values of the US society. Perhaps more importantly, they are not easily placed within the category of celebrities who are pro-establishment, but would seem to pursue their own humanitarian agendas. This is what sets them apart from more compliant celebrities, or those who seek to achieve their goals by pairing up with a particular politician. The exception here is George Clooney, who has a reportedly close relationship with President Obama; however, the former has been very reluctant to capitalize on this relationship. The three case studies that have been examined show clear sympathy with the view that foreign and security policy should be ethically inspired rather than simply couched within realist language. The fact that these celebrities were prepared to put their reputation and career at stake for the greater good of saving Iraqi and American lives alike, suggests at least a thin commitment to justice and peace within and beyond the bounded community.

References

Adams, Guy (2010), 'Hollywood star shows how aid helping Haiti', *NZ Herald*, http://www.nzherald.co.nz/world/news/article.cfm?c_id=2&objectid=10658061. Accessed 10 September 2010.

Associated Press (2003), 'Celebrities speak out against war with Iraq', http://www.ctv.ca/CTVNews/Canada/20030213/celebrities_war_030213/. Accessed 10 September 2010.

BBC News, 17 February 2003, 'Millions join global anti-war protests', http://news.bbc.co.uk/1/hi/world/europe/2765215.stm. Accessed 29 September 2010.

—— 20 January 2003, 'Clooney in anti-war protest', http://news.bbc.co.uk/1/hi/entertainment/2677881.stm. Accessed 12 September 2010.

Beitz, Charles R. (1979), *Political Theory and International Relations*, Princeton: Princeton University Press.

Brown, Chris (2002), *Sovereignty, Rights and Justice: International Political Theory Today*, Cambridge: Polity Press.

—— (2003), 'Moral Agency and International Society: Reflections on Norms, the UN, the Gulf War and the Kosovo Campaign', in Toni Erskine (ed.), *Can Institutions have Responsibilities: Collective Moral Agency and International Relations*, Basingstoke: Palgrave Macmillan.

Bishop, Matthew and Green, Michael (2008), *Philanthrocapitalism How the Rich Can Save the World and Why We Should Let Them*, London: A & C Black.

Brassett, James (2007), 'British Irony, Global Justice: Chris Brown, Banksy & Ricky Gervais on the Comedy of Ethics', *Paper Presented at Leicester University Politics and International Relations Seminar Series*, 7 November 2007.

—— (2009), 'British Irony, Global Justice: A Pragmatic Reading of Chris Brown, Banksy and Ricky Gervais', *Review of International Studies*, 35:1, pp. 219–245.

Buruma, Ian (2006), *Murder in Amsterdam: The Death of Theo van Gogh and the Limits of Tolerance*, Harmondsworth: Penguin.

Campbell, David (1992), *Writing Security: United States Foreign Policy and the Politics of Identity*, Manchester: Manchester University Press.

Caney, Simon (2005), *Justice Beyond Borders. A Global Political Theory*, Oxford: Oxford University Press.

Constantinou Costas, M., Richmond Oliver, P. and Watson, Alison M. S. (2008), 'International Relations and Challenges of Global Communication', *Review of International Studies*, 35 (S1), pp. 5–9.

Cooper, Andrew F. (2008), *Celebrity Diplomacy*, London: Paradigm.

Croft, Stuart (2006), *Culture, Crisis and America's War on Terror*, Cambridge: Cambridge University Press.

David Marsh, Paul Hart and Karen Tindall (2010), 'Celebrity Politics: The Politics of the Late Modernity?', *Political Studies Review*, 8(3), pp. 322–340.

'Discover the networks org', http://www.discoverthenetworks.org/individualProfile.asp?indid=1271. Accessed 2 October 2010.

Dower, Nigel (1998), *World Ethics*, Edinburgh: Edinburgh University Press.

Drake, Philip and Higgins, Michael (2006), 'I'm a Celebrity, Get Me into Politics': The Political Celebrity and the Celebrity Politician', in Su Holmes and Sean Redmond (eds), *Framing Celebrity New Directions in Celebrity Culture*, London: Routledge.

Erskine, Toni (2003), *Can Institutions Have Responsibilities? Collective Moral Agency and International Relations*, Basingstoke: Palgrave Macmillan.

—— (2004), '"Blood on the UN's Hands"? Assigning Responsibilities to an Intergovernmental Organization', *Global Society*, 18(1) (January 2004), pp. 21–42.

—— (2008), *Embedded Cosmopolitanism Duties to Strangers and Enemies in a World of Dislocated Communities*, Oxford: Oxford University Press.

Fox News, 26 March 2007, 'Sean Penn Leads California Town Hall Against Iraq War', http://www.foxnews.com/story/0,2933,261145,00.html. Accessed 1 September 2010.

Hansen, Lene (2008), 'Visual Securitisation: Taking Discourse Analysis form the Word to the Image', *Paper presented at the 49th Annual ISA Convention*, 26–29 March, San Francisco.

Higgins, Charlotte 'Gilbert and George unveil 7/7 works for retrospective' *The Guardian* 19 December 2006

Holmes, Su and Redmond, Sean (2006), *Framing Celebrity New Directions in Celebrity Culture*, London: Routledge.

Huliaras, Asteris and Tzifakis, Nikolaos (2008), 'The Dynamics of Celebrity Activism: Mia Farrow and the "Genocide Olympics" Campaign', *Karamanlis Working Papers in Hellenic and European Studies*, No. 7, The Fletcher School of Law and Diplomacy.

Hyde, Marina (2009), *Celebrity How Entertainers Took Over the World and Why We Need an Exit Strategy*, London: Harvill Secker.

Inglis, Fred (2010), *A Short History of Celebrity*, Princeton: Princeton University Press.

Kant, Immanuel (1795), *Perpetual Peace, and Other Essays on Politics, History, and Morals*, HPC Classics Series. Indianapolis

Klatell, James M. (2006), 'Sarandon Got Death Threats Over Iraq', http://www.cbsnews.com/stories/2006/04/30/entertainment/main1561644.shtml. Accessed 3 October 2010.

Lacy, Mark (2003), 'War, Cinema and International Relations', *Alternatives: Global, Local, Political*, 28:5, pp. 611–636.

—— (2007), 'Responsibility and Terror: Violence and Visual Culture in the Precarious Life', in Christina Masters and Elizabeth Dauphinee (eds), *The Logic of Biopower and the War on Terror*, London: Palgrave Macmillan.

Linklater, Andrew (1982), *Men and Citizens in the Theory of International Relations*, 1st ed., London: Macmillan Press.

—— (1998), *The Transformation of Political Community Ethical Foundations of the Post-Westphalian Era*, Cambridge: Polity Press.

Lyon, Alistair (2002), 'Sean Penn Says War in Iraq Is Avoidable', *Common Dreams*, http://www.commondreams.org/headlines02/1215-10.htm. Accessed 10 September 2010.

Marshall, P. David (2006), *The Celebrity Culture Reader*, London: Routledge.

Mathias Albert, Oliver Kessler and Stephan Stetter (2008), 'IR and the "communicative turn"', *Review of International Studies*, 34, Special Issue, pp. 21–42.

Mattelart, Armand (1996), *The Invention of Communication*, Minneapolis: Minneapolis University Press.

McCarthy, Ellen (2007), 'When the War Comes To the Home Front', *The Washington Post*, 14 September, http://www.washingtonpost.com/wp-dyn/content/article/2007/09/13/AR2007091300745.html. Accessed 1 October 2010.

Morales, Tatiana (2003), 'Sarandon To Bush: Get Real On War', CBS News.com, http://www.cbsnews.com/stories/2003/02/14/earlyshow/living/main540658.shtml. Accessed 1 October 2010.

Owen, Wilfred (1988), 'Dulce et Decorum Est', in J. Stallworthy (ed.), *The Oxford Book of War Poetry*, Oxford: Oxford University Press, pp. 188–89.

Peace FM Online, 2 September 2010 'George Clooney Fails To End Genocide In Darfur', http://foreign.peacefmonline.com/entertainment/201009/77758.php. Accessed 3 October 2010.

Penn, Sean (2002), 'An Open Letter to the President of the United States of America', *The Washington Post*, 19 October, http://www.peace.ca/seanpenn.htm. Accessed 10 September 2010.

Redmond, Sean (2006), 'Intimate Fame Everywhere', in Su Holmes and Sean Redmond (eds), *Framing Celebrity New Directions in Celebrity Culture*, London: Routledge.

Richey, Liza and Ponte, Stefano (2008), 'Better (Red) than Dead? Celebrities, consumption and international aid', *Third World Quarterly*, 29:4, pp. 711–729.

Saunders, Tim (2010), 'George Clooney Challenges Hollywood To Help Charity', *Look to the Stars the World of Celebrity Giving*, http://www.looktothestars.org/news/4981-george-clooney-challenges-hollywood-to-help-charity. Accessed 2 October 2010.

Sheahen, Laura (2005), 'The Power of One: Interview with Susan Sarandon', *Beliefnet*, http://www.beliefnet.com/Love-Family/Charity-Service/2005/07/The-Power-Of-One-Interview-With-Susan-Sarandon.aspx. Accessed 19 September 2010.

The Washington Post (2003), 'Iraq: Antiwar Voices With Susan Sarandon, Actor, Activist', http://www.washingtonpost.com/wp srv/liveonline/03/special/world/sp_world_sarandon021303.htm. Accessed 11 September 2010.

Updike, John (2006), *The Terrorist*, New York: Knopf.

Walzer, Michael (1977), *Unjust and Just Wars*, New York: Basic Books.

—— (1994), *Thick and Thin: Moral Argument at Home and Abroad*, Notre Dame: Notre Dame University Press.

Weber, Cynthia (2008), 'Popular visual language as global communication: the remediation of United Nations Flight 93', *Review of International Studies*, 35 (S1), pp. 137–154.

Part II

Transnational Celebrity Activism and Conflict

Chapter 4

'Creating a Groundswell or Getting on the Bandwagon? Celebrities, the Media and Distant Conflict'

Virgil Hawkins

Introduction

Much has been made of the apparently increasing involvement of celebrities in response to conflict situations, and it is often assumed that their actions have a major impact on the levels of outside attention that a conflict is able to attract. But how much of an impact do these celebrities really have? And why do celebrities choose to champion certain conflict situations over others? Are their choices somehow related to the impact they think they may be able to generate? This chapter aims to address these questions.

Celebrities have a long history of involvement in causes aimed at assisting those less fortunate than themselves, offering their fame, money, time, voices, songs, movie-making skills, parental services, and even breast milk, to assist those suffering from the ravages of conflict, poverty and disease. At times it appears that celebrity involvement in charity is not simply admired, but even expected. In December 2008, a spending spree on clothes at a boutique in Australia by Paris Hilton prompted a front page article in Australia's *Herald Sun* newspaper, complete with quotes from angry aid workers about how much that money could accomplish for an impoverished African village (Metlikovec and Magee 2008). The tone of the article was not that Hilton would have been praised and admired if she had given money to distant Africa, rather that she should be ashamed for not doing so.

When it comes to situations of conflict, celebrities have found a number of ways to involve themselves as part of a broader humanitarian and/or political response. They have worked to raise the profile of conflicts through media interviews, visits to refugee camps, making documentaries and participating in demonstrations; they have donated money for humanitarian assistance, and have engaged in advocacy aimed directly at policy-makers and corporations. Celebrities have been appointed as 'goodwill ambassadors' and 'messengers of peace' by the UN and its agencies (see Chapters 2 and 11 in this volume). Some have used their wealth to take out advertisements in major newspapers to protest against a war about to happen, or to raise public awareness about one that has already begun.

Some researchers and journalists have begun using the term 'celebrity diplomacy' (Cooper 2008), and we are told that 'an elite group of celebrities have gotten so involved in diplomacy that they are eclipsing true diplomats' (Chang et al. 2008). But celebrities lack perhaps the most critical ingredient of diplomacy – representation of a particular constituency or group (Evans and Newnham 1998). This is abundantly clear in Mia Farrow's defence of her outspoken approach over the issue of Darfur: 'I'm completely free to say anything I want [...] I have no trade agreements with anyone and I can be as incautious as I feel the occasion calls for' (Weir and Chang 2008). Celebrity activism (or 'actorvism') (Andrews 2007) is essentially the same as the lobbying, advocacy and activism conducted by other civil society and interest groups (who also engage in a blend of outspoken public pressure and private lobbying of policy-makers), except for the fact that celebrities generally have the initial advantage of a warmed-up media spotlight and often better access to financial resources.

Celebrity Impact and the Media

Just how much of an impact does such celebrity activism have? Jason McCue, a human rights lawyer who has worked with celebrities, tells us that we should not 'doubt the power of these people to put an issue in the public mind [...] Darfur was unknown to most Americans until Clooney took it on' (Wroe 2007). But is this really the case? Have celebrities really managed to pluck conflict-related humanitarian crises from obscurity and place them front and centre in the public agenda? John Prendergast, a former US government official who also works with celebrities, went even further in an interview in March 2008, stating that, a year earlier,

> there was no prospect of a U.N.-led peacekeeping force, and civilian protection was looking more and more elusive as the days ticked by. After intensive work by a number of these celebrities in coordination with work by strong activist groups, we have a unified Security Council authorizing a peacekeeping force, and China playing an assertive role behind the scenes in getting Sudan to agree to that force. (Traub 2008)

From what is already known about the politics of the UN Security Council and peacekeeping, the suggestion that celebrities played a key role in unifying the UN Security Council and getting troops on the ground in Darfur seems quite a stretch to say the least. These two sources, who are closely involved in promoting celebrity activism, can hardly be expected to serve as objective commentators, but there are many others in the media and beyond who glowingly appraise the power of celebrities in such causes (Boustany 2007; Philp 2008). Many NGOs also seem convinced of the value of celebrities, with some speaking of celebrities as essential in 'selling' a humanitarian campaign (Cottle and Nolan 2007: 868–69).

There seems to be evidence supporting the role of celebrities in short-term surges in financial donations, with reports, for example, of donations to certain aid agencies suddenly spiking on the day that a celebrity appears on CNN or the *Oprah Winfrey Show* (Boustany 2007). Voices from the donors can confirm the link between the celebrity and the donation. In one case, a donor who had contributed to a child feeding programme in Africa after seeing an interview with Drew Barrymore on CNN, remarked that the interview 'struck a chord with me [...] When I feel something is authentic, I respond [...] I could see the passion in her expression' (Boustany 2008). It must also be noted, however, that one study on emergency fund-raising for disaster relief found that just 12 per cent of respondents agreed or strongly agreed that celebrity endorsements would make an impact on their decision to donate, with 35 per cent disagreeing or strongly disagreeing (Bennett and Kottasz 2000). Of course these are responses to a hypothetical question and may not accurately represent the interviewees' motives for giving in the event of an actual disaster.

When it comes to media attention, however, it is considerably more difficult to pin down evidence of links between celebrity activism and coverage. The following sections look at celebrity involvement in response to conflict in Darfur and the Democratic Republic of Congo (DRC), and media attention to these conflicts in the USA. It is largely based on LexisNexis searches (during critical periods of attention and/or celebrity involvement) of US newspapers, as well as network (ABC, CBS and NBC) and cable news transcripts (CNBC, CNN, Fox News and MSNBC).[1]

The searches for the television transcripts included so-called 'hard news' programmes (the main news programmes) and 'soft news' programmes (such as ABC's *20/20*, CBS's *60 Minutes*, NBC's *Dateline*, CNN's *Showbiz Tonight* and Fox's *O'Reilly Factor*). Graphs of the results of these searches can be found in the appendix. Searches were also conducted of other soft programmes and publications, including the *Oprah Winfrey Show*, *Entertainment Tonight*, *Access Hollywood*, *E!*, *Vanity Fair* and *Daily Variety*.

Darfur

In the case of Darfur, media coverage and civil society initiatives began gathering momentum in 2004, in the absence of any major celebrity initiatives. The belated media interest (coming more than one year after the conflict had begun) was largely sparked by the claim by the UN Humanitarian Coordinator in Sudan, Mukesh Kapila, that the situation in Darfur was comparable to that in Rwanda (Reuters 2004). Critically, this claim came as the tenth anniversary of the Rwandan genocide approached. The comparison was picked up by the *New York Times* columnist, Nicholas Kristof (among others) (Kristof 2004). UN Secretary General Kofi Annan and US President George W. Bush expressed concern about the crisis in Darfur in statements commemorating the Rwandan genocide (Anon 2004). The association between Darfur and genocide was formed, and what had been until then sporadic coverage began to grow. At the end of June 2004, Annan visited Darfur with US Secretary of State Colin Powell. Other political initiatives followed, and media coverage was boosted to a new level. It is worth noting that roughly one month before media interest was sparked, Angelina Jolie, having visited refugees from Darfur in Chad in her capacity as a UNHCR goodwill ambassador, had made a 50,000 USD donation and urged individuals and corporations to also donate to the cause (UNHCR 2004). These efforts were not covered by US newspapers or television networks.

The association between Darfur and genocide proved powerful, and a civil society movement began to emerge. The Save Darfur coalition was established in July 2004, focusing solely on raising awareness and advocacy (not aid), and began to mobilize a large and well-funded support base. It began as a group led by Jewish groups such as the United States Holocaust Memorial Museum and the American Jewish World Service, but quickly expanded to encompass Christian and other groups. The portrayal of Darfur as a genocide

Number of articles/news stories in US media on Darfur, June-September 2004

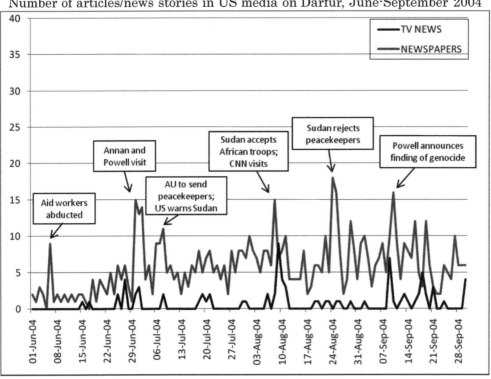

(raising comparisons with the Holocaust), and as one that was being perpetrated by 'Arabs' (perceived by many Jewish and Christian groups as a common 'foe'), certainly contributed to the emergence of such a strong movement (Prunier 2006; Eichler-Levine and Hicks 2007). The movement would gain momentum through 2005 and 2006, leading to the organization of a number of large-scale high-profile events.

Media coverage of Darfur had fallen in 2005, but resurged in 2006, partly because the conflict escalated, but also partly due to efforts in the US to draw attention to the conflict. By early 2006, celebrity efforts had also begun to gain momentum. George Clooney had visited the region and launched a documentary on his return. At the same time, Angelina Jolie paid for a letter to be published in the *USA Today* highlighting the humanitarian crisis in Darfur. These actions were timed to coincide with a nationwide rally (held four days after these celebrity events, on 30 April) organized by the Save Darfur coalition. The rally attracted 50,000 people in Washington DC alone. Speakers at the rally included George Clooney and Senator Barack Obama.

Media coverage of Darfur peaked at this point. There was heavy coverage of the rallies and the student, religious and other movements that had organized and held the event. Celebrity involvement was certainly covered, but it was by no means the central focus of

Number of articles/news stories in US media on Darfur, March-June 2006

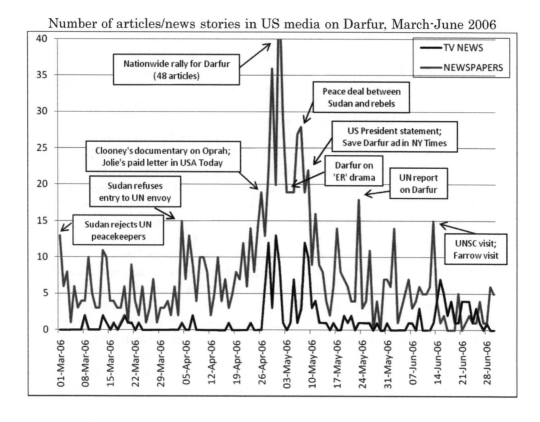

coverage. In a broadcast on ABC's 'World News Tonight' programme, for example, the reporter presented short interviews with three people: a victim of the conflict, Nicholas Kristof, and George Clooney (in that order) (Marquez 2006). It can be assumed that celebrity involvement served as a boost to the rallies and to the media coverage of them, but it is extremely difficult to separate the credit due to the organizers of the rallies, and that due to the celebrities who supported them. It is also worth noting that while the peak of newspaper coverage (48 articles on one day) is quite impressive for an African conflict, coverage of a conflict involving Israel at its peak is able to exceed this level for weeks at a time, on some days exceeding double the peak of coverage for Darfur.

Media coverage remained relatively high in the months that followed. There was heavy political activity, and there was heavy celebrity activity. A peace deal was signed between the Sudanese government and one of the main rebel groups. US political activity heightened, the UN released a report on the situation and a UN Security Council delegation visited the region. The Save Darfur coalition paid for a full-page advertisement in the *New York Times*. On the celebrity side, Darfur appeared as a setting for an episode of the hospital drama *ER*, and there were visits to the region by Bono and Mia Farrow. Again, it is difficult to separate exactly at what point the coverage was inspired by the politics and at what point by celebrity, but it is clear that celebrity activism was the object of some of the coverage.

The issue of Darfur also began to emerge (although sporadically) in soft news coverage from this point on, particularly in association with the celebrities involved in campaigning for Darfur. George Clooney's documentary was introduced on the *Oprah Winfrey Show* just prior to the Save Darfur rally (this was the first time the issue of Darfur appeared in depth on this programme) (Winfrey 2006). Fleeting references to Darfur (the announcement of screenings of or awards for documentaries about the conflict, for example) grew in publications such as *Daily Variety*. 'MTV' even facilitated the creation of computer games to raise awareness about Darfur (Ruiz 2006). This type of coverage may well have had some impact on public attentiveness. The image in the public eye of celebrity involvement on the issue of Darfur certainly became a strong one as seen in the parody sketch by Onion News Network, in which a mock panel debates how people in Darfur could be made more aware of what American celebrities were doing for them (Anon 2007).

Fast forward one year. Celebrities had become increasingly active and there were a number of political developments, but overall coverage had dropped somewhat, and the celebrity effect on the media coverage remained ambiguous. In early December 2007, two high-profile political events and three high-profile celebrity events focusing on Darfur happened in the space of just four days. A group of veteran statesmen (known as the Elders; for more on them, see Huijser and Tay in this volume), including Jimmy Carter and Desmond Tutu, released a report on the conflict and called for a ceasefire; and a nationwide student movement held a fast for Darfur – 'DarfurFast'. At the same time, a documentary, '*Darfur Now*', featuring Don Cheadle (among others), was released; Mia Farrow launched a fund to support Darfur; and a documentary narrated by George Clooney, '*Sand and Sorrow*' was aired. A spike in coverage was certainly unmistakable, but it could be considered relatively modest (considering the concentration of events), and perhaps revealing of some degree of media fatigue.

The connection between the Beijing Olympics and the conflict in Darfur (China was criticized for its support for the Sudanese government) kept the issue of Darfur on the media agenda for the following months. This debate was sustained by sectors of civil society, celebrities, and the media itself. Most notably, Steven Spielberg's withdrawal from his position as artistic adviser to the Olympics over China's stance on Darfur (following pressure from human rights groups, as well as Mia Farrow) caused a rise in coverage.

On 1 February 2008, George Clooney was appointed a UN 'messenger of peace', upon his return from a two-week trip with UN officials to Darfur, Chad and the DRC. This attracted some television coverage in the US. The following day, rebels in Chad entered the capital N'Djamena and the battle became the subject of media attention for the next few days. Later in the month, a visit to Africa by US President Bush caused another spike in media coverage on Darfur, as did a peace deal between Chad and Sudan in March. The latter happened to coincide with some coverage of a donation of 500,000 USD by the celebrity-led organization, Not On Our Watch, to sustain World Food Programme operations in Darfur.

Number of articles/news stories in US media on Darfur, December 2007-March 2008

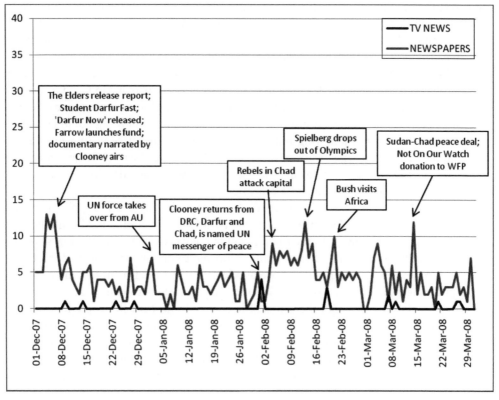

Overall, however, media coverage of Darfur by 2008 had fallen, not only well below the peak of 2006, but also below the 2004 levels, when the conflict had first managed to attract the outside world's attention. According to Google, Internet searches of Darfur originating from the USA reached their high points in 2006 and 2007, and began to decline in 2008.[2] This was despite increasing (and increasingly more organized) celebrity activity in support of Darfur, including the release of a pop video in September 2007 featuring a long list of stars including Matt Damon, Desmond Tutu, Elle Macpherson, Kanye West and the Will.i.am of the Black Eyed Peas (Wroe 2007).

The levels of media coverage seem to show some (albeit often highly ambiguous) evidence of very temporary impact by celebrities on the media agenda at some points in time in the case of Darfur. But how about long-term trends in public opinion polls, which perhaps better demonstrate the reach of celebrities to the public through a wider set of formal and informal information sources? Public opinion polls on Darfur over the years of the conflict reveal a moderate and largely unchanging level of public interest in the conflict. In a series of news interest index surveys conducted by the Pew Research Center for the People & the Press, respondents were asked whether they were following the conflict in Darfur very closely, fairly closely, not too closely, or not at all closely. Four surveys were conducted, in July 2004, May 2006, December 2006 and June 2007 (Pew 2009). Little change was observed in the results over time. The percentage of those following the conflict very closely began at 14 per cent in 2004 (prior to any major celebrity involvement), and rose to 16 per cent in May 2006 (at the peak of media and civil society engagement). By December 2006, it had fallen to thirteen per cent, and in June 2007, to twelve per cent. In the course of the four surveys, those following the conflict fairly closely remained steady at 22–23 per cent, those following not too closely at 27–29 per cent, and those following not at all closely at 33–36 per cent. In a fifth survey regarding the news of an arrest warrant being issued for the President of Sudan on charges of war crimes in Darfur, those following the issue very closely made up nine per cent of the respondents, while those following the conflict not at all closely made up 48 per cent.

These figures certainly do not reveal a groundswell of public interest, and appear to negate the existence of noticeable celebrity impact on public attention to Darfur. Public interest here appears to be roughly in line with the rise and fall of media coverage over the years, *not* the growing celebrity involvement. There remains, however, room for some speculation. It may be the case, for example, that in the absence of celebrity attention, Darfur would have fallen off the public agenda, but the work of celebrities helped sustain some degree of attention. It is also possible that, although there was little change in how much people followed the conflict, among those following the conflict not at all closely, many at least came to know of the existence of the conflict in Darfur through celebrity activity. Another possibility is that while the percentage of those that followed the story of Darfur very closely did not increase, many of those that were already following the story very closely were inspired by celebrities to become more actively involved, joining rallies and petitions or donating money.

Overall, in the case of Darfur, because of the powerful civil society movement already in place before celebrities arrived in force on the scene, it is difficult to isolate the celebrity effect from the effects of other movements. The Save Darfur coalition is well funded, well organized, and claims to have membership representing 130 million people. While it is certainly likely that celebrity activity has served as a welcome boost to civil society movements, the civil society movement was a highly powerful force in its own right.

Democratic Republic of Congo

The DRC is host to perhaps the 'greatest' stealth conflict of all time (Hawkins 2008). Despite drawing in armed forces from at least eight foreign countries and causing more deaths than any conflict the world has seen since World War II (5.4 million as of 2007), it has been largely ignored by the media and other key actors in international affairs. In 2004, when conflict in Darfur had begun to cause considerable outrage on humanitarian grounds, the known death toll in the DRC was some 80 times greater than that in Darfur. But the DRC conflict has remained largely 'off the radar', so much so that it does not even feature on public opinion polls – public awareness of the conflict is apparently not at measureable levels (or at levels considered worthy of measuring).

It took several years, but celebrities eventually found their way there. The DRC has been visited by such celebrities as Ben Affleck, George Clooney, Mia Farrow, Angelina Jolie, Jessica Lange and Lucy Liu. Benji and Joel Madden and Nicole Richie are among others who have become involved in raising awareness of the conflict. NBA star Dikembe Mutombo (from the DRC) used his celebrity status to raise money to build a hospital in the DRC. In January 2005, the *Oprah Winfrey Show* featured the conflict from the perspective of the sexual abuse of women (in a programme with a story about Ricky Martin's travels to meet tsunami orphans). Oprah Winfrey closed the programme saying, 'I know millions of people have not heard about what's going on in the Congo, but now that you have heard, you can't act like you didn't hear it' (Winfrey 2005). In October 2005, the travel log from Angelina Jolie's trip to the DRC was launched as an online exhibition by the US Holocaust Memorial Museum's Committee of Conscience. In December 2008, Ben Affleck, having made a number of exploratory visits to the DRC, released a short video called '*Gimme Shelter*' with Mick Jagger (the Rolling Stones song of the same title was used as the music for the video) as part of a UNCHR campaign to support humanitarian programmes in the DRC.

But these efforts appear to have made little impact on media coverage of the conflict. It is worth taking a look at media coverage around the beginning of 2008, a time that saw the screening of a documentary by Lisa Jackson about the DRC at the 'Sundance Film Festival', the release of a survey revealing a total death toll of 5.4 million people from the conflict, a visit to the DRC (as well as Darfur and Chad) by George Clooney and a visit to Rwanda by US President Bush. In the period from December 2007 to March 2008 coverage of the DRC was negligible, with only two relatively small spikes worthy of mention – that regarding the release of the results of the death toll survey and a peace deal, and another following an earthquake in Rwanda/DRC. NBC news did take advantage of the US President's visit to Rwanda to report from the DRC, but the association of the visit with the DRC remained weak.

The period between late 2008 and early 2009 is also worthy of observation, as it was a time of major developments in the conflict in the DRC, as well as of heightened celebrity activity. The most powerful rebel group in the DRC, Laurent Nkunda's National Congress for the Defence of the People (CNDP) launched a series of major offensives in eastern DRC, but this was eventually countered by an unlikely DRC-Rwandan alliance that resulted in the arrest of Nkunda. At the same time, an equally unlikely DRC-Uganda-Southern Sudanese alliance attempted to crush the remnants of Uganda's Lord's Resistance Army (LRA) in the DRC. The LRA retaliated, massacring as many as 500 civilians on Christmas Day 2008. The initial escalation of violence in late October and November 2008 attracted some media attention (although it must be noted that a large proportion of the articles appearing in the newspapers about the conflict were short news briefs), but this declined towards the end of

Number of articles/news stories in US media on the DRC, December 2007-March 2008

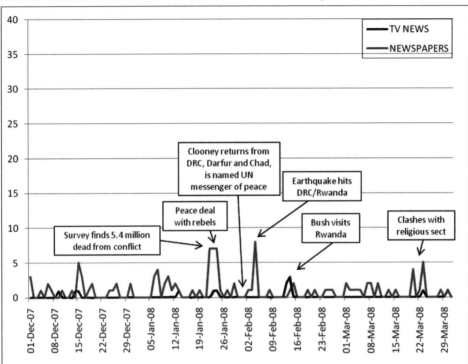

November. After a lull in media attention broken only by a spike when the LRA massacre was reported, a rise in newspaper coverage was seen in late January 2009 as Rwandan troops entered the DRC and Nkunda was arrested.

The same period saw visits to the DRC by Ben Affleck and Mia Farrow, as well as the release of two videos by Affleck – 'Gimme Shelter' and 'The Reporter' (the latter a documentary covering Nicholas Kristof's trip to the DRC in 2007 that premiered at the Sundance Film Festival). Also in January 2009, a fund-raiser for the DRC in Hollywood attracted a large number of celebrities, including Maria Bello, Mia Farrow, Emile Hirsch and Robin Wright Penn. These initiatives met with very limited media coverage. All television stories about the DRC for December 2008 (all except one were aired by CNN) were focused on the plight of the DRC's mountain gorillas, with the exception of one story about Ben Affleck's short documentary and another about Mia Farrow's trip to the DRC.

It is difficult to see any visible effects of celebrity involvement in the media agenda in the case of the DRC (except the few articles/programmes that directly covered the celebrities' activities). The moderate level of media response to the escalation of violence in late 2008

Number of articles/news stories in US media on the DRC, October 2008-Febraury 2009

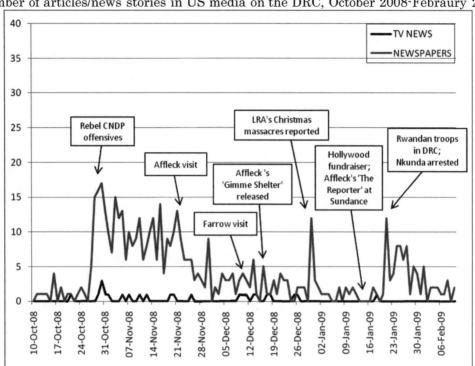

(a very rare occurrence for a conflict so uniformly ignored) did not follow any celebrity initiatives, and coverage in fact declined as celebrity involvement grew. It must be said that the combined effort levels that celebrities have devoted to raising awareness of conflict in the DRC are far below those for Darfur (for reasons that will be discussed below), despite the fact that a relatively large number of celebrities have visited and spoken out about the conflict. If the failure of those measuring public opinion to even conduct polls on the public's awareness of conflict in the DRC is any indication, it appears that celebrities are making little headway in drawing attention to the conflict in the DRC.

One problem with celebrity attempts to draw attention to a conflict situation is that the attention generated generally ends up being focused on the celebrity him/herself, with the issue the celebrity is trying to draw attention to remaining a background issue. As Simon Cottle and David Nolan point out, celebrity is 'used tactically to try and prise open the stubborn gates of media attention but these tactics are already shaped by the prevailing media logic and, as such, predisposed to produce fleeting, shallow or questionable coverage at best' (Cottle and Nolan 2007: 869). The media certainly seem attracted by the apparent mismatch of celebrities who are living in the lap of luxury, yet at times can be found visiting situations of abject poverty and suffering, or rubbing shoulders with world leaders. The image of Angelina Jolie as 'the superstar supermom who saves the world in between wiping runny noses' (Andrews 2007), for example, has appeal in this sense, and it is generally this aspect that keeps the limelight, rather than the issue being promoted.

George Clooney was interviewed by NBC's 'Today show' in 2008 about being named a UN messenger of peace, and the questions asked were clearly focused on him. This could be seen from the opening question, 'What do we call you, Envoy Clooney now?' to the closing question, in which Clooney is forced to choose which is more important to him, realizing success as an activist or getting an Oscar: 'Which one? Which one? No, compare it [...] Choose. I'm going to make you choose'. At one point, Clooney spoke of a woman in the DRC who had been raped and set on fire, to which the interviewer responded, 'You were affected by these women?' (Curry 2008). The same could be seen in a similar interview for CBS's *The Early Show*, in which questions included, 'Is this life-changing in some way for you?' and 'Are you up for some award or something?' (Smith 2008).

The 'softer' the news source becomes, the more pronounced this trend becomes. A search of the *Vanity Fair* magazine reveals 22 mentions of Darfur, but all except one (an article on China's relationship with Africa in 2007) (Junger 2007) mention Darfur only in passing, and usually in association with a celebrity. A *Press Association* article in February 2009 focusing on Joel Madden was based on comments made at a party to support charity work in the DRC. The reporter obviously attended the event, but the resulting article was almost entirely about Madden's family and who he hopes will win an Oscar at the upcoming awards ceremony (Press Association 2009). Readers will have the opportunity (that they may not otherwise have had) to see the words, 'Democratic Republic of Congo' in the article, but will not have the opportunity to know any more.

This is also reflected in the responses by the audience to the news of celebrity activism. News on the entertainment site E! Online of Ben Affleck's documentary about the DRC attracted twelve comments from readers but not one attempted to address the issue of the DRC. Instead, the comments were focused on Affleck's looks ('Time has not been kind to Mr Affleck', 'I think he still looks great') and his family responsibilities ('He has a newborn at home and he's going to Washington? Priorities, priorities [...] I give them 6 months') (Grossberg 2009).

Celebrity Choices: Making the Easy Sell?

The media may be attracted to stories of celebrities that double as activists, but they are not as easily swayed to take an interest in the objects of celebrity activism as some may think. Angelina Jolie's initial calls for help for Darfur in March 2004, for example, fell largely on deaf ears, and celebrity efforts in the DRC have met with very little enthusiasm from the media. The media have their own interests, their own agenda and their own reasons for covering or not covering certain world events, and visits to a conflict zone and/or words of concern from celebrities, or sometimes even from the president of the country may do little to change this.

When US President Bush visited Rwanda in February 2008, for example, he raised the issue of the neighbouring DRC at a press conference with his Rwandan counterpart (White House 2008). Yet the media were more interested in upcoming US elections, Cuban President Fidel Castro's announcement that he would resign, and the perpetrators of the Rwandan genocide, and had no questions about the DRC. The same applies to celebrities. In an interview on NBC's *Saturday Today* in 2006, *Blood Diamond* star Djimon Hounsou tried at three different points to raise the issue of child soldiers, but was diverted by the interviewer back to the topic of the movie itself and to the diamond industry's campaign to counter the bad publicity the movie was generating (Hollar 2007). The line of questioning was already fixed.

When it comes to selecting conflicts for coverage, a number of factors influence the media's decisions, among them national/political interest, simplicity, sensationalism, and the ability to identify and sympathize with the victims (Hawkins 2008: 189–195; Moeller 2006). The media almost completely ignored the conflict in Darfur for its first year, dismissing it as a 'tribal' conflict. But when it came to be portrayed as a case of 'Arabs' (the bad guys) victimizing 'blacks' (the good guys), and in the form of genocide, just as the tenth anniversary of the Rwandan genocide approached (with the ominous and guilt-laden 'never again' frame), the conditions of simplicity, sensationalism, and the ability to identify and sympathize with the victims fell into place. That is, even in the absence of celebrities, the media had its own reasons to be interested. The sheer complexity of the conflict in the DRC, on the other hand, made such a simplified Hollywood storyline untenable, and with no particular single 'ethnic' group that could fit the role of the innocent victim, media interest did not last, despite the unparalleled scale of the conflict. Close connections between certain key belligerents and the US did not help matters either.

Media-savvy celebrities are surely aware of what will sell and what will not, and may well choose to focus their attention accordingly. Both the media and its consumers (the general public) are more likely to be receptive to a simple and sensational plot in which there is an 'obvious' terrible injustice to be countered. Such a situation makes advocacy work much more effective: the plot is easier to understand, the message easier to deliver, and a reaction easier to generate. Furthermore, celebrities do not usually attempt to pluck conflicts from obscurity and bring them to the fore. Most conflicts that celebrities choose to target are those already on the media and public agendas – in fact it is often because of media coverage that they learn about the conflicts they choose to focus on. They essentially take up a cause that is already known and established, attempting to give a boost to existing attention and outrage.

Celebrities are sometimes faced with the charge that they are using their activist work to generate publicity for themselves. In a media interview featuring George Clooney, Brad Pitt and Don Cheadle, Clooney countered this suggestion with a simple, 'At what point do you think any one of us needs more publicity?' (Tourtellotte 2007). While this may be the case, what such celebrities surely want to avoid is bad publicity, and this may well factor into conflict choices. Avoiding bad publicity means staying on the side of the 'home team', going with the grain of what can often be fiercely aggressive nationalism/patriotism, not against it. In this sense, it is safe for those based in the US to criticize Sudan and China (for backing Sudan) over the issue of Darfur. Being critical of the US actions in Iraq (particularly once it had commenced its invasion), on the other hand, is far less safe. When the Dixie Chicks criticized US President Bush over the war in Iraq, they faced boycotts of their music from radio stations, and at least one station organized a public dumping of their tapes, CDs and concert tickets (Reuters 2003).

It is interesting in this sense to see the choices of the celebrity-led advocacy and aid organization, Not On Our Watch (founded by Don Cheadle, George Clooney, Matt Damon, Brad Pitt, David Pressman and Jerry Weintraub). This charity has chosen to focus on Darfur, Burma (Myanmar) and Zimbabwe. These are not the worst humanitarian situations in the world, and the governments there are not necessarily the most oppressive (Zunes 2008; Kekic 2007: 5). But they are certainly seen as the poster children for brutality and oppression – the popular bad guys. This makes advocacy work against these governments not only quite safe (in terms of celebrity image), but also more effective in generating support. Getting to the bottom of the conflict in DRC, on the other hand, would inevitably involve taking a close look at the US government's links with (and support for) Rwanda and Uganda, who have twice invaded the DRC, as well as the dubious actions of US mining corporations in the DRC (Montague 2002; Snow 2005). Probing in these directions would mean getting on the wrong side of the 'home team', which could well have negative consequences for the public image of the celebrities involved. Ben Affleck does not mention the role of natural resources in the DRC conflict in his short documentary, and interestingly is seen as being close to Rwanda (he has apparently taken Rwandan President Paul Kagame's children to baseball games, for example) (Snow 2009).

This is not to suggest that such calculations of what will sell and what might earn bad publicity are primarily, or always, behind celebrity selections. Celebrities may well be more receptive themselves to such simplified storylines. The 'day jobs' of actors are, after all, usually focused around storylines in which 'good' and 'evil' are clearly defined and separated, and celebrities are just as receptive as anyone else is to the power of emotive media coverage. George Clooney's interest in Darfur, for example, was sparked by Nicholas Kristof's emotive columns in the *New York Times*. For Don Cheadle it was his involvement in the movie *Hotel Rwanda* – the issue of 'genocide' was the connection.

Whatever their reasons, the fact is that many celebrity activists have spent time in both Darfur and the DRC, and are aware that the scale of suffering in the DRC is greater than that in Darfur, yet the focus of their activism almost invariably ends up being on Darfur, not the DRC. Angelina Jolie, for example, co-chairs the charity, Education Partnership for Children of Conflict, and while the homepage for this organization tells us that the DRC has more than double the number of out-of-school children than does Sudan, the DRC is not an option for those wishing to donate. Potential donors can choose to support projects in Haiti, Darfur, Iraq and New Orleans (the victims of Hurricane Katrina, not conflict). Ben Affleck may be an exception in this case, choosing to focus primarily on the DRC. He gave his reason as follows: 'I thought a lot of people are advocating on Darfur. I'd just be a very small log on a big fire. I started getting interested in Congo and I thought, this is a place where I can have a really big impact' (Powell 2008). The DRC was a 'niche' crisis. In general, celebrities returning from the DRC talk of the humanitarian suffering they encounter, but there is not the fiery 'this-must-be-stopped' enthusiasm that we hear from those returning from Darfur.

Conclusions

Using the examples of Darfur and the DRC, this study suggests that the impact of celebrities in drawing attention to foreign conflicts is not as powerful as is often assumed. In the short term, stories about celebrity activism in response to conflicts were at times taken up and became news stories, and occasionally caused a very brief rise in coverage. In the long term, an increasing and increasingly active set of celebrities did not seem to be able to increase or sustain media or public interest in either of the conflicts. Although evidence cannot be pinned down with certainty, celebrity activism could be interpreted as being somewhat effective (in temporarily raising attention) where there was already established political, media and public interest in the conflict (Darfur), and at times when the activism coincided with action by civil society and/or political leaders. This could also help explain why levels of celebrity interest and activity in response to Darfur were much higher than those for the DRC – with the former (having been framed in a simplified good-versus-evil storyline) being easier to 'sell'.

One limitation of this study is that it does not adequately cover the wide variety of soft news sources, and is unable to account for trends in the blogosphere and exchanges in social networking Internet sites, which may hold more clues about the impact of celebrities on public attentiveness and knowledge. By the same token, soft news sources tend to take their cues from trends in the hard news market (Baum 2003: 51), and as noted above, the 'softer' the news source becomes, the more likely a celebrity-mediated story about a conflict situation is going to be about the celebrity and not about the conflict situation. Soft news may help make news about distant conflicts more accessible to the public, who then become 'accidentally attentive', particularly in cases that are framed in simplistic and moralistic terms (Baum 2003: 18–56). But public opinion surveys in the case of Darfur suggest that the public were not becoming any more interested in following the conflict despite heavy celebrity involvement. Perhaps it can also be said that mainstream media interest was not quite high enough to cross over in a major way onto the soft and informal media agendas.

It would be unfair to judge the efforts of celebrities on whether they managed to single-handedly pressure their governments to intervene in conflict situations, mobilize massive grassroots networks and generate enough aid to stem the humanitarian suffering, or bring a conflict to a halt. But by the same token, it is important to be sober in evaluating the impact of celebrity activism. We should not confuse the grand presence of celebrities (the seemingly endless camera flashes and publicized interactions with presidents and prime ministers) for real impact in drawing substantial attention to conflict situations.

Celebrities seem to need a receptive and already active media and public, and can perhaps be most effective in boosting attention in established and ongoing responses to conflict, not in putting a conflict on the agenda in the first place, or in raising attention in cases in which substantial interest does not already exist.

References

Andrews, Helena (2007), '"Actorvists" make people care', *Politico*, 12 July, http://www.politico.com/news/stories/0607/4459.html. Accessed 28 April 2009.

Anon (2004), 'Bush, Annan call for end to Sudan fighting', CNN, 7 April.

—— (2007), 'How can we raise awareness in Darfur of how much we're doing for them', Onion News Network, http://www.theonion.com/content/video/how_can_we_raise_awareness_in. Accessed 20 April 2009.

Baum, Matthew (2003), *Soft News goes to War: Public Opinion and American Foreign Policy in the New Media Age*, Princeton: Princeton University Press.

Bennett, Roger and Kottasz, Rita (2000), 'Emergency fund-raising for disaster relief', *Disaster Prevention and Management*, 9:5, pp. 352–360.

Boustany, Nora (2007), 'Hollywood stars find an audience for social causes', *Washington Post*, 10 June.

Chang, Juju (2008), *Good Morning America*, ABC News, 9 March.

Chang, Juju, Desiree Adib, Desiree and Sterns, Olivia (2008), 'Celebs give U.N. star-power punch', ABC News, 9 March, http://abcnews.go.com/GMA/Story?id=4413688&page=1. Accessed 20 April 2009.

Cooper, Andrew (2008), *Celebrity Diplomacy*, Boulder: Paradigm Publishers.

Cottle, Simon and Nolan, David (2007), 'Global humanitarianism and the changing aid-media field', *Journalism Studies*, 8:6, pp. 862–878.

Curry, Ann (2008), *Today*, NBC News, 1 February.

Education Partnership for Children of Conflict (2009), 'Understanding the issue', http://www.educationpartnership.org/theissue. Accessed 28 April 2009.

Eichler-Levine, Jodi and Hicks, Rosemary (2007), '"As Americans against genocide": the crisis in Darfur and interreligious political activism', *American Quarterly*, 59:3, pp. 711–735.

Evans, Graham and Newnham, Jeffrey (1998), *The Penguin Dictionary of International Relations*, London: Penguin Books.

Grossberg, Josh (2009), 'Sundance notebook: Ben Affleck turns reporter', E! Online, 19 January 2009, http://www.eonline.com/uberblog/b79694_sundance_notebook_ben_affleck_turns.html#comments. Accessed 28 April 2009.

Hawkins, Virgil (2008), *Stealth Conflicts: How the World's Worst Violence is Ignored*, Aldershot: Ashgate.

Hollar, Julie (2007), 'Bono, I presume? Covering Africa through celebrities', *Extra!* May/June.

Junger, Sebastian (2007), 'Enter China, the giant', *Vanity Fair*, July.

Kekic, Laza (2007), 'The Economist Intelligence Unit's index of democracy', The World in 2007, *Economist*, pp. 1–11.

Kristof, Nicholas (2004), 'Will we say 'never again' yet again?', *New York Times*, 27 March.

Marquez, Laura (2006), *World News Tonight*, ABC News, 30 April.

Metlikovec, Jane and Magee, Antonia (2008), 'Paris blast: shopping spree sparks anger', *Herald Sun*, 30 December.

Moeller, Susan (2006), '"Regarding the pain of others": media, bias and the coverage of international disasters', *Journal of International Affairs*, 59:2, pp. 173–196.

Montague, Dena (2002), 'Stolen goods: coltan and conflict in the Democratic Republic of Congo', *SAIS Review*, 22:1, pp. 103–18.

Pew (2009), 6–9 March 2009 News Interest Index Omnibus Survey, Pew Research Center for the People & the Press, http://people-press.org/reports/questionnaires/497.pdf. Accessed 29 April 2009.

Philp, Catherine (2008), 'How stars turned spotlight on an unfolding crisis', *Times*, 15 February.

Powell, Anita (2008), 'Ben Affleck returns to the Congo', *Huffington Post*, 20 November, http://www.huffingtonpost.com/2008/11/20/ben-affleck-returns-to-th_n_145119.html. Accessed 29 April 2009.

Press Association (2009), 'Madden backs Pitt's part', in *Wiltshire Times*, 19 February, http://www.wiltshiretimes.co.uk/uk_national_entertainment/4138025.Madden_backs_Pitt_s_part_/.Accessed 28 April 2009.

Prunier, Gerard (2006), 'The politics of death in Darfur', *Current History*, May.

Reuters (2003), 'Dixie Chicks pulled from air after bashing Bush', CNN.com, 15 March, http://edition.cnn.com/2003/SHOWBIZ/Music/03/14/dixie.chicks.reut/. Accessed 29 April 2009.

—— (2004), 'Sudanese atrocities likened to Rwanda', *Toronto Star*, 20 March.

Ruiz, Susana (2006), 'Darfur Is Dying', http://www.darfurisdying.com/. Accessed 20 April 2009.

Smith, Harry (2008), 'Early Show', CBS News, 1 February.

Snow, Keith Harmon (2005), 'Rwanda's secret war', *Z Magazine*, February.

—— (2009), 'America's war in Central Africa: unpacking Western whiteness, war and propaganda', *San Francisco Bay View*, 28 March.

Tourtellotte, Bob (2007), 'Pitt, Clooney, Cheadle move spotlight to Darfur', *Reuters*, 26 May, http://www.reuters.com/article/entertainmentNews/idUSN2443704420070526. Accessed 24 April 2009.

Traub, James (2008), 'The celebrity solution', *New York Times Magazine*, 9 March.

UNHCR (2004), 'Jolie donates to Chad emergency, urges others to follow suit', UNCHR News Stories, 9 March, http://www.unhcr.org/cgi-bin/texis/vtx/home/opendoc.htm?tbl=NEWS&id=404de25e4&page=news. Accessed 26 April 2009.

Weir, Bill and Chang, Juju (2008), 'Good Morning America', ABC News, 9 March.

White House (2008), 'President Bush participates in joint press availability with President Kagame of Rwanda', White House Press Releases, 19 February.

Winfrey, Oprah (2005), *Oprah Winfrey Show*, 24 January.

—— (2006), *Oprah Winfrey Show*, 26 April.

Wroe, Martin (2007), 'Sing after me: do they know it's genocide?', *Sunday Times*, 16 September.

Zunes, Stephen (2008), 'African dictatorships and double standards', Foreign Policy in Focus, 1 July, http://www.fpif.org/fpiftxt/5333. Accessed 29 April 2009.

Notes

1. The search filtered articles/stories with at least three occurrences (including in indexing) of the term 'Darfur'. The same conditions were repeated for the term 'Congo'. Results were manually filtered for repetition and items unrelated to the situation in Darfur or Congo (the plight of a dog in the US named Congo that was involved in a mauling incident, for example).
2. Web search (using 'Darfur' as search term) of Google Insights for Search, 2004 to present. See http://www.google.com/insights/search/#q=Darfur&geo=US&cmpt=q. Accessed 30 April 2009.

Chapter 5

Can Celebrity Save Diplomacy? Appropriating Wisdom through 'The Elders'

Henk Huijser and Jinna Tay

Introduction

U2 singer and social activist Bono has described his celebrity status as valuable 'currency' that can be used productively in the fight against Third World poverty. Furthermore, he is unapologetic about the deliberate exploitation of his celebrity status, affording him and Bob Geldof unprecedented access to world leaders to champion their cause to 'make poverty history', and thus casting them in the role of 'celebrity diplomats' (Cooper 2007). In short, it is precisely their celebrity status that draws attention to the cause they champion, via blanket media coverage, and it is their celebrity status that puts pressure on current political leaders to be seen to engage with them: popularity by association.

In July 2007, rock singer Peter Gabriel and 'celebrity' business tycoon Richard Branson, who has made effective use of his own carefully cultivated celebrity status, introduced a new initiative that aims to take celebrity diplomacy to a new level: the establishment of a group of 'Elders' that includes Desmond Tutu, Jimmy Carter, Kofi Annan, Mary Robinson, and the ultimate beacon of global wisdom, Nelson Mandela. Their brief goes beyond fighting global poverty and includes conflict resolution through diplomacy. However, this is not diplomacy in its traditional guise, but rather aims to take the traditional elements that often block effective solutions out of the equation: political ambition and conflicting interests. The initiative aims to resurrect the function of elders in traditional societies, and is specifically modelled on the role and status of elders in African village societies. Central to the initiative is the fact that none of the Elders holds public office, which allows them to work for the common good, rather than external political interests. It thus aims to overcome the considerable limitations of the current context of political diplomacy. Similarly, it avoids some of the connotations of 'celebrity activism', as something that celebrities do as an image-building exercise, since the Elders are well past the need for image building.

While the self-conscious exploitation of celebrity status within this initiative has the potential to make a positive impact on both the levels of fund-raising and of awareness in a western context, the 'traditional' role of celebrity in this process is at the same time fraught with profound contradictions. 'Goodwill ambassadors', in the form of pop singers and movie stars, have long been employed for a variety of political causes. However, similar to politicians, the effectiveness of celebrities from the entertainment world is limited to some extent, as they can easily be 'accused' of exploiting these political causes to enhance their own celebrity status and provide them with an 'aura' of credibility. In other words, these celebrities can easily be perceived to have vested interests, in a similar way that politicians do, which potentially affects their effectiveness. Again, the Elders initiative appears to cut through such perceptions.

This chapter will explore the role of 'celebrity diplomacy' (as a specific form of 'celebrity activism') in the Elders' attempts to effect change and engage with politics and poverty at a global level. The central question is whether their celebrity status, as well as the celebrity status of their founders, will limit them to awareness-raising alone, or whether they can effect meaningful change and a shift in the way diplomacy operates on a global level. This chapter will argue that while 'celebrity' has the potential to create awareness, raise much-needed funds, and drive 'political action', this potential is at the same time firmly wedded to contemporary politics of entertainment and media consumption, thus potentially limiting its ability to effect structural change.

Defining Celebrity

An analysis of the role and status of the Elders in relation to their status as celebrities requires a working definition of the concept of celebrity. In other words, there are different ways of approaching celebrity, and the concept of celebrity has undergone a series of important changes, particularly under the influence of the explosive growth of the global media. As Bonner et al. have noted, 'the concept of celebrity is itself a little slippery, partly because its constitutive discourses have leaked into such a wide range of media formats and practices' (1999: 56). If visibility is the oxygen of celebrity, then the opportunities to achieve such visibility are becoming ever more widespread. Conversely, however, visibility alone is not enough, and *attention*, or rather the ability to attract attention, is increasingly becoming the main currency that drives celebrity status. As Marshall has noted, celebrity status itself 'confers on the person a certain discursive power within society, and the celebrity is a voice above others, a voice that is channelled into the media system as being legitimately significant' (1997: 10). This suggests that celebrity is seen as 'significant' in itself, and therefore deserving of attention. Holmes and Redmond (2006) cite Couldry (2004) who talks in this respect about the 'myth of the media centre' [...] in which mediated space is constructed as 'special' and significant, and to enter it, or even pass through it, is to receive a form of symbolic capital' (2006: 10). However, we would argue that there are divergent degrees of such symbolic capital, which in turn command divergent degrees of attention, and some celebrity currencies offer better exchange rates than others. Within the global media context, there are thus different degrees of celebrity, and it is no coincidence that the most 'celebrated' of all are those celebrities that cut across different media spheres, and thereby achieve a kind of blanket visibility.

For example, there is little doubt that Robert De Niro is a celebrity, but he is first and foremost a Hollywood movie actor and his visibility is largely restricted to the films in which he appears, and perhaps the odd appearance on the *Oprah Winfrey* show. His celebrity status is nevertheless global, unlike many localized celebrities, especially those whose status is derived from localized reality television shows such as *Big Brother*. If we continue to follow this logic, it becomes clear why someone like Angelina Jolie has now achieved the status of 'super celebrity', for not only is she hyper-visible across all media spheres, but she also commands attention for a number of different reasons, and thus from different media audiences and publics. Within this context, her celebrity status in itself can be seen as a product or commodity and it serves as valuable currency, which is subsequently being appropriated for different political causes. However, to keep this currency as valuable as it is requires her to maintain her celebrity status on all fronts (e.g. Hollywood movies, television talk shows, fashion and gossip magazines), as they reinforce each other. As Junod puts it, 'she became the most famous in the world because despite her willingness to take on the world's suffering – no, precisely on *account* of her willingness to take on the world's suffering – people suspected that she was still crazy' (2007). Thus, it is the suspicion of 'craziness', derived from her carefully constructed media persona that keeps commanding attention, and this attention can then be diverted into other directions; for example, political causes. If, as Rojek argues, 'celebrity = impact on public consciousness' (2001: 10), then Angelina Jolie is indeed a 'super celebrity'. Of course, Angelina Jolie is only one example here, and it works in similar ways for others, although arguably not to the same extent.

The different types and degrees of celebrity outlined above are usefully reflected in Turner, Bonner and Marshall's extensive definition (2000: 13):

> Celebrities are brand names as well as cultural icons or identities; they operate as marketing tools as well as sites where the agency of the audience is clearly evident; and they represent the achievement of individualism – the triumph of the human and the familiar – as well as its commodification and commercialisation. Like all commodities, however, their trade needs to be organised and controlled and, as a result, the production and commercialisation of celebrities has become an industry too.

Graeme Turner's definition of celebrity refines the concept further (2004: 9):

> Celebrity is a genre of representation and a discursive effect; it is a commodity traded by the promotions, publicity, and media industries that produce these representations and their effects; and it is a cultural formation that has a social function we can better understand.

Both these definitions stress the constructedness of celebrity, which is echoed in Rojek's much shorter conceptualization of celebrity as 'the attribution of glamorous or notorious status to an individual within the public sphere' (2001: 10). In short, in all these accounts celebrity is seen as something that is 'done to someone', as something that is constructed by the media industry. Indeed, Rojek goes as far as to say that 'celebrities are cultural fabrications' (2001: 10), who are stage managed by a faceless media machine. This is then tempered somewhat by his distinction between three different categories of celebrity: *ascribed* (following bloodlines, e.g. royal families); *achieved* (due to perceived accomplishments, e.g. sports people); and *attributed* (result of representation of an individual as noteworthy by cultural intermediaries) (Rojek 2001). Despite allowing for 'achievement' as the basis of a particular form of celebrity, the maintenance of that celebrity status is still largely seen as dependent on mediated stage management. Although we acknowledge that mediated (and therefore constructed) elements are central to celebrity culture, these definitions do have a tendency to deny specific celebrities any form of agency. This becomes problematic when we begin to think about how all of this applies to the Elders under investigation here. In other words, to what extent is their status based on 'stage management' by the media? This in turn becomes an important question if one tries to evaluate their potential effectiveness. While the Elders were brought together for explicitly *political* reasons, their status (and thus their 'currency') is intimately linked to the celebrity status of their founders. Aung San Suu Kyi, for example, is the latest inclusion to the Elders, despite, or perhaps *because* being under continued house arrest in Burma,[1] she demands considerable attention. Her participation is therefore more of a symbolic gesture of support, as is the fact that the other Elders leave an empty chair for her during their meetings. To explore these subtle (or perhaps not so subtle) gestures in more depth, we will now turn to the relationship between celebrity and politics.

Celebrity and Politics

The relationship between celebrity and politics has received considerable academic attention, and this attention is usually focused on two main variants that John Street (2004: 435) identifies as: the elected politician or candidate who uses elements of 'celebrityhood' to establish their claim to represent a group or cause. The second is the celebrity – the star of popular culture – who uses their popularity to speak for public opinion. Both are often seen as leading to a phenomenon called 'celebrity politics', which is, in turn, often seen as something to be profoundly concerned about, primarily because it is considered to undermine the democratic process (West and Orman 2002; Meyer 2002). 'The assumption is that the political use of popular culture is a cynical expression of a desperate populism, one in which presentation and appearance substitute for policy and principle. What is being signified is a crisis of representation, not a realisation of it' (Street 2004: 436). This crisis in representation is symbolized by the apparent rise in importance of public relations firms and spin doctors in the political process, or what Gamson (2000) has called the 'celebrification process' in politics. In short, critics of celebrity politics are concerned about this development, because they believe that 'representatives should be judged in terms of the quality of their policy proposals, the ideological coherence of their manifesto, the sophistication of their political skills or the legitimacy of their selection procedures' (Street 2004: 443), rather than on their appearance or their skill in front of the cameras. This is a common critique and one with a very long history (Drake and Higgins 2006). However, it has gathered pace under the influence of a fast-changing mediascape.

In *Media Democracy*, Thomas Meyer focuses on this changing mediascape and the ways in which it affects democratic politics. The central question he asks is: 'in what sense and to what degree, (if at all) are democratic procedures jeopardised when the rules of the media system displace those of the political system?' (2002: xvi). The rules of the media are manifold in Meyer's opinion, and they include factors of time (emphasis on the present; difference between media time and political time), news values, the rules of 'media stage management', personification (read *celebrification*), and parasitic publicity. All of this creates a situation that places major constraints on traditional politics. It leads Meyer to conclude that, 'in so far as the elite actors in the political system put their faith in the basic equation of media democracy – publicity equals success – they yield to the time-constraints of media production, because they suppose that is the price they have to pay to win public support' (2002: 45). The reason for singling out Meyer here is that his study rightly takes the changing mediascape seriously, but that it is at the same time fairly typical of many critiques of the media's influence on contemporary politics. Within such critiques, celebrity politics exemplifies everything that is wrong with contemporary politics, and is thus customarily dismissed outright. However, we agree with Street that it is rather more useful to see celebrity politics in a much wider context, as that would allow us to specifically identify characteristics of celebrity politics that can be appropriated to effect social or political change. Street (2004: 445) sums it up like this:

> In analysing forms of political representation in modern democracies, we need to be aware of the ways in which this relationship is constituted and experienced aesthetically. From this perspective, the phenomenon of the celebrity politician takes on a different aspect. It is not to be dismissed as a betrayal of the proper principles of democratic representation, but as an extension of them. Celebrity politics is a code for the performance of representations through the gestures and media available to those who wish to claim 'representativeness'.

The attraction of this formulation is that it widens the possibilities of what counts as 'political', and therefore allows for the crossing of boundaries between 'politicians' and 'celebrities', or indeed, 'celebrity politicians'.

Drake and Higgins identify two main positions with regard to celebrity politics, which are important for our purposes here: one is pessimistic and the other more optimistic. The pessimistic position is outlined above and is based on the view that 'politics proper' has come to rely too much on image and spin and not enough on 'rational argumentation' (2006: 89). Underlying this view is a sense of nostalgia and longing for a time when politics was characterized by 'rigorous debate' rather than 'trivial celebrity gossip'. McKee (2005) has debunked these myths to some extent, but in doing so, it is important to incorporate the changes in the wider media sphere.

The other more optimistic position does precisely that. Corner and Pels draw on performance theory to argue that a 'performative restyling of politics does not have to be viewed in a negative manner but might be fashioned to the service of a more *inclusive* political culture' (2003: 16). The inclusiveness they refer to suggests a more democratic political environment with wider public participation.

The role of politicians in this mediated political environment has changed in the sense that they have much less time to get their political ideas across, and that they compete for attention (for example, with celebrities) in a cluttered and largely commercialized media environment. This has an enormous impact on the role of politicians, and it changes the ways in which they communicate and perform. Jessica Evans argues that the 'function of celebrities is to convert very complex economic and political arguments [...] into digestible and easily understandable chunks of information that will fit into the contexts of media viewing' (2005: 42); the same role can be ascribed to politicians in the contemporary media scape, and the distinction between 'celebrity' and 'politician' is thus very blurred in this view.

The question, according to Drake and Higgins, becomes: 'to what extent do celebrities, and politicians endorsed by celebrities, engage a public disengaged from formal politics: that is, do they enable political issues to be aired to a wider audience?' (2006: 99).

In relation to the case of the Elders, we can then ask the question of whether there are any shades of grey in these descriptions. In other words, the categories of 'politician' and 'celebrity' are both applicable to the relationships between the Elders themselves and their founders. Hence, they function partly as celebrities that attract attention and therefore have the potential to 'engage a disengaged public', and they function partly as people with enormous political prestige and status (many of them are Nobel Peace Prize winners).

In the former case, their function is to create public awareness and support for specific causes, through their knowledge of the requirements of contemporary media communication, while in the latter case, their status itself demands respect on a political level, and thus potentially allows them to be very effective diplomatically. Indeed, the fact that they are recognized as 'Elders', who have already earned their stripes, and have therefore nothing left to prove, nor have any pressure from being elected representatives, may make them much *more* effective than traditional diplomats.

Turner notes that 'these days, public relations touches most facets of commercial and public life: managing corporate relations with the public, providing advice to politicians about how to build their public image, or designing a government public information campaign' (2004: 44). But what if politicians are relieved of the need to manage their public image, by virtue of their status and 'retirement' stage of their 'proper' political careers? This applies to the Elders, and again, it may make them potentially much more effective, because it allows them to navigate with ease around media-imposed constraints that affect 'normal' politicians. In addition, Turner argues about celebrities that they 'may have achieved things that suggest they 'deserve' their eminence, but that is not going to protect that individual from the celebrity process, nor affect how it actually operates over time' (2004: 19). Again, the status of the Elders may mean that they are 'relieved' from the pressure to 'prove' that they deserve their political status and their celebrity status respectively, which in a sense contrasts with other 'political celebrities' like Bob Geldof or Richard Branson — who have been integral to the organizing of The Elders but have discreetly stayed on the side lines, leaving the diplomatic work to those who have demonstrated expertise in the international arena.

Celebrity Diplomats: Celebrities or Diplomats?

Given the calibre and standing of this group we surmise that the question is not whether the term 'celebrities' is applicable to this group, but *how* it is applicable and enacted in a changing global mediascape, in which the roles and performance of diplomats and political figures may be better understood through the prism of 'celebrity'. In order to further this argument, we specifically look at who the Elders are and examine their profiles to gain an understanding of how the framework of celebrity is enacted in this context.

Nelson Mandela	First elected black President of South Africa, international symbol of freedom after 27 years as political prisoner, Nobel Peace Prize winner.
Graça Machel	International advocate for women and children's rights, President of the Foundation for Community Development, Mozambique.
Desmond Tutu	First black Archbishop of Cape Town, Chairman of South Africa's Truth and Reconciliation Commission; pursues conflict resolution by advocating forgiveness and reconciliation.
Kofi Annan	The 7th Secretary-General of the United Nations, reformer of UN global policy aims to focus more on national civil societies and grass roots formation, Nobel Peace Prize winner.
Ela Bhatt	Entrepreneur in grassroots development, founder and chair of the Self-Employed Women's Association and the All India Association of Micro Finance Institutions in India.
Lakhdar Brahimi	Pursuer of liberation and peace keeping role in Algeria and Indonesia, Ambassador for Algeria, lectures internationally and is based in the Institute for Advanced Study at Princeton.
Gro Brundtland	Physician, public health administrator and former Prime Minister of Norway, Chair of the World Commission of Environment and Development (the Brundtland Commission).
Fernando H Cardoso	Former Senator, Minister of Foreign Relations, Minister of Finance and President of Brazil for two successive terms, currently Professor across several international universities.
Jimmy Carter	Former President of the United States of America, he founded the Carter Center dedicated to advance global health and peaceful resolutions, Nobel Peace Prize winner.
Mary Robinson	First female President of Ireland, UN High Commissioner for Human Rights, Founder and President of 'Realizing Rights: The Ethical Globalisation' initiative.
Muhammad Yunus	Established 'micro banking': the Grameen Bank Project (Bangladesh), Nobel Peace Prize winner for establishing grassroots economic and social development.

Aung San Suu Kyi   Freedom fighter for a democratic Burma (Myanmar) and winner of the Nobel Peace Prize, the Sakharov Prize from the European Parliament, the United States Presidential Medal of Freedom, and the Jawaharlal Nehru Award from India.

* www.theelders.org

It is clear from this list that the group of individuals that make up the Elders are not exactly average diplomatic figures but most of them are larger-than-life personalities that have wrought political, social and cultural change in their countries and institutions. They are more than just famous; they are celebrities because they are leaders who represent a kind of global conscience, which the public can identify with.

They are famous for what they have achieved (*actions*) as well as for how they *appear* and for the attention they command; the consequences of their contributions are experienced *en masse* by the very poor or the politically disenfranchised. They are classic examples of figures that 'deserve' to be famous and to be celebrities, before celebrity became what it is today. Yet, in our everyday use and understanding of celebrities now, the term sits uneasily with these leaders precisely because celebrity has been popularized and tabloidized.

However, as we have pointed out through John Street's work, taking the celebrity approach (as opposed to, say, the political marketing one) is expressive of the cultural and stylistic changes that have marked political change in recent times and that are characteristic of contemporary political culture, which further allows us to examine their 'value […] in their meaning as texts' (2004: 444). In other words, this allows us to understand and negotiate their role and performance as cultural hegemonic figures in their world rather than what they can offer as commodities or products. This is important because as political diplomats and Elders, and to some extent as activists, it is not just *what* they 'do', but *how* they do it; their performance is their role and that approach is instrumental to the process of diplomatic negotiation. What they can offer is themselves, and their personification as symbols of the possibility of a peaceful resolution. Indeed, because they are able to attract attention due to their historical track record (including their historical mediated record), their comment on a given situation is valuable. Evidently, the represented figure, its fame and capacity to perform in a context of urgency, attracts media interest and this is far removed from the cynical understanding of politicians/diplomats as merely offering a bag of 'political lollies'.

Umbrella organizations usually serve to create and foster a larger identity for the individuals they represent. Yet in this case, it is the other way around as each Elder's reputation exceeds the group. While we may not have heard of all the Elders in the group, each of them is nonetheless 'world famous' in the context in which their work is relevant, while some of them have far outgrown that context and are therefore truly 'world famous'. The question then becomes whether being brought together allows them to function more effectively.

The Elders' website has a strong articulation of its own identity. The logo and banner consist of a constellation of stars (reflecting the gathering of the Elders, and with strong religious connotations of 'wise men') anchored to an inscription of 'The Elders' (in Sans Serif). This then opens up to a larger editorial layout with a picture of Nelson Mandela attached to his speech at the launch of The Elders. Desmond Tutu is the chair of the group, which originally started with eleven Elders but has since recruited Burmese freedom fighter Aung Sung Suu Kyi to its ranks. Under 'Global Village' on the website, 'netizens' are asked to e-mail suggestions of other celebrity diplomats they think could be part of The Elders, demonstrating the openness of the initiative to grow but also 'who' the public thinks would have the right calibre to join these luminaries. In a sense, this could be interpreted as a kind of democratization of celebrity status; in other words, the public vote ensures celebrity status for the next recruit. In his speech at the launch of The Elders, Mandela pointed out the qualities that would make them different from other activists or diplomatic groups:

> This group derives its strength not from political, economic or military power, but from the independence and integrity of those who are here. They do not have careers to build, elections to win, constituencies to please. They can talk to anyone they please, and are free to follow paths they deem right, even if hugely unpopular (< http://dl.groovygecko.net/ anon.groovy/clients/akqa/projectamber/press/The_Elders-Speech.pdf>).

These Elders have won their personal battles, and it is their accumulated expertise and international success that they bring to the group; more importantly, as Nobel Prize winners and symbols of nurturers and humanitarians, their involvement guarantees a certain amount of global media coverage and worldwide interest. Since the launch of the group in 2007, they have worked on four projects: Cyprus, Zimbabwe, Human Rights and Sudan. A case in point is a visit to Cyprus in October 2008 where Desmond Tutu, Jimmy Carter and Lakhdah Brahimi went to support the on-going negotiations between Greek and Turkish Cypriots to reunify their island in a peaceful manner. The website hosts the 'summary of their report' and news of the latest developments of the island, along with pictures detailing their involvement and meetings with the community. They instigated conversations across the diverse sections of the community; from the political leaders of the two sides to young people, civil groups, and ambassadors. As a demonstration of the political impasse, they heard from students who reported that they had to carry their passports across the border twice a day in order to attend school, due to the border regulations. Archibishop Tutu made it clear that their role in Cyprus was purely in a support capacity (listening, providing examples, talking) within the process rather than as negotiators (in this case), because the Cypriots were making the resolutions themselves. This is an important aspect of the form of diplomacy (rather than direct activism) the Elders practice, as it removes the pressure of having a direct stake in the process, while at the same time allowing the main protagonists to keep a sense of ownership (read agency) over the process. The Cyprus trip represents a short, succinct project whereby the Elders attracted global press coverage about the peace process in Cyprus; simply being there guarantees such coverage, based on the celebrity status of Jimmy Carter and Desmond Tutu alone. Their story of political progress was thus widely reported by news agencies around the world.

In a sense, this visit resembles others made by political attachés and celebrity Goodwill Ambassadors such as Geri Halliwell or UNICEF's Mia Farrow, where their primary role is similarly to raise attention to a cause as a means of raising funds and awareness of a particular political or humanitarian crisis. However, political lobbying, a particularly important aspect of effecting change is not something Goodwill Ambassadors are capable of doing effectively, despite having the ability to attract media attention. It is precisely the proven capacity to exploit this media attention, through their political nous, which makes The Elders potentially much more effective. A central criticism levelled at the Goodwill Ambassadors, is the suggestion that they have only a superficial understanding of the political situations they find themselves in without the required depth of knowledge, and this may inadvertently produce more damage than good (Huliaras and Tzifakis 2008). It is clear that The Elders bring with them diplomatic knowledge (*the commodity*), plus the celebrity goodwill (*representation*) that will draw in global media interest. If we look at Mandela, his individual status and widely known personal and political (as with all celebrities, a combination of public and private) history juxtaposes the representational figure (survivor, leader) and the values he stands for (strong ethics, strength, freedom, justice) depicting him as an authentic and affective figure in world politics, yet allowing the public to identify with him because of his suffering and triumph, and because his public persona is not restricted to the label 'politician'. As an embodiment of the values outlined above, we are drawn to Mandela as a saviour of sorts, a Christ-like figure who has suffered and survived a form of racial politics that the global public is eager to view as history, and who has emerged victorious with humility and forgiveness for his captors. Thus, Mandela represents what is possible without resorting to violence, which is doubly symbolic if we consider that The Elders were founded during the latter part of a hawkish Bush era.

To return to Mandela's speech, he also points to another critical aspect of their participation: networks – the integral lifeblood of modern-day relations. As he notes, 'through [the other Elders'] friends in business, they can mobilise up to date technology, and raise not only awareness of forgotten issues, but also help locate the resources to address them' (Mandela 2007). The connexion to people, ideas, technology and knowledge is at the forefront of the global developmental agenda and not only are the influential Elders able to access it – they have the financial backing through their supporters such as United Nations Foundations, Richard Branson, Humanity United, the Bridgeway Foundation, Peter Gabriel, Shashi Ruia and others, to fulfil these needs. This even gives them the added advantage of being able to offer or promise financial backing for some projects, and the ability to deliver on such a promise. Overall then, as achieved and attributed celebrities, these Elders defy the typically easy arguments about the lack of agency that are often targeted at entertainment celebrities – the fact is that they are known for their ability to overcome adversity, deliver outcomes, operate outside the box and they are at the same time without the burden of the explicit political agenda of any contemporary national or intra-national agency.

On closer inspection, The Elders are represented as a unique organization and one that is worthy and deserving because it brings together such valuable attributes (embodied in these individual leaders) and unites them as a global problem-solving taskforce. However, the question of why now is perhaps not amiss here – for, historically, there have always been great humanitarians (Mahatma Gandhi and Mother Teresa would surely need to be part of The Elders if they were still alive). However, it seems that the factors that make the coming together of this group of people possible at this particular juncture in history, is not only the calibre of leadership and humanitarianism, but a particular constellation of mediating factors and a huge exercise in global philanthropy: from Peter Gabriel and Richard Branson who initiated the idea, to the tremendous financial injection required to bankroll such a global project. The Elders' newly launched website lists this financial support from not-for-profit foundations such as Virgin, the United Nations, the Peter Gabriel Foundation, the Skoll Foundation, and individual philanthropists such as Shashi Ruia and Richard Tarlow. The other key features that make it possible for an international collaborative institution such as The Elders to exist are the current context of global media, direct public participation/engagement, and access to a global audience. More importantly, we argue that these are precisely the same factors that have enabled the rise of the 'celebrity age' (Turner 2004), which is characterized by a proliferation of media channels and outlets, as well as a proliferation of social networking media that allow for easy public participation (or at least the perception thereof). The paradox in this context is that the '15 minutes of fame' form of celebrity is relatively easy to achieve, but sustainable celebrity status (and the advantages that accompany its currency) is much harder to establish; The Elders clearly possess the latter form of celebrity in spades. As mentioned above, the same attributes that allow globalized public identification with Nelson Mandela (and some of the other Elders to a lesser degree), are evident here, and these are the same attributes (ability to overcome adversity, deliver outcomes, operate outside the box, and lack of explicit political agenda) that allow us to identify with their achievements, and thus their leadership.

Celebrity Politics and Celebrity Diplomacy: How Effective can the Elders be?

Basing the roles of the Elders on the idea of African village elders, immediately raises certain connotations and questions. One assumes that the traditional elder serves as a guide and moral compass, so how should 'global village' elders act in these scenarios? Do they assist only in an advisory capacity? Or, can they intercede, negotiate, officiate, or, indeed, force certain outcomes? What are the boundaries of their humanitarian endeavours? Of course, some of the Elders like Mary Robinson, Nelson Mandela, Jimmy Carter, Gro Brundtland and Fernando Cardoso, who are experienced Prime Ministers and Presidents, carry the required expertise and status to assist in policy advice. But how effective are they? Beyond their media status, the celebrity connections and their individual strength – how do they work as a group? This depends on how effectiveness is measured, and while it is probably too early in the process to come to any firm conclusions in this respect, we have to note that firstly, the political hotspots they focus on have been unresolved diplomatic black holes for a long time. Second, the continued sustainability of The Elders as a stable, diplomatic project would in itself indicate a degree of success. For most Chinese knots do not lend themselves to immediate resolution, but rather require slow ongoing negotiations within different social and cultural milieux and political contexts. Apart from that, not all the projects that the Elders are involved with are specific *political* problems; some are ravages of war that require the diverse international support that media coverage and public awareness would bring. For now, it is too early to tell whether The Elders will primarily be successful in ensuring the establishment of humanitarian interventions *after* political meltdowns, or whether they will be able to prevent such political meltdowns in the future.

For example, *Every Human Has Rights* (EHHR) is another Elders project based around the UN's universal declaration of human rights, rather than dealing directly with a specific political context. Unlike the rest of the projects, this is a portal to a substantive website – www.everyhumanhasrights.org – that asks 'netizens' to participate by pledging to uphold the declaration of human rights through signing the petition. At present count (November 2009), there are 52,591 signatures. The site also provides links to civil rights groups in different countries, where local action and more participation could be achieved. Furthermore, organizations such as the Self Employed Women's Association (SEWA), founded by Ela Bhatt, are profiled, stories and reports from Nigeria are available, a book by National Geographic on human rights is discussed and the EHHR Media Awards are reported on. On one level, this site simply provides information, but may also increase levels of participation (schools, individuals, youth centres, civil society groups) through association with these celebrity Elders. When one signs the declaration, the site provides you with Internet-savvy promotions such as widgets, badges and links that one can display on personalized social networking sites to promote and demonstrate one's affiliation with this campaign; this is a form of political action by association.

In the Media Awards section, Elders such as Kofi Annan are at hand to promote the event and mingle with attendees (blogpost by Colours of Bohemia). The video portal is a huge archive of detailed field work by various Elders, and the short video clips provide in-depth coverage of how some of the Elders are carrying out their work 'in the field'. For example, Mary Robinson on her road trip around Liberia trying to create decent work in Africa; Archbishop Desmond Tutu's partnering with UNICEF to campaign for children's rights; and the opening and report of the Poverty Hearings of the Millennium Development Goals. Each project portal carries detailed descriptions through individual blogs, videos and reports of the kinds of work that is being carried out in the 'fields' and opportunities for participation. What is unclear, however, is how each 'project' gets selected, and whether or not the supporters, as the financial providers, have a say in where they choose to direct their finances.

What is clear from an analysis of the Elders' site is that effectiveness, in the sense of 'key performance indicators' is perhaps the wrong yardstick to account for global developmental projects. While projects such as 'the Cyprus project' have a clear political outcome within a relatively short period of time, many of the other projects are long-standing complex political deadlocks such as political freedom and starvation in Zimbabwe or the Human Rights campaign. Indeed, in the current global climate of political and ideological inconsistency and uncertainty, perhaps the outcomes that can be asked of the Elders are a combination of what they have claimed for themselves and what non-governmental organizations set out to achieve: social transparency, financial accountability, the installation of long-term sustainable processes, engagement with the public, creating public awareness and education, and promoting and representing universal values such as freedom, democracy and human rights. In each of these instances, the Elders lead by example, and the fact that many of them have celebrity status (visibility and access to the media) only serves to stimulate identification.

Straddling the divide between politics and celebrity, The Elders, as a group, demonstrate an embodiment of celebrity diplomacy. It is perhaps fitting in today's global media age, that while many may enter the world of advocacy and developmental agencies, doing the slow grassroots groundwork of education and volunteerism, it is these celebrity diplomats who may carry the strongest impact on public consciousness (Rojek 2001).

Conclusion

In the ever-growing kingdom of celebrities, the celebrity diplomat, as embodied in the Elders, represents a new breed and somewhat of a different take on global celebrity culture, with potentially very wide and convergent access to media attention and global funding. While many of these Elders have charities and foundations of their own, their extra role of being an Elder perhaps gives them, and their celebrity founders, the hard currency in a media sphere characterized by celebrity inflation. Alongside the many NGOs and competing international agencies, the Elders stand out as a unique organization of 'super diplomats' with celebrity status. Perhaps most tellingly, one is not able to join the Elders (the organization), but rather one is chosen based on strict but unspoken criteria. One of these criteria is celebrity status built on past endeavours, 'good deeds' or strong leadership, while another is political experience and clout. At the same time, however, being an Elder means that on a personal level, the political stakes are not as high as they would be for politicians who are still relying on the popular vote for their career advancement. In other words, the Elders have already achieved everything they possibly can in terms of their personal careers, which ostensibly frees them up to pursue clear agendas for positive change, rather than agendas that may be partly clouded by the ambiguity of necessary political compromise. Overall then, the combination of their celebrity status and their political credentials is perhaps the most powerful combination for change in a contemporary global context. Time will tell.

References

Bonner, F., Farley, R., Marshall, P. D. and Turner, G. (1999), 'Celebrity and the Media', *Australian Journal of Communication*, 26:1, pp. 55–70.

Cashmore, E. (2006), *Celebrity/Culture*, Abington & New York: Routledge.

Colours of Bohemia (2008), 'Every Human Has Rights Media Award', <http://coloursofbohemia. blogspot.com/search/label/human%20rights>. Accessed10 December 2008.

Cooper, A. F. (2007), *Celebrity Diplomacy*, Toronto: UTP.

Corner, J. and Pels, D. (eds) (2003), *Media and the Restyling of Politics*, London: Sage.

Couldry, N. (2004), 'Teaching Us to Fake It: The Ritualized Norms of Television's "Reality" Games', in S. Murray and L. Ouellette (eds), *Reality TV: Remaking Television Culture*, New York: New York University Press.

Drake, P. and Higgins, M. (2006), '"I'm a Celebrity, get me into Politics": The Political Celebrity and the Celebrity Politician', in S. Holmes and S. Redmond (eds), *Framing Celebrity: New Directions in Celebrity Culture*, London & New York: Routledge.

Evans, J. (2005), 'Celebrity, Media and History', in J. Evans and D. Hesmondhalgh (eds), *Understanding Media: Inside Celebrity*, Maidenhead: Open University Press.

Gamson, J. (2000), 'The Web of Celebrity', *American Prospect*, 11:20, pp. 40–41.

Holmes, S. and Redmond, S. (2006), 'Introduction: Understanding Celebrity Culture', in S. Holmes and S. Redmond (eds), *Framing Celebrity: New Directions in Celebrity Culture*, London & New York: Routledge.

Huliaras, A. and Tzifakis, N. (2008), 'The Dynamics of Celebrity Activism: Mia Farrow and the "Genocide Olympics" Campaign', *Karamanlis Working Papers in Hellenic and European Studies*, no. 7, July 2008.

Junod, T. (2007), 'Angelina Jolie dies for our sins', *Esquire*, 5 October 2007, <http://www.esquire.com/print-this/women-we-love/Jolie0707/>. Accessed 3 April 2009.

Mandela, N. (2007), 'Mr Nelson Mandela's Speech at the Launch of The Elders', 18 July 2007, <http://dl.groovygecko.net/anon.groovy/clients/akqa/projectamber/press/The_Elders-Speech.pdf>. Accessed 5 April 2009.

Marshall, P. D. (1997), *Celebrity and Power: Fame in Contemporary Culture*, Minnesota: University of Minnesota Press.

McKee, A. (2005), *The Public Sphere: An Introduction*, Cambridge: Cambridge University Press.

Meyer, T. (with Hinchman, L.) (2002), *Media Democracy: How the Media Colonize Politics*, Cambridge UK: Polity.

Rojek, C. (2001), *Celebrity*, London: Reaktion Books.

Street, J. (2004), 'Celebrity Politicians: Popular culture and popular representation', *The British Journal of Politics and International Relations*, 6: 4, pp. 435–452.

The Elders, <www.theelders.org>. Accessed 15 October 2009.

Turner, G. (2004), *Understanding Celebrity*, London: Sage.

Turner, G., Bonner, F. and Marshall, P. D. (2000), *Fame Games: The Production of Celebrity in Australia*, Cambridge UK: Cambridge University Press.

West, D. and Orman, J. (2002), *Celebrity Politics*, New Jersey: Prentice Hall.

Note

1. Aung San Suu Kyi is a human rights advocate, Nobel laureate and symbol of freedom for Burma. She was placed under house arrest by the military junta in 1989 when her political party, The National League for Democracy won the general elections. She has been offered freedom if she were to leave the country but she has refused; instead she practices Mahatma Ghandi's philosophy of non-violence. She is also the daughter of General Aung San, widely believed to be responsible for the birth of modern Burma.

Chapter 6

Fighting Superior Military Power in Chiapas, Mexico: Celebrity Activism and its Limitations

Roy Krøvel

Introduction

Global news travels fast. I recall reading first about the Zapatistas in the *International Herald Tribune* while having a cup of coffee in a street-side restaurant in Cairo, Egypt. The waiter told me he had seen a masked spokesperson on television the night before. Everything was less than clear, but the name, 'Zapatista', caught my attention. I had read about Emiliano Zapata in a book I found in a Norwegian bookshop just a few weeks before. I contacted my editor upon returning to my hometown in Norway, and he later agreed to send me, along with a photographer, to Chiapas to cover the conflict.

The Zapatistas Army of National Liberation (EZLN) seemed to come from nowhere when they marched into San Cristobal de las Casas and a few other small towns in the southern Mexican state of Chiapas on 1 January 1994. They took everyone by surprise, but were also slightly taken aback themselves by the massive attention they got from national and international media. That very day Mexico, the US and Canada formally formed a free trade area (NAFTA) and EZLN were there to spoil the party. Thousands of tourists, who had spent New Year's Eve in San Cristobal de las Casas, woke up in the middle of dramatic events. Many called home; others called the newspapers and television.

A great number of articles and books have since been written and published on the rebellion and its aftermath. One large group of authors see the rebellion in a constructivist or postmodern perspective, highlighting the role of the media, the Internet, journalists, global activists, networks of solidarity and so forth (Beverly 1995; Castells 1996, 1997a; Cleaver 1998; Cleaver and Holloway 1998; Holloway 1998, 2005; Leyva-Solano 2003; Leyva Solano and Abdala 2006; Nugent 1995). Others see material conditions taking precedence over the production of information, networks of solidarity and the media, while exclusion of peasants and labourers still play a pivotal role in explaining social change for many authors (Morton 2002; Nugent 1995; Petras and Veltmeyer 2001; Petras et al. 1994; Veltmeyer et al. 1997). A number of authors argue that the rebellion should be read from an indigenous perspective, identifying affinities with earlier indigenous rebellions (Gosner 1996). Overall, more than 500 books have been published on the Zapatistas, and the variety of approaches is too wide for even pretending to give a fair representation within a short chapter.

The early 1990s was a good moment for a local, indigenous movement with national ambitions to build global alliances. The Internet had arrived in Chiapas just a few months earlier, and a number of NGOs had direct access to global networks of solidarity. A global movement of indigenous peoples was growing in size and influence. Many travelled to

Chiapas to demonstrate their solidarity with the Zapatistas and indigenous peoples, ordinary people, and a few celebrities, or at least well-known artists, musicians or authors, alike.

In this chapter I will analyse this kind of celebrity activism, taking the violent events that took place in a few small villages in the municipality of Zinacantan in 2004 as my starting point. I will put these events into a historical perspective, trying to evaluate practices of celebrity activism in Chiapas, before returning to the debate on celebrity diplomacy in the light of the Chiapas events.

Existing literature on celebrity activism relevant for the study of the Zapatistas

Existing literature on celebrity activism can enrich the understanding of the Zapatistas and the conflict in Chiapas. I also contend that the practice of celebrity activism in Chiapas and Mexico can deepen our understanding of celebrity activism in general, particularly in relation to a number of issues. First, I will build on Huliaras and Tzifakis (2008) to elaborate on the dynamics of celebrity activism in order to facilitate analysis of the interaction between celebrities and the solidarity movement in Chiapas. Second, I will comment on Chandler's claim that these activists are first and foremost using the indigenous cause to construct their own identities by making us aware of their awareness (Chandler 2004, 2007). An alternative view is developed using Tarrow's term 'rooted cosmopolitans' (Tarrow and Della Porta 2005). According to Tarrow, these activists emerge from domestic political or social activities, they are better educated and better connected than their compatriots and they normally return to domestic activities. Finally, this chapter also intends to built on the theoretical framework of celebrity activism as an activity practiced by more mainstream celebrities who have taken up less politically controversial (in the West, at least) issues linked to human rights compared to the few politically engaged celebrities of the 1960s and 1970s.

According to Huliaras and Tzifakis (2008), from the 1970s onwards, there was a shift in the field of international relations, away from focusing mainly on states, statesmen and other political leaders, towards a more complex understanding of international relations. This opened up the field of international relations for including other actors and other types of activity, for instance, that of celebrity activists. The ensuing body of literature is helpful when trying to make sense of the particularities of activism in solidarity with the Zapatistas in Chiapas. Understanding the practices of celebrity activism in Chiapas requires close attention to the cooperation and interaction between activist celebrities, NGOs and individual activists in the global solidarity movement. A few words on NGOs and global social movements in the international relations literature are therefore needed, as this will clarify how and why celebrity activism might work, especially in relation to issues involving indigenous peoples.

Robert Keohane and Joseph Nye were among the first to focus on the many social activities outside state control with significant political impact (Keohane and Nye 1970; Nye 1990). Many writers have since focused on the explosive growth, both in numbers and influence of Non-Governmental Organizations (NGOs), leading to a much more complex understanding of international politics. Another group of authors, often defined as *constructivists*, have contributed to the literature on the global indigenous movement. Allison Brysk's understanding of the term 'power' is a useful starting point, especially because she is particularly concerned with the development and growth of a global indigenous movement. According to Brysk, symbols of identity belonging to indigenous peoples have been converted into something that can be used or exploited for political end (Brysk 2002a, 2002b; Khagram et al. 2002; Klotz 2002; Price 1998). Power can be exercised directly by forcing someone to act in a prescribed way, but also in more indirect ways through symbols, institutions and social structures. Brysk sees social movements as actors struggling to *construct meaning*. According to Manuel Castells, some individuals can have a similar effect on how meaning is constructed: '[…] their identity may enter the realm of symbolic struggles, and stand a chance of seizing power' (Castells 1997b: 361). This, according to Castells, applies to subcomandante Marcos, the military leader of the Zapatistas.

Taking a constructivist perspective on international relations, by focusing on the struggle to construct meaning using information and symbols of identity, can also help us understand how and why practices of celebrity activism may or may not work in Chiapas. Celebrities can use their 'celebrityhood' to disseminate information, thus reaching a wider audience than other activists. Information that is new to the audience, or that is presented from a different angle, can thus 'enter the realm of symbolic struggles' (Castells 1997b). In the case of the 'symbolic struggle' on indigenous peoples, social movements have contributed to constructing meanings or understandings of 'being indigenous', which are profoundly different from those constructed only a generation ago (Brysk 2002a, 2002b). These alternative understandings of indigenous peoples have normative, ideological and political implications.

Returning to the constructivist literature on indigenous identity, Brysk explains that systems of meaning are exercised through norms of different types. Norms are constantly constructed and reconstructed and new types of interaction, new information and new actors can contribute to reconstructing the underlying 'scripts' of social life. New information can thus contribute to the formulation of new stories that again lead to changes in the political system by mobilizing collective action based on identity, change the social agenda or challenge the legitimacy of the current regime. In my view, celebrity activists in Chiapas seek to do exactly that.

Some argue that celebrity activists might be more interested in constructing their own image than the causes they take up, and that activism is more a question of egoistic branding than an altruistic attempt of doing something good (see Virgil Hawkins, this volume). Chandler has proposed a similar type of understanding of activists in the global network of solidarity operating in Chiapas (Chandler 2004). According to Chandler, the activists in Chiapas are mainly engaged in constructing identities free of commitments instead of taking part in real communities with real commitments at home. This type of activism could thus be described as a form of escape; the activists are 'illusory participants' and mainly engaged in constructing themselves, using the various causes to produce symbols of identity, with the intent of making us aware of their cause (Chandler 2007). While this perspective is interesting and possibly fruitful for the study of individuals in international relations, it is based on a very limited number of sources, mostly media representations of a handful of activist intentions.

Why all the fuzz? Celebrity activism and solidarity in Chiapas

The value of a case study of Chiapas celebrity advocacy lies in the particularities of Chiapas activism. While a few high-profile celebrities participated in making news from Chiapas 'newsworthy' in the eyes of editors and journalists, it was the writers, authors and musicians who contributed most to developing new framings and understandings of the conflict in Chiapas, thus giving 'voice to the voiceless' (Thomassen 2007: 111–126). The ripple effects of this collaboration meant that being 'seen' by celebrities and activists also affected the ways in which the insurgents saw and represented themselves. To better understand the complex interactions and communications among insurgents, indigenous peoples, celebrities, activists and the media, we need to take a closer look at a couple of examples.

For the purposes of this chapter, which draws from my doctoral thesis (Krøvel 2006), I conducted a content analysis of newspapers and online sources regarding the violent clashes that took place in a few small villages in the Zinacantan municipality in 2004. The purpose of the content analysis was to understand the communication and interaction between celebrities and the global social movement supporting the Zapatista cause. This would facilitate the analysis of the case in relation to existing literature on the relation between celebrity activism and social movements; for instance, Marks, Cooper, Thrall and Meyer (Cooper 2007; Marks and Fischer 2002; Meyer 1995; Meyer and Tarrow 1998; Thrall et al. 2008). I will return to this literature as the analysis progresses.

Both celebrities and left-leaning activists descended on Chiapas over the next few years. Bianca Jagger, the Nicaraguan ex-wife of rock star Mick Jagger, was among the first to arrive (DeParle 1995; Ryan 2006: 260).[1] Hundreds of journalists and photographers also travelled to Chiapas to cover the conflict, and the authorities set up a press centre at one of the more fashionable hotels, in San Cristóbal de las Casas. The massive media coverage stimulated unprecedented cooperation and activity between the insurgents and activists around the world. Only some six or seven months after the initial fighting took place, at least 5,000 solidarity activists convened in a small indigenous community on the outskirts of the Lacandon jungle to dialogue directly with the Zapatistas. The experience was repeated the following year. International activists set up dozens of solidarity camps and organized projects all over the region over the next years, while the Zapatistas themselves organized both national campaigns, caravans to different regions of Mexico and global solidarity activities. A 'referendum' on indigenous rights organized by the Zapatistas in 1999 attracted close to three million participants, mostly from Mexico, but also many in Europe and elsewhere in America (Ross 2000).

Some of those engaged in Chiapas belonged to a small circle of very famous celebrities, like Bianca Jagger. Hollywood director Oliver Stone could also be counted in this group. He investigated the possibility of making a documentary on the Zapatista struggle. Danielle Mitterrand, widow of the late French President François Mitterrand, said that she was filled with a new vital force after speaking with the Zapatistas (Froehling 1997; González de Pazos 1997). But the large majority of celebrities engaged in the conflict in Chiapas, did not belong to this type of celebrity. They were famous mainly in more closely defined circles, for instance, among those interested in art, literature, music or politics. Typical examples are the Nobel laureates José Saramago and Gabriel García Márquez who both met and interviewed subcomandante Marcos and other Zapatistas, musicians like Manu Chao and members of the group Rage Against the Machine and political activists like Naomi Klein and Noam Chomsky (although he did not travel to Mexico himself). The list should also include Regis Debray, Eduardo Galeano, John Berger, Manuel Vázquez Montalbán, Carlos Monsiváis, Saul Landau and many more. While these artists and writers arguably are not as famous as Stone and Jagger, they are still able to create headlines. Within their fields, they are undoubtedly among the most well known and respected.

These artists, writers and musicians did not merely travel to Chiapas to 'witness' what was going on or make statements to the media; instead, in contrast to the majority of celebrities in the existing literature on celebrity diplomacy, they typically set out to formulate their own histories on the conflict and the Zapatistas, framing the conflict and communicating directly with their audience, or at least without depending on journalists to mediate their messages. This resulted in numerous texts written by the celebrities themselves (Chomsky 1999; Debray 1996; Galeano 1996; Garcia Marquez 2001; Landau and Hayden 2002; Monsiváis Aceves 2001; Saramago 1999; Taibo Ii 1994).

Another aspect of the conflict in Chiapas also stands out from many other cases where celebrities have been engaged: the combined efforts of journalists, individual activists, NGOs, the solidarity movement and celebrity activists made at least one of the Zapatistas become a sort of celebrity himself, at least for a moment. Benetton reportedly offered subcomandante Marcos a lucrative contract for the rights to use his image in an ad (Knudson 1998; Marcos and Vodovnik 2004). The *Associated Press* later said that subcomandante Marcos was 'on his way to becoming the most marketable masked man on the planet' (Watson 2001: 1). In many publications, Marcos, for instance, appears as a co-author of a number of books together with several of the celebrities mentioned previously.[2] This indicates that the celebrity diplomacy observed in Chiapas differed from what is described by Huliaras and Tzifakis on, for instance, the campaign against human rights abuses in Sudan (Huliaras and Tzifakis 2008). The celebrity activists did not merely represent the Zapatistas' cause internationally; they were also engaged in a dialogue with the Zapatistas on how to understand the cause.

Methods used: a short note on the sources investigated

The research is based on two types of articles. First, I have selected all relevant articles from the two newspapers *La Jornada* and *Cuarto Poder* from 2004. *Cuarto Poder* is the dominant daily in Chiapas. *La Jornada* is a national newspaper and is particularly interesting because it is historically closely related to The Partido de la Revolución Democrática (PRD), the party of the new generation of local leaders in Zinacantan, and at the same time is supportive of the Zapatistas. Second, I have selected online articles from various NGOs in San Cristobal de las Casas, such as El *Centro de Derechos Humanos Fray Bartolomé de Las Casas* (*www.frayba. org.mx/*), CIEPAC (www.ciepac.org) and CAPISE. (www.capise.org.mx). The latter were distributed and adopted for local audiences by a large number of solidarity organizations, among them Latin-Amerikagruppene i Norge (www.latin-amerikagruppene.no/), *Ya Basta* (www.yabasta.it), *La plataforma de solidaridad con Chiapas* (www.nodo50.org/pchiapas/plataforma.htm).

In addition, I draw on approximately 100 interviews I conducted between 1994 and 2004. These interviews include individual activists, members of foreign NGOs, local NGOs, civilian Zapatistas, Zapatista military leaders, members and leaders of organizations of peasants and political parties and others.

While the previously mentioned channels of communication made it possible for Zapatistas and solidarity activists to communicate directly with each other, they also mobilized activists both at home and in Chiapas, including the celebrities who published open letters in support of the Zapatistas in Zinacantan. These sources therefore present us with an opportunity to study the interaction of celebrities, networks of activists and the Zapatistas.

A representation of the conflict in Zinacantan

A little background information is necessary to understand the dynamics of celebrity activism and social movement in the conflict in the Zinacantan municipality. Zinacantan is a municipality of approximately 30,000 inhabitants in the mountainous area just outside San Cristobal de las Casas. A handful of indigenous leaders dominated local politics in Zinacantan in close cooperation with the often authoritarian The Institutional Revolutionary Party (PRI) until the late 1990s, when a group of successful small business owners challenged the hegemonic alliance. This group of small business owners had successfully shifted to producing flowers and vegetables when an economic crisis hit the region in the 1970s and 1980s, thus becoming serious contenders for political positions in the municipality (Camacho 2004). Other groups also challenged the status quo in Zinacantan, leading to increasing volatility of the political system in the region.

The local elections in 2000 totally changed the political landscape in Chiapas; the PRI lost both at the state level and in Zinacantan. The group of small business owners formed the backbone of the new local government in alliance with the opposition PRD. But any illusion of fundamental changes in the way politics was conducted in Zinacantan soon disappeared. Access to common goods like schools, roads and water supply were used to construct a new corporative system in Zinacantan, often by authoritarian means. Human rights organizations fought a hard and mostly unsuccessful battle against the impunity in the municipality. Two members of the PRI were, for instance, lynched and killed by a politically motivated mob in 2003. The crime was not properly investigated and the killers walked free ('El saldo, dos muertos y 15 lesionados; PRD y PRI acuerdan di logo permanente. Firman la no agreción en Zinacantan' 2003). The conflict in Zinacantan to a large degree evolved around differing understandings of local tradition. For those who had governed in alliance with PRI for two generations, tradition included belonging to the Catholic Church and voting for the right political party (PRI). Tens of thousands were expelled from their villages in highland Chiapas for joining a Lutheran church or an opposition party.

The leaders of the new corporative system in Zinacantan entered before long into a long and violent conflict with local Zapatistas on rights to water and religious obligations related to what was seen as the 'traditional' way of organization in the region. Falling prices of local products led to rising levels of poverty in Zinacantan, and many poor started to blame the local corporative system. Many of the disgruntled families joined the Zapatistas. The EZLN therefore grew rapidly among the very poor in small villages like Jechvó, Elambó Alto, San Isidro and Elambó Bajo. This was a challenge to traditional ways of doing politics in the region. The conflict intensified when the Zapatistas refused to accept tasks assigned to them by local leaders. The local leaders decided to punish the Zapatistas for 'breaking local tradition' by cutting off access to the water supply system (Krøvel 2005a). Similar punishment was also imposed on others, for example, those who had converted from Catholicism to evangelical churches.

The local Zapatistas received support from other Zapatistas in the region. On 10 April 4000 Zapatistas from the region marched in Zinacantan in solidarity with those of Jechvó, Elambó Alto, San Isidro and Elambó Bajo. The march was peaceful until a group of local police and supporters of the corporative system ambushed the Zapatistas outside one of the small villages (my own observations). Attacking the march with guns and rocks, they injured at least twenty Zapatistas who had to seek medical care at a nearby hospital. One hundred and twenty-five families fled the four villages. The mayor of Zinacantan claimed that the violence was nothing more than traditional 'enmity between rival indigenous groups', thereby obscuring the political dimension and the involvement of both local leaders and local police (*Cuarto Podér* and *La Jornada* 11, 12 and 13 April 2004). The local leaders tried to de-politicize the interpretation of the conflict, but were unsuccessful.

The confrontation provoked renewed fears of increased levels of violence and armed conflict in Chiapas, and therefore generated much interest in both national and international media. Nine non-governmental organizations (NGOs) participated in delegations to investigate the violence in the villages of Zinacantan. They presented their findings in a conference in San Cristobal de las Casas on 12 April, giving a wholly different picture of the events and leaving the mayor in an awkward position. The nine NGOs concluded that the attack had been planned in detail in advance and was politically motivated.

A long list of international media participated at the press conference in San Cristobal de las Casas, and reports were published all over the world. In addition, the nine NGOs used alternative online channels of information to distribute their findings. It did not take long before the first reactions started to pour in. Within a week, prominent activists like Nobel Prize laureate in Literature, Jose Saramago, musician Manu Chao, author John Berger, author Carlos Taibo and 800 others had signed a petition supporting the exiled Zapatistas. The petition was published in several newspapers, among them *La Jornada*; a newspaper that had traditionally been seen as very supportive of the PRD.

The PRD was one of two main national opposition parties in Mexico, and could not easily ignore the criticism. It therefore sent a delegation to investigate the situation. The PRD was in a particularly sensitive position since the party had been founded precisely in protest of the often authoritarian corporative politics of the PRI, which dominated Mexican politics for 60 years. Adolfo Gilly, one of the founding members of the PRD, had only recently published an open letter criticizing the party for becoming more and more like the PRI (Gilly 2004). The PRD was forced to react. The delegation published a report heavily criticizing the local leaders of PRD. On 18 April, the PRD published an ad in several Mexican newspapers saying the party 'fully supported the demands of the EZLN' and promised to 'do something' about the problems in Zinacantan (PRD, 'Posición del PRD Acerca del Problema Politico en Zinacantan, Chiapas', Cuernavaca 18 April 2004). The state governor of Chiapas was forced to publish a counter-ad distancing himself from those responsible for the violence in Zinacantan (Gobierno de Chiapas, 'Zinacantan: posición y acciones del Gobierno de Chiapas', *La Jornada* 20 April 2004). The pressure against the mayor of Zinacantan increased further when the PRD threatened to suspend him ('El PRD suspenderá derechos politicos al edil de Zinacantan', *La Foja* 20 April 2004).

The leaders of the PRD in Zinacantan, meanwhile, defended themselves by saying that the Zapatistas represented a threat to local tradition because they refused to comply with local traditions of organizing in the villages. They used a language very similar to that of the Zapatistas to defend the repression, using terms like 'tradition' and 'indigenous rights'.

The conflict in Zinacantan proved that the global solidarity network of activists and celebrities could act fast when mobilized by local human rights organizations. The extent and gravity of violence provoked spontaneous reactions from organizations and individuals alike. The reactions further motivated national PRD leaders, putting additional pressure on local leaders so that the refugees could return home. But a year later not much had changed in the villages of Zinacantan. The families still lacked access to the water system, and the Zapatistas of the region had to spend a substantial part of their resources on transporting water to the affected families (Krøvel 2005b). The Zapatistas of Zinacantan continued to be the poorest of the poor of the region.

A number of evangelical families were denied access to water in the following months; water continued to be one of the most powerful weapons used to discipline political and religious opposition in Zinacantan. In my view, the global network of solidarity activists and celebrities was effective as long as the human rights violations caused substantial media interest around the world. But when the lights were turned off, and the attention was on something else, it was back to business as usual in the small villages of Zinacantan. The global networks could contribute to putting restrictions on the abuse of power only as long as the human rights violations were seen as dramatic enough to be newsworthy. News of the daily 'small' abuses of power did not manage to penetrate the many barriers filtering the news before it, eventually, reached an audience (Bob 2005). Global activism and protest could possibly set limitations on the exercise of power, but fundamental processes producing and reproducing power remained unaltered in Zinacantan.

Notwithstanding the limitations of celebrity activism in relation to human rights abuses in Zinacantan, the case offers some insights in relation to existing literature on celebrity activism and social movements. Left-wing criticism has often expressed frustration for the attractiveness of celebrity diplomacy. According to Cooper, it defuses or suffocates more radical forms of protest (Cooper 2007). In the case of Zincantan, this did not happen. In fact, it was some of the most radical groups supporting the Zapatistas that initiated mass protest and activated the celebrities. The latter were used not only to highlight human rights abuses, but also to draw attention towards the Zapatista cause and its revolutionary politics. In this case, then, this differs from the Marks and Fischer contention that celebrities have become the chief vehicles for the simulation of political consent, and buttressing existing political order (Marks and Fischer 2002). On the contrary, in Zinacantan, celebrity activists joined the social movement by demanding radical changes to the political order. Meyer argues that when celebrities speak in favour of a movement, they frequently soften the claims of that movement to more consensual kinds of politics (Meyer 1995). The celebrities in the case of Zinacantan did indeed focus on a few particularly violent human rights abuses. But it would be unfair to claim that this amounts to a softening of the claims of the social movement supporting the Zapatistas. In fact, these celebrities were well known for their radical or revolutionary politics and were long-time supporters of the Zapatistas. In relation to the case of the Zapatistas, it would be more fitting to understand the dynamics of celebrity activism within the framework proposed by Thrall et al. (2008). Celebrities played an important role in an emerging strategy for political advocacy made possible by the evolution of technology and stimulated by the difficulty most groups have in making news (Thrall et al. 2008).

Understanding celebrity activism and global networks of solidarity in Chiapas

The previous representation of the conflict in Zinacantan makes clear some of the many security concerns involved with being a solidarity activist in Chiapas. This is a challenge when investigating the interaction between celebrities and social movements. I observed the demonstrations in Zinacantan, conducted a large number of interviews and collected a large number of reports and news items on the conflict. But because of the precarious security situations, the majority of those participating in the demonstrations preferred to avoid anything that could help identify them. In fact, most of the foreigners participating in the demonstrations in Zinacantan wore masks making identification virtually impossible.

Having visited Chiapas at first as a journalist, and later as an investigator periodically for some fifteen years, I nonetheless feel it is possible and necessary to make some very general comments. The group of a few dozen 'outsiders' on 10 April consisted of both Mexicans and foreigners. Among the foreigners many, probably the majority, represented European or North American NGOs cooperating with the nine NGOs making the initial investigation into violence. Many thus were members of a more or less formal network of NGOs, even though they might have participated in the demonstration as individuals rather than acting formally as representatives of their respective NGOs. In addition, I also observed a few representing delegations of trade unions on a mission to study the conflict in Chiapas. Some had joined the protest to cover the conflict for alternative or community media, for instance, *Indymedia*, but no one, as far as I could judge, could be described as 'celebrity'; this group was mobilized later by other grassroot activists in the global network.

Chandler has painted a bleak picture of this type of cosmopolitan activism, with activists being mainly engaged in constructing themselves, raising awareness and producing symbols of identity (Chandler 2007). My investigation has not provided evidence to support Chandler's claim. All the activists I interviewed had a history of social and political activity behind them. Most had been members of political organizations of some kind in their home countries, or elsewhere in Mexico, in the case of Mexicans. Many could be said to belong to a loosely defined counter-cultural movement, some living in squatted houses or doing voluntary work in 'autonomous' cultural centres. All those that I interviewed had been engaged in many types of solidarity activities before Chiapas. Some had a long history of solidarity with colonized peoples in Africa or elsewhere. A few could tell stories of demonstrations against the Vietnam War, while many had protested against the apartheid in South Africa.

The vast majority had also participated in more local activities in home towns or neighbourhoods, often related to traffic or the environment. Some had participated in trade unions or in demonstrations supporting workers on strike, for instance. The variety of activity is too great to make generalizations, but the point is that these activists were not detached from local real communities with real obligations. I found no evidence of escapism. I would rather describe these activists as 'hyper-political', constantly engaged in local and global causes, always involved in debates and reflexion on the meaning of their activities. This does not mean that they were not 'constructing' themselves as they went along, using images to convey political preferences. In fact, it is difficult to imagine anyone not actively or passively taking part in a constantly on-going construction of identity. We all need symbols to imagine ourselves in the various communities we feel a part of. This is also true for activists in Chiapas, I believe, but is not a defining characteristic of this group of people; it is not something that distinguishes this group from others.

Tarrow has adopted the term 'rooted cosmopolitans' to describe increasing global activism (Tarrow 2005). Tarrow has described three common features of such activists: they emerge from domestic political or social activities, they are better educated and connected than their compatriots and they normally return to domestic activities. All the activists I interviewed emerged from domestic political activities, most had studied at universities and many or most returned to domestic activities. The term 'rooted cosmopolitans' thus fits the group of activists in Chiapas much better than the description given by Chandler.

Grenier has found that 'a good education and a relatively privileged upbringing give certain advantages' in relation to being a 'pioneer' in the 'new global civil society' (Grenier 2004: 122–157). Building on Grenier, I would also argue that the majority could be defined to have had 'a good education and a relatively privileged upbringing'; they would definitely have what Grenier describes as 'strong motivation'. Curiously, though, most activists in Chiapas do not easily fit some of the characteristics put forward by Grenier for such activists. This is especially true for one 'enabling condition' facilitating the emergence of a 'pioneer', namely 'access to material resources' (Grenier 2004: 122–157; Huliaras and Tzifakis 2010: 258). Compared with their compatriots, many could be described as relatively poor, at least with lesser economic resources than the majority. Many would work for months to save enough for a ticket to Mexico. And when in Mexico, most could survive for weeks or months because the cost of living in Mexico is relatively much lower than in their home countries. In relation to ordinary Mexicans, though, these activists would still have access to substantial material resources.

In my view, communities must be imagined or constructed in continuously on-going processes. Terms like 'home', 'domestic' and 'foreign' are also subjected to constant processes of interpretation and change, just like notions of 'us' and 'them'. The activists in Chiapas are engaged in this on-going process of constructing communities, and have much in common with those engaged in constructing the communities we today take for granted; for instance, 'nation' or 'working class'. Rather than escaping from domestic communities and responsibilities, they could be described as protagonists in the process of reconstructing the borders of existing imagined communities in response to the global processes of change.

The list of celebrities engaged in Chiapas makes a few points clear: First, the typical celebrity engaged in Chiapas was not the typical Hollywood celebrity. While internationally famous, they appealed first and foremost to a specific audience, not the general public. The activities of these celebrities must be understood and analysed in close connexion with the networks of global activists. Second, these celebrities did not have to worry about their image or reputation. For most of them solidarity with the indigenous population of Mexico was not very different from other political activities they had been engaged in. Saramago and Garcia Marquez, for instance, both had long histories of involvement with political and social movements, often taking sides on controversial issues. In contrast to Hollywood activists, they did not have to worry about the next role or what the audience might think. Because of their long-standing involvement with social issues, it is difficult to accuse them of embracing the cause in order to 'remain celebrities' or of self-serving image building (Huliaras and Tzifakis 2008). These celebrities have more in common with the 1960s celebrities who embraced controversial issues like the fight against the Vietnam War and the struggle for equal rights in the US. Their engagement in Chiapas seems to be rooted in conviction rather than in public relations.

Third, their activism was something more than just supporting the Zapatistas. In fact, many of these activists have criticized the Zapatistas and would feel uncomfortable with being grouped together under the umbrella 'solidarity activists'. While many of their articles could fairly be described as supporting the general goals of the Zapatistas, these celebrity authors are clearly out to be active participants in a global dialogue, presenting their own analysis and points of views, even when these are divergent from the views of the Zapatistas (Berger 2006; Galeano 1996; Garcia Marquez 2001; Klein 2001; Landau and Hayden 2002; Saramago 1999; Taibo Ii 1994; Vázquez Montalbán 1999).

As we have seen, celebrity activism in Chiapas contributed to turning Marcos at one point into something like a celebrity himself. The war, the media, the global network of solidarity activists, celebrity activists and the Zapatista's own keen sense for public relations, all contributed to his celebrityhood. At one point, the *Associate Press* described him as 'becoming the most marketable man on the planet' (Associated Press 2001). While this, in retrospect, grossly exaggerated his fame, it nonetheless helps to explain some of the influence he exerted on the radical, so-called 'anti-globalization' movement in Europe and North America. While the buzz surrounding celebrities had clear benefits for mobilizing support among a broader audience, the Zapatistas themselves could communicate and appeal directly to a large audience both in Mexico and outside. The Zapatistas made use of radio, television and the Internet to mobilize support and engage in debates with supporters. Marcos himself published books and articles, and with many of them translated into a large number of languages, he was responsible for one of the meta-narratives for the understanding of indigenous peoples and their struggles.

Zapatistas, solidarity activists and celebrities were in many cases successful in stopping or limiting human rights violations, for instance, in Zinacantan. Solidarity activists could, in close cooperation with NGOs in Chiapas, engage celebrities in specific issues; for instance, in banning military campaigns or facilitating the return of refugees. Celebrities had significant influence over segments of both the Mexican political community and civil society, and could be quite effective in mobilizing support for change, especially when the campaigns managed to direct media-attention towards human rights abuse. Celebrities and activists thus had some success in raising public awareness, though their efforts were limited due to a number of factors.

First, their fund-raising capabilities were very weak. Compared with Guatemala, El Salvador or Nicaragua in the 1980s and 1990s, the number of international NGOs engaged in Chiapas was very small, and those engaged were mostly without financial muscle. This was probably because of the very political nature of the conflict; both the Zapatistas and their supporters continued to use a revolutionary language in their communication. Mainstream western NGOs seemed to prefer less political calls for 'indigenous rights', as presented by organizations in Central America, to the combination of revolutionary rhetoric and demands for indigenous rights by Marcos. The United Nations also kept a very low profile in Chiapas, even though Mexico had adopted the International Labor Organizations' (ILO) Convention 169 on indigenous affairs, and the specialists of ILO often criticized Mexico for its handling of indigenous affairs.

Second, political lobbying also faced difficulties. While lobbying the PRD to some extent was effective in Zinacantan, the liberal government in Mexico proved a much more difficult target. Many had been engaged in the struggle to have Mexico accept a negotiated peace agreement signed by the Zapatistas and government representatives in

San Andres in 1996. This agreement was to give indigenous peoples a number of rights, both individually and collectively – among them collective rights to territories including resources below the surface. In spite of massive political lobbying from indigenous groups, NGOs and celebrities, the Mexican congress in 2001 chose to adopt a much weaker wording, granting indigenous groups lesser collective rights. This is just one of many examples of the limitations of the effectiveness of activism in Chiapas. The Zapatistas decided to withdraw from any negotiations or dialogue with the Mexican authorities as a consequence of the lack of political will to accept the peace agreement reached in 1996.

Conclusions

The case of celebrity activism in Chiapas potentially offers several insights, especially in relation to the literature on celebrity activism and social movements. First, the case shows how celebrity activism must be understood in close relationship to social movements, both local and global NGOs and networks of solidarity activists. Much more investigation is needed on the interplay between celebrities and activists, especially in cases where the causes embraced are overtly political, such as in the case of the Zapatistas.

The case of Chiapas also calls for a broader understanding of what constitutes celebrity. Hollywood stars are definitely celebrities, but many of the effects of celebrity activism can also be observed in activism by other and less famous individuals. Novelists, artists and academics can act as celebrities reaching and mobilizing support and action in groups with significant cultural capital in their respective audiences. Working together, several such celebrities could potentially have significant influence over political events. This type of activism was, in my view, effective in reducing the general level of violence in Chiapas, and sometimes also succeeded in stopping human rights abuse. It can arguably also be credited with limiting the scope for authoritarian abuse of power in Chiapas. Nonetheless, it proved much less effective against long-term, 'quiet' structural violence; for example, poverty, hunger, exclusion (Galtung 1969).

Celebrity activism in Chiapas should also lead us to question the effect celebrities have on the causes they adopt. The celebrities in Chiapas were in general very engaged with social and political issues, and also engaged the Zapatistas in dialogue on the meanings of the rebellion itself. While the Zapatistas initially presented themselves within the framework of a Marxist revolutionary guerrilla, much along the lines defined by Che Guevara (Guevara 1997; Loveman and Guevara 1997), outsiders often saw something else, highlighting other elements of the struggle they adopted. They, instead, focused on the indigenous elements of the reality in Chiapas. The first declaration of the Zapatistas paid little attention to the fact that the vast majority belonged to indigenous peoples, highlighting other aspects of their identity, such as being Mexicans and peasants. Little by little, though, being indigenous moved to the forefront of the Zapatista discourse, thereby facilitating a wide variety of alliances with other indigenous groups or organizations supporting indigenous causes.

Some social scientists have claimed to see profound changes in the Zapatista rebellion in relation of power in the world. Some have called the Zapatistas the first 'postmodern' guerrillas (Burbach 1994). Others have seen a new form of a powerful individual in Marcos, powerful in the sense that he can supposedly change the way in which people think about the world, thus being a modern 'prophet' (Castells 1997a: 362). In hindsight, though, the effects of the Chiapas rebellion, including the activism of both celebrities and others, seem to be much less dramatic, but this should not divert us from trying to understand the many ways in which modern social movements, organizations and individuals influence international relations. The Zapatista rebellion, the global network of activists and many celebrities did play important roles in defining both modern Mexico and its relationship with the world.

References

Berger, J. (2006), 'Against the great defeat of the world', *Race and Class*, 40:2–3 (October 1998–March 1999), pp. 1–4.

Beverly, J., Aronna, M., & Oviedo, J. (Eds.). (1995). *The Postmodern Debate in Latin-America*. Durham, N. C.: Duke University Press.

Bob, C. (2005), *The Marketing of Rebellion. Insurgents, Media, and International Activism*, Cambridge: Cambridge University Press.

Brysk, A. (2002a), *From Tribal Village to Global Village. Indian Rights and International Relations in Latin America*, Stanford, CA: Stanford University Press.

—— (2002b), *Globalization and Human Rights*, Berkeley, Calif: University of California Press.

Burbach, R. (1994), 'Roots of postmodern rebellion in Chiapas', *New Left Review*, (May/June), pp. 113–114.

Camacho, D., & Lomelí, A. (2004). El ascenso de la Violencia en Zinacantán. Ojarasca / The ascent of Violence in Zinacantán, *La Jornada*, pp. 3–4

Castells, M. (1996), *The Rise of the Network Society*, Cambridge, Mass: Blackwell Publishers.

—— (1997a), *The Power of Identity*, Oxford: Oxford University Press.

—— (1997b), *The Power of Identity*, Malden, Mass.: Blackwell Publishers.

Chandler, D. (2004), 'Building Global Civil Society "From Below"?', *Millennium – Journal of International Studies*, 33:2, pp. 313–339.

—— (2007), 'The possibilities of post-territorial political community', *Area*, 39:1, pp. 116–119.

Chomsky, N. (1999), *Profit over People: Neoliberalism and Global Order* (Seven Stories Press 1st ed.), New York: Seven Stories Press.

Cleaver, H. (1998), 'The Zapatista Effect: The Internet and the Rise of an Alternative Political Fabric', *Journal of International Affairs*, 51:2, Spring, pp. 621–640.

Cleaver, H. (1998). The Zapatistas and the Electronic Fabric of the Struggle. In J. Holloway & E. Pelaez (Eds.), *Zapatista!: Reinventing Revolution in Mexico* (pp. 81–103). London: Pluto Press.

Cooper, A. (2007). Celebrity Diplomacy and the G8: Bono and Bob as Legitimate International Actors. Retrieved 22.05.2010, from SSR: http://ssrn.com/abstract=1019091

Debray, R. (1996), 'Talking to the Zapatistas', *New Left Review* (218, July/August), pp. 128–137.

DeParle, J. (1995, June 4), 'Bob (Torricelli) and Bianca (yes, that one) to the rescue', *New York Times*.

Henriquez, E. (2003, 07.03.2003). El saldo, dos muertos y 15 lesionados; PRD y PRI acuerdan diálogo permanente/ Final result is two dead and 15 injured; PRD and PRI agree on permanent dialogue. *La Jornada*.

Froehling, O. (1997), 'The Cyberspace "War of Ink and Internet" in Chiapas, Mexico', *Geographical Review*, 87:2, pp. 291–307.

Galeano, E. (2002). Chiapas Cronicle. In T. Hayden (Ed.), *The Zapatista Reader. A Literary Anthology* (pp. 48 – 50). New York: Nation Books.

Galtung, J. (1969), 'Violence, Peace, and Peace Research', *Journal of Peace Research*, 6:3, pp. 167–191.

Márquez, G. G., & Pombo, R. (2001, 28.03.). Habla Marcos/ Marcos Speaks. *Revista Cambio*.

Gilly, A. (2004, 26.03.). El PRD, un partido lejano del pueblo (carta abierta a Leonel Godoy) / PRD is a party far removed from the people (an open letter to Leonel Godoy). *La Jornada*.

González de Pazos, M. (1997), 'Mexico Since the Mayan Uprising: Government and Zapatista Strategies', *10 ST. THOMAS L. REV* (159, 160).

Gosner, K., & Ouweneel, A. (1996), *Indigenous Revolts in Chiapas and the Andean Highlands*, Amsterdam: CEDLA.

Grenier, P. (2004), 'The New Pioneers. The People Behind Global Civil Society', in H. K. Anheier, M. Glasius and M. Kaldor (eds), *Global Civil Society 2004/5*, London: Sage.

Guevara, E. (1997), *La guerra de guerrillas*, Hondarribia: Argitaletxe HIRU.

Holloway, J. (1998), *Zapatista! Reinventing Revolution in Mexico*, London: Pluto Press.

—— (2005), *Change the World without Taking Power*, London: Pluto Press.

Huliaras, A. and Tzifakis, N. (2008), 'The Dynamics of Celebrity Activism: Mia Farrow and the "Genocide Olympics" Campaign', *Karamanlis Working Papers in Hellenic and European Studies* (No 7/July), 26.

—— (2010), 'Celebrity Activism in International Relations: In Search of a Framework for Analysis', *Global Society*, 24:2, pp. 255–274.

Keohane, R. and Nye, J. (1970), *Transnational Relations and World Politics*, Cambridge: Cambridge University Press.

Khagram, S., Riker, J. V. and Sikkink, K. (2002), *Restructuring World Politics : Transnational Social Movements, Networks, and Norms*, Minneapolis: University of Minnesota Press.

Klein, N. (2001), 'The Unknown Icon', *The Guardian*.

Klotz, A. (2002), 'Transnational Activism and Global Transformations: The Anti-Apartheid and Abolitionist Experiences', *European Journal of International Relations*, 8:1, pp. 49–76.

Knudson, J. W. (1998), 'Rebellion in Chiapas: insurrection by Internet and public relations', *Media Culture Society*, 20:3, pp. 507–518.

Krøvel, R. (2005a), José Jimenez Peréz. Secretario Municipal. PRD. Interview. Zinacantan.

—— (2005b), Junta de buen gobierno, Interview. Morelia.

—— (2006), *Fra gerilja til globale solidaritetsnettverk i Chiapas, Mexico/ From Guerrilla to Global Networks of Solidarity in Chiapas, Mexico. Unpublished PhD, Norges teknisk-naturvitenskapelige universitet, Det historisk-filosofiske fakultet, Institutt for historie og klassiske fag / Norwegian University of Science and Technology, The department of History and classical studies*, Trondheim.

Landau, S. and Hayden, T. (2002), 'The Zapatista Army of National Liberation. Part of the Latin American Tradition – But also very Different', *The Zapatista Reader*, pp. 146–152.

Leyva-Solano, X. (2003), 'Neo-zapatista advocacy networks, from local to global experience', 6 March 2003, *Conference on Global Protest Movements and Transnational Advocacy Networks: Another World is Possible!*, Dublin.

Leyva Solano, X. and Abdala, B. J. (2006), 'El Neozapatismo: De Guerrilla a Social Movement Web', *Portos Flutuantes*, pp. 355–370, São Paulo.

Loveman, B., Davies, T. M., & Guevara, E. (1997), 'Introduction. Guerrilla Warfare, Revolutionary Theory, and Revolutionary Movements in Latin America', *Guerrilla warfare*, pp. 1–38, Wilmington.

Subcomandante Marcos and Vodovnik, Z. (2004), *Ya basta! : ten years of the Zapatista uprising*, 1st ed., Oakland, CA: AK Press.

Marks, M. P. and Fischer, Z. M. (2002), 'The King's New Bodies: Simulating Consent in the Age of Celebrity', *New Political Science*, 24:3, pp. 371–394.

Meyer, D. S. (1995), 'The Challenge of Cultural Elites: Celebrities and Social Movements', *Sociological Inquiry*, 65:2, pp. 181–206.

Meyer, D. S. and Tarrow, S. G. (1998), *The Social Movement Society: Contentious Politics for a New Century*, Lanham: Rowman & Littlefield Publishers.

Monsiváis Aceves, C. (2001, 04.03), *El indígena visible.(movimiento por los derechos civiles de pueblos indígenas en México)/ The Visible Indigenous (Indigenous Peoples Civil Rights Movement in Mexico) El Proceso.*

Morton, A. D. (2002), '"La Resurrecci¢n del Ma¡z": Globalisation, Resistance and the Zapatistas', *Millennium: Journal of International Studies*, 31:1, January, pp. 27–54.

Nugent, D. (1995), 'Northern intellectuals and the EZLN', *Monthly Review*, 47, June/August, pp. 124–138.

Nye, J. S. (1990), *Bound to Lead. The Changing Nature of American Power*, New York: Basic Books.

Petras, J. and Veltmeyer, H. (2001), *Globalization Unmasked Imperialism in the 21st Century*, Halifax, N.S: Fernwood Publ.

Petras, J., Veltmeyer, H., & Leiva, F. I. (1994), *Democracy and poverty in Chile. The limits to electoral politics.* Boulder and Oxford: Westview Press.

Price, R. (1998), 'Reversing the Gun Sights: Transnational Civil Society Targets Land Mines', *International Organization*, 52:03, pp. 613–644.

Ross, J. (2000), *The War against Oblivion. The Zapatista Chronicles*, Philadelphia: The Read & Resist Series.

Ryan, R. (ed.) (2006), *Clandestines: The Pirate Journals of an Irish Exile*, Oakland: AKPress.

Saramago, J. (1999), 'Moral Force versus the State. Chiapas, land of hope and sorrow', *Le Monde Diplomatique, English version.*

Taibo Ii, P. I. (1994), 'Zapatistas. The Phoenix Rises', *The Nation.*

Tarrow, S. G. (2005), *The New Transnational Activism*, New York: Cambridge University Press.

Tarrow, S. and Della Porta, D. (2005), *Transnational Protest and Global Activism*, Lanham, Md.: Rowman & Littlefield.

Thomassen, L. (2007), 'Beyond Representation?', *Parliam Aff*, 60:1, pp. 111–126.

Thrall, A. T., Lollio-Fakhreddine, J., Berent, J., Donnelly, L., Herrin, W., Paquette, Z. et al. (2008), 'Star Power: Celebrity Advocacy and the Evolution of the Public Sphere', *International Journal of Press/ Politics*, 13:4, pp. 362–385.

Vázquez Montalbán, M. (1999), *Marcos, El Señor de los Espejos/ Marcos, The Lord of Mirrors*, Barcelona: Aguilar.

Veltmeyer, H., Vieux, S. and Petras, J. (1997), Neoliberalism and class conflict in Latin America a comparative perspective on the political economy of structural adjustment, Houndmills, Basingstoke, Hampshire and New York, N.Y: MacMillan Press Ltd

Watson, J. (2001), 'Guerrilla's image generates sales', *Associated Press*, 1 March 2001.

Notes

1. I personally witnessed her visit in May 1994 at a hospital in one of the areas where the fighting had been most intense.
2. Marcos's own publications include essays, political commentaries and novels. A search on amazon. com results in 28 titles, although some are translated versions of the same books (January 2010).

Chapter 7

'Hollywood Goes to the Eastern Mediterranean: Spiro S. Skouras and 'Unorthodox Power', 1940s and 1950s

Evanthis Hatzivassiliou and Georgios Kazamias

Introduction

Celebrity activism has become the subject of an ongoing debate on the theoretical problems that arise from activist intervention in the public sphere, including international initiatives. Although celebrity activism was developed mainly in the post-Cold War era, scholars also note that this phenomenon can be traced to earlier periods, for example, the mobilization of film stars during the two World Wars, the campaign to support UNICEF, the peace protests of the 1960s and the case of the Ethiopian famine in the 1980s (Street 2004; Huliaras and Tzifakis 2010). Indeed, during the post-1945 era, the ascent of international organizations and the emphasis on transnational problems such as famine, the Cold War, peace or the environment played an important role in legitimizing ventures at this kind of activism. At the same time, technological advances and cultural changes affected patterns of communication, and consequently politics (West and Orman 2002; Turner 2004). During the 1990s the UN's effort to employ 'goodwill ambassadors' (Alleyne 2005), and the ascent of the non-governmental organization (NGO), including the employment of the World Economic Forum (Cooper 2008: 70–90), provided the necessary framework of external 'enabling factors' (Huliaras and Tzifakis 2010: 257–8). Although it has been argued that many of these celebrities practice a kind of 'diplomacy' (on the grounds that they enter into deliberations with the official diplomatic community – Cooper 2008: 7), the authors of this chapter take the view that diplomacy remains a more narrowly defined function, and requires official representation and official roles in the settlement of international problems.

This chapter takes a historical approach by presenting a case study of an early attempt at celebrity activism, by the chairman of 20th Century Fox, Spiro S. Skouras. Skouras was initially mobilized in the context of a humanitarian cause, and headed the Greek War Relief Association (GWRA) in the early 1940s. Although his charity work continued in the following years, he also strove to become involved in political issues as well. In 1944–45, he attempted to effect an Anglo-American understanding (including more involvement by the US) on the future of Greece; in the mid-1950s, he sought to mediate in the Cyprus question. This chapter will focus on these two ventures. The first part of the chapter discusses Skouras' career and the nature of his activism in the light of the ongoing theoretical discussion. The following two parts present his attempts at political mediation in the 1940s and the 1950s. In the conclusions, his efforts, as well as the response of foreign policy bureaucracies, are evaluated.

A Transnational Greek?

Spiro S. Skouras (1893–1971) is the archetypal American dream success story. Born in a poor, ten-member family in the Peloponnese, Greece, he migrated to the US in the 1910s, where he worked with his two brothers (Charles and George) in St Louis, Missouri. The brothers went into the then budding movie theatre business, pooling savings to buy a 'nickelodeon'. They soon controlled 30 theatres, which they sold to Warner Brothers in 1929. While all three brothers made their name and fortunes in the movie industry, Spiro became the most visible. A media magnate, in 1942 he became chairman of 20th Century Fox (a company he had helped form earlier, with the merger of Fox and 20th Century Films). He remained in this position for the next twenty years, helping the movie industry survive the early onslaught of television. He also signed Marilyn Monroe for 20th Century Fox and had numerous classics made in the company studios. He lost his position in 1962, following the box office failure of the film *Cleopatra*, and gradually moved away from the industry and into shipping, until his death from a heart attack in 1971.[1]

During his media magnate time, he practiced celebrity activism in the 1940s and 1950s, in issues linked with his homeland, Greece. It is crucial, however, to distinguish between two patterns of activities: during the first half of the 1940s, chairing the Greek War Relief Association (GWRA), he worked for a largely humanitarian cause. Formed after the Italian attack against Greece in 1940, the GWRA initially aimed at collecting financial aid for the Greek war effort; in this, it proved highly successful, as it also was in lobbying for Greece, mainly by managing to mobilize the Greek-Americans through a network that spread far and wide in the US. Skouras was chosen to head the GWRA in the US in 1940. The choice was obvious: at the time Skouras was the most visible Greek-American businessman, and also a member of the top layer of the powerful motion pictures industry. Following Greece's occupation by the Germans, Italians and Bulgarians in spring 1941, and the outbreak of famine in the country in the following winter, Skouras and the GWRA lobbied the US government for relief supplies. This largely successful mass mobilization effort helped secure relief for Greece during the war (the only such large-scale effort for an occupied country straddling the conflict's front lines); it also worked as the springboard for the post-war entry of Greek-Americans in US politics as well as for the formation of the early 'Greek lobby' in the US (Saloutos 1964; Vlachos n.d.; Kazamias 1991; Kyrou 2008; Hionidou 2006). However, Skouras' two next ventures, which are examined here, centred on more narrowly defined political issues.

Although not an artist, Skouras was a film magnate falling under the category of celebrity activists who 'use their status and the medium within which they work to speak out on specific causes and for particular interests with a view to influencing political outcomes'; his venture was based on the political attention he could attract, 'e.g. a willingness by politicians to meet to discuss the particular concerns' (Street 2004: 438). His case is an early example of transnational activism rather than the manifestation of an emerging 'Greek lobby' in the US, or a case of informal diplomacy. In both his later attempts to mediate in political disputes, he did not work within a framework of the Greek-American lobby (even though he drew part of his 'strength' from it), and did not act as the representative, even an informal one, of a nation state. Furthermore, as will be shown, his efforts to intervene in the diplomatic deliberations of his time were unsuccessful: foreign policy bureaucracies were (more or less) willing to listen to him, but also too eager to ignore him (however politely). His motivation was complicated: Skouras tried to intervene both as a Greek-American who took an interest in political problems of his country of origin, but also as a member of the American civic society, trying to bring Britain and the US closer, in political problems which involved the eastern Mediterranean at a time when there was the possibility that the Soviets might take advantage of the differences of the two major western powers and infiltrate the region. He tried to act in defence of an emerging international western (or, in 1950s parlance, 'atlantic') community. Although confined by the context of one of the competing 'worlds' of the Cold War, the transnational character of his intervention cannot be overlooked.

Dealing with Anglo-American Relations and the Future of the Homeland, mid-1940s

As the Second World War was coming to a close, the future of pivotal strategic positions in the eastern Mediterranean, such as Greece, became a contested political problem. Starting in October 1943, civil war had erupted in occupied Greece between the pro-western and the communist-led resistance organizations, with the Security Battalions of the collaborator government fighting their own cause (Fleischer 1995; Close 1993; Kalyvas 2000). At that moment, Greece's post-war fate seemed to hang in the balance: Greece was primarily an area of British, rather than US interests, and London aimed to secure the return of the (unpopular) King George II (Papastratis 1984). Although the country was liberated from German rule in October 1944, new clashes occurred in December between the forces of the communist-led National Liberation Front (EAM) on one side, and the army of the Greek government and the small British expeditionary force on the other; these ended with the defeat of the communists in early 1945 (Iatrides 1972). The suppression of the communist rebellion, however, was strongly denounced in the US, where the press (and largely the government) criticized British methods. It is indicative that Soviet reactions to British policy were far more moderate than American reactions: Stalin had already agreed with the British Prime Minister, Winston Churchill, that Greece was going to be an area of prime British interest; and in itself this act was a kind of division of spheres of influence with which Franklin D. Roosevelt strongly disagreed. By 1945, the US and Britain were not in full agreement over the future of the country, whereas the rapid Soviet advance in eastern Europe had turned Greece into a frontline state between the western-controlled Mediterranean coastline and the Soviet-controlled eastern European hinterland. The emerging post-war order, Greece's slippery slide to a new phase of civil war and the possibility of further Anglo-American disagreements formed the background of Skouras' intervention.

Skouras made his first appearance onto this scene in February 1944, after the eruption of the first phase of Greek civil war. Coming highly recommended with letters of introduction,[2] he arrived in London and was received by no less a person than Anthony Eden, the British Foreign Secretary. Such a reception was to be expected: the film magnate had behind him a long list of services to the allied cause (mainly through the film industry), but for the Foreign Office (FO) there was also the home US politics angle. AS an FO official noted:

The Greeks in the US, form a large and fairly influential body and have been very critical of our policy of support for the King of Greece. Since Mr. Skouras must have considerable authority amongst them, I think it would be valuable if the S[ecretary] of S[tate] could see him.[3]

The meeting between Eden and Skouras took place on 29 February 1944. Skouras suggested to Eden to entrust the task of uniting the Greeks to 'a Greek with no political views or ambitions but who understood all the ramifications of the Greek situation', and promptly put forward his younger brother George, 'an influential but non-political Greek', who could be sent to the country with some British (and American) officers to effect reconciliation.[4]

Skouras' suggestion was mooted in several quarters: Foreign Office representatives discussed it with John Gilbert Winant, the US Ambassador in Britain, while it seems to have also been discussed with Colonel William Donovan, the wartime Head of the Office of Strategic Studies (OSS, a precursor of the CIA); and a telegram was sent to Reginald Leeper, the British Ambassador to the Greek government-in-exile. However, British officials were skeptical of the proposal: 'I do not see how anything could possibly come of this proposal',[5] minuted an FO official; the telegram to Leeper suggested that George Skouras 'could obviously not be let loose in Greece to do what he likes'.[6] Although there was some further correspondence,[7] the FO was apparently not ready to accommodate amateurs with strong views on Greek politics. Friends in high places notwithstanding, Spiro's attempt to propel his brother into Greek politics was a failure.

His next move was both more carefully prepared and far reaching. It all started with the obvious: a visit to Greece, officially for fact-finding on the United Nations Relief and Rehabilitation Administration (UNRRA) relief. In November 1944 the Earl of Halifax, the British Ambassador in the US, formally expressed the hope that Britain would authorize Skouras' visit to Greece, stressing his political value and connections in the US:

[Skouras is] powerful, not only in the Greek community in this country, but also outside it. [...] He is a typical poor boy grown rich, a shrewd, jovial, cynical bon viveur who likes to throw his weight about in New York and Hollywood society and is cultivated by Democrats as a 'deliverer' of the Greek vote.[8]

The initiative, however, was delayed by the fighting in Athens in December 1944 and January 1945. Skouras returned in March 1945. His opening move was a letter to Anthony

Eden, where he praised him for the role the latter had played in relation to Greece – the connotation being clear, that he aimed to voice no criticism for Britain's crushing of the Greek communists in the previous December. This was a great relief for the British, whose actions in Athens had been severely criticized in the US. Eden and Skouras agreed to meet, but the funeral of Franklin D. Roosevelt (which Eden attended) made this impossible.[9]

By now the FO was fully aware of Skouras' access to power in the US. The correspondence describes Skouras as 'a Greek-American of considerable importance in the United States of America. He is in fact the most influential Greek-American and has recently given full support to our policy in Greece'.[10] In a telegram to Athens, Skouras was described as 'an extremely influential American. When he gets back he will certainly go straight to the President and his view of conditions in Greece will have a marked effect upon the attitude of the United States Administration'.[11] Skouras had asked for Colonel C.M. Woodhouse to accompany him during his visit to Greece and the Foreign Office concurred gladly, as this would fend off the 'danger of itinerant Americans falling under bad influences and with anyone as influential as Mr Skouras this would be a pity'.[12] Woodhouse was promptly dispatched to Greece.

Skouras' trip to Greece took place between 29 April and 27 May 1945 (he also toured Egypt and Palestine). In Athens, he gave a conference for the Greek press, in the *Grande Bretagne* Hotel, on the work of the GWRA (*Eleftheria*, Athens, 9 May 1945). In conversations with Woodhouse, he mentioned that he had met, privately, the leaders of the Greek Communists and

> used the occasion [...] to dress them down. He told them that their behaviour in December had put back democracy in Greece by 25 years, and that they were idiots if they thought they could run their country without British friendship.[13]

However, the main political axis of Skouras' efforts was Anglo-American cooperation in Greece. As Woodhouse reports,

> [Skouras] deplore[s] the bitterness created between Great Britain and the U.S.A. over Greece. This does not mean that he sees everything from our point of view [...] Mr. Skouras believes, however, that the role of the U.S.A., where it disagrees with us, should be not to criticise after the event, but to work out an agreed policy in advance.[14]

In Skouras' thinking, Greek problems would be solved by more relief supplies (to help restore the economy) and by a sharing of responsibility for Greece between the US and Britain. He suggested that he hoped to use his influence to pass on to the 'proper quarters' (meaning both Truman and Churchill, whom he was hoping to meet) the view that 'Greece's future lies in Anglo-American understanding'.[15] Skouras further suggested that US troops be sent to Greece to equal the British forces in number, and a joint Headquarters be formed, accompanied by 'a parallel integration in the diplomatic sphere'; he was certain such proposals would be accepted by both President Truman and General Marshall.[16] Woodhouse's reaction to all this is perhaps indicative of the puzzlement experienced by a relative layman, faced with the potential of celebrity involvement in foreign policy formation:

It is still impossible to be sure whether Mr. Skouras is fooling himself; or fooling me; or simply stating the facts. If the last be the case (which is perhaps worth assuming as an experiment) he is a man of immense and unorthodox power. Much of his talk sounds like Hollywood self-advertisement; as for instance when he took me aside to whisper 'They wanted to give Stettinius the push, but I told them not to'. It is difficult to take this sort of thing seriously; but it would probably be unwise to dismiss Mr. Skouras as a mere buffoon. He certainly gives the impression of being powerful as well as energetic: and it may be that *'potest quia posse videtur'*. Equally certainly he is a very good friend and champion of England. My impression from a month's close acquaintance with him is that it would be a pity not to make use of this combination.[17]

The postscript to Skouras' proposals was written in mid-1945. On 22 June, Skouras was reported to have telegraphed Woodhouse that, having 'convinced the US authorities', he was 'confident that, if [the British] now ask the Americans to share responsibility in Greece on a 50/50 basis, they will agree to do so'.[18] The British reaction was, again, one of mistrust: on 23 June 1945, a Foreign Office official expressed discomfort with the activity of this unusual celebrity channel.[19]

While Woodhouse was prepared to give Skouras and his schemes at least the benefit of the doubt, the Foreign Office was much more wary. While professing readiness to accept US help in Greece, the minutes discussing Skouras' proposals more or less condemn an Anglo-American power sharing, though they now claimed that the US would be reluctant to accept it.

During his initial approaches, Skouras was a relative unknown to the diplomatic establishment: when he was introduced to Eden by film mogul Darryl Zanuck, the Foreign Office officials did not quite know Skouras in his business capacity; he was only known as President of the Greek War Relief Association; evidently, they did not even know Zanuck.[20] On this occasion, it appears that the recommendations that accompanied Skouras, the political clout he claimed to have, and his well-known pro-Britishness, were not enough for the British diplomatic establishment to accept his unsolicited proposals. In fact, it could be argued that the British government declined his advances in 1944–45, partly because traditional British diplomacy was not 'in synchronisation' with this particular brand of celebrity activism. It is also highly debatable whether he had really talked the US administration into sending troops in Greece in 1945. Undaunted, Skouras was to return to the scene, in the mid-1950s, with the crisis over Cyprus.

Mediating in the Cyprus Conflict, mid-1950s

In 1954, agitation in Cyprus for *Enosis* (i.e. union with Greece) was mounting. Greece was planning to appeal to the UN asking for the application of the principle of self-determination in Cyprus, while the British were determined to resist any attempt to have the issue discussed in the international organization, on the grounds that it involved their internal jurisdiction. In July 1954, the British offered a very restricted Constitution to Cyprus, accompanied by the remark of the Minister of State for the Colonies, Henry Hopkinson, that Cyprus belonged to those strategically placed colonies that would 'never' become independent. This caused an outcry in the Greek world, and Athens duly submitted its appeal to the UN in August (Holland 1998: 33–41). The US found itself in an embarrassing position. When asked by London to state their opposition to *Enosis*, the Americans refused to indicate that western interests would only be served by the continuation of British sovereignty (Stefanidis 1999: 184–6; Nicolet 2001: 44–7). At the same time the Americans were against a UN appeal, which could offer opportunities for Soviet involvement in an infra-western dispute. The US Secretary of State, John Foster Dulles, strongly warned the Greeks, early in 1954 and again in July, that the US would not back them in such a debate (Xydis 1966; Stefanidis 1999: 189).

Things deteriorated sharply in the following two years. In December 1954 the Greek appeal to the UN was defeated, and in April 1955 the Greek Cypriot armed revolt against the British started. That summer, Britain called a Tripartite Conference in which Greece and Turkey also participated; this conference collapsed when riots took place in Istanbul against the Greek minority and the Oecumenical Patriarchate, while Greek officers serving in the NATO Headquarters at Izmir were also attacked. As the armed confrontation between the British and the Greek Cypriots intensified and Greek–Turkish relations deteriorated, the British also tried to negotiate with the Greek Cypriot leader, Archbishop Makarios. However, the discussions led nowhere and the British deported Makarios to the Seychelles in March 1956. This, in turn, led to a further intensification of fighting within Cyprus, to a severe crisis in Anglo–Greek relations, to the rise of anti-Americanism in Greece and to popular demands for Athens' withdrawal from NATO. By the summer of 1956, fears were expressed of a Greek–Turkish war, which would destroy NATO cohesion in the region (Holland 1998: 55–119; Xydis 1967: 3–32; Hatzivassiliou 1997: 23–70; Stefanidis 2007: 169–215). Once more, therefore, in 1954–56 an infra-western problem was surfacing, one indeed involving Greek interests, but also one that could weaken the western alliance and offer opportunities to the Soviets. Again, Skouras tried to mediate, to help bring about a 'western' solution and prevent a confrontation between two NATO members as well as a disagreement between Britain and the US.

In May 1954, as the Greeks were becoming convinced that they should appeal to the UN over Cyprus, Skouras came forward once again. This time, he could count on a stronger political base in the US, namely a politically active Greek-American community. As the US Ambassador to Athens, Cavendish Cannon, had told his British counterpart, Sir Charles Peake, the US government was reluctant to support British policy, among others 'because of powerful Greek Zionism [sic] in Washington'.[21] In September 1954, Henry Cabot Lodge, the US Permanent Representative at the UN, drew the attention of his British colleague to the position of the Greek-Americans, although the Foreign Office considered that the electoral strength of the Greek-American community (dispersed in the country) was being exaggerated.[22] Skouras was an incontestable leader of this community, but also an important and well-connected US businessman in his own right. A Foreign Office minute stressed that 20th Century Fox was 'the biggest interest in the American film world', while Skouras was known for his support of Dwight D. Eisenhower's presidential campaign of 1952. The same British official also seemed to have an exaggerated picture of Skouras' political role in the past, suggesting that he had influenced the decision-making process, which had led to the 1947 Truman Doctrine.[23] Thus the British were not prepared to rebuff him – at least not directly.

On 31 May 1954, Skouras saw the British Minister of State for Foreign Affairs, Lord Reading; it was a general discussion, with the Greek-American businessman indicating his desire to assist in toning down the dispute.[24] In August 1954, the stakes had been raised considerably for a meeting with Prime Minister Winston Churchill to become possible, with the intercession of his old acquaintance, C.M. Woodhouse. On 21 August, Skouras met Churchill in London and suggested that the British indicate to Athens their readiness to discuss Cyprus after a period of ten years, without any commitment for eventual Enosis; receiving such a British assurance, the Greeks would refrain from pressing on with their UN appeal. Skouras then returned to the US and informed the State Department of his contacts. However, Churchill was not receptive to his ideas, and another attempt by Skouras to see Lord Reading in mid-September was politely refused.[25] As the Foreign Office stressed to its Washington Embassy, Whitehall was determined to give no indication for a future negotiation on Cyprus: this would give the Greeks an additional motive to continue their campaign of 'agitation' in the hope of extracting more concessions.[26]

Skouras' August 1954 intervention was fully in line with the US preference to avoid an embarrassing public quarrel between NATO members. However, as was usually the case in the Cyprus question, such wider political considerations tended to become confused when it came down to the individual priorities of the parties concerned. The British were determined to avoid a promise to discuss the issue even in the future. Moreover, the Churchill government had just made the immense sacrifice of agreeing to withdraw from the Suez Base: with Conservative backbenchers (the 'Suez rebels') accusing the government of 'selling out' the Empire, Whitehall could not appear 'soft' on Cyprus, a Crown Colony (Holland 1998: 36–40).

After the outbreak of the armed revolt in Cyprus, and following the calling of the 1955 Tripartite London Conference, Skouras appeared again on the scene. In early August 1955, once more through Woodhouse, he asked to see Eden, who now was Prime Minister, but the British replied that he was not available.[27] In fact, a senior FO official, William Young, reflected the Department's attitude when he minuted that 'there is no evidence that his advice about Cyprus is taken very seriously by the Government of either country' [i.e. Greece or the US]. Skouras finally saw Lord Reading, and expressed his concern at the deterioration of Anglo-Greek relations.[28] However, at that moment the British were set on a specific policy for the Tripartite Conference, which could not be influenced by Skouras' initiative. Failing once more to be received by Eden, Skouras met Lord Reading again in late September, after the collapse of the Tripartite Conference; he professed to have seen the Greek leaders, whom he had urged to be moderate; he hoped that the Turks would accept the recent British proposals (tabled at the Tripartite Conference), thus forcing Athens to follow the same course.[29] His suggestion was obviously unrealistic: there was no prospect of a Greek acceptance of the British proposals after the Istanbul riots.

Things continued to deteriorate. After Makarios' deportation to the Seychelles in March 1956, parts of the Greek public demanded Greece's withdrawal from NATO. In summer 1956, the Suez crisis erupted, following Gamal Abdel Nasser's nationalization of the Canal. In June 1956, the British put a proposal of their own to the Turks, who reacted adversely (Hatzivassiliou 1997: 70–3). London's priority now was to keep up with Turkey, a valuable Middle Eastern ally, during a period of Middle Eastern turmoil. Once more tension was running high in the region, and again Skouras tried to step in.[30]

In June 1956, Skouras communicated with the British, indicating that he had the encouragement of President Eisenhower to put forward his suggestions. Indeed, the US embassy in London recommended Skouras' effort to the British. Although the Foreign Office, rather impatiently, described him as a 'peripatetic gentleman of some influence in America',[31] his overtures could not be ignored. On 20 June, he was received by the British Foreign Secretary, Selwyn Lloyd. Skouras suggested that Greece and Turkey cease all activity regarding Cyprus, including propaganda; after violence had ended, the British should bring Makarios back from exile and negotiate a settlement with him. Selwyn Lloyd then minuted to Eden that Skouras was a wealthy man, and could damage Britain's image on the level of publicity; thus the British government should allow him to come forward; his plan was 'too simple to work', and the likely Turkish reaction would anyway 'educate him'.[32] Skouras then met Eden, and on 26 June, before departing for Athens, again saw Selwyn Lloyd.[33]

Meanwhile, the Greek government was trying, unsuccessfully, to convince the Americans to mediate.[34] From Athens' point of view, the intervention of the film magnate with the impressive links to the White House was welcome. Early in July 1956, Prime Minister Constantinos Karamanlis met Skouras and indicated his government's suggestion for an eventual settlement: NATO should fix a date for the application of self-determination in Cyprus in the future; Makarios should be released from exile; for the interim period, a liberal Constitution should be introduced in Cyprus. In case of eventual *Enosis*, NATO would determine limitations of Greek troops in Cyprus; one or two free ports would be established for trade between Cyprus and Turkey to move without passing through Greek customs; the Turkish Cypriots could acquire double nationality (Greek and Turkish), would not serve in the Greek army, and their position would be guaranteed by the UN.[35] Similar ideas were communicated by the Greek government to London through the Labour MP, Philip Noel Baker and the Italian Foreign Minister, Gaetano Martino.[36] Skouras communicated this proposal to the British.

Again, no result came out of this activity. Skouras' effort was strongly resented by the FO (officials minuted that he was 'naïve' and that he had 'swallowed the Greek line pretty thoroughly'), and when he again met Selwyn Loyd on 24 July, the Foreign Secretary refused to comment on Karamanlis' proposals.[37] However, Skouras' Turkish experience in early August was traumatic. President Çelâl Bayar and Prime Minister Adnan Menderes refused to see him; he was received by the President of the Grand National Assembly, Refik Koraltan, with no success; more ominous was the fact the British Ambassador to Ankara, Sir James Bowker, also refused to meet him, as the British were alarmed that the Turks might think that he had their acquiescence to mediate.[38] This was an indication of the degree to which British policy in Cyprus was now, after the eruption of the crisis in Suez, becoming a hostage to Turkey. This marked the end of Skouras' attempt. Early in 1957 he made a last effort to meet the new British Prime Minister, Harold Macmillan, who, however, refused to receive him; indeed, this time Selwyn Lloyd, who continued to be Foreign Secretary, himself advised the Prime Minister against meeting him.[39]

In fact, Skouras' chances of success were slim from the start. His mission was entangled in the web of misunderstanding and bitterness that had engulfed Anglo–Greek relations. Since Makarios' deportation in March 1956, the British Embassy in Athens had insisted that the Karamanlis government was 'hostage to the extremists', and could not be trusted to act 'responsibly' in foreign affairs; according to Ambassador Peake, only the complete isolation of Athens would bring about a 'moderate' Greek position. This was a mistaken assumption, but Athens' efforts to open alternative channels of communication were simply ignored by Whitehall, which had anyway turned its attention to the Middle Eastern crisis and (with respect to Cyprus) to retaining Turkish friendship. Karamanlis' paper to Skouras was dismissed by the British since, as a non-paper, it was 'officially non existent'.[40] The very unofficial status of Skouras (or, for that matter, Noel-Baker) allowed the British to kill their suggestions as mediators. Peake's comment of the Noel Baker mediation could easily stand for Skouras' effort as well:

> I have said that at the present juncture we should not count on the Greeks in any way, unless, of course, they make an approach to us through the diplomatic channel which would put a different complexion on the question [...] Thus, it would be fatal if at this juncture any enthusiastic amateur (Noel Baker or else) were allowed to represent himself as a mediator [...] encouraging the Greeks to raise their sights.[41]

In other words, setting the Skouras mission aside was part of a general British mental attitude at that time. By late August the Americans decided that they needed to step onto the Cyprus scene; this led to the Julius Holmes mission of autumn. Despite Greek jubilation at securing, at last, a formal US mediation, this also led nowhere, exactly because of the Suez crisis. At a moment when a crisis of confidence occurred between themselves and the British, the Americans were hardly in a position to break the vicious circle of mistrust between their three allies. The Holmes mission was dismissed by London (Nicolet 2001: 85–94; Hatzivassiliou 1997: 77–84). 1956 was not the best time for mediators on Cyprus, official or otherwise: nerves were stretched to the extreme in the Eastern Mediterranean, and Skouras had little chance of success.

Conclusions

At a time when the rich and famous went into politics in the conventional way, Spiro Skouras chose his transnational identity to make his mark in international relations, focusing on a humanitarian issue and the need to uphold Anglo-American cooperation in the 1940s, and on the need to safeguard western unity in the 1950s. Despite his partial success on the humanitarian level, in either of his political initiatives he failed to make a lasting impact. However, there was more in his failure than Britain's mistrust of an 'amateur', who apparently was susceptible both to American anti-colonialism and Greek influence. In 1945, it was by no means certain that Skouras' suggestion of moving US troops to Greece would be met with enthusiasm by the US administration or, indeed, the US Congress; and in the mid-1950s the Eisenhower administration, despite giving him a vague blessing, did not appear to expect much from his endeavours.

The Skouras cases raise a series of questions involving a *political* initiative by a celebrity: regardless of the latter's commitment to a cause, how far does he/she accurately understand the aims of the actors that he/she wants to bring closer? How far can a celebrity initiative be 'integrated' in a consistent foreign policy? How could a celebrity counter the inevitable mistrust of the professionals or the inflamed public opinions, a combination that often forms the fatal nexus of an international dispute? Is there a necessary mix of good will and knowledge of particular circumstances that might guarantee success?

In trying to answer these questions, the theoretical propositions of recent scholarship can prove useful. Skouras' initiatives show that a precondition of the celebrity's success is the desirability of the celebrity's involvement by all concerned. For example, Skouras' proposals in 1944–45 for solving Greece's political problems were politely tolerated by Britain, which knew they could not be enforced; the fact that by then Britain was the junior partner in the emerging Atlantic relationship made polite toleration possible. In Skouras' 1956 attempt, it was clear that the Greeks were anxious for it, the Americans did not mind, but the British and the Turks did; and Greece did not possess the international 'clout' to support his initiative. Skouras' failures are also indicative because he lacked another of the preconditions of the success of later forms of celebrity activism, namely, an external 'enabling factor', such as UN concurrence or the support of an important NGO. A lone rider (albeit rich and influential in his home political milieu) could not achieve results. Skouras' relative success as a head of a humanitarian organization (an early form of an NGO) and his failures as an individual mediating in political disputes confirm that an organizational framework is crucial in maximizing the impact of a celebrity; and thus 'celebrities are not very influential, on their own, in affecting policy outcomes' (Huliaras and Tzifakis 2010: 254).

The Skouras incidents suggest that even at this early stage celebrity diplomacy was more likely to be successful in humanitarian crises. When it came to the settlement of highly political issues, Skouras was evidently helped by his aura of an enormously successful US media magnate with good links to US politics. This opened for him the doors of the political offices, but could by no means guarantee the success of his efforts: his 'unorthodox power' as a celebrity had narrow limits. He was bound to fail, facing sensitive political inter-state balances and the 'professionalism', snub and impatience of diplomatic services and political establishments, who, especially at that time, were not prepared to appreciate similar ventures. At least within the Anglo-Saxon establishment of the 1940s and the 1950s, few were ready to accept the blurring of the line delimiting international affairs as the exclusive domain of government.

References

Alleyne, M. D. (2005), 'The United Nations' Celebrity Diplomacy', *SAIS Review*, XXV:1, pp. 175–185.

Close, D. H. (ed.) (1993), *The Greek Civil War, 1943–1950: Studies of Polarization*, London and New York: Routledge.

Cooper, A. F. (2008), *Celebrity Diplomacy*, Boulder and London: Paradigm Publishers.

Curti, C. (1967), *Skouras, King of Fox Studios*, Los Angeles, CA: Holloway House Publishing Company.

Fleischer, H. (1995), *Στέμμα και Σβάστικα*/The Crown and the Swastica, vol. 2, Athens: Papazisis.

Hatzivassiliou, E. (1997), *Britain and the International Status of Cyprus, 1955–59*, Minneapolis: Minnesota Mediterranean and East European Monographs.

Hionidou, V. (2006), *Famine and Death in Occupied Greece, 1941–1944*, Cambridge: Cambridge University Press.

Holland, R. (1998), *Britain and the Revolt in Cyprus, 1954–1959*, Oxford: Clarendon Press.

Huliaras, A. and Tzifakis, N. (2010), 'Celebrity Activism in International Relations: In Search of a Framework for Analysis', *Global Society*, 24:2, pp. 253–272.

Iatrides, J. O. (1972), *Revolt in Athens: the Greek Communist 'second round'*, Princeton: Princeton University Press.

Kalyvas, S. N. (2000), 'Red Terror: Leftist Violence during the Occupation', in M. Mazower (ed.) *After the War was Over: Reconstructing the Family, Nation, and State in Greece, 1943–1960*, Princeton: Princeton University Press, pp. 142–183.

Kazamias, G. (1991), 'Allied Policy towards Occupied Greece: The 1941–44 Famine', Ph.D. thesis, UK: University of Bradford.

Kyrou, A. K. (2008), 'The Greek-American Community and the Famine in Axis-occupied Greece', in R. Clogg (ed.), *Bearing Gifts to Greeks, Humanitarian Aid to Greece in the 1940s*, London and New York: Palgrave Macmillan, pp. 58–84.

Nicolet, C. (2001), *United States Policy Towards Cyprus, 1954–1974: Removing the Greek-Turkish Bone of Contention*, Manheim and Möhnesee: Bibliopolis,

Papastratis, P. (1984), *British Foreign Policy towards Greece during the Second World War*, Cambridge: Cambridge University Press.

Saloutos, T. (1964), *The Greeks in the United States*, Cambridge, Mass.: Harvard University Press.

Stefanidis, I. D. (1999), *Isle of Discord: Nationalism, Imperialism and the Making of the Cyprus Problem*, London: Hurst.

—— (2007), *Stirring the Greek Nation: Political Culture, Irredentism and Anti-Americanism in Post-War Greece, 1945–1967*, Aldershot: Ashgate,

Street, J. (2004), 'Celebrity Politicians: Popular Culture and Political Representation', *The British Journal of Politics and International Relations*, 6:4, pp. 435–452.

Turner, G. (2004), *Understanding Celebrity*, London: Sage.

Vlachos, J. P. (ed.), *From Lamb, to Lion, to Goat, and back, Memoirs of Peter Voudoures* (n.p., n.d), in http://www.annunciation.org/photoarchive/boudoures/index.html, accessed 20 March 2010.

West, D. M. and Orman, J. (2002), *Celebrity Politics*, New Jersey: Prentice Hall.

Xydis, S. G. (1966), 'Toward "Toil and Moil" in Cyprus', *The Middle East Journal*, 20:1, pp. 1–19.

_____ (1967), *Cyprus: Conflict and Conciliation, 1954–1958*, Columbus, Ohio: Ohio State University Press.

Notes

1. On Skouras see Curti (1967); Cf., 'Hands across the sea', *Time*, 5 June 1944; also Gino Gullace, 'Πώς εξεθρονίσθη ο Σπύρος Σκούρας'/How Spiro Skouras was dethroned, *Eleftheria* (Athens), 18 July 1962.
2. See London, The National Archives (TNA), FO 371/43758/4435. These included a telegram from the film mogul Darryl Zanuck (9 February 1944), and support from the British Ministry of Information, the North American Department and the Southern Department of the FO.
3. FO 371/43758/4435, FO minute (Laskey), 14 February 1944.
4. FO 371/43758/4435, Note, 29 February 1944. The original suggestion mentioned only British officers; however, when elaborated to the FO, the plan had developed to include 'a high grade British and American officer'. FO 371/43758/4435, FO minute (Howard), 16 March 1944.
5. FO 371/43758/4435, FO minute (Howard), 16 March 1944.
6. FO 371/43758/4435, FO to Leeper, 20 March 1944.
7. We only have indications of further discussions, as four folios of the file FO 371/43758 (R6024, R7478, R7943 and R 18591), have been retained by the Foreign Office. George Skouras did reach London during 1944 and 'was keen at that time to be allowed to go to Greece, where he thought he could settle all the difficulties in a big way. He was a burden to all of us and we were thankful when he returned to the States'. FO 371/48361/1012, FO minute (Howard), 12 January 1945.
8. See FO 371/41191/1599, Washington to FO, 24 November 1944.
9. See FO 371/48361/6200. Skouras' letter (dated 7 March 1945), was answered on 15 April 1945. It is indicative of the tone of the letter that the title given to Folio 6200 is 'Mr Spiros P. Skouras' personal tribute to Mr Eden'.
10. FO 371/48361/6200, FO to Caserta, 26 April 1945.
11. FO 371/48361/6200, FO to Athens, 26 April 1945. While planning the trip Skouras had successfully enlisted the support of the British Embassy in Washington, the US State Department, and UNRRA – indeed he travelled as UNRRA voluntary society personnel, essentially depriving the British from any grounds for objecting to the visit.
12. FO 371/48361/6200, FO to Athens, 26 April 1945.
13. FO 371/48361/9353, Woodhouse to H.M. Ambassador to Greece, 'Final Report on Mr Skouras' visit to Greece, May 1945, 30th May 1945'.
14. FO 371/48361/9686, 'Report on Visit to Crete and Middle East'.
15. FO 371/48361/9686, 'Report on Visit to Crete and Middle East'. Woodhouse commented: 'This [reference to proper quarters] presumably referred to President Truman, who is his intimate friend' and 'If he [Skouras] does see Mr Churchill, the P.M.'s impression may well be of something unique – an American who sympathises with both EAM and the British'.

16. FO 371/48361/9353, 'Final Report'.
17. FO 371/48361/9353, 'Final Report'. The latin phrase translates as 'it is possible if it looks possible' or, more loosely, 'he can do it if he thinks it is possible'.
18. FO 371/48361/9353, FO minute (Laskey).
19. FO 371/48361/9353, FO minute, (sign. Illeg.), 23 June 1945.
20. See eg. FO 371/43758/4435, FO minute (Laskey), 14 February 1944: 'I do not know much about M. Skouras, but the Greek War Relief Association, of which he is President, has made and is making very generous contributions in connection with relief to Greece and the care of Greek refugees in the M.E.'. On Skouras' referee see Sir Orme Sargent's note: 'Who is W [sic]. Zanuck?' in FO 371/43758/4435, minutes.
21. FO 371/112843/11, Peake to FO, 4 February 1954.
22. FO 371/112863/602, Dixon to FO, 20 September 1954, and FO minute, 27 September 1954.
23. FO 371/112847/142, FO minute (Glutton), 28 May 1954. It is not clear whether Skouras had played such a role.
24. FO 371/112847/143, FO minute (Duff), 1 June 1954.
25. London, TNA, FO 800/764, Scott to FO, 27 August 1954. See also FO 371/112854/359 and 363, Washington Embassy to FO, 27 August 1954; and No.10 to Stark (FO), 21 August 1954; FO 371/112862/576, Brief, 15 September 1954. For the Churchill-Skouras meeting see also Stefanidis (1999: 75); and the correspondence in London, TNA, PREM11/1869, including two letters by Skouras to Churchill, one undated, the other of 31 August.
26. FO 800/764, FO to Washington Embassy, 30 August 1954. The British also rebuffed another attempt by the American journalist Fleur Cowles to mediate in the dispute: see Stefanidis (1999: 76).
27. See Woodhouse's correspondence with No. 10 at PREM11/1869.
28. FO 371/117647/791, FO minute (Graham), 4 August 1955, and FO minute (Young), 8 August 1956; FO 371/117649/819, FO minute (Lord Reading), 12 August 1955.
29. FO 371/117661/1147, FO minute (Lord Reading), 24 September 1955.
30. Eden and Skouras had corresponded in December 1955, when the British Prime Minister congratulated him for his work on charity: see PREM11/1869, Eden to Skouras, 2 December 1955, and Skouras to Eden, 9 December 1955.
31. PREM11/1869, de Zulueta (No. 10) to Eden, 14 June 1956; FO 371/123899/1254, FO to Ankara, 23 June 1956.
32. FO 371/123903/1422, Record (Selwyn Lloyd-Skouras), 20 June 1956; FO 800/731, Selwyn Lloyd to Eden, 22 June 1956.
33. FO 371/123903/1421, FO to Athens Embassy, 27 June 1956, and FO minute (Thomson), 29 June 1956.
34. FO 371/123898/1210, Peake to FO, 14 June 1956.
35. FO 371/123906/1504, Lambert (Athens) to FO, 5 July 1956; FO 371/123911/1671, FO to Athens, 26 July 1956.
36. FO 371/123902/1381, Makins to FO, 25 June 1956.
37. FO 371/123909/1580, Young to Lambert, 20 July 1956; FO 371/123911/1670, FO minute (Thomson), 23 July; FO 371/123911/1671, FO minute (Laskey), 25 July.
38. FO 371/123912/1687, Bower to FO 26 July 1956, and FO minute (Thomson), 27 July 1956; FO 371/123917/1814, Bowker to Ward, 7 August 1956.
39. PREM11/1869, de Zulueta (no. 10) to Macmillan, 15 February 1957, and de Zulueta to Graham (FO), 18 February 1957.
40. FO 371/123915/1786, Lambert to FO, 8 August 1956.
41. FO 371/123903/1426, Peake to Ward, 6 June 1956.

Part III

Celebrity Activism, Global Humanitarianism and the Global South

Chapter 8

Consuming Ethics: Conflict Diamonds, the Entertainment Industry and Celebrity Activism

Sue Tait

Introduction: The Burden of the Witness and Globally Oriented Citizenship

Conflict diamonds, or blood diamonds, are diamonds that fund conflict, usually in West Africa. Diamonds have, of course, been used to fund colonial endeavours and apartheid, but the adjectives 'conflict' and 'blood' have become attached to diamonds in order to describe conflicts in which black people brutalize one another, rather than the brutalizing of black people by white people. Civil wars in Angola, Liberia, Sierra Leone and the Democratic Republic of Congo have largely been ignored by the western media (Carruthers 2004). However, the issue of conflict diamonds has received attention from the entertainment industry in the US, including Kanye West's Grammy-winning 'Diamonds from Sierra Leone', released in 2005, the film Blood Diamond (Zwick 2006), which was nominated for five Academy Awards, and the documentary Bling: A Planet Rock (Cepeda 2007). Each of these texts focuses on conflict diamonds in relation to Sierra Leone.

The politicizing of the issue of conflict diamonds by Hollywood and the US hip hop community has served to memorialize the atrocities perpetrated during Sierra Leone's civil war. Within the narratives of fiction and documentary films, songs, public relations and marketing campaigns, consumers have been interpolated as agents in relation to the issue of conflict diamonds at the point of purchase. Within this context, consumer capitalism becomes the means through which to render collective justice: wearing diamonds becomes an ethical issue, but only insofar as those diamonds can be certified 'conflict free'. As I elucidate, this elides broader issues regarding the predication of consumer capitalism on a globalized system of inequity. The issue becomes *blood diamonds*, bloodied by amputated hands, arms, ears, lips, legs and noses, rather than the embodied subjects who bear the consequences of these atrocities, and the nations they are rebuilding.

Producing Witnessing Publics

Implicit within any response to atrocity is the paradox that, through representation, we can only ever memorialize suffering that is already consigned to history. However, this commemoration is the first step in the production of witnessing publics. Commemoration provides (ostensible) justification for the images and narratives that can never convey the experience of trauma, which must objectify subjective experience and in that process translate it into a commodity. Central to the reproduction of global capitalism are the linked processes of competition and fashion. This extends to humanitarian issues on the global stage, which must compete for attention within a mediated environment driven by ratings and funded by advertising. The role of celebrity activists is to garner this attention: celebrities are able to draw public attention towards humanitarian issues through public fascination with celebrity (Huliaras and Tzifakis 2008: 15). This is not confined to the rise of 'soft' news: celebrity activism enables the mainstream press to cover what is normatively the purview of the entertainment press, and lends sobriety to celebrity coverage (Little 2008). The issue, however, is that once attention is drawn to a 'cause', publics must be interpellated in ways that transform a cause, which is subject to both fashion and commodification, into meaningful and constructive action. The formation of witnessing publics requires facilitating a sense of empowerment to act towards the prevention of atrocity, which requires being able to imagine how history can be prevented from reoccurring. It requires being able to imagine a collective response as a possibility, and as a possibility that will change the conditions that have produced suffering.

Cynthia Rentschler (2004), following Barbie Zelizer (1998, 2002) argues that witnessing 'means far more than just "watch" or "see"; it is also a form of bodily and political participation in what people see and document that is often masked by their perceived distance from events' (Rentschler 2004: 298). Rentschler summarizes arguments by Zelizer and Sontag that the presentation of atrocious events within the media may impede our ability to bear witness because 'without a politically mobilizing news media, witnesses are left to 'feel' with little or no direction for how to act' (Rentschler 2004: 300). This argument must be extended to texts produced by the entertainment industry, which commemorate suffering but fail to address publics in ways that enable them to imagine intervention in cycles of atrocity. I contend that the role of celebrity activists, who may have no special knowledge of a humanitarian issue, but who become ethically burdened by attaching that cause to their 'brand' (Littler 2008), should be to provide models for public action. Commemoration is not enough.

My first issue then, is the way the entertainment industry has rendered the issue of conflict diamonds through the production of specific texts which site the issue as a global public concern. My analysis of these texts is guided by the work of Ngwarsungu Chiwengo (2008), who highlights the way the suffering of some victims is made to matter over the suffering of others. Her comparative analysis of representations of the Rwanda genocide and the civil war in the Democratic Republic of Congo suggests that attention to the former has impacted on the virtual indifference of the West to the latter (see also Virgil Hawkins, this volume). In the media coverage of Congo, the role of the West in the conflict is elided, particularly the role of foreign interests in mineral resources, such as copper, zinc and diamonds. Chiwengo's paper addresses how the subjective experience of pain can be communicated in such a way that it enables the audience to empathize with the victim, recognize their humanity and equality, and the specificity of their suffering. This provides a set of criteria for assessing texts that memorialize the civil war in Sierra Leone.

Globally Oriented Citizenship

The second theoretical framework motivating my analysis is Bhikhu Parekh's (2003) discussion of globally oriented citizenship. Parekh argues that it is a fundamental ethical principle that all humans are of intrinsic and equal worth (2003: 5). Because of this, conditions that denigrate any individual's worth must compel our collective attention. Our responsibilities here are twofold. We must not act in ways that produce another's suffering, and we have a duty to alleviate the suffering of others insofar as our capabilities allow (2003: 6). Our duty to others consists of general duties to the species, and special duties to those with whom we have intimate ties, and Parekh applies this framework to the obligations of global citizenship. We must acknowledge a dual citizenship: we have a particular investment in our local and national political community; our home. We also have duties to the global community, and these are a product of our shared humanity, colonial legacies, economic interdependence and collective need for security in the face of environmental destruction, disease and munitions that are not constrained by national borders (2003: 8–11). Globalization has thus produced a '*moral* community', within which the West, with its disproportionate resources, has the responsibility to 'set new moral and political norms, and give rise to a new awareness of global obligations' (2003: 11). Parekh contends that within this emergent moral order, the group to which we have political allegiance is expanding, and that our obligation to this group must be discharged via politics rather than charity.

Parekh uses the term 'globally oriented citizenship' to render the specific nature of this identity. Unlike global citizenship and cosmopolitanism (Littler 2008), which presuppose primary allegiance to the species and no political 'home' consisting of special local attachments (Parekh 2003: 12), globally oriented citizenship is a dual citizenship. Parekh argues that there are three components to globally oriented citizenship: we must be vigilant in relation to the politics of our home state and ensure that it promotes the interests of humankind. This means we cannot be apathetic; political apathy serves no one. Second, globally oriented citizenship involves an active engagement with the affairs of other nations, and requires our response when rights are violated. Third, we have a responsibility to participate in creating a mutually beneficial and ethical world order, at the very least because no one is safe in a world where injustice and inequality breed violence (2003: 12–13).

Parekh's model of globally oriented citizenship, in conjunction with Chiwengo's criteria for assessing texts for their ability to bear witness as texts, and thus facilitate the formation of witnessing publics, provides a framework for assessing the nature of celebrity activism. It is this framework I bring to bear on the specific texts through which the entertainment industry has rendered the issue of conflict diamonds in Sierra Leone. Central to this assessment is the degree to which these sites of memorialization equip publics to understand the nature of the civil war, and the ways they interpellate viewers and listeners as witnessing publics through the way they frame the audience's obligation to the other.

Blood Diamond: The Movie

Activism regarding conflict diamonds did not begin with the entertainment industry. NGOs put the issue on the agenda of international politics in the 1990s. Global Witness, an international NGO founded in 1993, which seeks to 'break the links between the exploitation of natural resources, and conflict and corruption' (Global Witness 2009), lobbied international agencies, regarding the role of diamonds and oil, in funding Angola's civil war of 1975–2002. One of the outcomes of Global Witness' initiatives has been the Kimberley Process Certification Scheme. The Kimberley Process, a series of UN-backed negotiations between governments, NGOs and the diamond industry, initiated in 2000, culminated in a certification process, which specifies the origins of diamonds and requires jewellers to self-regulate in order to halt the trade in conflict stones (Gaber and Wynne Willson 2005: 102). The certification scheme was introduced in January 2003, and in the lead up to its introduction, it was NGOs, without celebrity participation, who staged public protests in the UK, garnering international media attention, which put pressure on the diamond industry to take the introduction of new codes of conduct and practice seriously (Gaber and Wynne Willson 2005: 103). The work of NGOs in raising public awareness of the issue of conflict diamonds was reflected by a survey conducted for ActionAid, a UK-based charity. The survey showed that knowledge of the issue among the British public had increased from 9 per cent in 2001 to 25 per cent at the start of 2003 (Gaber and Wynne Willson 2005: 106).

In a *New York Times* article, Marc Santora notes that prior to the release of *Blood Diamond*, conflict diamonds had become a 'fashionable concern among entertainment figures, with stars ranging from Leonardo DiCaprio to Kanye West to Raekwon from the hip hop collective Wu-Tang Clan speaking out about the need for consumer vigilance' (2006: 2.1). However, for many people, particularly in the US, it was the film *Blood Diamond*, released in December 2006, which put both the issue of conflict diamonds and Sierra Leone on the map. This extended to broadcast media: over the eleven years of Sierra Leone's civil war, news programmes on the major networks in the US – ABC, NBC and CBS – cumulatively mentioned the role of diamonds in funding the war an average of just over twice a year (Hollar 2007). Following the release of *Blood Diamond*, the same programmes mentioned this issue eleven times in one week (Hollar 2007).

Directed by Edward Zwick and starring Leonardo DiCaprio, Djimon Hounsou and Jennifer Connelly, *Blood Diamond* is set in 1999 during the Revolutionary United Front's (RUF) siege of Freetown, Sierra Leone's capital. The film provides scant detail with regard to the complexities of the civil war, which had beleaguered the nation since 1991, highlighting, instead, some of the most brutal (and narratively simple) aspects of the conflict. The film begins by establishing Solomon Vandy's (Hounsou) character as a loving family man, a fisherman who aspires for his son to become a doctor. The idyll of domestic life is shattered as RUF soldiers descend upon the village, blaring rap music, and soldiers, including children, massacre villagers. Vandy helps his family to flee, but is captured by the RUF and corralled with others doomed to have a hand amputated. Exposition from the RUF leader

162

explains for the audience that the amputation of the hand is a means to prevent the citizenry from voting. In a particularly graphic sequence, a villager's forearm is then chopped off with an axe. While this serves a crucial narrative function of foregrounding the atrocities perpetrated by the RUF, and rendering them as agents of evil, it simultaneously provides a reductive portrait of who practiced amputation within the war, and why this was so. Research conducted by Sierra Leone's Truth and Reconciliation Commission details that all armed groups within the conflict, including the Sierra Leone Army, practiced amputation as a strategy of terror, that amputation as a practice of war was not indigenous to Sierra Leone (it was probably introduced to Africa under King Leopold's regime in Congo), and was a tactic used to disrupt social organization, bond recruits to the rebels and perhaps a calculated attempt to gain international attention (Park 2007).

Vandy escapes amputation and is, instead, enslaved to work on the alluvial mines, where he finds and buries a valuable pink diamond. Freed by government troops, but imprisoned in a Freetown jail, Solomon and his diamond become known to Danny Archer, a Rhodesian (Zimbabwean) mercenary who had been caught attempting to smuggle diamonds into Liberia, which he had received from the RUF in exchange for arms. The men escape from Freetown to recover the diamond, on the proviso that Archer will help Vandy find his family. The RUF's abduction of children to conscript as soldiers is a central plot point via the capture of Vandy's son, while the role of child soldiers in the government's army is omitted (see chapter by Michael, Cynthia and Rachel Stohl, this volume). The men are joined for part of their quest by an American journalist, Maddy Bowen (Connelly), who helps the men in exchange for Archer's testimony revealing the role of a pre-eminent diamond corporation in the trafficking of conflict stones so that she can break the story of 'blood diamonds' and the complicity of western corporations and consumers.

It is through the character trajectories of Archer and Bowen that the responsibility of the westerner to the Other is played out, albeit through a frame of rescuing Africans from Africa, the assuaging of colonial guilt, the reinscription of primitivist discourse and the circumscription of the western audience's burden to 'ethical shopping'.

Through the course of the narrative, Archer and Bowen are redeemed of their complicity with systems of western oppression. Archer's complicity as a mercenary, and the racism that underpins this, is made comprehensible as we learn of the rape and murder of his mother, and decapitation of his father during the conflict to end white minority rule in Rhodesia. Archer's racism is rendered most explicitly following an incident where Solomon has jeopardized their lives. As Archer skins a baboon for bush meat, he reminisces about his childhood hunting:

Baboons, they were the hardest to catch, they're cunning creatures. Fast, strong, got good eyesight. We'd always find them by the smell of their shit. And that's how we learned to track your black terrorists in Angola. By the smell of your shit, it's not the same as a baboon's. But you know, after you skin it, the flesh of a baboon isn't that much different from a man's you know. I tell you, I can track anything.

As Archer cleans the blood from his knife, then points it in Solomon's face, he continues 'you risk my life like that again, and I'll peel your face back off your head. Do you understand?' Yet we are drawn to consider Archer's savagery as a product of his quest for survival within the violent continent, and a fight between the two men, during which Archer calls Vandy 'kaffa' (a racial slur synonymous with 'nigger') and pulls his gun on him, is resolved by Archer empathizing with the other man's love for his child, and thus his redemption begins. The men's moral equivalence plays out as Vandy also becomes a killer. He is sprayed with the blood of the RUF leader who kidnapped his son as he smashes him with a spade. In the course of the fighting during which the diamond is secured from the mercenaries Archer formerly collaborated with, Archer is shot. Vandy carries him to the top of the ridge where the plane will meet them – the white man literally, but temporarily, becoming the black man's burden. Archer demands to be left behind in order to hold back the men pursuing them, and facing certain death tells his companion that 'I'm exactly where I'm supposed to be'. Thus Archer's sacrifice enables the father and son to escape to London with the diamond, and the West becomes the site of salvation and reconciliation.

The film ends with a scene depicting the Kimberley Process hearings. Solomon Vandy is introduced to the delegates by the Chair:

> The natural resources of a country are the sovereign property of its people, they are not ours to steal, or exploit in the name of our comfort, our corporations or our consumerism [...] The Third World is not a world apart, and the witness you will hear today speaks on its behalf. Let us hear the voice of that world, let us learn from that voice and let us ignore it no more.

Vandy receives a standing ovation, but before he speaks, the film ends. Thus, while the resolution to the narrative is an exhortation to hear the Other, he is silenced. Further, the Chair imagines a singular voice of the Third World, and that voice, the one ostensibly permitted to speak, is a heroic voice, one that we may assume will speak of suffering and survival from a position that has been explicitly moralized throughout the film, rather than a voice speaking to the ambiguities of conflict. Aside from the profit imperative and desire to entertain audiences, Edward Zwick's motivation to tell this story was to render

> the responsibilities of a consumer society that has to reckon with the fact that the purchase of something here has implications somewhere else. By putting your credit card down, you're essentially endorsing the practices that are involved in getting a resource. This place and that place are, in fact, interconnected. (Foreign Policy 2006)

The agenda of the director then, suggests a commitment to fostering a sense of global citizenship. However, this is framed only in terms of consumption, and the complicity of the West is rendered only in terms of those who buy, and the corporations that traffic in, conflict stones. The film thus channels the issue at stake into 'ethical shopping', rather than the nations from which diamonds are extracted. Sierra Leone is left behind as a site of *political* obligation.

Bling: The Hip Hop Community and Conflict Diamonds

The release of *Blood Diamond* met with a multi million-dollar public relations campaign from the diamond industry to counter negative publicity (Hollar 2007). De Beers hired PR firm Sitrick and Co. (which specializes in celebrity scandals), while the wider diamond industry launched a website (diamonfacts.org), and ran full-page ads online and in the press (Snead 2006). On one hand, this illustrates that pressure regarding the issue of conflict diamonds forced those who profit from the trade in diamonds to publicly frame the possibilities of both ethical consumption and extraction. On the other, it channels the issue of ethical consumption into the purchase of 'conflict-free' stones. While this is a critical issue, the discursive production of 'conflict diamonds' or 'blood diamonds' enables unethical gems to be circumscribed to those linked with atrocity. The less sensational or cinematic issues of local and global inequalities around class, race, gender, nation, (post)coloniality, and the paradoxes intrinsic to global capitalism must be sublimated in order for some diamonds to be signified as 'conflict free'.

Russell Simmons, hip hop and fashion mogul, founder of Def Jam records, Phat Farm fashion, and Simmons Jewellery Company participated in the diamond industry's PR offensive. Simmons' personal fortune is estimated to be between US $325 million and US $500 million (Fetterman 2007). He works with the South African De Beers Company on his jewellery line, a company notorious for its history of monopolistic practices, price fixing, and brutal labour practices, particularly under apartheid (Roberts 2003). Bonnie Abaunza, the Los Angeles-based director of Amnesty International's 'celebrity outreach programme' arranged a pre-release screening of *Blood Diamond* for Simmons (Snead 2006), who subsequently took part in a 'fact-finding' mission to South Africa and Botswana from 26 November to 4 December 2006. Simmons' return, and the publicity his trip generated, thus coincided with the release of *Blood Diamond* in US theatres on December 8. Simmons claimed that his trip was an attempt to draw attention to the way the countries he visited were benefiting from the diamond industry, and reflected his concern that 'too much attention was being placed on the illicit "conflict diamonds" that are the focus of *Blood Diamond*' (Reuters 2006). Thus, at a press conference upon his return, Simmons announced the launch of his 'Green Initiative' range of jewellery, a quarter of the profits from which would be paid into a fund he would establish, the Diamond Empowerment Fund. The fund currently finances education initiatives in South Africa and Botswana.

News coverage around the release of *Blood Diamond* focused on the diamond industry's response to the film, and the rift between the film's director Edward Zwick and Russell Simmons. Zwick criticized Simmons as a 'PR puppet' of the diamond industry, and one article hyperbolized this disagreement as Africa's 'new civil war' (Africa Resource 2006).

Broadcast journalism also focused on the diamond industry's response to the film, thwarting attempts of star Djimon Hounsou to use the film's publicity to draw attention to the issue of child soldiers (Hollar 2007).

Simmons' Green Initiative jewellery includes a bracelet of malachite beads sourced from Africa with a rough diamond attached. Twenty dollars from the sale of each bracelet, which retails for US$125, is donated to the Diamond Empowerment Fund (National Jeweller 2007). The bracelet is worn by a raft of celebrities including Beyoncé, Chris Tucker, David Beckham, Naomi Campbell, Ludacris, Penelope Cruz and Serena Williams (Daniels 2007). Bill Clinton wore the bracelet on a national television appearance (Ecorazzi 2007). In January 2008, Simmons Jewellery Company donated over US$ 300 000, proceeds from the sale of Green Initiative products, to the Diamond Empowerment Fund (Diamond Empowerment Fund 2009).

In a manner analogous to the Product (RED)TM campaign, whereby a portion of profits of RED branded products are paid into The Global Fund to Fight AIDS, Tuberculosis and Malaria, Simmons' Green Initiative renders the possibility of 'heroic shopping' and 'compassionate consumption' (Richey and Ponte 2008: 713). Russell Simmons' PR for the diamond industry and his Green Initiative explicitly deflected attention from the issue of conflict diamonds in order to reinscribe the legitimacy of consumption and profit accumulation as signifiers of philanthropy. Wearing the Green Initiative brand enables the consumer to perform a cosmopolitan identity that signifies an engagement with 'African-ness', and like the product RED campaign, 'is about individual consumption, not about public engagement in activism or advocacy' (Richey and Ponte 2008: 717). As I detail in the following section, the documentary *Bling* (2007) attempts to extend the hip hop community's attention on the issue of conflict diamonds beyond personal consumption. However, the need to justify the prominent role 'bling' plays within hip hop culture means the documentary's project of critique is marked by paradox.

Bling: A Planet Rock

Raquel Cepeda's documentary *Bling: A Planet Rock* (2007) explores the role of diamonds, or 'bling' within the hip hop community. Cepeda claims that she began working on her treatment for the documentary in 2001, while she was chief editor of Russell Simmons' *Oneworld* magazine. Her goal as editor was 'to promote the notion of global community. I believed it was important to inspire our demographic to travel, to become citizens of Earth rather than just America' (Cepeda 2009). This commitment to promoting global citizenship underpinned her production of *Bling*.

Within the documentary, the practice of signifying success through hyperbolic displays of diamonds is situated in a historical and political context. The paradoxes of consumption of both diamonds and hip hop within global markets, and the ways in which history produces the present are rendered through what is said by people on screen, and through juxtaposing historical and contemporary footage. The director does not smooth over these contradictions; rather, she allows the complexities of who or what is 'good' or 'evil' to trouble her narrative, eschewing closure or solution. Sierra Leone is represented as a nation where little has been 'solved' and where answers to the nation's problems lie outside the familiar paradigm of private charity and development aid.

In *Bling*, hip hop artists draw on personal biographies of poverty and broader systems of raced exploitation in order to render an entitlement to their current wealth and perform a brotherhood of African-ness. In the film's prologue, Kanye West explains

> It's in us to want to shine, from the days of the kings and the queens, to show off the jewellery, to show off the gold. So it's our rightful place to want to show off our jewellery, but they've taken it away from us. We've had, for so many years, chains around our necks. But this time we've got diamonds in 'em [...] This is our way to almost make ourselves be truly citizens, to move up in the caste system, it's just ironic that what made black people feel so empowered was completely demoralizing and destroying other black people.

West's account is intercut with stills from *National Geographic* of contemporary Africans adorned in gold and old line drawings and photographs of slaves in chains of bondage. This segment functions to frame the desire to display wealth as natural, innate to 'black culture', and its denial an expression of exploitation. At the same time, West renders conflict diamonds as a historical issue, concealing that the ascendance of some black people within the caste system remains premised on profound local and global inequities in access to resources.

The prologue of *Bling* focuses on West because his Grammy-winning single 'Diamonds from Sierra Leone', released in July 2005, was the first time many in the hip hop community had heard of conflict diamonds and their role within the civil war in Sierra Leone.[1] West himself had revised an earlier song, 'Diamonds are Forever', following prompting from other artists to consider the role of diamonds in funding West African conflicts. The video accompanying the single is shot in black and white, connoting both realism and sophistication, and begins with West's epigraph: 'Little is known of Sierra Leone and its connection to the diamonds we own'. The video opens with a scene of black adults and children working in mines. An accented Sierra Leonean voice (which is subtitled) explains that these are 'the children of the blood diamonds', some of whom have been forced by the rebels to kill their families before they were enslaved. The sequence cuts to a white jeweller examining gems. The narrative of the blood diamond continues with a white man putting an engagement ring on a white woman's finger, which begins to run with blood, and scenes of wealthy white shoppers. An end title asks the viewer to 'please purchase conflict-free diamonds'.

West's video elides the role of 'bling' within the hip hop community. He stands with the 'children of the blood diamond', who in a feigned mobility haunt the shoppers in Prague. Instead, the white woman's romantic fantasy, which culminates with a diamond ring, becomes the site through which the graphic signifier of blood is rendered as it literally drips from her hand. This simplifies the globalized politics of diamonds by deflecting attention from the men within the hip hop community who wear diamonds, and the gendered politics that produces female desire for an engagement ring, signifying the aspiration of 'belonging' to another. Further, by restricting the viewer's duty to the Sierra Leoneans memorialized by the video to purchasing conflict-free diamonds, the obscenity of ostentatious consumption rendered within the video is necessarily deflected due to West's obvious 'success' within that system of stratification.

A substantive portion of *Bling* follows a trio of the first US hip hop artists to have visited Sierra Leone. The trip took place in 2006, and the documentary follows the group as they tour Freetown, visit alluvial diamond miners, the industrial mine of Sierra Leone Selection Trust (SLST), rehabilitation centres for amputees and 'bush wives' (girls kidnapped and raped during the war) and visit a hip hop club. As the artists travelling to Sierra Leone are introduced, the themes of entitlement and brotherhood established by West are reiterated. White Southern rapper Paul Wall explains that diamonds are how he rewards himself for overcoming poverty (Wall is renowned for the diamond-encrusted grills, jewellery worn over the teeth, he wears and markets. His partner in this enterprise, jeweller 'TV Johnny', accompanies him to Sierra Leone). Tego Calderon, a Reggaeton and hip hop artist who immigrated to the US from Puerto Rico as a child, explains that while he considers the flamboyant display of wealth by hip hop artists disrespectful to their impoverished communities, his community demands to see the signifiers of his success.

The artists are accompanied on the trip by Ishmael Beah, an author and former child soldier, who is returning home from the US for the first time in ten years. Beah's return home is something quite different from Calderon's references to returning to the motherland; the former kissing the ground as he lands on the soil of 'home'. Beah has, like the protagonists of *Blood Diamond*, only succeeded through leaving Africa. He ruminates over his luck, and the guilt attending it as he visits old friends 'still in the same place as I left them', which, he says, highlights that 'the factors responsible for causing the war still continue on to this day'. Beah's testimony and opinions are woven throughout the documentary through responses to an unseen interviewer and sequences of the three US performers listening to him describe his experiences during the war. He is the primary figure through which the complexities of the globalized past and present play out.

Beah is introduced within the documentary through his testimony about his experience as a child soldier, and he links that experience to diamonds and hip hop:

The first day of battle was actually the worst, just to see it and to actually shoot someone – most of the young recruits couldn't do it. But your friends next to you were being killed and you were covered in blood, and you just start shooting. And after that it just became as simple as drinking water or eating a meal. I think the diamonds played a very, very big role in the war, the reason there were lots of guns in Sierra Leone [...] [was because] they were being exchanged for diamonds [...] Hip hop has a big influence because the majority of the big [American] hip hop artists wore a lot of really expensive diamonds.

The connection Beah makes here between the war and hip hop is simplistic, but it gestures towards the mongrel consequences of global capitalism; a discordance which troubles the film. This is made explicit by BBC journalist Lansana Fofana, who explains that in lieu of military uniforms, RUF combatants often wore t-shirts bearing the image of Tupac Shakur.[2] When the Americans are told by Sierra Leonean artists about the role rap played in the conflict; that lyrics that fetishized using guns and killing legitimized these practices, Wall responds that rap is about *testifying* to experience, and was not intended to *glorify* it. Implied here is that the correct mode of reception for this music is witnessing; a subject position based on empathy for the one who testifies, and requires taking on a burden to respond with ethical action as a result of that knowledge (Rentschler 2004; Zelizer 1998, 2002).

Bling, like *Blood Diamond,* memorializes atrocities that are consigned to history; however, unlike the fiction film, *Bling* also documents the continued suffering of people mentally and physically maimed by war, and the abject poverty of the Freetown slums and alluvial diamond miners. The viewer must assume that the pain on screen, while recorded in the past, has not been resolved. Thus, the documentary interpellates viewers to bear witness in multiple and shifting ways: to the testimony of survivor witnesses articulated to the hip hop artists (who may be read as acting as the viewer's proxy); to the testimony of the hip hop artists who have been in the presence of suffering, to the testimony of survivor witnesses directed to the camera, and to the narrative constructed by the director, which incorporates imagery of atrocity and renders an argument regarding the reproduction of colonial exploitation via the incorporation of archival footage.

Yet throughout the documentary, the US hip hop artists fail to model a witnessing subject position that might enable viewers to foster a sense of obligation to the other. While the director may intend to facilitate a sense of global connection and duty among her audience, this is possible only if viewers read the interactions between the US artists and Sierra Leoneans they meet critically, and as part of that acknowledge that the whiteness, which is foregrounded by both the narrative structure and the US artists as the locus of oppression, poses a reductive account of contemporary raced inequities.

The hip hop artists visit the National Commission for War Affected Children, a rehabilitation centre for 'bush wives'. The focus of the segment is the distribution of a gift of a pair of Reebok sneakers to each girl, which Wall has arranged as a result of promotional work he has done for the brand. The shoes, albeit a practical gift, become a site through which the semiotic space around the brand, and the artists, are imbued with a sensibility of compassion and philanthropy. This functions to obfuscate globalized gender politics. Elsewhere in the documentary, the US visitors are told by Sierra Leonean hip hop artists that in lieu of wealth 'the women are our bling'. There is no connection made by any of the artists, or the director, between the sexual politics of hip hop and the status of women. The music videos through which the US performers promote their music typically render buxom, scantily clad women as the trappings of success – their identities secondary to their value as signifiers of masculine prowess and achievement. While these women consent to this role, it is part of a spectrum of objectification, and a performance of availability, which informs an imaginary of male entitlement to the bodies of women.

The artists' visit to a resettlement camp for amputees on the outskirts of Freetown is the sequence within which the task of bearing witness is performed through its most conventional framework, whereby the visitors constitute an audience for amputees who present testimony of suffering. On the way to the camp, Gavin Simpson, a representative from the Truth and Reconciliation Commission, explains to the men that they will be meeting with people who 'have lost their hands, their feet, some of them have lost their ears, they've lost their lips'. Raekwon (a member of Wu Tang clan) responds, 'That's what we're going to see? Ah man, why the fuck did I smoke a blunt?' Simpson must then coax Raekwon, for quite some time, to leave the bus because he does not want to see the amputees. This scenario reveals the performer's lack of engagement with the tour schedule, and a failure to approach the trip with the requisite sobriety; breaching a line between dark tourism and empathizing with the other in pain. However, by including this footage of Raekwon the director allows viewers to make this judgement, and perhaps to consider what the obligations to the other might be under these circumstances.

During the crew's visit to miners working the river, and Koidu Holdings' industrial mine, the director edits in BBC archival footage from 1969, directing us to observe how little has changed and to connect this with the continued control of the diamond industry by neo-colonial interests. At the mine in Koidu, Calderon waits at the razor wire while the others enter, saying 'They clean diamonds and shit here right?' They're guilty of the suffering of the people then right?' Inside the compound the rappers debate with the white manager, accusing him of producing the suffering they have seen. In response to the manager's contention that diamonds did not cause the civil war, Raekwon responds,

> what was the cause of the war was poverty. Was people not having nothing. People not having no water, no food, no electricity – how could you live without these things – so therefore you're walking dead.

While these comments are legitimate, the artists' preoccupation with imagining themselves part of a brotherhood exploited by external forces enables them to abdicate responsibility for their participation in the globalized dynamics of 'bling'.

Ishmael Beah shows the group around the Freetown slums, and it is during some of these scenes that the local people take on roles other than recipients of celebrity patronage. Some of the Sierra Leoneans do not want to be filmed, and a distressed man shouts at them,

> we are suffering, we are suffering in this country, I have no place to sleep. We are shelterless. Why in my own country am I shelterless? It must not be in my own country. We are feeling the pain. No progress man. We are the youth of today. Look at me I am 20 years old. Only sleeping and working. No future plan in this country, no future plan.

After leaving the area, and having ruminated on the locals' misunderstanding that the men had a higher purpose than tourism, and the danger the situation posed, Calderon concludes 'doesn't feel right, cos I ain't doing nothing. At least if I was doing something it would be different. But yeah, it makes me uncomfortable to see my brothers living that way'. To which Wall responds 'its heading right back to 1991. Its gonna happen again, that's what it looks like'.

The sense of powerlessness the performers convey here reveals the impossibilities intrinsic to their trip, and the limitations of celebrity activism (see Roy Crovel in this volume). While the documentary attempts to enable audiences to bear witness to the continued suffering in Sierra Leone, it fails to direct viewers to unpack the intersections of violence, masculinity and wealth as signifiers of status and success. There is a fundamental incompatibility of celebrity (Littler 2008: 243); the embodiment of personal wealth and conspicuous consumption, with activism on behalf of the impoverished and marginal.

Conclusion

My analysis of the entertainment industry's discursive production of, and response to, the issue of conflict diamonds reveals the circumscription of the western/northern audiences' obligation to the Other to commodity relations. Kanye West's video 'Diamonds from Sierra Leone', the film *Blood Diamond* and the documentary *Bling: A Planet Rock*, all function to memorialize the civil war and the role of the illicit trade in diamonds within it. However, rather than modelling a subject position for audiences of the globally oriented citizen, the requirement of which is to bear witness to suffering in order to take *political* responsibility towards alleviating that suffering, political responsibility is occulted. By rendering the issue as diamonds, and the ethical consumption of them, the nations from which diamonds are extracted are left behind.

The battle to define the semiotic meaning of the stones, as either 'blood diamonds' or 'conflict free', consumes the embodied Other who suffers; signs to conceal those bodies are produced in order to position consumption as 'justice'. By positing 'ethical consumption' as the requisite response to the role of diamonds within conflicts, the imaginary around diamonds may be cleansed of violence. If diamonds are made to signify 'conflict' or 'blood' only when linked to atrocity, the consumer's conscience may be assuaged rather than pricked by focusing on the certification of their purchase, or purchasing Green Initiative products. The role of diamonds within the ostentatious display of wealth, within celebrity culture, and, specifically the role of 'bling' within hip hop, is elided as a signifier of global class stratification.

The entertainment industry's articulation of the issue of conflict diamonds provides representations that may facilitate empathy for the other, but audiences are not instructed in how they may act on that empathy, other than by shopping. The privileged are asked to consume as means to address inequity, leaving intact the paradigm that who we are is expressed through what we buy. Further, while diamonds remain the issue and the commodity links the western consumer to the Other, what remains off the agenda are the manifold issues within post-conflict nation building. We are not asked to consider that there may be something inherently wrong with global capitalism; rather, the problem is rendered as that capitalism has not extended far enough. What gets covered over is that capitalism requires globalized structural inequities, enabling profit accumulation via access to cheap labour and resources. Celebrity advocacy in response to conflict diamonds functions to protect global capitalism, rather than challenging its constituent inequalities.

The texts I have analysed reveal that public culture does not equip us with the tools to think with about our obligations and responsibilities as globally oriented citizens. In order for hip hop artists to maintain their legitimacy as consumers and producers of diamond jewellery, the role of 'bling' (and rap) within Sierra Leone's civil war must be deflected. While Cepeda intends her documentary to pose hip hop as a vehicle for unity, a critical reading demonstrates the inability of hip hop in its current form to engage with the consequences of the way masculinity and power is constituted.

References

Africa Resource (2006), 'Russell Simmons and Ed Zwick dispute over *Blood Diamonds*', AfricaResource. com, http://www.africaresource.com/index.php?option=com_content&view=article&id=247:russell-simmons-and-ed-zwick-dispute-over-blood-diamonds&catid=111:hip-hop&Itemid=327. Accessed 10 November 2008.

Carruthers, Susan (2004), 'Tribalism and Tribulation: Media Constructions of "African savagery" and "Western humanitarianism" in the 1990s', in S. Allen and B. Zelizer (eds), *Reporting War: Journalism in Wartime*, New York: Routledge, pp. 155–173.

Cepeda, Raquel (2007), *Bling: A Planet Rock*, Chatsworth, California: VH1 and Article 19 Films.

—— (2009), '*Bling: A Planet Rock*: Frequently asked questions', djalirancher.com, http://djalirancher. com/blog/?tag=conflict. Accessed 1 August 2009.

Chiwengo, Ngwarsungu (2008), 'When wounds and corpses fail to speak: Narratives of violence and rape in Congo (DRC)', *Comparative Studies of South Asia, Africa and the Middle East*, 28:1, pp. 78–92.

Daniels, Karu F. (2007), 'Russell Simmons: Diamond initiative garners special honour', *Black Voices*, 27 September, http://www.bvnewswire.com/2007/09/27/russell-simmons-diamond-initiative-garners-special-honor/. Accessed 10 November 2008.

Diamond Empowerment Fund (2009), 'Green bracelet', http://www.diamondempowerment.org/ green-bracelet/. Accessed 10 November 2008.

Ecorazzi (2007), 'Former President Clinton takes the dare and wears the Green Bracelet', 27 September, http://www.ecorazzi.com/2007/09/27/former-president-clinton-takes-the-dare-and-wears-the-green-bracelet/. Accessed 10 November 2008.

Fetterman, Mindy (2007), 'Today's entrepreneur: Russell Simmons can't slow down', *USA Today*, 23 May, http://www.usatoday.com/money/companies/management/2007-05-13-exec-simmons-usat_ N.htm. Accessed 10 November 2008.

Foreign Policy (2006), 'Seven questions: A chat with *Blood Diamond* Director Ed Zwick', December, www.foreignpolicy.com/story/cms.php?story_id=3648. Accessed 10 November 2008.

Gaber, Ivor and Wynne Willson, Alice (2005), 'Dying for Diamonds: The Mainstream Media and the NGOs – A case study of ActionAid', in W. de Jong, M. Shaw and N. Stammers (eds), *Global Activism, Global Media*, London: Pluto Press, pp. 95–109.

Global Witness (2009), 'History', http://www.globalwitness.org/pages/en/history.html. Accessed 1 August 2009.

Guerin, Frances and Hallas, Roger (2007), *The Image and the Witness: Trauma, Memory and Visual Culture*, London: Wallflower Press.

Hamilton Smith, Summer (2008), 'Raquel Cepeda', *Clutch Magazine*, 1 January, http://clutchmagonline.com/lifeculture/feature/raquel-cepeda/#2. Accessed 10 November 2008.

Hollar, Julie (2007), 'Bono, I presume? Covering Africa through celebrities', *Fair Extra!* May/June, http://www.fair.org/index.php?page=3119. Accessed 10 November 2008.

Huliaras, Asteris and Tzifakis, Nikolaos (2008), 'The dynamics of celebrity activism: Mia Farrow and the "Genocide Olympics" campaign', *Karamanlis Working Papers in Hellenic and European Studies*, The Fletcher School of Law and Diplomacy, July, Number 7.

Jarosz, Lucy (1992), 'Constructing the Dark Continent: Metaphor as geographic representation of Africa', *Geografiska Annaler*, 74:2, pp. 105–115.

Jones, Steve (2006), 'Music, film open eyes to war in Sierra Leone', *USA Today*, 27 September, http://www.usatoday.com/life/music/news/2006-09-27-refugee-all-stars_x.htm. Accessed 10 November 2008.

Littler, Jo (2008), '"I feel your pain": Cosmopolitan charity and the public fashioning of the celebrity soul', *Social Semiotics*, 18:2, pp. 237–251.

National Jeweller (2007), 'Simmons Jewellery Co.'s 'Green Bracelet' to benefit DEF', March 1, http://www.nationaljewelernetwork.com/njn/content_display/diamonds/e3i9410da3dd7ac1a5611124f1345e8b9c1?imw=Y. Accessed 10 November 2008.

Parekh, Bhikhu (2003), 'Cosmopolitanism and global citizenship', *Review of International Studies*, 29:1, pp. 3–17.

Park, Augustine (2007), 'Making sense of amputations in Sierra Leone', *Peace Review: A Journal of Social Justice*, 19:4, pp. 579–587.

Rentschler, Cynthia (2004), 'Witnessing: US citizenship and the vicarious experience of suffering', *Media, Culture & Society*, 26:2, pp. 296–304.

Reuters (2006), 'Simmons, rights groups clash over diamonds: Hip-hop mogul defends trip to African mine', *MSNBC*, 6 December, http://www.msnbc.msn.com/id/16062603/. Accessed 10 November 2008.

Richey, Lisa Ann and Ponte, Stefano (2008), 'Better (Red)TM than Dead? Celebrities, consumption and international aid', *Third World Quarterly*, 29:4, pp. 711–729.

Roberts, Janine (2003), 'The underside of De Beers Diamonds', in R. Kick (ed.), *Abuse Your Illusions: The Disinformation Guide to Media Mirages and Establishment Lies*, New York: The Disinformation Company, pp. 120–126.

Santora, Marc (2006), 'Hollywood's multifaceted cause du jour', *The New York Times,* 3 December, http://www.nytimes.com/2006/12/03/movies/03sant.html?_r=3&oref=slogin&pagewanted=all. Accessed 10 November 2008, p. 2. 1.

Snead, Elizabeth (2006), '*Blood Diamond's*' PR war', *LA Times*, 10 October, http://theenvelope.latimes.com/movies/env-et-diamonds10oct10,0,5836118.story?page=1. Accessed 10 November 2008.

Wall, Melissa (2007), 'An Analysis of News Magazine Coverage of the Rwanda crisis in the United States', in A. Thompson (ed.), *The Media and the Rwanda Genocide*, London: Pluto Press, pp. 261–273.

Zelizer, Barbie (1998), *Remembering to Forget: Holocaust Memory Through the Camera's Eye*, Chicago: The University of Chicago Press.

—— (2002), 'Finding aids to the past: Bearing personal witness to traumatic public events', *Media, Culture & Society*, 24:5, pp. 697–714.

Zwick, Ed (2006), *Blood Diamond*, Los Angeles: Warner Brothers.

Notes

1. West's video for Diamonds from Sierra Leone is available to view online at http://www.youtube.com/watch?v=Fgqd80026xU.
2. Shakur, a rap icon assassinated in 1996, wrote lyrics expressing his disenfranchisement as a young black man in the US. Lyrics, which may have resonated with the rebels, include the following, from 'Trouble Some 96': 'Menacing methods/Label me a lethal weapon/Making niggas die […] A guerrilla in this criminal war we all rebels/Death before dishonour […] Young, strapped, and I don't give a fuck […] this is dedicated to the real niggas/all the real troublesome soldiers on the street'.

Chapter 9

The Global Politics of Celebrity Humanitarianism

Riina Yrjölä

Introduction

Historically, the high profile of celebrities involved in political causes is a somewhat radical political change from the past. When in the 1960s, celebrity activists were seen mostly arguing against politicians on issues relating to the Vietnam War, many of the most visible celebrities acting on behalf of Africa's poor have moved from counter-culture to mainstream politics by sharing the same stages on various conferences, panels and seminars with politicians and other leading decision-makers. The key difference between these two types of politically active celebrities is that whereas previously celebrities were engaged in anti-war activism (perceived as openly political and radical), the contemporary humanitarian action, which attempts to alleviate suffering, is perceived as ethical action aiming at a more humane, co-operative and peaceful global world. As Kofi Annan has argued, celebrity humanitarians 'help instill in young people the values of understanding, solidarity, respect and communication across cultures [...] so that those values come to them naturally for the rest of their lives' (UN Chronicle Online Edition: 27 June 2002).

Lately, political scientists have also acknowledged the role of celebrities in endorsing humanitarian causes. According to Andrew Cooper (2008) several 'celebrity diplomats' have become enormously successful in mobilizing, channelling and mediating their causes into international public policy. This optimistic view has not been shared by all. Criticism has emerged on celebrities' legitimacy and accountability in humanitarian politics, as well as the effectiveness of the aid policies they promote in Africa (Dieter and Kumar 2008; Richey and Ponte 2008; Moyo 2009).

The current academic debate on the suitability and accuracy of celebrity humanitarian actions, however, leaves important questions unasked. These questions are not 'what-and-who' questions, but rather how celebrities act and represent the African poor to global citizens and what kind of truths celebrities, with their representations, create themselves. In effect no specific empirical research exists on their media representations of Africa. Since their campaigns are fundamentally moral, doubting the rightness of their humanitarianism seems difficult, if not impossible (Douzinas 2007: 19) – not only for the general public, but also for academic researchers.

By aiming to fill the gaps in contemporary research and to further theorize the essence as well as the effects of contemporary celebrity humanitarianism, specifically the discourses, ideals and imaginaries of and by them, the objective of this chapter is to critically examine the different visual and textual representations of Bob Geldof and Bono in the British media.

In short, my aim is to reveal the 'historically developed, socially embedded interpretations of space and identity' (Shapiro 2009: 18) these celebrity discourses perform. In order to execute this task, the focus of this chapter is twofold. First, to examine how Geldof and Bono – the two most visible spokespersons acting on behalf of Africa – are constituted in the British media as legitimate humanitarian actors and truth-tellers, and second, to analyse how 'Africa' and its place in a world system becomes produced through these discourses.

The research material consists of major media articles between 2002 and August 2008 reporting Bono's and Geldof's humanitarian work in Africa. I approach these articles through a Foucaultian discourse-theoretical analysis as sites where political meanings are debated, evaluated, built and exchanged (Turner 2004; Marshall 1997; Dyer 1998, 2004). For my main media sources, I have selected two leading British news publishers, the *Daily Telegraph* and the web news service of the British Broadcasting Corporation, 'BBC News'.[1] In addition, *TIME* magazine, even though a US source, has been included as one of the leading newsweeklies both in the United Kingdom as well as in Europe.

The chapter is divided in two parts. Part one details my theoretical approach towards a more critical, historized and thus politicized analysis on the discursive effects of celebrity humanitarianism. In part two, which is based on an empirical analysis of the selected media articles on Bono and Geldof, I identify some historical western archetypes that arise in the media's discourses. I conclude that the discourses of Bono and Geldof cement both the western celebrities as well as Africa into specific hierarchical subject positions, which elaborate colonial formations and imaginaries. It follows that more critical research on celebrity humanitarian discourses and imaginaries as sites of cultural governance is urgently needed.

Reading and Viewing Celebrity Humanitarianism Politically

The view on celebrities as governmental tools of modern capitalist societies is widely shared. As many researchers have argued, celebrities as ideological texts of a 'common man' provide a fundamental mechanism through which the discursive linkages between consumer capitalism, democracy and individualism are constructed and maintained in secular western societies (Adorno and Horkheimer 2002; Marshall 1997; Rojek 2001).

However, as icons and deities of contemporary media culture, celebrities do not only have a central function in the legitimization of capitalist economies, but they are also an essential part of personalized western politics where mediated political identities are increasingly built by cultural containment: symbol management, affections and imaginaries of being and becoming (Kellner 2003; Street 2002, 2003; Van Zoonen 2005; Corner and Pels 2003). To a great degree, political authority is today constucted through emotional attachments, making aesthetic stylization a central feature of mass politics in its mediated form. Politics, entertainment and media have become intricately interwoven affecting both the representation practices as well as legitimation processes of western political systems making media visibilities, issues of style, image management and authenticity the key forms of how a political persona is constituted and maintained.

In contemporary political times, power works increasingly through imaginaries on individual development, life politics and moral re-education. Choosing, deciding, shaping individuals who aspire to be the authors of their lives and the creators of their identities is the central characteristic of our time (Beck 2001: 165). In these contexts the significant role of celebrities has been widely acknowledged (Louw 2005: 172–193; Street 2001: 187–192; 2002, 2003, 2004; Yrjölä 2008). Acting as lenses of understanding (Marshall 2006: 5) and as vehicles for cultural memory and cohesion (Braudy 1997: 15) celebrities – through their imaginaries – unify, explain and shape everyday life by providing sites of belonging, recognition and meaning (Rojek 2001; Dyer 1998). As wider cultural discourses, celebrities not only articulate and express specific cultural norms, values and ideals, but through them imaginaries and world-views are opened, shaped and built.

Throughout history, western hegemony in Africa has been built through symbolic cultural practices, as much as with force, and shaped the actions, beliefs and orientations of its citizens. These representations of Africa have been eminently recoverable and variable, and as such they tell us more about the nexus of European interests in African affairs than they do about Africa and Africans (Coombes 1994: 3). As such, these representations cannot be reduced to mere 'ideological expressions, or manifestations of specific people's will, but rather [should be figured as] interpretative contentions, negotiations, between cultures' (Shapiro 1999: 47). During colonialism and imperialism, fictional stories and travel writing were at the heart of the construction and management of Africa, forming and shaping its realities with imperial and anti-imperial attitudes (Said 1994; Hall 2000; Pratt 1992). The representations of the explorers, novelists and missionaries constituted Africa as a dark continent – savage, different, dangerous – and justified western intervention in the name of progress, reason and civilization. Later, popular literature, music halls, theatre and cinema formed the centre where from the message was conveyed further (Pieterse 1995; MacKenzie 1984; Landau and Kaspin 2002). These various representations provided the western public with a widely shared view of their role in Africa on moral, religious and national grounds. Power spoke through culture with one voice: 'there was only one "civilization", one path to "progress" and one "true religion"' (Brantlinger 1986: 185). Civilizing Africa was 'not about politics but about duty, a deed to be done' (Mayer 2002: 107).

Today, global imaginaries, mental environments and mediascapes play a central role within a new global governance of which celebrity humanitarian imaginaries constitute a part (Oliver 2001: 555). Arguably, in recent years, humanitarianism has 'turned into the ultimate political ideology bringing together the well-being of the West with the hardships of the global South' (Douzinas 2007: 11). In other words, humanitarianism has become the key-frame of contemporary world politics – an essential expression of what is meant by 'international community' and the contemporary world order behind it (Aaltola 2009). Humanitarian agencies and actors, of which celebrity humanitarians are an increasingly visible part, are not only imprinted in this culture, but are also the carriers of its message and principles by generating humanitarian obligations and duties.

In these contexts, celebrity humanitarians and their representations are as important for African affairs as analysing official political decisions, speeches or documents. As instances of international relations, celebrity humanitarians produce the imagined terrains of world order by structuring the relationships between people, cultures and nations. Through their mediations, biological bodies are forged into social bodies by foregrounding connections between knowledge and forms of human community – of ways of being in the world. In other words, celebrity humanitarians are engaged in 'systems of meaning production [which] are intimately related to practices of power – the power to define and defend "reality"' (Shepherd 2006: 21). To ignore how their mediated texts produce surfaces, boundaries, orientations and past associations through emotional attributes and calls (Ahmed 2004) misses out on the complex interaction between violence and the systems of oppression that are constituted, performed and constructed in these texts.

Different representations do not simply disseminate information, or reflect 'reality'. Rather they can be seen as historical event-makings, as 'ambivalent texts of projection and introjection [...] displacement, overdetermination, guilt [and] aggressivity' (Bhabha 1994: 82). As power-invested enactments they wage war on intelligibilities, producing their discursive objects, the difference and sameness, by containment and capture (Foucault 1982). These social realities and truths are fundamentally acts of power that not only constitute discursively the speaker (i.e. celebrity), but in them the object of speech (Africa) also becomes ascribed. The latter is not only a consequence of how Africa is envisioned by these celebrity humanitarians and/in the media, but also a performative repercussion of the characteristics and possibilities of these western celebrities in contrast to those of Africa. It is exactly the physical realization of the performative roles designated in media texts that sketch both celebrities and Africa into subject positions, cementing them firmly into these assumed spaces as their logical and natural positions and roles in world politics.[2]

Performing Global Humanity

Today, Bob Geldof and Bono are the most media-visible and prize-awarded celebrities acting on behalf of Africa. They met originally in 1984 when Bob Geldof initiated the Band-Aid project in order to raise funds for famine relief for Ethiopia, followed by the 'Live Aid' concerts in London and Philadelphia in 1985. It, however, took over fifteen years – until 1999 – for Geldof and Bono to reach their current visibility in the media as global humanitarians through their involvement in the Jubilee 2000 campaign – a worldwide movement set up to eliminate Third World debt. Since then, both men have been increasingly involved in various campaigns and events to help ease African suffering, by establishing, for example, the lobby group DATA (Debt, AIDS, Trade, Africa) and launching the RED campaign that aims to aid African AIDS sufferers through commercial means. Their latest global involvement was in 2005 when they organized the 'Live8' concerts in G8 countries as well as in South Africa. These events supported the Make Poverty History Campaign message, aimed at pressuring world leaders to erase the debt of the world's poorest nations, increase and improve aid, and negotiate fair trade rules in the interest of poorer countries.

Even though Bono and Geldof do not formally participate in the decision-making processes on African issues, they can be seen playing a significant role as producers of knowledge, truths and facts about Africa through the performative qualities of celebrity (Street 2002: 2004). For many western citizens, Bono and Geldof are today anti-hegemonic heroes who act against the western power elites and their policies by truthful reasoning and selfless engagements (Oxfam 2005, 2006); various media discourses reflect and build upon these assumptions. It is precisely because Bono and Geldof are represented as outsiders to, or even challengers of, conventional politics, that they can be seen to enjoy such a degree of mass support as apolitical humanitarian actors.

Bob Geldof: Uncompromising Pioneer

Following a critical discourse analysis of the chosen media texts and images, Bob Geldof can be seen to become represented through two dominant and overlapping discourses – defined here as the discourses of the Judge and the Discoverer.

In the discourse of the Judge, Geldof was a man of justice. This image was achieved predominantly through contrasting Geldof's actions with the immaterialized and empty promises of western politicians to help Africa. In the BBC News headlines, he was, on occasion, reported to 'push', 'set out' and 'urge' western politicians to help Africa (e.g. BBC 31 May 2005a; BBC 6 July 2005; BBC 29 June 2006). Admired for being free of favours and obligations, he was labelled as 'an outspoken campaigner' and 'ragged-trousered pragmatist' whose 'credibility [was] intact (BBC 13 July 2006; BBC 4 June 2003). As an arbitrator, Geldof became depicted as an honest man with the ability to question and challenge political and economic authorities as well as reward them through praise (BBC 10 March 2007; BBC 27 September 2006; BBC 8 July 2007). He was reported to give an account to George Bush's administration as 'the most radical – in a positive sense – in its approach to Africa since Kennedy', and qualifying the talks at Tony Blair's Commission for Africa as 'radical and progressive' (BBC 28 May 2004; BBC 7 October 2004). According to *The Telegraph*, Geldof and Bono were 'a dynamic duo of African aid', men who were not 'hemmed in by narrow national interests and party policy' (*Telegraph* 2 July 2005). To the BBC, Geldof was 'the clearest example of a modern day hero [...] (p)olitical and empathetic, but not a politician' (BBC 2 July 2002). As a judge, in these media representations Geldof became viewed as an impartial, neutral and apolitical figure, i.e. possessing the core principles of traditional humanitarians (Barnett and Weiss 2008: 2).

This outsider status, which articulated his credibility and moral authority, was directly dependent on the connection with direct and live interviews of summits and conferences attended by Geldof alongside political leaders. Framed as an on-site reporter and a qualified advisor who gave his own personal judgements and reflections on the African implications of western policies, Geldof was a man capable of reasonably assessing the extent of the crimes and progress made against Africa by western political elites (e.g. BBC 11 March 2007; BBC 30 June 2006; BBC 9 July 2008; BBC 20 December 2005). Judging on the correct and achievable policies to end African poverty, Geldof called for action 'to change our debt, aid and trade policies and Africans to deal with issues of governance as above' (BBC 13 July 2006). His views on the actors qualified to take action in Africa were evident. He argued that

> even with the 'undoubtable leadership' taken by the United Kingdom on Africa, 'the vacuum of our (European leaders) lack of fulfilment have stepped the Chinese, who do not care about the values of democracy, transparency and accountability [...] (and who say) we'll give you the money so long as we have influence over your resources and your politics'. (BBC 13 July 2006)

Geldof's final verdict was explicit: 'it was the time for the Old Economies to come to Africa' [...] 'to protect Africa through aid for trade scheme as the US did for Europe after the WWII' (BBC 30 November 2007).

This discourse of the Judge overlapped with the discourse of the Discoverer, which depicted Geldof as an authority who knew and understood Africa with an exceptionally deep knowledge. This discourse was built mostly on news stories of Geldof mingling and travelling with western business and political elites to Africa. For example, *TIME* magazine assigned Geldof to travel with President George W. Bush into Africa (TIME 28 February 2008). This allocated task reflects and builds Geldof's status as a wise man, a neutral and respected observer whose words are trusted and truthful. The media images of the magazine feature further built this status. The magazine portrayed him mingling in the streets in a white suit and a camera, as if observing the progress and compliance of Africa.

Indeed, Geldof's long career on African issues was widely celebrated. *TIME* wrote that Geldof had 'spent much of the last 25 years stressing to world leaders the importance of Africa' (*TIME* 28 February 2008). It was Bob Geldof, the BBC continued 'who helped put Ethiopia on the map' over two decades ago (BBC 10 May 2007). Also, the then World Bank President, Paul Wolfowitz, celebrated Geldof as 'an inspirational man' with a 'wide surprising breadth of knowledge and intellectual curiosity'. He continued that Geldof was a 'volcanic force of nature' who acted out 'visionary acts' (*TIME* 13 November 2006). Geldof travelled to Africa and his forceful nature became well documented in the six-part BBC series 'Geldof in Africa' (2005). This documentary, according to the BBC, supplied Geldof's 'own unique take on this extraordinary land' in 'provocative, informative, funny, poignant and endlessly entertaining ways', and brought 'the colours and contradictions of Africa to life' (BBC 23 May 2006).

Wearing khaki trousers, a Havana hat and sunglasses, as if following the trajectory of the great nineteenth-century British explorers, Geldof was shown to be riding in buses, planes and trains through Africa, sleeping in rough lodgings and experiencing his physical and mental limits. In an interview with the BBC, Geldof argued that his TV series was 'not a promo clip for Africa [but] an attempt to explore it the way Africans see it themselves' (BBC 10 June 2005). Putting himself in the shoes of the Africans, becoming their eyes, Geldof was, however, not only seeing and reporting Africa, but as a Discoverer, he was forging an identity that combined courage, curiosity and undoubtable white knowledge over Africa.

Geldof's personal relationships with and access to politicians were widely reported in the media (e.g. BBC 26 February 2004; BBC 27 February 2004a; BBC 27 February 2004b, BBC 11 March 2005). In these stories, Geldof was seen specifically as a man on a mission to be completed at any cost, even if it meant battling political demons. The *Daily Telegraph* reported his willingness to 'take it up with the devil on his left and the devil on his right if it would help Africa' (*Telegraph* 9 June 2007). His actions, according to the BBC were 'passionate and groundbreaking', giving his words 'the same weight – if not more – as big name politicians from Clare Short up to Tony Blair' (BBC 2 July 2002). This knowledge and a fearless attitude can be seen to culminate in Geldof's answer to President Bush, who questioned the 'international best selling' status of his 'Geldof in Africa' book. *TIME* reported Geldof's confident and attacking words back to the President: 'That's right. It's called marketing. Something you obviously have no clue about or else I wouldn't have to be here telling people your Africa story' (*TIME* 28 February 2008).

Once more the images attached to the news stories consolidated Geldof's presence, uniqueness and authority. Photographs of Tony Blair listening seriously to Geldof's speech in the United Nations (BBC 16 September 2005), Geldof sitting at a dinner table with President Bush, Secretary of State Condoleezza Rice and members of the Peace Corps, and President Bush explaining America's African strategy to him on board Air Force One (*TIME* 28 February 2008), emphasized further a story of an independent man on the political frontline who was listening to, and was listened to by politicians. Read together, the photographs conveyed further an image of the knowing and acting West, constantly planning, observing, watching and grading Africa's progress in the present and the near future.

Bono: Passionate Revolutionary

In articles on Bono's humanitarian efforts, he was viewed through two interlocking discourses that overlap with the discourses of Geldof the Judge and the Discoverer. This is not surprising, taking into consideration the nature of their humanitarian activities as well as their background. However, when it comes to Bono, new characteristics emerged, which broke the historical and repetitive narrations of knowing (western) subjectivity in Africa and added new global superhuman aspects into it. These were the discourses of Bono the Superman and the Revolutionary.

When the media depicted Geldof as someone from within this world, Bono was depicted as someone from without. *TIME* wrote that he was more 'like Superman turning into

Clark Kent' (*TIME* 4 March 2002a) than vice versa, as if he was in reality a superhuman in the guise of a human. The published images of Bono intensified this perception. On *TIME*'s cover Bono was pictured looking seriously straight in the eyes of the reader/viewer, alone, afloat in a space of emptiness. His superhumanity was apparent in the cover title, which asked if Bono 'can save the world'. This otherworldness became further advocated when Bono, along with Bill and Melinda Gates, was chosen as *TIME*'s Person of the Year in 2005. *TIME* wrote that it was for such extraordinary and dignified achievements as 'for being shrewd about doing good, for rewiring politics and re-engineering justice, for making mercy smarter and hope strategic and then daring the rest of us to follow' (*TIME* 19 December 2005). Bono was in a league of his own. Having 'no rivals', he had 'transform(ed) himself into the most secular of saints', *TIME* concluded (*TIME* 4 March 2002a).

As with Geldof, the wealthy and extravagant lifestyle of Bono the rock star was often sidelined and, instead, his phenomenal moral strength was the object of awe and applause. He came through as a man of simplicity, sincerity, and rare abilities, and a persuasive voice of influence. According to *TIME*, Bono was as 'a modern day Samaritan' continuing that 'such is the nature of Bono's fame that just about everyone in the world want(ed) to meet him' (*TIME* 19 December 2005). However, whereas for Geldof it was related to his dealings with politicians, for Bono it was more in the context of action and rationality over dreaming. His arguments were 'pragmatic, not preachy' [...] 'refrain(ing) him from treating Africa as an emotional issue' (*TIME* 4 March 2005a). *TIME* continued: 'Bono knows he has to make the case for aid with his head, not his heart'.

In the Person of the Year article, his alliance with the Gates was portrayed as 'unlikely, unsentimental, hard nosed, clear eyed and dead set on driving poverty into history' (*TIME* 19 December 2005). His conviction and sureness on his African mission are reported to be so convincing that 'it took about three minutes with Bono for Gates to change his mind'. The BBC reported that he had an 'ability to secure an audience with world leaders' [...] 'with the ear of Tony Blair, Gordon Brown, George Bush (BBC 23 December 2006). Leading with his words and by example, the BBC wrote, Bono was 'the man of mission' (BBC 22 May 2002), 'a televangelist persona who talks with righteously candid words about global justice for Africa' (BBC 23 December 2006).

However, Bono was neither a monk nor an ascetic: he was also a man of enjoyment and high life who was reported to like his fine wines and modern art and enjoying the world of the rich and famous in celebrity hotspots (*Daily Telegraph* 4 January 2008). However, this discourse on the hedonistic Bono was scarce and emerged usually outside the African context. If it did emerge, the humanitarian Bono took prominence. For example, *TIME* wrote that although rock stars are normally 'designed to be shiny, shallow creatures, furloughed from reality for all time', Bono was a 'busy capitalist' who moved 'in political circles like a very charming shark' (*TIME* 19 December 2005).

The scale force of Bono's activities made him a Superman, but the nature and depth of change achieved was deemed revolutionary. The BBC reported on how he had made modern history through the Make Poverty History Campaign by influencing the G8 summit to 'take big steps' for humanity (BBC 31 December 2005). Not only the changes he had succeeded in bringing about, but his whole persona were seen to be revolutionary. Bono's appearances in a number of photographs also transmitted this image, specifically when wearing the green cap and army jacket that recalls Che Guevara. The connection to Guevara, and hence guerrilla warfare, became reflected on Bono's body, metaphorically paralleling it to his struggle against the suffering or even oppression of Africa. As Che, Bono referred widely in his speeches to injustice, oppression, poverty, hunger and disease. However, Bono was 'not an advocate of pity or charity, but [of] passion and hope' (*TIME* 19 December 2005). Charity, as *TIME* argued in its article on Bono and Gates, was 'not the model for the current crusaders or the message for these extraordinary times' (*TIME* 19 December 2005). Nor was Bono rebelling against the world capitalist system. Rather, he was 'a right man on a right time' (4 March 2002b), realizing his revolution from within the system as a business venture, rather than with 'misty-eyed or bleeding- heart helping emotionalism' (*Daily Telegraph* 27 January 2006).

As a revolutionary prophet, Bono understood the situation in Africa and saw the future to come. The BBC reported that his 'mission' in Africa was aimed to 'show that development aid could work effectively' (BBC 22 May 2002). On 'BBC Radio 4', Bono spoke about his vision of a Marshall Plan for Africa that would 'liberate' and 'build' Africa, a comment that also held connotations about the rebuilding of the continent from the remains of colonialism, against the enemies of the West (BBC Radio 4, 9 September 2003). Linking contemporary fight against poverty in Africa to western experiences and memories of WWII, he called for 'a fight against world poverty as noble as the previous generations battle against Nazis during WW2' (BBC 29 September 2004). This action for Africa, Bono argued, would bring 'effective' and 'enduring' results as well as provide 'grace' for the West by making people 'feel proud for generations' to come (*TIME* 4 March 2002a).

This man, who was reported to be 'spiritual, gentle, inspired and inspiring acts of grace' (*TIME* 13 November 2006), warned the people in the West on the possible catastrophe which loomed in Africa. As with the Marshall plan, which during the Cold War worked 'against sovietism', today 'rebuilding Africa' would act 'as the bow-work against extremism', something that Bono called the 'Hot War' (BBC Radio 4, 9 September 2003). According to Bono there were 'potentially another 10 Afghanistans in Africa', making Africa's poverty a 'financial and security issue' for the West (*TIME* 4 March 2002a). In the BBC he argued,

in these distressing and disturbing times, surely it is cheaper, and smarter, to make friends out of potential enemies than it is to defend yourself against them [...] Africa is not the frontline in the War on Terror, but it could be soon. Justice is the surest way to get to peace. (BBC 31 September 2004)

Conclusions: The Cultural Politics of Celebrity Humanitarianism

The discourses on Bono and Geldof not only shed light on the different ways in which political agency is distributed and allowed among different subjects, but also are informative of a broader construction of North–South world relations. Through words and images, Bono and Geldof became portrayed as charismatic authorities – norm setters, teachers, truth-tellers and preachers – men who with grace, knowledge and independence were reported to guide the world forward to a rightful and compulsory fight against poverty in Africa.[3] As the ideals of cosmopolitan humanitarian individuals – altruistic, self-sacrificing, apolitical world citizens – they were described to be on a historical 'crusade' and 'mission' to promote equality and empathy for Africans, who were outside the processes of development, progress, peace and human security of the North.

These discourses not only frame humanitarianism specifically as a western activity, but also through them Africa emerges as an unwordly continent void of intelligence, will or capability to take care of itself. For Geldof, Africa was 'the great wound of the 21st Century' (BBC 31 May 2005b). Alongside Bono, this pain was closely linked to western memories of the unimaginable horrors of the Nazi Holocaust. As unimaginable horror, Africa became an injury – bodily disfigurement – which called for the West's corrective restoration. Healing the maimed Africa became a western parental responsibility, and failure to do so would reflect badly not only on the West, but also have an adverse affect on the well-being of the entire family – the world.

The cultural specificities of nations change over time. Alongside them are also transformed the national artefacts, which form imaginations and national self-understandings (Hayward 2000: 81–94) – collective memories of the glorious past, constructed by selective insomnias. Inasmuch as the history of nationhood has required these continious scriptings, symbolic conversions and cultural performances (Shapiro 2004). Today the global liberal order, of which humanity is a central part, also needs cultural management and legitimation. A wide range of liberal governance's keywords, such as 'freedom' and 'justice', feature consistently in Bono's and Geldof's speeches, as do the current development policy's buzzwords of 'transformation' 'participation', 'good governance' and 'empowerment' (Cornwall and Brock 2005). Furthermore, their criticism of the morality and legitimacy of the existing western trade arrangements and policies towards Africa implies that only through trade and economic development will Africa be able to break free from poverty. As Geldof argues: 'aid is not the answer', (t)he continent of Africa and its people must trade its way into the global market and sit where it rightfully belongs, negotiating as equals with the rest of us' (*Independent* 16 May 2006). These commonsensical calls towards societal reconstruction, backed up by narrations of moral responsibilities for governments, and NGOs alongside societies, to work together so as to construct global economic governance and achieve a more just, democratic and equal world, are not apolitical acts. Rather, they can be seen as the cultural part of the ways in which the power and authority of northern governments are put on use to reassert their authority along a North–South axis (Duffield 2001: 8).

Collective memories of the glorious past and visions of triumphant futures are a crucial part of these constructions. In Geldof's and Bono's humanitarian discourses, saving Africa through western humanitarian aid became an act of justice, fairness and intelligence. As an ethical action, it aimed to transform the lives of millions of people in Africa: to help the unfortunate poor to survive, to give African children a future through basic education, and to provide HIV-antiviral drugs for the affected.

In these discourses, the West was articulated as an actor who did not have any economic, strategic or political interests in Africa. On the contrary, its interest in African issues was too insignificant, as both Geldof and Bono argued. As a consequence, celebrity criticism turns, almost paradoxically, into a call for increasing western action in Africa. By repeating the old narratives from the western past in the African context – the heroic actions of the British and Americans ending WW2 and taking action against the Holocaust – Africa became framed as a specifically western destiny and calling. The role to build and maintain world order was assigned to the westerners who, with their knowledge, assets and high morals, became the natural leaders in world politics. Consequently, other countries such as China, which has been increasingly active in Africa, as well as other influences coming outside the western hemisphere, most notably Islam, became framed as a danger to this western moral hegemony in Africa.

Bono's and Geldof's fine moral arguments and framings carry a considerable normative power and lend legitimacy to western actions and actors over Africa. As a result, these celebrity discourses, rather, end up repeating and maintaining western authority over Africa, than radically opening up new ways for Africa to be or become. Nowhere to be seen or heard in these celebrated humanitarian stories are any accounts of African refugees who arrive at European shores alive, only to be taken into refugee camps before they are expedited back.

The role of the UK and the US, as the world's leading arms traders in Africa's 'burning landscapes' or 'holocausts', also went amiss. These immoral and less glamorous stories of western actions and interests were not part of these celebrity humanitarians history writing and truth games. A vast silence covers a number of issues that would somewhat question the role of the West as a rightful, neutral and heroic actor in global politics.

There are many 'truthful' worlds to be made out of words and images of Africa. As Jutta Weldes has argued, the reproduction of commonsensical notions about international relations and policies cannot be restricted to the representational practices of state actors or other political elites alone (Weldes 1999: 133). How celebrity humanitarians police, maintain, produce or break the borders of political imagination through their humanitarian performances is also a crucial task for political scientists to take. Doing so, these mediations might open critical insights on how western power and authority is (re)produced in the current war on the hearts and minds where culture, the media and the globalized humanitarian imaginaries form their key battlegrounds.

References

Aaltola, M. (2009), *Western Spectacle of Governance and the Emergence of Humanitarian World Politics,* New York: Palgrave Macmillan.

Adorno, T. and Horkheimer, M. (2002), *Dialectic of Enlightenment,* Stanford: Stanford University Press.

Ahmed, S. (2004), *The Cultural Politics of Emotion,* Edinburgh: Edinburgh University Press.

Barnett, M. and Weiss, T. G. (2008), *Humanitarinaism in Question,* New York: Cornell University Press.

Beck, U. (2001), 'Living your Own Life in a Runaway World: Individualisation, Globalisation and Politics', in W. Hutton and A. Giddens (eds), *On the Edge,* Cambridge: Polity Press, pp. 164–75.

Bhabha, H.K. (1994), *The Location of Culture,* New York: Routledge.

Brantlinger, P. (1986), 'Victorians and Africans: The Genealogy of the Myth of the Dark Continent', in H. Gates (ed.), *Race, Writing and Difference,* Chicago: Chicago University Press, pp. 185–222.

Braudy, L. (1997), *The Frency and Renown,* New York: Vintage Books.

Corner, J. and Pels, D. (eds) (2003), *Media and the Restyling of Politics: Consumerism, Celebrity and Cynicism,* London: Sage.

Cornwall, A. and Brock, K. (2005), *Beyond Buzzwords,* Geneva: United Nations Research Institute for Social Development.

Coombes, A. (1994), *Reinventing Africa: Museums, Material Culture, and Popular Imagination in Late Victorian and Edwardian England,* New Haven: Yale University Press.

Cooper, F. A. (2008), *Celebrity Diplomacy,* London: Paradigm Publishers: Boulder.

Dieter, H. and Kumar, R. (2008), 'The Downside of Celebrity Diplomacy: The Neglected Complexity of Development', *Global Governance,* 14:3, pp. 259–64.

Douzinas, C. (2007), 'The Many Faces of Humanitarianism', *Parrhesia,* No. 2, pp. 1–28.

Duffield, M. (2001), *Global Governance and the New Wars. The Merging of Development and Security,* London & New York: Zed Books.

Dyer, R. (1998), *Stars,* London: British Film Institute.

—— (2004), *Heavenly Bodies. Film Stars and Society,* London: Routledge.

Foucault, M. (1982), *This is Not a Pipe,* Berkley and London: University of California Press.

—— (2001), *Fearless Speech,* Los Angeles: Semiotext(e).

Hall, C. (ed.) (2000), *Cultures of Empire,* Manchester: Manchester University Press.

Hayward, S. (2000), 'Framing National Cinema', in M. Hjort and S. MacKenzie (eds), *Cinema and Nation,* Oxon: Routledge, pp. 81–94.

Kellner, D. (2003), *Media Spectacle,* London and New York: Routledge.

Landau, P. and Kaspin, D. (eds) (2002), *Images & Empire,* Berkley: University of California Press.

Louw, Eric (2005), The Media and Political Process, London: Sage.

Marshall, P. D. (1997), *Celebrity and Power. Fame in Contemporary Culture,* Minneapolis: University of Minnesota Press.

—— (ed.) (2006), *The Celebrity Culture Reader,* New York and London: Routledge.

Mayer, R. (2002), *Artificial Africas: Colonial Images in the Times of Globalization,* Hanover and London: University Press of New England.

MacKenzie, J. (1984), *Propaganda and Empire,* Manchester and New York: Manchester University Press.

Moyo, D. (2009), *Dead Aid,* New York: Farrar, stras and Giroux.

Oliver, T. (2001), 'Techniques of Abstraction', *Millenium* 30:3, pp. 555–570.

Oxfam (2005), 'Make Poverty History Survey', http://www.oxfam.org.uk/generationwhy/blog/2005/12/survey-make-poverty-history-has.html. Accessed on 10 December 2005

—— (2006), 'Britons say they can do better than politicians in the fight against poverty. Oxfam press release', http://www.oxfam.org.uk/press/releases/iminpollresults_110506.htm. Accessed 18 July 2006.

Pratt, M. L. (1992), *Imperial Eyes,* New York: Routledge.

Pieterse, J. (1995), *White on Black: Images of Africa and Blacks in Western Popular Culture*, New Haven and London: Yale University Press.

Richey, L. A. and Ponte, S. (2008), 'Better (Red)™ than Dead? Celebrities, consumption and international aid', *Third World Quarterly*, 29:4, pp. 711–29.

Rojek, C. (2001), *Celebrity,* London: Reaktion Books.

Said, E. (1994), *Culture and Imperialism,* London: Random House.

Schmitt, C. (1985), *Political Theology*, Chicago: University of Chicago Press.

Shapiro, M. (1999), *Cinematic Political Through: Narrating Race, Nation and Gender*, Edinburg: Edinburg University Press.

—— (2004), *Methods and Nations*, New York and London: Routledge.

—— (2009), *Cinematic Geopolitics*, Abingdon: Routledge.

Shepherd, L. (2006), 'Veiled References. Constructions of Gender in the Bush Administration Discourse on the Attacks on Afghanistan post-9/11', *International Feminist Journal of Politics*, 8:1, pp. 19–41.

Street, J. (2001), *Mass Media, Politics and Democracy*, Hampshire: Palgrave.

—— (2002), 'Bob, Bono and Tony B: the popular artist as politician', *Media, Culture and Society*, 24:3, pp. 433–41.

—— (2003), 'The Celebrity Politician: Political Style and Popular Culture', in Corner John and Pels Dick (eds), *Media and the Restyling of Politics: Consumerism, Celebrity and Cynicism,* London: Sage, pp. 85–98.

—— (2004), 'Celebrity Politicians: Popular Culture and Political Representation', *British Journal of Politics & International Relations*, 6:4, pp. 435–452.

Turner, G. (2004), *Understanding Celebrity*, London: Sage.

Van Zoonen, L. (2005), *Entertaining the Citizen – When Politics and Popular Culture Converge*, Oxford: Rowman & Littlefield Publishers.

Weldes, J. (1999), 'Going Cultural: Star Trek, state Action, and Popular Culture', *Millenium*, 28:1, pp. 117–134.

Yrjölä, R. (2008), 'Pehmeitä kuvia ja kovia sanoja: Afrikkaa tuottamassa ja purkaamassa', *Politiikka*, 50:4, pp. 279–92.

'BBC News' (including BBC Audio & Video archives)

'Bono begins African mission', 22 May 2002

'Geldof's political power', 2 July 2002

'Bono hails Bush's Aids funding', 29 January 2003

'Campaigners welcome US Aids Plan', 28 May 2003

'Bob Geldof: ragged-trousered pragmatist', 4 June 2003

'Problems without Passports – Bono Interview', BBC Radio Four, 9 September 2003

'Blair launches Africa commission', 26 February 2004

'Geldof backs African commission', 27 February 2004

'Blair unveils 'Africa action-plan', 27 February 2004

'Get real' on Africa, urges Bono', 29 September 2004
'Bono pushes the right buttons', 31 September 2004
'Geldof positive on Africa talks', 7 October 2004
'Blair and Geldof unveil Africa report', 11 March 2005
'Geldof sets out global poverty goals', 31 May 2005a
'Geldof cast as Mr Bloody Africa', 31 May 2005b
'Bob Geldof on the sofa with Jonathan Ross', 10 June 2005
'Poverty Campign was a big step', 31 December 2005
'Geldof in Africa from BBC Audiobooks', 23 May 2006
'Geldof pushes G8 on aid to Africa', 29 June 2006
'Geldof thoughts on G8 promises', 30 June 2006
'Bob Geldof answers your questions', 13 July 2006
'Geldof on Blair and Brown', 27 September 2006
'Voice of influential U2 frontman', 23 December 2006
'Bob Geldof speaks two years after the G8 Gleneagles', 11 March 2007
'Geldof attacks European leaders', 10 March 2007
'Blair passes on his African vision', 10 May 2007
'Geldof: G8 summit a farce', 8 July 2007.
'Geldof unveils African trade plan', 30 November 2007
'Geldof on G8 commitment to aid', 9 July 2008

TIME magazine
'Bono's Mission', 04 March 2002a
'Right Man, Right TIME', 04 March 2002b
'The Good Samaritans', 19 December 2005
'Bono & Bob Geldof', 13 November 2006
'Geldof and Bush: Diary from the Road', 28 February 2008

The Daily Telegraph (London)
'Bob & Bono's excellent adventure', 02 July 2005
'Bono marketing his Red badge of virtue', 27 January 2006
'Portrait of Blair as a worn down global hobnobber', 21 February 2007
'A chorus of anger, but Geldof and Bono will be back', 9 June 2007
'When our politicians go pop', 14 July 2007
'Hooking up', 4 January 2008
'Is Davos our last resort?', 20 January 2008a
'WHO'S OFF PISTE?', 20 January 2008b

Other
'Celebrity Advocacy for the New Millennium'. UN Chronicle, 27 June 2002
'Bob Geldof: Aid isn't the answer. Africa must be allowed to trade its way out of poverty'. The
    Independent, 16 May 2006.

Notes

1. *The Daily Telegraph* is the leading morning paper in the UK with an average daily circulation of 857,871 copies and 'BBC News' service (www.bbc.co.uk) is the nations leading web-news service measured by page traffic (sources: ABC UK Jan–June 2008; Alexa).
2. For more elaborate analysis on these discourses' gendered and raced implications, see Yrjölä and Repo (in press), 'The Gender Politics of Celebrity Humanitarianism in Africa' *International Feminist Journal of Politics* (IFJP) (Accepted for publication September 2009).
3. This does not mean that Bono and Geldof were celebrated without any criticism in the media. Their close relationships with western politicians did invoke it, but this criticism tended to target the efforts by politicians to build themselves a favourable and 'cool' media image through their association with Bono and Geldof. See for example: *The Sunday Telegraph*, 20 January 2008a; *The Telegraph*, 20 January 2008b; *The Daily Telegraph* 14 July 2007; *The Daily Telegraph* 21 February 2007.

Chapter 10

Madonna's Adoptions: Celebrity Activism, Justice and Civil Society in the Global South

Graham Finlay

Introduction

The American-born international celebrity Madonna has embarked upon three adoptions in Malawi: her adoption of David Banda, which was finalized on 28 May 2008; her attempt to adopt Chifundo 'Mercy' James, rejected by a Malawian judge in April, 2009 and granted by the Malawian Supreme Court of Appeal on 12 June 2009; and, finally, her adoption of Malawi itself, through the charity she co-founded, 'Raising Malawi'. The adoptions of the two children were vigorously contested by a coalition of Malawian Human Rights NGOs, the Human Rights Consultative Committee (HRCC), although the HRCC has not contested the larger initiative.

All three adoptions are intricately linked with each other and with Madonna's celebrity. In the course of making her documentary, *I Am Because We Are*, which describes the efforts of 'Raising Malawi', Madonna met David Banda and decided to adopt him. Even before she had been to Malawi, Madonna had seen both David Banda and, allegedly, Mercy James on video from the film and another video shot by her then husband, film director Guy Ritchie, respectively. It has been claimed that Madonna decided to adopt Mercy James first, but difficulties with adopting her due to resistance from her extended family led to David Banda's adoption instead. This eventually succeeded, despite a challenge from the HRCC and some resistance from David Banda's father, Yohane Banda, who was said to be confused about what Madonna's adoption of David meant. Madonna persisted, however, in her adoption of Mercy, at least partly to counter allegations by the HRCC that her adoption of David Banda separated him from his Malawian culture (Peretti 2009).[1] In the end, it was her activism on behalf of Malawian orphans that allowed her to win her appeal and to adopt Mercy James.[2]

The intertwining of Madonna's personal and family life and her celebrity activism is no coincidence. Celebrities' power to attract attention and donations relies, in no small degree, on the blurring of the distinction between their personal and public lives, since the strong identifications consumers of celebrity culture have with celebrities do not respect this distinction. Similarly, Raising Malawi and the related film mix Madonna's personal history, her corporate brand and personal religious beliefs with the humanitarian work of the charity.

Madonna's adoptions raise a number of ethical issues surrounding the role of celebrities in the Global South and the role of 'civil society' in both humanitarian development by northern NGOs and in the Global South itself. One problem *is a problem of justice*: Madonna's attempts to adopt David Banda and Mercy James and her humanitarian work in Malawi, all raise ethical questions about individual responsibility to alleviate global poverty, what actions produce the best outcomes, and what distributive effects those actions have.

The second problem *is one of democracy*: celebrities, particularly in their roles as freelance activists, have been accused of undermining democracy because of their lack of democratic legitimacy and accountability and because they distract from the details of the issues involved.[3] This democratic problem becomes more acute when we consider celebrity activism on behalf of the poor citizens of another polity or polities.

In this chapter, I will evaluate these charges against celebrity activism from the point of view of both democratic theory and international distributive justice. Despite democratic concerns about the role of unelected NGOs and civil society networks themselves, I conclude that the benefits of Madonna's adoption of Malawi – and the benefits to David Banda and Mercy James from Madonna's adoption of them – are complicated by the need for the recipients of aid to determine the conditions under which it is received and by the importance of any celebrity intervention to respect the appropriate process for determining people's needs and the rule of law. When there are other ways of engaging in humanitarian action that avoid the problems of the model of celebrity activism that Madonna has chosen, there is a moral obligation on celebrities who sincerely want to improve the conditions of poor people in other countries to choose that alternative approach.

Raising Malawi

Madonna is one of the world's richest and most recognizable celebrities. In *Forbes Magazine*'s 2009 list of the world's most powerful celebrities, Madonna ranked number 3, after Angelina Jolie and Oprah Winfrey. The same list estimates her earnings for the previous year at $110 million (Forbes 2009). She is also an important businesswoman, having run her own record label, Maverick, between 1992 and 2004, as well as having significant real estate interests and her own line of clothing for H&M (Norman 2007).

In *I Am Because We Are* (Rissman 2008), Madonna credits her interest in Malawi to a telephone call from Victoria Keelan, a Malawian businesswoman who is also active in several NGOs. Having contacted Madonna through the 'Spirituality for Kids' programme of the Los Angeles Kabbalah Centre, with which Madonna is strongly identified, Keelan told her about the plight of AIDS orphans in Malawi, who number one million of Malawi's population of twelve million. As Madonna recounts in the film, Keelan chose her because of her celebrity, saying to her: 'You're a person with resources. People pay attention to what you say and do' (Rissman 2008).

Even before visiting Malawi or Africa, Madonna created Raising Malawi with the Kabbalah Centre's Co-Director Michael Berg and his wife, Monica, and promised to raise three million dollars for Malawian orphans and poverty relief, working with local NGOs and the UN's Millennium Village project (Luscombe 2006). She also began *I Am Because We Are* (Rissman 2008) as a documentary about her efforts in Malawi, using one million dollars of her own money. The film, 'written and produced by Madonna' and directed by her former gardener, Nathan Rissman, was shown at various film festivals, on Time Warner Cable and the Sundance Channel and photographs of children featured in the film have appeared in *Time* and in the book of the film. In March 2009, Madonna made the entire film available on www.youtube.com and www.Hulu.com.

Since 2006, 'Raising Malawi' claims to have helped many thousand children and adults through their health, education, hunger, poverty, psychosocial, capacity-building and awareness initiatives. The actual expenditure is difficult to establish and has been questioned by some of Madonna and Kabbalah's critics, most pointedly by *Fox News* (Friedman 2009). In particular, *Fox News* questions whether the $3.7 million generated by a controversial fundraising event involving 'Raising Malawi', UNICEF and Gucci at the United Nations – which also promoted Gucci's new flagship store in New York – money which was to be divided between 'Raising Malawi' and UNICEF, went to either of the charities. 'Raising Malawi' performs much of its work through other northern-led initiatives, like the Clinton Global Initiative and Jeffrey Sachs's Millennium Village project – both Bill Clinton and Jeffrey Sachs appear in *I Am Because We Are* along with development 'celebrities', Desmond Tutu and Paul Farmer – and through cooperation with both local and northern-sponsored local institutions like the Mchinji District Government Hospital, the Harvard College of Dental Medicine and the Kindle Orphan Care Clinic. It also has particular institutions that it especially devotes its resources to including the Home of Hope Orphanage, Consol Homes Orphan Care and the projected Raising Malawi Academy for Girls. It is these latter institutions that feature most prominently in *I Am Because We Are*.

Madonna's approach to development in both 'Raising Malawi' and *I Am Because We Are,* (Rissman 2008) is remarkably personal. She discusses her own mother's death when she was six.[4] As a result, she thinks she 'has a connection to children who lose their parents' (Rissman 2008). She makes a deal with one child, Fanizo, that if he studies hard, she will send him to a private school and they 'shake on it'. Most important, she meets David Banda. His mother died giving birth and his siblings are also all dead. Madonna says, 'No one knew where his father was'. On Madonna's return trip she finds David very sick with both pneumonia and malaria. Given the inability of the Home of Hope Orphanage to treat his diseases, she asks, 'What was I prepared to do? If I was challenging people to open up their minds and their hearts, then I had to be willing to stand at the front of the line' (Rissman 2008). Madonna decides to adopt him and although pictures of a happy David are shown during the credits, no further mention of the adoption saga is made in the film. Sonia Sachs, a public health academic and coordinator with the Millenium Villages project – and wife of Jeffrey Sachs – has said that David would have died of his illnesses the first night he spent with Madonna, if she and Sonia Sachs had not rushed him to a private clinic (Luce 2009). The children in the orphanage are shown reading Madonna's English Roses books, which feature London schoolgirls (Rissman 2008). Since the film was made, the books' main illustrator has joined Raising Malawi, along with Madonna's personal trainer, Tracy Anderson. The Raising Malawi website also ran a blog by Madonna's 'oxygen facialist', Michelle Peck (Peck 2009).

Madonna's influence is also felt in the development approach of the film and charity. The developmental argument of *I Am Because We Are* (Rissman 2008) is that food, medicine and improved agricultural practices are not enough. Madonna says, near the beginning of the film, 'We can raise awareness. We can build orphanages. We can make medicine more accessible. And we can help diversify their crops. These things are essential. But are they enough? This is a story about Malawi, but perhaps it's a story about all of us. As technology brings us together, we seem to be a world spinning out of control' (Rissman 2008). Much of the film and a significant part of the programme of 'Raising Malawi' involves 'Spirituality for Kids' (now 'Success for Kids') the Kabbalah Centre's teaching of what the film calls 'universal concepts', including 'cause and effect', 'resiliency' and 'believing in yourself' (Rissman 2008).

Although not the largest component of Raising Malawi's work, in terms of numbers of children involved, the Spirituality for Kids programme (SfK) is Raising Malawi's 'psychosocial initiative'.[5] The curriculum of SfK is tightly controlled by the Kabbalah Centre: Madonna's publicist has acknowledged that the Malawian teachers of SfK were flown to the Centre in Hollywood for training and in the film one of the teachers explains SfK's concepts wearing a t-shirt reading 'Hollywood' in gold letters (Friedman 2008; Rissman 2008).[6] A number of the northern interviewees in *I Am Because We Are* are SfK workers. One says, 'Looking at the extremes of a place like Malawi, of course it's necessary to provide basic needs for these children. No one can deny that. But the question is, is that enough, when we have a situation as extreme as here' (Dr Heath Grant, SfK in Rissman 2008).

The case for the psychosocial initiative begins with a discussion of orphans' 'spiritual needs' by Desmond Tutu, but is somewhat at odds with the view of Jeffrey Sachs, who seems to believe that providing these basic services is enough:

Sometimes people look at the situation in Africa and think it's hopeless and that it's overwhelming. But when you look at the spirit of Africans, you see not only is it not hopeless, the solutions are right there in front of us. They start with the Africans wanting to be empowered, ready to take up the challenge. They just need the tools to get themselves out of poverty. (Rissman 2008)

Paul Farmer's advocacy of community-based health care also implies that no spiritual transformation of the beneficiaries is required and that community-based initiatives create jobs and impart knowledge: 'People can be agents of change. People can be involved in improving their communities' (Rissman 2008). Like Sachs's prescription for development, however, and unlike Farmer's, Raising Malawi's programme is based on a recipience model, only it includes receiving lessons in spiritual empowerment as well as resources.[7]

The Morality of Adoption

How should we evaluate Madonna's adoptions? The adoptions of David Banda and Mercy James are the most dramatic examples of the arbitrariness of birth. Adoption by Madonna means that, in an instant, they are transported from being members of the world's very worst off to the world's very best off. In David Banda's case, the difference was between death and extreme luxury.[8] Although it is clear that Madonna's desire to adopt David Banda and Mercy James is based on a genuine love and commitment to the children, such a clear-cut material case was also made by Madonna herself, by Bono and by many other commentators in the countless newspaper articles, Internet posts and blogs devoted to the question.[9] This simple consequentialist argument invokes a well-known claim by Peter Singer: that when we can save a life without any significant sacrifice on our part, or in its stronger version, any equally significant sacrifice on our part, we should do so (Singer 1972).

The problem with such an argument as a justification for adopting David Banda and Mercy James is that it does not allow you to stop at these two adoptions. There are over 500 children in the Home of Hope Orphanage and 125 children in Mercy's Kondanani Orphanage who would equally benefit from being adopted by Madonna (Rissman 2008; Kondanani 2006). Why stop at one? Some might benefit more: Madonna has been criticized by the international NGO Save the Children for not choosing a child with a disability, for example (Campbell 2009). The same NGO has criticized her adoptions in general, saying that inter-country adoption should be a last resort. The problem is compounded, they argue, by Madonna's celebrity status:

It doesn't help to take one child out of an orphanage to a huge palace and buy them a pony. All these children who may only have one parent, or no parent, cannot be transported to Notting Hill by pop stars. Madonna's heart may be in the right place, but other mothers will look up to her and she's setting a terrible example (Campbell 2009).

Madonna herself seems to acknowledge the moral problem: 'You hold these children and you think, how can I save them all, how can I make their lives better, what is their future' (*Vanity Fair* 2007). In turn, however, Madonna uses the question of the example she is setting in her favour, arguing that the criticism she received for adopting David Banda will discourage other people from adopting the 'orphans of Africa' ('British Broadcasting Corporation' 2006). Although she cannot save all the orphans of Malawi, let alone Africa, Madonna could, with a personal fortune estimated at $490 million, save a great number of them, even if she could not bring all of them home ('CBS News' 2008).

The problem of providing parents for orphans is rendered more acute by the way that parenthood is constructed by the film. As noted above, *I Am Because We Are* emphasizes not just the material needs of the children it portrays, but also their 'psychosocial' needs. After discussing everyone's material needs, Madonna says, 'Some of us need guidance. Everyone needs parents. But what if there are no parents? And whose job is it then to look after these motherless children?' (Rissman 2008) In its portrayal of the children, the film emphasizes their plight as orphans above other worries. Adoption, then, becomes a necessary strategy to meet that need for parents.

The solution to this ethical problem proposed by both Save the Children and by Madonna's critics in Malawi, the Human Rights Consultative Committee, is an institutional one, one that privileges the children's need for access to their culture and language over their need for parents. Citing Article 20 of the Convention on the Rights of the Child (CRC), the HRCC emphasizes a sentence from paragraph 3 'When considering solutions, due regard shall be paid to the desirability of continuity in a child's upbringing and to the child's ethnic, religious, cultural and linguistic background' (Mwakasungura and Bamusi 2009; Convention on the Rights of the Child 1989). The HRCC calls on the Malawian government to honour its responsibilities to all orphans under the CRC, including provision for their basic needs, and to enforce the residence requirement of eighteen months for inter-country adoption under Malawian law, so as not to set a precedent for exceptions that might lead to trafficking in children. Finally, the HRCC turns Madonna's 'psychosocial' needs argument against her, arguing that: 'Children need to be taken care of within their communities and where their psychosocial needs are satisfied'. According to the HRCC, then, Mercy James needs to be taken care of in her community and in contact with members of her extended family (Mwakasungura and Bamusi 2009).

These cultural arguments have been urged against inter-country adoption generally (Saunders 2007; Bartholet 1993; Selman 2000).[10] Although it is impossible to do full justice to the complexity of these issues here, it should be noted that much of the demand for inter-country adoption has been produced by laws or policies that prevent parents from adopting children of another race in their own countries, most particularly the United States. This was altered in the United States by the 1994 Multiethnic Placement Act (Bartholet 2007). The link between the claim that the most important priority in the care for a child is that the child be raised by its own 'race', and the claim that it should be raised in its own culture, shows just how problematic such claims are. When we are deciding priorities, clearly basic needs come first: 'due regard' to ethnic, linguistic and cultural claims need not mean 'absolute regard'. This is the argument that was used in the decision of the Supreme Court of Appeal, which carefully examined both the interpretation of the CRC and of the relevant international precedents (In Re: CJ A Female Infant 2009: 9–15, 23–25). Leaving a child in the care of a Malawian orphanage does allow the children in question to be raised within their Malawian culture. The question is: how does this relate to the provision for their other needs? Similar arguments based on the stark difference between provision for the children's basic needs and other, more speculative, potential harms might be made against other criticisms of Madonna's adoption of Mercy James, like her ongoing divorce and future status as a single parent.

The argument that the Malawian government is using Madonna's adoptions as a way of avoiding its responsibilities to these two children has some merit. The duty to fulfil the orphans' rights to have their basic needs met falls first on the Malawian state. In the case of Malawi, however, the state seems genuinely unable to meet those needs and the reason is not that it is particularly corrupt or uninterested in doing so, but because it is poor. Malawi ranks 160 out of 182 on the latest United Nations Development Programme Human Development Index, with a GDP per capita of 761 US Purchasing Power Parity (PPP) dollars (United Nations Development Programme 2009). After the end of the dictatorship of Hastings Kamazu Banda in 1993, Malawi has become a multi-party democracy, with a relatively free press and an anti-corruption campaign that has had some effect, although accusations of partisanship have been made.[11] Malawi ranks 115 out of 180 countries on Transparency International's Corruption Perceptions Index for 2008. As Onora O'Neill argues, when states that are the 'primary agents' of securing justice for and the fulfilment of the human rights of their populations cannot do so, the obligation falls on organizations – and we could, using Singer's argument, extend this to individuals – that can (O'Neill 2004: 254–255).

The best case against Madonna's adoption made by the HRCC is one based on the process of adoption and respect for Malawi's adoption policies and laws. Although the 'fostering requirement' that requires an adopting parent to reside in Malawi and foster the child for at least eighteen months has been portrayed as a 'policy' and not a part of the law, the Supreme Court of Appeal treated the question of residence as a matter of Malawian adoption law (Embassy of the United States, Lilongwe, Malawi 2008). The ruling in Madonna's favour regarding Mercy James explicitly interprets the requirement as having been met by Madonna's visits to Malawi as part of her work with Raising Malawi:

> The Appellant has plans to travel to Malawi frequently with her adopted children in order to instil in them a cultural pride and knowledge of their country of origin. The Judge in the court below had evidence before her indicating that the Appellant had a project in Malawi which had noble and immediate ideas of investing in the improvement of the lives of more disadvantaged children in Malawi. It is clear from this evidence that the Appellant in this case is not a mere sojourner in this country but has a targeted long term presence aimed at ameliorating the lives of more disadvantaged children in Malawi. (In Re: CJ A Female Infant 2009: 23)

Further, the decision argues, 'It has for some time now been the law that a man may have more than one place at which he resides' (In Re: CJ A Female Infant 2009: 21). The decision notes Madonna's homes in Beverly Hills and London, and suggests that 'by her lifestyle she is herself a child of the world' (In Re: CJ A Female Infant 2009: 26).

The fostering requirement had been put in place out of concerns for child trafficking, concerns that also animate the Hague Convention on inter-country adoption of 1993. Child trafficking is a problem in Malawi, although most of the abuses are through informal in-country adoptions (Kariuki 2007).[12] The fostering period also allows relatives of the child in question to assert their rights to custody, important in a country in which children are often temporarily placed in an orphanage while their families are unable to care for them and in which kinship relations and extended family are particularly important (Peretti 2009). In the cases of David Banda and Mercy James, these rights have been waived by their current guardians, although a man claiming to be Mercy James's father continues to claim his rights, and the children have been removed from the country.

Given these important reasons for the fostering requirement, it is reasonable to ask Madonna to abide by them. While it would necessarily involve some sacrifice on her part, given the global nature of her business, compliance with the adoption policies of the Malawian government would not be impossible, nor would they keep her from all of her engagements elsewhere. The Supreme Court of Appeal's decision declared Madonna a resident in Malawi for the purposes of adoption, but did not provide for one of the chief roles of the fostering period, namely the opportunity for members of the child's extended family to assert their rights. Madonna no doubt fears the loss of control compliance which the policies entails – including vulnerability to claims by the children's relatives – and, as everyone notes, is used to having complete control over her affairs.[13]

Indeed, one hallmark of Madonna's celebrity brand has been the kind of control she exercises over its management, signing deals that involve control over all aspects of her production and promotion (Pareles 2008). In this she exemplifies the greater autonomy of modern celebrities, and, accordingly, their greater ability to speak out, noted by Daniel W. Drezner (2007). Nevertheless, the fact that she could have complied with the policies, suggests that she should have. In this way, she is less vulnerable to the charge that exceptions are being made in her case because of her superior wealth and celebrity, and the process of adoption would have been better respected. The power of her example and its effect on the institutional aspects of adoptions in Malawi, including concerns about child trafficking, also argue in favour of her respecting policies and processes that protect future children from such harms. This is despite the Supreme Court of Appeals' unwillingness to consider such hypothetical future child traffickers.[14]

> In short, because a morally superior way of adopting both David Banda and Mercy James was available – one that was more responsive to the outcome for all those affected by the decision, including Mercy James's extended family and the families of future adoptees – Madonna should have chosen it. By the consequentialist logic invoked by her defence of her adoptions, Madonna is also required to continue her humanitarian work in Malawi. How much time and resources she should devote to such work is a further question, addressed by both Peter Singer's institutional recommendations and by the large literature that has grown around his work (Singer 2009).

How she should go about her humanitarian work is a different matter. Questions about the process involved and respect for the agency of all those affected also arise regarding Madonna's developmental model in Raising Malawi. Although many urban Malawians are said to view Raising Malawi as Kabbalah's attempt to take over the country, the consequentialist defence of the adoption of the two children also applies to Malawi itself. Mercy James's uncle, Peter Baneti, claims that such criticisms of Madonna's development work are based on the contempt of the urbanites for the welfare of poor rural people. In contrast, Madonna is said to have an almost religious popularity in the rural areas of Malawi (Peretti 2009). I have already noted, above, the recipience-based view that animates Raising Malawi's conception of human beings and how their needs might be met through development. A developmental model that makes the democratic input of communities that are the targets of development central to its developmental approach is another option that was available to Madonna as a developer, but is one that has not been taken. Every aspect of Raising Malawi bears her personal stamp, including the role of the Kabbalah Centre and its Spirituality for Kids programme in the charity and in its humanitarian work.

Although Madonna is not bringing a market-based approach to her development work, she shares some characteristics with the 'philanthrocapitalists' critically examined by Michael Edwards from the point of view of civil society. Edwards notes:

> Having inherited their wealth or made it very quickly, the philanthrocapitalists are not in the mood to wait around for their results. In business, scaling-up tends to be direct (more consumers and larger markets), whereas in civil society scale tends to come through indirect strategies that change policies, regulations, values and institutions – for example, the rules within which individual producers operate in order to generate a bigger, systemic impact. (Edwards 2008: 65)

Edwards further analyses the effects of the dominance of this approach on civil society: 'In civil society, however, processes of engagement with other institutions and constituencies may be more important as a measure of impact than tangible outputs or the direct products of each organization, and impact relies on forces – like government action – that are usually out of their control' (Edwards 2008: 66). Edwards contrasts this civil society approach with individual philanthropists' desires for results.

It is not surprising that celebrities, as the *raison d'être* of celebrity activism, often take an approach to development that leaves them democratically accountable to no one. Given the extent to which Madonna and the Kabbalah centre control Raising Malawi, we can see how this charge might be levelled against Madonna's humanitarian work. This is particularly true given the state of democracy in Malawi. The country has a 'vibrant civic society' and freedom of the press has improved since the elections of 2004, when the government allowed the police to engage in extensive interference with press activities.[15] One of the most remarkable aspects of Malawian political life is the independence of the judiciary. The Freedom House report on Malawi notes: 'In general, higher courts have in recent years demonstrated substantial independence, ruling against the government in several cases that were considered politically sensitive'.[16] Indeed, the difficulties that Madonna has experienced in adopting David Banda and Mercy James stem from the independence of the judiciary and civil society groups' ability to contest those adoptions. Madonna certainly has the government's support. She has been supported throughout the adoption processes by Joyce Banda, who has recently been elected Vice President of Malawi and was previously Minister for Foreign Affairs. Joyce Banda's foundation is supported by Raising Malawi's Hunger and Nutrition Initiative (Nicholl 2009; Raising Malawi 2009b).

It might well be argued that the support of Malawi's elected government for Madonna's adoptions, notwithstanding the imperfect nature of Malawi's multi-party democracy, and the decision by the Supreme Court of Appeal lend democratic credibility to Madonna's efforts. We might also examine the democratic credentials of Madonna's civil society opponent, the HRCC – a network of 66 different civil society organizations.[17] The hearing of Madonna's appeal regarding Mercy James's adoption, led to an interesting conflict between Malawian human rights institutions. Both the Malawi Human Rights Commission, a constitutionally established, independent body that reports to parliament, who favoured the adoption, and Eye of the Child, a member of the HRCC, which opposed it, were made *amicus curiae* or friends of the court, and both made submissions on human rights and inter-country adoptions (In Re: CJ A Female Infant 2009: 26).

The HRCC is a genuine human rights network, with concerns beyond Madonna's adoptions. Nevertheless, its capacity to democratically represent the people of Malawi could be challenged. It seems to suffer from the familiar problems of civil society networks in the Global South: donor capture and problems of representation. Broadly speaking, there is a tendency for civil society networks in the Global South to switch their focus from representing their members' concerns to advocating the goals of their principal donors, who are usually institutions based in the Global North. Although the HRCC was not one of the networks studied, Rick James and Chiku Malunga have studied Malawian civil society networks and have found that such challenges characterized all the networks they did study. When a civil society network receives funding, it establishes a secretariat. The secretariat then becomes independent of the member civil society organizations and gains its own identity, but loses its representative character in the process. The secretariat becomes an 'advocacy NGO' rather than the representative of the network (James and Malunga 2006: 59). Exercising its leadership role, it then takes strong stands on issues that divide the individual members of the network (James and Malunga 2006: 51–52). Donors, especially donors focused on 'rights-based' approaches to development or advocacy, look for 'quick results' and support the network, rather than the individual civil society organizations (James and Malunga 2006: 54, 56). In this way, donors who patronize civil society organizations and networks, often share the same logic with philanthrocapitalists and many celebrity activists. Major donors to the HRCC include the Norwegian Agency for Development Cooperation (NORAD), DanChurchAid (DCA) from Denmark, and the Danish Centre for Human Rights, as well as the Danish Institute for Human Rights. The HRCC has established procedures for elections of officers to the network.[18] Regardless of these procedures, however, the HRCC can still be criticized from a more basic point of view for being insufficiently democratic. The recipients of its human rights work have not voted, and in the case of children could not have voted for the representations made on their behalf.

How do we evaluate the collision between an unelected, highly personalized charity like Raising Malawi, and an unelected, by the individual beneficiaries, civil society network?

The answer is not, I submit, to defer to the attitudes of the elected government of Malawi. The Malawian government itself seems to be suffering from donor capture in the case of Madonna and Raising Malawi. The solution, I would argue, is to press both for improvements in the representativeness of civil society organizations in networks like the HRCC, and to urge the creation of real mechanisms of participation and accountability for humanitarian charities like Raising Malawi. Hopes for the democratic role of the HRCC are warranted by the transformative potential Edwards has identified in civil society, a potential even he acknowledges requires constant attention. The need for a more democratic approach by Raising Malawi is based on the demonstrably better outcomes that occur when beneficiaries are given a meaningful say in setting development and humanitarian priorities, and in how the money raised by such charities is spent. This will allow the beneficiaries to decide on the hierarchy of needs that they prefer, and would allow Raising Malawi to respond to criticisms that its real goal is the indoctrination of poor Malawians into the beliefs of Kabbalah (Peretti 2009). Given real input, the older children, young offenders, guardians and HIV-positive parents, who are the subjects of *I Am Because We Are* and the beneficiaries of Raising Malawi, could decide for themselves how important their psychosocial needs are compared to more material needs, and what the form of those meeting those psychosocial needs should take. In the cases of both organizations, the practicalities of the state of civil society in Africa may suggest the use of kinship ties to facilitate this democratization. It is, perhaps, not too great a stretch to suggest that the lack of consideration for kinship ties in Madonna's adoptions of David Banda and Mercy James are analogous to the neglect of kinship relations by donor-centric approaches to civil society in Africa.[19] Thus, as with her adoption of the two children, there is an approach to humanitarian assistance that Madonna and her charity could have taken, which would have led to better outcomes, but that Raising Malawi has thus far failed to take.

Conclusion

Of the various possible approaches to celebrity activism, we can distinguish three. There is the individually controlled and less accountable approach, where humanitarian work is strongly identified with one celebrity's personality and brand. This is the one chosen by Madonna, Bono and Bob Geldof, among others. There is also a more multilateral approach, which involves working through established international institutions that preceded the celebrity's own initiative and have their own mechanisms of accountability, like the United Nations High Commission for Refugees or the Red Cross. This is the approach taken by Angelina Jolie and all the other, less well-known, UN goodwill ambassadors. Finally, we can imagine an approach to celebrity activism that embraces participatory development and lets the people who are supposed to benefit from development and humanitarian actions set their own priorities and define their own understanding of development. This latter approach, with all its complexities and difficulties, has not been pursued, to my knowledge, by any internationally well-known celebrity activist except, perhaps, by Natalie Portman's championing of microfinance as an 'Ambassador of Hope' for the Foundation for International Community Assistance (FINCA) (Traub 2008). Nevertheless, I argue that the superior outcomes and regard for the democratic process of development, despite any losses of efficiency that may occur, suggest that this is the approach that celebrity activists in these areas are morally obliged to take. It might be asked whether celebrity activism, with its emphasis on 'charismatic leadership' is essentially incompatible with such an approach.[20] There are reasons to suspect this. Celebrities are effective because of whatever aspect of their lives resonates with a wide public. Often this depends on the force of their personalities and the strength of their convictions, forcefully expressed. Nevertheless, if those convictions include a strong commitment to democracy and to seeing poor people as people, as agents capable of deciding how to live their own lives, then the power of celebrity can be effectively harnessed to more complex development projects. After all, the international media will pay as much attention to Madonna sitting down in dialogue with the beneficiaries of Raising Malawi as it will to her writing cheques for orphans' education or for her adoption of individual African children. It was the contested nature of these adoptions that generated the immense international coverage of the two cases, not the fact of the adoptions themselves. We need only contrast the proportions of coverage devoted to another celebrity adopter, Angelina Jolie, where her adoptions from Cambodia, Ethiopia and Vietnam have taken a back seat to her Goodwill Ambassador role and her participation in high level foreign policy fora.

Celebrity activism is increasingly important to the global dialogue about issues of humanitarian assistance, development and human rights. More and more, the work of prominent people like Madonna on such causes shapes ordinary people's understanding of their own relationship to the global poor. This is not surprising, since, as my very brief allusions to the literature on individual moral responsibility for the distant needy suggest, celebrities' greater power to act brings with it greater responsibility to do so. This is a responsibility that many celebrity activists acknowledge. In this chapter, however, I have argued that this responsibility is not simply to do something, but to do it in the right way, in a way that respects legal and democratic processes, and the agency of the people you are trying to help. But celebrity activism is not enough: it cannot replace individual, state or international action. One way in which celebrity activism would not achieve better outcomes overall would be for it to become a surrogate for action by ordinary individual citizens of the world's wealthy countries and by the wealthier citizens of poor countries, so that the fans of a particular celebrity limit themselves to vicarious participation in the celebrity's good deeds. The theory of responsibility that emerges from an examination of the role of celebrities in global causes places obligations on everyone with the power to help.

References

Bartholet, Elizabeth (1993), *Family Bonds, Adoption and the Politics of Parenting*, New York: Houghton Mifflin.

—— (2007), 'Slamming the Door on Adoption', *Washington Post*, 4 November 2007.

—— (2010), 'International Adoption: The Human Rights Position', *Global Policy*, 1:1, pp. 91–100.

British Broadcasting Corporation (2006), 'Madonna's Oprah Interview: in quotes', 25 October <http://news.bbc.co.uk/2/hi/entertainment/6085032.stm>. Accessed 15 June 2009.

Campbell, Lori (2009), 'Madonna's adoption is like a puppy parade. It's terrible', *The Sunday Mirror*, 29 March 2009.

CBS News (2008), 'How Will Madonna and Guy Split Their $$?', CBSnews.com, <http://www.cbsnews.com/stories/2008/10/16/earlyshow/main4526065.shtml>, 16 October 2008. Accessed 9 June 2009.

Clements, Jo (2009), 'Is he really my daddy, Madonna? Star takes David to meet his real father…but he doesn't recognise him', *The Daily Mail*, 1 April 2009.

Comaroff, John L. and Comaroff, Jean (1999), 'Introduction', in J. L. Comaroff and J. Comaroff (eds), *Civil Society and the Political Imagination in Africa: Critical Perspectives*, Chicago: University of Chicago Press.

Convention on the Rights of the Child (1989), <http://www.unhchr.ch/html/menu3/b/k2crc.htm>. Accessed 9 June 2009.

Dieter, Heribert and Kumar, Rajiv (2008), 'The Downside of Celebrity Diplomacy: The Neglected Complexity of Development', *Global Governance*, 14:3, pp. 259–264.

Drezner, Daniel, W. (2007), 'Foreign Policy Goes Glam', *The National Interest*, November/December.

Edwards, Michael (2008), *Just Another Emperor? The Myths and Realities of Philanthrocapitalism*, London: Dēmos: A Network for Ideas & Action, The Young Foundation.

Embassy of the United States, Lilongwe, Malawi (2008) 'Malawi and the US Commemorate National Adoption Month', <http://lilongwe.usembassy.gov/latestembassynews11113.html>. Accessed 12 June 2009.

Forbes (2009), '#3 Madonna – The 2009 Celebrity 100', Forbes.com, 6 March, http://www.forbes.com/lists/2009/53/celebrity-09_Madonna_KMJ4.html. Accessed 8 June 2009.

Friedman, Roger (2008), 'Madonna Gets Gucci $$$ for Kabbalah', FoxNews.com, <http://www.foxnews.com/story/0,2933,321228,00.html?sPage=fnc/entertainment/celebrity/madonna>. Accessed 9 June 2009.

—— (2009), 'Madonna's Missing Millions', FoxNews.com, 31 March <http://www.foxnews.com/story/0,2933,511737,00.html>. Accessed June 8 2009.

Harvard Law School (2009), Press release: 'Save the Children from Save the Children', <http://www.law.harvard.edu/faculty/bartholet/Save_the_Children2.pdf>, April, 2009. Accessed 12 June 2009.

Human Rights Consultative Committee (2006), 'Minutes of 4th Annual General Meeting, Human Rights Consultative Committee', <http://www.hrccmalawi.org/pressroom/agm%20reports/2006%20AGM%20minutes.pdf>, 2006. Accessed 13 June 2009.

—— (2009), 'Member's List', <http://www.hrccmalawi.org/hrcc%20members%20list.pdf>. Accessed 12 June 2009.

In Re: CJ A Female Infant (2009). In Re: CJ A Female Infant of C/o P.O.Box 30871, Chichiri, Blantyre 3 (Msca Adoption Appeal No. 28 of 2009) MWSC 1, 12 June. <http://www.saflii.org/_mw/cases/MWSC/2009/1.pdf>. Accessed 15 June 2009.

James, Rick and Malunga, Chiku (2006), 'Organisational challenges facing civil society networks in Malawi', *KM4D Journal*, 2:2, pp. 48–63.

Kabbalah Centre (2006), 'Raising Malawi', <http://www.youtube.com/watch?v=UoUSS1Qcwus>. Accessed 15 June 2009.

Kamons, A. (2007), 'Celebrity and Politics', *SAIS Review*, 27:1. pp. 145–146.

Kariuki, Brenda (2007), 'Stop Child Abuse campaign asks for a change at policy level', UNICEF, <http://www.unicef.org/infobycountry/malawi_40938.html>. Accessed 12 June 2009.

Khaila, Stanley (2006), 'Freedom House Country Report – Malawi', <http://www.freedomhouse.org/template.cfm?page=140&edition=7&ccrcountry=121&section=73&ccrpage=31>.Accessed 11 June 2009.

Kondanani (2006), 'Kondanani', <http://www.kondanani.com/index-uk.html>. Accessed 15 June 2009.

Luce, Jim (2009), 'Madonna, Africa and Child Mortality', huffingtonpost.com, 15 May.

Luscombe, Belinda (2006), 'Madonna Finds a Cause', *Time*, 6 August.

Maina, Wachira (1998), 'Kenya: The State, Donors and the Politics of Democratization', in A. Van Rooy (ed.), *Civil Society and the Aid Industry*, London: Earthscan.

Marks, Michael P. and Fisher, Zachary M. (2002), 'The King's New Bodies: Simulating Consent in the Age of Celebrity', *New Political Science*, 24:3, pp. 371–394.

Mwakasungura, Undule and Bamusi, Mavuto (2009), 'Redefining the Boundaries Between Child Adoption and Child Kidnapping', Press Release by the Human Rights Consultative Committee, <http://www.hrccmalawi.org/madonnastatement.pdf>, 30 March 2009. Accessed 9 June 2009.

Nicholl, Katie (2009), 'Will Madonna now look to adopt a baby in Lesotho – and is that why she saw Prince Harry at the polo?', *The Daily Mail*, 8 June 2009.

NME (2006), 'Bono defends Madonna's adoption', NME.com, <http://www.nme.com/news/madonna/25047>, 13 November 2006. Accessed 15 June 2009.

Norman, P. (2007), 'Madonna's New H & M Clothes a Hit on eBay', People.com, <http://www.people.com/people/article/0,,20015890,00.html>, 23 March. Accessed 8 June 2009.

O'Neill, Onora (2004), 'Global Justice: Whose Obligations?', in D. K. Chatterjee (ed.), *The Ethics of Assistance*, Cambridge: Cambridge University Press, pp. 242–259.

Pareles, Jon (2008), 'Material Woman, Restoring Her Brand', *New York Times*, 27 April.

Peck, Michelle (2009), 'Raising Malawi', <http://www.raisingmalawi.org/blog09.php>. Accessed 9 June 2009.

Peretti, J. (2009), 'Madonna, Mercy and Malawi: her fight to adopt a second African child', *The Guardian*, 12 June.

Raising Malawi (2009a, 2010), 'Our Impact', <http://www.raisingmalawi.org/acmp-emp.php>. Accessed 9 June 2009 and 8 February 2010.

—— (2009b), 'Raising Malawi Hunger and Nutrition Initiative', <http://www.raisingmalawi.org/acmp-nut.php>. Accessed 11 June 2009.

Rissman, Nathan (2008), *I Am Because We Are*, Semtex Films, London.

Saunders, Robert A. (2007), 'Transnational Reproduction and its Discontents: The Politics of Intercountry Adoption in a Global Society', *Journal of Global Change and Governance*, 1:1, pp. 1–23.

Selman, Peter (ed.) (2000), *Intercountry Adoption: Developments, Trends and Perspectives*, London: British Agencies for Adoption and Fostering.

Singer, Peter (1972), 'Famine, Affluence, and Morality', *Philosophy and Public Affairs*, 1:1, pp. 229–243.

—— (2009), *The Life You Can Save: Acting Now to End World Poverty*, New York: Random House.

Transparency International (2008), '2008 Corruption Perceptions Index', <http://www.transparency.org/news_room/in_focus/2008/cpi2008/cpi_2008_table>. Accessed 11 June 2009.

Traub, James (2008), 'The Celebrity Solution', *New York Times Magazine*, 9 March.

United Nations Development Programme, 'Human Development Report, 2009', http://hdrstats.undp.
org/en/countries/country_fact_sheets/cty_fs_MWI.html. Accessed 9 February 2010.
Vanity Fair (2007), 'Saving Malawi's Children', VanityFair.com, <http://www.vanityfair.com/politics/
features/2007/07/kim200707?currentPage=1>, 5 June 2007. Accessed 9 June 2009.
West, D. M. and Orman, J. M. (2003), *Celebrity Politics*, Upper Saddle River: Prentice Hall.

Notes

1. Madonna refers to seeing David Banda on video before going to Malawi in her interview with Oprah Winfrey, as transcribed in British Broadcasting Corporation, 2006.
2. It is also her celebrity that caused the lower court judge to refuse the adoption of Mercy James on the grounds that Madonna was not resident in Malawi. The judgment of the Supreme Court of Appeal criticizes the lower court judge for relying on reports in the 'global media' rather than the evidence presented to her. For this criticism and the importance of Madonna's celebrity work to the judgment, see the full text of the decision granting adoption, (In Re: CJ A Female Infant 2009: 15–16 and 26, respectively.
3. For example, Darrell West and John Orman have claimed, 'Celebrity politics accentuates many of the elements in our society that drain substance out of the political process and substitutes trivial and non-substantive forms of entertainment. [This] endangers the ability of ordinary citizens to hold leaders accountable for their policymaking decisions' (West and Orman 2003: 113, cited in Kamons 2007: 145–146).
4. Madonna's own loss of her mother at a young age and her taking 'on a maternal role to her younger siblings, assuming responsibility of housecleaning, cooking and babysitting' is cited in her support in the Supreme Court of Appeal's decision. Also cited in support is her personality and character: 'It is clear from the evidence on record that the appellant who was before the court is an intelligent, articulate and outgoing individual of strong character. She is also a determined, independent and hardworking person of compassion who comes from a God fearing family'. While no one can doubt that Madonna is 'intelligent', 'determined, independent' and 'of strong character', the Supreme Court of Appeal, in accordance with its refusal to consider reports in the global media, is clearly not concerning itself with Madonna's musical career. See In Re: CJ A Female Infant (2009: 26).
5. '1500 children are receiving SFK classes and personalized mentorship through Community Based Organizations', '300 youths…through juvenile prisons and reformatory schools, 200 children […] through orphanages'. Raising Malawi (2009a, 2010). By 8 February 2010, the programme had been renamed 'Success for Kids' and references to it in the Raising Malawi website had been changed to reflect this.
6. The training of the teachers in the US is also noted in the Kabbalah Centre's own film urging donations to Raising Malawi, which also argues: 'Kabbalah believes, that to make a real difference, we must empower children by teaching them skills of independence and that change can only occur from within', Kabbalah Centre 2006.
7. Sachs's model is criticized, along with its use of celebrity activism in Dieter and Kumar 2008.
8. After David's meeting with his father in March 2009, his father expressed approval of how David was doing with Madonna and reported the following dialogue with him: '"He asked me whether I ride horses", Mr Banda said later. "I told him horses are for the rich and he asked me why I am poor. He told me his mum likes riding horses and that he too rides horses"'.. Later he added, 'It's

amazing how David has grown; I can't believe he is the same small and sickly baby we left at Home of Hope', Clements (2009).

9. Bono said, 'Madonna should be applauded for helping to take a child out of the worst poverty imaginable and giving him a better chance at life' *NME* 2006.

10. Elizabeth Bartholet and other legal academics have released a press statement supporting Madonna's adoption of Mercy James called 'Save the Children from Save the Children', Harvard Law School 2009. Elizabeth Bartholet has written more extensively about Madonna's adoption cases in Bartholet 2010, where she strongly endorses the Malawi Supreme Court of Appeal's waiving of the residence requirement, p. 98.

11. 'Anticorruption and Transparency' in Khaila (2006).

12. Malawi has not signed the Hague convention.

13. An American couple interested in adopting from Malawi described these concerns at a US embassy sponsored event in Lilongwe. See Embassy of the United States, Lilongwe, Malawi, 2008.

14. The Supreme Court of Appeal decision argues that neither the 'imaginary unscrupulous individuals' or the 'imaginary children' who would be their victims are before the court. See In Re: CJ A Female Infant (2009: 26).

15. 'Accountability and Public Voice' in Khaila (2006).

16. 'Rule of Law' in Khaila (2006).

17. At time of writing. The number fluctuates over time. See Human Rights Consultative Committee (2009).

18. As of 2006, the latest year for which an annual report is available. See Human Rights Consultative Committee 2006.

19. This neglect is frequently complained of by observers of the relationship between aid and civil society in Africa. Examples include, Comaroff and Comaroff (1999) and Maina (1998).

20. For celebrities as 'charismatic leaders', see Marks and Fisher (2002).

Part IV

Transnational Celebrity Activism, 'Celebrityhood' and Media Representations

Chapter 11

Linking Small Arms, Child Soldiers, NGOs and Celebrity Activism:
Nicolas Cage and the *Lord Of War*

Michael Stohl, Cynthia Stohl and Rachel Stohl

'Diplomacy is not just carried out by diplomats',

U.S. Secretary of State Hillary Clinton
Cape Verde. August 2009

Introduction[1]

In the past 50 years, the role of citizen diplomacy and the participation of celebrities in the process have greatly expanded. From the appointment of Danny Kaye as a global ambassador for UNICEF from 1953 to 1987 to the work of more contemporary celebrities like Angelina Jolie, Brad Pitt, Mia Farrow, Sir Bob Geldof and Bono, celebrities are prominently associated with humanitarian work and political activism across the globe. Their prominence has focused an increasingly linked global audience upon a wide variety of issues and causes.

The interdependent issues of small arms and child soldiers are important and timely concerns that we examine to illustrate the role of celebrity and citizen diplomacy in contemporary international affairs. Our focal celebrity is Nicolas Cage, who produced and starred in the film *Lord of War* because he was convinced that he could bring attention to, as well as dramatize, the connected issues. Cage allied himself with Amnesty International and the Joint Control Arms campaign effort of Amnesty International, the International Action Network on Small Arms (IANSA) and Oxfam International. Through Amnesty International, in his role as an organizational steering committee member, Cage is also connected to the Coalition to Stop the Use of Child Soldiers. In the course of his work for these causes, Cage became a spokesman for both these organizations and their campaigns, and produced public service announcements on their behalf.

In considering Cage's activities, we will explore the ways in which Cage has promoted these causes and attempted to mobilize public support. In our analysis, we address five basic questions about celebrity activism raised by scholars, journalists, and public responses to celebrity involvement in diplomacy (and public policy in general): (1) Is celebrity activism emerging as a new and distinct intellectual factor in international politics? (2) What communicative and organizational factors enhance celebrity involvement in political affairs? (3) Are celebrities capable of making (and do they intend to make) governments review aspects of their policies and shape the international agenda? (4) Are celebrity actions fundamentally addressed to staying in the spotlight? and (5) What are the unintended consequences of celebrity activism?

To answer these questions, we begin by placing the study of celebrity diplomacy in the historical and communication context of the growth of what international relations scholars and historians have labelled 'the new diplomacy'. We do this by examining the characteristics of the opportunities that public diplomacy provides for celebrities to engage and influence the process. We consider the new diplomacy in the context of the growth of global civic society, a context Philip Cerny (1995: 596) has described as the enabling condition for individuals to adopt a more active international role.

Public Diplomacy and Celebrity Activism in Context: The New Diplomacy

Huliaras and Tzifakis (2008: 11–15) argue that globalization drives celebrity activism for global issues and that the most important factors associated with globalization are the technological advances in communication and the increased capabilities and opportunities for organizing. In addition, in the current era, celebrity diplomacy is clearly linked to the growth of NGOs, the emergence of campaigns for corporate social responsibility and, what Huliaras and Tzifakis characterize as 'the reemergence of private philanthropy'. While there is no doubt that this web of factors, commonly referred to as globalization, has dramatically altered and eased the ability of citizens to engage in global affairs, we should also recognize that celebrity activism existed prior to the 'age of globalization' (Cooper 2008: 1). By first considering the dynamics of celebrity activism in this earlier period, we suggest that we gain insights into contemporary celebrity activists, their engagement and the effects of their efforts.

Two nineteenth-century examples are illustrative. They demonstrate that although different eras have different types of artists as major celebrities, it is the potential influence of prominence itself that makes celebrities attractive as advocates, rather than the particular medium in which they operate. While in the contemporary period, television, film and recording artists are the most prominent celebrities and the most recognized celebrity activists, in past eras, artists and writers were the major celebrities. For example, in the nineteenth century, artists JMW Turner and William Blake provided visual representations of slavery, having been recruited by Thomas Clarkson to the anti-slavery campaign, both because they could provide dramatic images and because their 'celebrity' brought additional attention to the campaign. Samuel Clemens (Mark Twain), who, for the most part used his author's celebrity to earn income as a public speaker, became an active and quite vocal speaker for the anti-imperialist league in the aftermath of the Spanish–American War using his celebrity to attract interest in the political cause. The *Springfield Republican*, the leading anti-imperialist daily newspaper in the US at the time, editorialized that, 'Mark Twain has suddenly become the most influential anti-imperialist and the most dreaded critic of the sacrosanct person in the White House that the country contains' (Zwick 1992: xix).

Huliaras and Tzifakis further identify five factors that explain celebrity activism in the modern context. The first three factors are rooted in changes in the organizational landscape: (1) the evolution of UN, efforts to engage celebrities; (2) the growth of NGOs and (3) changes in the studio system and the movie industry. The final two factors are rooted in interpersonal network dynamics: (4) celebrities need to remain in the public consciousness and (5) a bandwagon effect takes place in which celebrities bring others along. Before we expand upon these factors, we briefly review the important dynamics identified by Huliaras and Tzifakis.

For Huliaras and Tzifakis, the history of celebrity activism begins in the post-WWII international community. The UN first introduced the idea of goodwill ambassadors with the appointment by UNICEF of Danny Kaye in 1953 (the appointment was made a year after Kaye had starred in the movie *Hans Christian Andersen* and become associated with the character's identity and relationship with children). UN Secretary General Kofi Annan greatly expanded the idea of goodwill ambassadors for the UN during his tenure and after 1997, as Huliaras and Tzifakis (2008: 11) indicate, there was a 'spectacular growth of goodwill ambassadors', with the result that as we write, more than 30 celebrities were involved in 2009.

In 1997, the Secretary General also created the role of messengers of peace, distinguished individuals, carefully selected, as are the goodwill ambassadors, from the fields of art, literature, music and sports, and who have agreed to help focus worldwide attention on the work of the United Nations. Thus far seventeen persons have been honoured with the positions. Princess Haya Bint Al Hussein, Daniel Barenboim, Ross Bleckner, George Clooney, Paulo Coelho, Midori Goto, Michael Douglas, Jane Goodall, Yo-Yo Ma, Charlize Theron and Elie Wiesel are currently serving, while Luciano Pavarotti, Wynton Marsalis, Enrico Macias, Anna Cataldi, Vijay Armitraj and Muhammed Ali had the honour of serving in the past. The diversity of arenas from which these individuals come demonstrates that celebrity still comes in many forms, with artists, musicians, sports figures and authors still prominent among the stage, screen and television actors, and that different celebrities resonate with different parts of the global audience. The UN agencies have also sought out celebrities to help them spread their message, and the list of celebrities attached to these agencies includes hundreds of nationally and internationally known stars across a wide range of fields.

Second, Huliaras and Tzifakis argue that in addition to the UN, NGOs have also 'understood that global celebrities can direct media attention on certain issues, raise public awareness and provide access on the highest levels of government' (2008: 12), thus extending the organizational possibilities for celebrities. Although not the focus of Huliaras's and Tzifakis's work, governments too have realized the power of celebrity. Both the US and the Soviet Union employed celebrities in their public diplomacy during the Cold War. In the late 1950s, both Dizzy Gillespie and Louis Armstrong, two jazz giants, were sent on tours around the world by the Department of State. Shortly thereafter, the Soviet Union sent three of their cultural icons, the Bolshoi and Kirov Ballet companies and the Moiseyev Dancers to tour the West. In a later period, Cuba allowed their baseball players to tour, again to create positive human stories to assist its national image.

Each nation also learned a lesson about the unanticipated diplomatic dangers that celebrities as 'cultural ambassadors' might entail. For example, in 1957, Louis Armstrong cancelled a State Department-sponsored tour and criticized President Eisenhower for refusing to send troops to Little Rock to protect black students who were attempting to desegregate Central High School. At an appearance in North Dakota, Armstrong declared that 'the government can go to hell'. Armstrong also stated that 'Eisenhower's got no guts', and called Arkansas's Governor Faubus 'a fool' and 'an uneducated ploughboy' (Bradbury 2003: 112). In the Soviet case, the celebrities let their feet 'do the talking', as Rudolf Nureyev in 1961 and Mikhail Baryshnikov in 1974 defected from the Kirov ballet, while Alexander Gudonov defected from the Bolshoi in 1979. The Cubans in turn have also more than 150 of their prominent baseball stars defect, including 28 who have played in major league baseball, dimming the propaganda value of their national team's triumphs on the playing field.

Huliaras and Tzifakis (2008: 12), along with Daniel Drezner (2007), also argue that because the movie industry has become less authoritarian, movie stars enjoy far more freedom to act (author's note, we imagine no pun intended) than some decades ago. We certainly agree that the movie and media stars' freedom to choose if, how and when to engage and use their star power is an important factor in explaining the willingness of these celebrities to become involved. We, however, identify the cause of this freedom in the structural decline of the 'studio system' rather than the waning of authoritarian bosses.

Huliaras and Tzifakis contend that the fourth factor, 'Celebrities embrace global causes or take political initiatives in order to remain celebrities' (2008: 13) is the most important. There is no question that celebrities may engage in causes to help their images but it is also the case that numerous celebrities have embraced political causes at clear costs to their celebrity and careers (e.g. Jane Fonda, Vietnam; Vanessa Redgrave, the Palestinians; and the Dixie Chicks, the Iraq War being only a few prominent examples). Jane Fonda found it difficult to be cast in mainstream Hollywood films for some years; Vanessa Redgrave suffered widespread blacklisting after her acceptance speech at the Academy Awards for best supporting actress in 1978 when she gave a pro-PLO speech and the Dixie Chicks were banned from conglomerate Clear Channel's radio stations (more than 1000 in the US) after singer Natalie Maines said during a concert in March 2003 that she was ashamed Mr Bush was from Texas (St John 2003).

The fifth factor that Huliaras and Tzifakis (2008: 14) identify is rooted in network connectedness, i.e., celebrities mobilize other celebrities. Celebrities have the capacity to bring to bear their professional networks to engage wider numbers in a particular cause. These networks possess the possibilities of mobilizing across many different sectors and may create the opportunity to mobilize multiple publics beyond the reach of any individual celebrities. Thus, the mobilization of music celebrities from many different musical forms and locales by the UN family has led to benefit concerts by the likes of Luciano Pavarotti and others. These collaborations widened the reach of Pavarotti beyond his opera audience to also include the fans of rock music's Bono, country music's Dixie Chicks, the jazz samba of Gilberto Gil, the pop of MiriamYeung and the fusion pop of Youssou N'Dour, thus connecting not simply styles of music but continents as well (for further elaboration, see Cooper 2008, and Smith 2009.)

The Context of Citizen Diplomacy: Origins and Unintended Consequences

As suggested above, to understand more fully the factors associated with the current role of celebrity diplomacy, it is useful to frame the organizational and network factors within a historical/communicative context. We suggest that rather than arising strategically in the post-WWII UN context, celebrity diplomacy can be seen as an outgrowth of the 'new diplomacy' that emerged as a result of Woodrow Wilson's Fourteen Points speech and the establishment of the League of Nations. Unlike the overt actions of the UN, which established a formalized role for celebrities, it is the unintended consequences of Wilson's actions that strongly influence the development of celebrity activism today.

In particular, Wilson's January 8, 1918 speech to a joint session of Congress that enunciated the Fourteen Points had as its first point a call for 'open covenants, openly arrived at'. The structural changes in the interaction of states that followed this speech (see Mayer 1959) are still evident in international affairs today. While Wilson was primarily interested in the negative effects of the secret agreements of the 'old diplomacy', which had resulted in the escalation of the Serbian assassination of Archduke Ferdinand into the 'Great War', the longer-term results of his call for openness were the 'democratization' of foreign policy, because it focused much greater attention on the citizen and public opinion within democracies, and the establishment of open forums in which to discuss diplomatic affairs. These open forums eventually drew in citizens to act as both expert witnesses on behalf of governments, and as lobbyists attempting to influence the activities of these government representatives discussing international affairs in an open session.

The 'new diplomacy' has grown over the past nine decades to include not only openness and organizational structures for discourse and information dissemination, but has also expanded to include the media and public diplomacy. This trend is particularly evident as governments and others seek to sway public opinion and other governments in the pursuit of diplomatic objectives, as well as influence conference and multilateral diplomacy centred on particular issues such as landmines, the law of the sea, the environment and women's rights. The new diplomacy has been facilitated by features of globalization and the emergence of new communication technologies, but at the core, it is the fundamental communicative principles of the new diplomacy that have resulted in changes in both organizational and network factors associated with celebrity activism.

The new diplomacy has created both a greatly expanded set of actors who participate in diplomatic processes, i.e., more international organizations, more corporations, more non-governmental organizations, and a new set of diplomatic approaches and routines. In comparison with the old, the new diplomacy depends on far greater openness of communication; greater accountability of governments to their publics; greater attention to public opinion at home and abroad; and simultaneous bargaining with political factions and publics at home and other nations and publics abroad. There are also much greater levels of media intrusion in the process of diplomacy and therefore many more opportunities and incentives to employ the media by those engaged in the diplomatic process, whether they be diplomats, corporations, non-governmental or governmental organizations as well as private citizens and activists.

The more active media role also provides a basis for indirect conversation among governments, citizens and their counterparts worldwide. The media may function to provide set(s) of facts and opinions that all sides can monitor and employ in their talks, and may be employed to substitute or supplement face-to-face conversations, depending on how actively governments engage the media in their activities. Governments may use the media to send up trial balloons to determine whether there will be a likelihood of support or opposition to various positions, and may gain insights into modifications of positions that may be necessary to obtain approval. The media may also serve to alert governments and other interested parties of the potential problems faced by governments vis-à-vis their domestic publics or other actors.

Here again, the new communicative practices are grounded in historical precedent. About 25 years ago, Joseph Montville, a diplomat working within the US State Department, was interested in the significance of the growing numbers of unofficial dialogues taking place with respect to conflict resolution for those working in the diplomatic service. Montville introduced the term 'track two diplomacy' to capture the evolution of the participants in the diplomatic community (Montville and Davidson 1981). The second track was defined as 'unofficial, informal interaction among members of adversarial groups or nations with the goals of developing strategies, influencing public opinion, and organizing human and material resources in ways that might help resolve the conflict' (Montville and Davidson 1981: 155). Significantly, the various forms of what would henceforth be labelled as track two diplomacy were not completely new – they had emerged as early as the First World War, and even earlier, as citizen groups pressed governments to engage in disarmament. These peace societies accelerated after Wilson's Fourteen Points and had noticeable success in pushing Secretary of State Frank Kellogg into acceptance of these principles; they also led to the successful negotiation of the Kellogg–Briand pact of 1928 in which nations (none too successfully as it transpired) agreed to outlaw war (Chatfield 1971, 1992; deBenedetti 1980).

In the past few decades, both before and after Montville and Davidson's article appeared, in addition to the problem-solving workshops that Montville envisioned, numerous other forms of multinational political dialogues amongst citizens have emerged. These too have set the stage for modern-day celebrity diplomacy because they emphasize the important role of multiple forms of citizen involvement in what has become known as 'public diplomacy'. These programmes normalized the right and expectation that citizens would participate in activities that had diplomatic dimensions. For example, the Fulbright Programme, created by Senator J. W. Fulbright in 1946, was developed to promote international goodwill through the exchange of students in the fields of education, culture and science. It was subsequently expanded to include teachers, journalists and scholars and is based on a bilateral exchange model. The assumption was that individual citizens could serve as 'ambassadors' for their respective nations and these citizens could bring awareness of the 'other' to both their own and host societies. In 1956, President Eisenhower employed the same underlying idea to create the People to People programme as part of the United States Information Agency. As he left office, he privatized the organization and created People to People International as an NGO. People to People sponsors the exchange of citizens extending the Fulbright idea to the wider society. Both of these organizations, thus, institutionalized the idea of the citizen as diplomat, and NGOs have emerged to push the idea to an extent never dreamed of by Fulbright or Eisenhower (Alger 1980; Alger and Mendlovitz 1984).

In the context of the Cold War and as a consequence of the Helsinki agreements in 1975, there was also a great burst of cultural and scientific exchanges, travelling artists, sports teams, and many other contacts between people groups representing the sides in the Cold War that were part of public diplomacy. Significantly, this network-building model was adopted by many other groups whose nations were seen as currently engaged in intractable conflicts or who identified common conflicts that those nations might cooperate in confronting for their common good. For example, the US-based NGO Search for Common Ground, founded in 1982, created citizen workshops and collaborations on conflict and negotiation.

Overall, throughout the 1990s, we have seen citizen diplomacy taking hold, utilizing track two diplomacy, relying on the media to get out a message, and using celebrity to highlight issues and bring additional media attention and pressure on governments. The most successful campaign was that of the International Campaign to Ban Landmines (ICBL), which inspired governments and civil society to tackle the use of these deadly and indiscriminate weapons. The Campaign got a significant boost when Diana, Princess of Wales, visited demining centres and met with landmine survivors. After only five years – an extraordinarily short time in the world of contemporary treaty negotiations – the Mine Ban Treaty (formally the Convention on the Prohibition of the Use, Stockpiling, Production and Transfer of Anti-Personnel Mines and on their Destruction) was adopted and the ICBL won the Nobel Peace Prize. The Campaign's success was buoyed by the role of celebrity and the push of civil society. The success of the ICBL also had another effect: it inspired other NGOs to attempt similar practices to push their own agenda. One such effort has been the quest to address the negative consequences of small arms proliferation and misuse, and achieve an Arms Trade Treaty. Below we describe the critical communicative features of the case as we examine the contributions of Nicolas Cage, Andrew Niccol and the *Lord of War*.

Nicolas Cage and the *Lord of War*

Andrew Niccol, the screenwriter and director of the movie *Lord of War* became interested in the issue of small arms after reading investigative news stories about arms trafficking.

The film seeks to explore not only the arms trade, but also the personal dilemmas, or lack thereof, of a person who traffics weapons for a living and the experiences of government pursuers. Niccol recruited Nicolas Cage to star in the film and according to Niccol, Cage, who also became an executive producer on the film

> ... was drawn to the material and he wanted to also explore that darker side of human nature and this project gave him that, so he attached his company to this project. I think he was also interested in the issue itself. He made Amnesty International a big part of it; he made sure they were one of the groups to benefit from the film. (Axmaker 2005)

As with any actor, clearly at the start of the project, Cage's professional commitment was to his craft, rather than the cause, but, as the project unfolded, Cage's personal network became an instrumental component of the campaign. Cage had first started supporting and then working with Amnesty International's United States chapter (AIUSA) some years before the film in connection with the Stop Violence Against Women Campaign. During the filming of *Lord of War*, Cage developed a growing interest in the problem of arms trafficking beyond the making of the film. Because of his familiarity with the various aspects of Amnesty International's work, Cage approached Amnesty International on how he could help with their Control Arms campaign. Through Cage, AIUSA became involved with promoting *Lord of War*.

Cage's involvement spanned a number of fronts. Cage and Niccol each wrote a letter to AIUSA activists urging them to take action to push US Secretary of State, Condoleezza Rice, to support a global agreement on arms brokering and to address arms trafficking issues in the Democratic Republic of the Congo. Cage also recorded a Public Service Announcement (PSA) about arms brokers for the launch of the movie, using the text that Amnesty International prepared. Cage then wrote the text himself and recorded a second PSA in which he linked the issue of arms trafficking and child soldiers. The PSA was first aired in New York, during the occasion of the United Nations Review Conference on the Program of Action on Small Arms. In addition, Cage pledged two million dollars to AIUSA and the International Secretariat of Amnesty International to positively impact the lives of child soldiers. Most of the money, $1.5 million, was designed in consultation with AI as pass-through grants to World Vision for their child soldier rehabilitation centre in Uganda and the International Rescue Committee for similar centres in Nepal and Sudan. Amnesty split the remaining $500,000 between AIUSA and the Amnesty International's International Secretariat for research and advocacy as well as campaigning on issues related to child soldiers and arms trafficking. As agreed by Cage, Amnesty, World Vision, and the International Rescue Committee prepared six-month updates on their work after initial conversations about how they would use the resources provided. Cage was asked for his input when the organizations sought to deviate from the work plan. The announcement of the gift and the airing of the PSA occurred prior to, and during, a concert whose purpose was to raise awareness of the Control Arms Campaign. The concert featured live performances by a number of international stars including four-time Grammy nominee, Angelique Kidjo, South African actor and musician Zola, and Colombian band Alma Parlantes, who played guitars fabricated from guns. In addition, testimonies from survivors of armed violence were read by actresses Rosario Dawson and Piper Perabo, who also had become part of the Control Arms campaign.

Cage's PSA included the following lines:

> Think about the nine months it took for your child to be born; think about all the care you put into teaching him how to cross the street and look both ways or to read a book or to simply have good manners. Then imagine a warlord dropping a gun into his hand and forcing him to kill someone. He's eight years old. He hasn't kissed a girl yet or fallen in love, but he's killed a man. What does that do to a child's mind? Sounds like a nightmare? It's reality for some families.

Cage also injected discussions about arms and child soldier issues during private interviews with press during his many promotion appearances for *Lord of War*.[2]

It appears that Amnesty International was quite happy with Niccol's and Cage's work on behalf of the organization and the opportunities that the film *Lord of War* provided them for bringing attention to the Control Arms campaign and the related issue of child soldiers. They were able to use the film to create briefings for various governments whose assistance they sought on the issues. Thus, for example, on 1 November 2005, AI and Oxfam arranged a U.K. parliamentary screening of *Lord of War*. Several parliamentarians and many parliamentary researchers attended the screening and signed up to the Control Arms Million Faces petition. An 'Early Day Motion' was passed at the House of Commons concerning the proliferation of the illegal arms trade following the screening. A similar event was organized by the Swedish Action Network on Small Arms (SANSA) together with the Parliamentary Forum on Small Arms and Light Weapons for a parliamentary screening of the film in the Swedish parliament (see IANSA 2006).

While Amnesty International reports that Cage expressed a sincere interest in going on an Amnesty mission to Africa to support the Control Arms campaign or the child soldier issue on two occasions, they were unable to schedule the mission.[3] Cage also expressed interest in maintaining involvement. Cage indicated that he wanted to do more than simply record his PSAs and make a generous gift before moving on to his next film. However, while several attempts were made to keep Cage involved with AI work, for example, by inviting him to go on an AI mission to Africa, doing media work on a launch of a report that Cage himself funded, or engaging in face-to-face lobbying with US congressional staff, Cage's professional filming commitments appear to have prevented any further public involvement with the organization. Thus, although Amnesty International worked with Cage and Cage's agent, as well as distributor Lion's Gate, to help AI with promotional work, nothing further developed. Ironically, although Cage's network linkages prior to the film helped make him a celebrity advocate, part of the problem for Cage's lack of further involvement seems also to involve network connections uncovered by Alice Okeeffe of the Observer. She writes:

> Arms campaigners were delighted with their new celebrity recruit, and both Amnesty International Worldwide and the Control Arms campaign snapped up interviews with him for their websites [...] However, Cage's campaigning career has hit a snag. He is unable to become an ambassador for the anti-arms cause because he remains a fully paid-up member of the National Rifle Association of America [author's insert, which not only does not support the Control Arms Campaign or their goals but also actively opposes them].

Okeeffe continues:

> Anna Macdonald, campaigns director at Oxfam, said: There were some discussions about getting Nicolas Cage to support the Control Arms campaign. 'We're very supportive of the issues raised in Lord of War, but we have no direct relationship with Nicolas Cage'. (Okeeffe 2005)

Although Cage himself came to AIUSA with the significant political baggage of his NRA membership, Cage's lack of follow-up and involvement may also be attributed to organizational changes within AIUSA. In June 2009, AIUSA altered its approach to the arms trade and children in armed conflict project shifting from a project staffed by full-time paid staff members to one relying on the work and time of volunteers. Although Amnesty's International Secretariat remains part of the Control Arms Campaign (and individual country campaigns can take part in Control Arms activities and campaigning at their own discretion), AIUSA has chosen not to make Control Arms the focus of their campaigning efforts. The result of this is that there are no funds that will be employed on the project beyond Cage's original donation. Without the staff and funds AIUSA will not advocate as effectively for the arms trade and children and armed conflict agenda and is also unlikely to attempt to mobilize the identified celebrity commitment to the cause and project.

It is important to note that there are other stars who have become involved with AI on these interrelated issues such as Jennifer Connelly, who was one of the stars of the film *Blood Diamond*. As with *Lord of War*, AIUSA participated in advertising and marketing for the movies, and Connelly shot a PSA on child soldiers as part of the public awareness campaign around the movie. She also became a spokesperson for AIUSA's Human Rights Education programme. Indeed, Amnesty International, Oxfam and the IANSA, through the Control Arms campaign were extraordinarily successful in employing 'celebrity' to highlight the campaign and keep the global public audience aware of the issue. Literally, hundreds of celebrities are on the 'Million Faces' portion of the campaign and many of them have been utilized for important public events along with interested government legislators and leaders to maintain pressure on national states and international organizations such as the UN, to pass a small arms trade treaty. Thus, for example, on 23 April 2007 Liberian President, Ellen Johnson-Sirleaf (who had been Director of the United Nations Development Programme's Regional Bureau for Africa and had been involved in issues of small arms), Oscar-winning actress Helen Mirren, and former Irish President, Mary Robinson, together with twenty prominent journalists, asked governments 'to deliver a tough Arms Trade Treaty rooted in international human rights and humanitarian law to stop arms transfers that fuel global violence and conflict.'[4]

Thus, this case illustrates that celebrity notoriety may be a double-edged sword. Groups associated with particular causes may get more than they bargained for when they enlist a celebrity. Not only does their celebrity focus attention on the issue for which they are recruited, but also their celebrity focuses attention on other connections and vulnerabilities. For example, Angelina Jolie, a United Nations Goodwill Ambassador has spent a decade highlighting the problem of refugees and donating substantial sums on their behalf. Nonetheless, her 2003 film *Beyond Borders,* which focused on humanitarian aid organizations that operate in war zones, suggests that the doctor played by Clive Owen, who is at the centre of the film with Jolie, in order to secure delivery of needed medical supplies, works with the CIA and allows the smuggling of weapons. Aid groups immediately attacked the film because of the underlying message, which they said had the potential of putting their staff at risk because their aid workers would be seen as CIA agents. As Duncan Campbell reported: 'Medical aid organizations are particularly anxious to distance themselves from any governmental links after the attack on the International Committee of the Red Cross building in Baghdad […]' (Campbell 2003).

There are also some additional ironic twists to Cage's and Niccol's work on *Lord of War* which, for the most part, escaped the public's notice. In the production of the film, as Niccol has pointed out in various media interviews, he modelled the characters after real dealers, such as the notorious Viktor Bout, and even spent time with some of them to better familiarize himself with how they operated so as to go beyond the factual material he had gathered.[5] Niccol also indicates that he did business with illegal arms dealers in order to make the film. As Niccol observes, purchasing arms from dealers was simply cheaper than finding replicas or legally acquired props. The scene in which Cage as Yuri Orlov walks through a Ukrainian warehouse of Soviet AK-47s actually has 3000 real guns in it, which were there because of a buy-and-sell-back procedure to which Niccol contracted with the dealer. Niccol describes the process:

That plane you saw in the movie belongs to one of the most notorious arms dealers in Africa. He's Russian. You say to yourself, 'I know these guys fly Antanovs in and out of here all the time. I'm going to need an Antanov. Where does the production get an Antanov?' From an arms dealer. And that same plane had been running real guns into the Congo the week before I filmed it […] .(Axmaker 2005)

It is quite possible that the arms dealer described here is Viktor Bout as he was one of the few dealers who owned an Antonov cargo plane (Masland and Cohen 2005). Thus, while filming a movie whose purpose was to mobilize international action against the trade in small arms, Niccol actively engaged and brought profits to the same arms traffickers.

Conclusions

Our analysis addressed five basic questions related to celebrity activism. The first focused on whether celebrity activism is emerging as a new and distinct factor in international politics. It certainly is the case that because of changing structural changes in the news industry and emerging communication technologies, celebrities today have increased opportunities for activism. Specifically, the time and space devoted to soft vs hard news in broadcast and print media has dramatically increased as a direct result of the twin processes of concentration and conglomeration of media. Cross-platform internal corporate advertising of movie, television and music entertainment, sports, and publishing across the global conglomerates of Fox, Bertelsmann, Disney, General Electric, and Viacom means that entertainers have much greater prominence as part of the news, and therefore greater opportunities to gain air and print time. Moreover, there are several technological changes that enhance the likelihood and efficacy of celebrity activism. These include (1) *acceleration*, technologies are eliminating time constraints and (2) *transparency*, readily available information is taking more power out of the hands of governments. Other enhancement factors include (3) *ease of mobilization*, information stirs people into action, and the Internet and cell phones enable people to coordinate behaviour without the accoutrements of formal large-scale organizations and (4) *virtuality*. There is a decline in face-to-face social interactions and a corresponding increase in electronic interaction. New forms of social media, such as Twitter, Facebook, and YouTube enable celebrities to personally connect with mass audiences in ways that heretofore required face-to-face interaction. Overall, new information communication technologies are mechanisms that allow activists instead of organizations to take on the role of brokerage (Burt 2005), i.e. the 'linking of two or more unconnected social actors by a unit that mediates their relations with one another and/or with yet other sites' (Tarrow 2005: 190). Nonetheless, our analysis indicates that even without these conditions, as the case of Mark Twain and William Blake, celebrity activism has been a powerful and commonplace phenomenon.

Our second question addressed what communicative and organizational factors enhance celebrity involvement in political affairs. Besides the emergence of new forms of organization and technology, it is also important to note that films provide a 'frame' for news stories, which keeps the celebrity activist in the spotlight. For example, when arms dealer Viktor Bout was arrested in Thailand last year, the arrest was framed by many news agencies in terms of the film character in *Lord of War* and references to Nicolas Cage having portrayed the arms dealer. Thus, the *Times of London* headlined the news article 'Lord of War' arms dealer Viktor Bout arrested in Thailand and its first sentence read 'A Russian arms dealer thought to have inspired the lead character in the blockbuster film *Lord of War* was arrested in Bangkok today'.[6] Although the film continues to appear in government and IGO documents as a reference point for the issue of arms sales, ironically little media attention has been given to Bout's thus far successful attempts to avoid extradition to the US to face arms trafficking charges.

The next two questions focused on celebrities' efficacy and commitment to political campaigns and causes. In general, there is a wide range of celebrity activism. Some celebrities, such as Mira Sorvino, who helped Amnesty on Darfur issues, want to be deeply involved in many aspects of the work. Sorvino helped steer advocacy work, was a spokesperson and a lobbyist for AIUSA, and participated in an online chat with the American public, among other activities.[7] Others, such as Cage, publicly may state that they want deep involvement, but in actuality, either because they are not that interested or are too busy with other work and interests, only get involved intermittently. Further, there are numerous celebrities who are long-time major donors to a particular issue or organization, but do not engage in public campaigns in their support for a cause. Finally, naturally there are also celebrities who involve themselves in a cause for a short period of time, perhaps for reasons of publicity, without any long-term financial or personal commitment.

Our final question addressed the unintended consequences of celebrity activism. It is usually taken as a given that celebrities can bring critical media attention by adding saliency and credibility to an issue. However, our analysis also suggests that there are several unintended consequences of their involvement. Perhaps, most importantly for our work is the critical role the celebrity's own network and past connections play in their involvement in an issue. As in the case with Cage, memberships in other organizations and network linkages outside the focal cause have a significant impact on their advocacy. As with all citizen diplomacy, it is important to consider the implications of these connections when examining the efficacy of celebrity activism.

Presented with the potential benefits and costs of celebrity, at the end of the day, most organizations and causes are likely to calculate that a celebrity champion, regardless of the level of financial or personal commitment will bring a surplus of benefits to their cause. In addition, there is a clear push-and-pull relationship between celebrities and NGOs. While celebrities may use issue platforms for their own careers or for altruistic purposes, organizations are also keen to encourage celebrity involvement in their fund-raising, advocacy and political strategies. In the end, unless organizations have a fundamental problem with a celebrity's involvement, Nicolas Cage's support of the NRA, for example, being unpalatable to Oxfam, organizations are quite happy to accept the trade-offs of time and resource expenditures that accompany celebrity involvement for the possibilities of focusing public attention on their issues. As media continues to penetrate an ever greater range and scope of global public life, the interest and opportunities for celebrities and organizations to engage with each other in pursuit of diplomatic actions will continue to increase, and celebrity diplomacy is likely to become ever more pervasive.

References

Alger, C. F. (1980), 'Empowering people for global participation', *International-Transnational Associations*, 12, pp. 508–510.

Alger, C. F. and Mendlovitz, S. (1984), 'Grassroots activism in the United States: Global implications?', *Alternatives*, 9:4, pp. 447–474.

Axmaker, S. (2005), 'Andrew Niccol Finds a World of "Macabre Absurdity"', 16 September 2005, Available at: http://www.greencine.com/article?action=view&articleID=234. Accessed 1 September 2009.

Bradbury, D. (2003), *Armstrong*, London: Haus Publishing.

Burt, R. (2005), *Brokerage and Closure: An Introduction to Social Capital*, Oxford: Oxford University Press.

Campbell, D. (2003), 'Agencies fear film about doctor in league with gunrunners could put staff at risk Hollywood Tale of Aid Worker in Cahoots With CIA Sparks Dismay', *The Guardian*, 15 November 2003, Available at http://www.guardian.co.uk/world/2003/nov/15/usa.film. Accessed 1 March 2009.

Cerny, P. G. (1995), 'Globalization and the Changing Logic of Collective Action', *International Organization*, 49:4, pp. 595–626.

Chatfield, C. (1971), *For Peace and Justice: Pacifism in America, 1914–1941*, Knoxville, Tennessee: University of Tennessee Press.

—— (1992), *The American Peace Movement: Ideals and Activism*, New York: Twayne Publishers.

Cooper, A. (2008), *Celebrity Diplomacy*, Boulder: Paradigm Publishers.

DeBenedetti, C. (1980), *The Peace Reform in American History*, Bloomington, Indiana: Indiana University Press.

Drezner, D. (2007), 'Foreign Policy goes Glam', *The National Interest*, November/December, pp. 22–28.

Hularias, A. and Tzifakis, N. (2008), 'The Dynamics of Celebrity Activism: Mia Farrow and the "Genocide Olympics Campaign', *Karamalis Working Papers in Hellenic and European Studies*, Fletcher School of Law and Diplomacy, p. 7.

IANSA Parliamentary Action to Stop Gun Violence (2006), Available at: http://www.iansa.org/control_arms/parliamentary_action.htm. Accessed 15 August 2009.

Marks, J. and Beliaev, I. (eds) (1991), *Common Ground on Terrorism*, New York: WW Norton & Co.

Mayer, A. (1959), *Political Origins of the New Diplomacy 1917–1918*, New Haven: Yale University Press.

Masland, T. and Cohen, A. (2005), 'Deal With the Devil. *Newsweek*, Web exclusive', 23 September 2005, Available at: http://web.archive.org/web/20060529083830/http://www.msnbc.msn.com/id/9442606/site/newsweek/. Accessed 15 August 2009.

Montville, J. V. and Davidson, W. D. (1981), 'Foreign Policy According to Freud', *Foreign Policy*, Winter 1981–82, pp. 145–157.

Okeeffe, A. (2005), 'NRA snag for Cage as arms curbs icon', *The Observer*, Sunday 4 December 2005, Available at: http://www.guardian.co.uk/world/2005/dec/04/usgunviolence.film. Accessed 1 April 2009.

Rousselet, P. (2006), 'Lord of War', official website available at http://patriotpictures.com/low/production.htm. Accessed 30 April 2009.

St John, W. (2003), 'The Backlash Grows against celebrity activists', *The New York Times*, March 23, Available at http://www.nytimes.com/2003/03/23/style/the-backlash-grows-against-celebrity-activists.html. Accessed 15April 2009.

Smith, C. H. (2009), 'The Effectiveness and Value of Celebrity Diplomacy An edited transcript of a panel discussion at the USC Annenberg School for Communication and Journalism 21 April', Available at: http://www.learcenter.org/images/event_uploads/celebritydiplomacy.pdf. Accessed 15 September 2009.

Tarrow, S. (2005), *The New Transnational Activism*, Cambridge: Cambridge University Press.

Zwick, J. (ed.) (1992), *Mark Twain's Weapons of Satire: Anti-Imperialist Writings on the Philippine-American War*, Syracuse: Syracuse University Press.

Notes

1. The authors thank Alan Cooper for his diligent research for this project.
2. See http://www.amnestyusa.org/artists-for-amnesty/lord-of-war/page.do?id=1104972 to view the PSAs.
3. Interview with former AIUSA staff member, April 2009.
4. Campaign to End Gun Trade Ramps Up Available at: http://www.commondreams.org/archive/2007/04/24/711. Accessed 1 September 2009.
5. 'At an AIUSA-sponsored screening of 'Lord of War' at the Library of Congress in Washington, DC, Niccol told author Rachel Stohl that he used her research and publications in writing the script of the movie.
6. 'Lord of War' arms dealer Viktor Bout arrested in Thailand, 6 March 2008. Retrieved on 1 August 2009 from http://www.timesonline.co.uk/tol/news/world/asia/article3498795.ece.
7. The online chat may be found at http://www.amnestyusa.org/askamnesty/live/display.php?topic=44

Chapter 12

Calling a New Tune for Africa? Analysing a Celebrity-led Campaign to Redefine the Debate on Africa

Dorothy Njoroge

What we are facing in Africa is an unprecedented threat to human dignity and equality. […] I'd like to be clear about what this problem is, and what this problem isn't – this is not all about charity, this is about justice.[1] (Bono, 2005 TED prize acceptance speech)

Introduction

The statement above encapsulates the main thrust of the Make Poverty History Campaign organized by rock stars Sir Bob Geldof, formerly of Boomtown Rats, and U2's Bono, along with film-maker Richard Curtis, as well as hundreds of charities and citizen groups, to encourage a debate on debt cancellation and trade justice for Africa during the G8 summit in Gleneagles in 2005. The goal of the campaign was to raise consciousness, rather than money, about the African crisis. The trio sought to use the power of pop music by planning concerts around the world on the theme of poverty eradication. Convinced that if the global community and world leaders understood the issue of African poverty in moral terms, more could be done to alleviate the suffering on the continent, the campaigners used media appearances and events to promote the message of debt relief and fairer trading terms for Africa.

Geldof and Bono's activism has outlasted many of their celebrity counterparts' faddish flirtation with causes. Geldof was involved first and recruited Bono during the 'Live Aid' concerts of 1985, which raised money for the Ethiopian famine. After U2's performance in that concert, Bono and his wife Ali quietly spent a month in an orphanage in Ethiopia where his conversion to the African cause became complete. The U2 lead singer's involvement grew as one of the star faces on *Jubilee 2000* debt relief campaign before creating his own *Debt, Aids, Trade, Africa* (DATA) advocacy network (Cooper 2008: 36). He launched a campaign, ONE, (see also Varihi Scott's chapter, this volume) to fight against poverty and for debt relief in Africa, and has engaged many of his celebrity friends in the effort – including Brad Pitt, George Clooney, and Matt Damon (Freydkin 2006).

Bono and Geldof are an integral part of a growing celebrity activism that is gradually being consolidated. Bono's angst for Africa, Bob Geldof's searing rage over the world leaders' inaction in Africa, Madonna's latest adoption of a Malawian girl and George Clooney's Darfur campaign are just a few examples of how the Hollywood glitterati become involved in the continent (see also Graham Finlay and Virgil Hawkins, this volume). What is the cause of the phenomenon? Is it the stars' larger-than-life-egos; a highly developed social conscience; or shameless publicity ploys? What are the implications for international development? Most critically, can they really change the world and our view of it?

This chapter analyses celebrity involvement in international issues by examining celebrity efforts to influence the debate on African development through the Make Poverty History campaign in 2005. It will assess how their message of justice fared in the media coverage of the campaign by examining how the British press (*Financial Times* and *The Times*) discursively constructed the African crisis during the campaign in the summer of 2005. But first, let us have a look at the African crisis.

The African Crisis

After a short dawn of hope in the 1960s following the independence of many African nations from colonial powers such as Britain, France, Portugal and Belgium, many held out the hope that African nations would join the community of prosperous and advancing nations of the world. But, after almost half a century of political independence, this dream is not even close to being realized. African problems, most notably grinding poverty, continue to escalate. To counter this, several bilateral assistance programmes such as the UK's Department for International Development (DFID), Canadian International Development Agency (CIDA), Norwegian Agency for Development Cooperation (NORAD), United States Agency for International Development (USAID) operate in the continent to jumpstart African development. The objectives of these assistance programmes include manpower training, agricultural innovations, democratic governance and other positive ends. In addition, various international financial agencies, particularly the World Bank and the International Monetary Fund (IMF), have taken up the job of drawing up economic programmes to help African nations lift themselves out of poverty. These ranged from structural adjustment programmes (SAPs) in the 1980s and 1990s, to poverty reduction strategy plans (PRSPs) presently. Historically, religious organizations have also been an integral part of attempting to provide services to Africans such as education and health. The foundations of the educational system in modern-day Africa were established by missionaries who generally used education as a tool for conversion. Despite all these efforts the situation remains dire. Thus, not just saddled with failed development programmes, but also riddled with diseases that flourish in tropical climates, such as malaria and tuberculosis, and weighed down by crushing poverty, natural disasters and unstable political systems, Africa has come to symbolize the face of hopelessness and despair. While this reality repels some, it has also served as a magnet that draws many philanthropists, economic innovators, industrialists, celebrities, religious leaders and other interested types of every shape and form to the continent to craft solutions to these endemic problems.

As a result, no longer is the discussion on African debt, declining trade, or the HIV/AIDs in the hallowed halls of the World Bank, the United Nations or academia. Global civil society, including individuals, grassroots organizations, NGOs and celebrities alike, convene to articulate their vision of a fairer world given the failures of international governance institutions to provide adequate and lasting solutions to the world's most pressing problems.

The Rise of Celebrity Activism

Celebrity involvement has grown significantly as individuals amass vast personal fortunes and want to extend their influence through philanthropy. Oprah Winfrey's Angel Network focuses on education and other social projects; the Clinton Foundation targets HIV/AIDS in Africa; Angelina Jolie focuses on refugees serving as a United Nations Refugee Agency (UNHCR) goodwill ambassador; George Clooney raises awareness on the Darfur crisis, among many others. Many of these celebrity activists' and philanthropists' attention has focused on Africa for obvious reasons – it is the continent most in need. As far as causes go, 'AIDS, Africa and the environment are the hottest now' (Freydkin 2006).

Famous individuals or celebrities, through the media, have 'a greater presence and wider scope of activity and agency than those who make up the rest of the population. They are allowed to move on the public stage while the rest of us watch' (Marshall 1997: ix) and their fame does not rely on institutional positions of power (Freydkin 2006). Street distinguishes between two kinds of celebrity politicians: (1) those who used to be entertainers but have taken up elective politics as their vocation, like Arnold Schwarzenegger and (2) those entertainers who make political statements or otherwise engage in political activities (Street 2004). Our focus here is on the latter. The 'cult of celebrity' is drawn from personalities in film, television, politics, music, sport, business and all forms of entertainment (West and Orman 2003: 17). Cooper points out that the categories from which star power is drawn has widened from entertainment to include global celebrities like the late Princess Diana – a 'glamorous enthusiast of the highest rank whose activities embedded her into the world public diplomacy' (Cooper 2008: 17).

Celebrities may take on the task of philanthropy or advocacy, or both. Bill Gates and George Soros are mainly philanthropists; for example, they contribute to Bono's DATA – Debt, AIDS, Trade, Africa (Cooper 2008: 11); Bono is mainly an advocate and solicits money from others; Angelina Jolie is both – Jolie, being the highest paid actress in 2008,[2] reportedly gives a third of her earnings to charity (Freydkin 2006). There are many reasons that account for celebrity political involvement. Street postulates that celebrities could be just like everyone else, though they have certain values that may influence their participation (Street 2002). Second, they are also products of their time, which may explain John Lennon's involvement with politics in the 1960s, a period of great political upheaval due to the Vietnam War, the struggle for women's rights and civil rights in the US. Similarly, singer Miriam Makeba's political engagement in her native South Africa during the apartheid was fostered by the political situation at the time. Third, celebrities may also be responding to audience interests. Thus, if audiences are politicized, the stars may try to tap into that (Street

2002). However, as Street rightly argues, these factors can only offer a partial explanation. Depending on the circumstances, this involvement may be costly or may simply be political gesturing.

Activist celebrities are part of a much wider global social justice movement made up of grassroots organizations, NGOs and global activist publics. According to Pompper, celebrities play three key roles in social movements: (1) as they possess substantial personal wealth, they contribute financially to movements they support – Oprah donated $51.8 million to charity in 2005; (2) they use their media skills as spokespersons for their causes and record public service announcements and make appeals; (3) they have a network of contacts they can employ to give movements access to elites in the political and financial sectors (Pompper 2003: 158–9).

They also legitimize the causes they support by lending their credibility and popularity to them. The drawback is that they can overshadow the movements and hog the spotlight for themselves and should a celebrity be involved in a scandal, he or she might take the movement down with them. But most ominously, celebrity support can lead to deradicalizing the movement (Pompper 2003: 158–9). For example, critics objected to the Make Poverty History campaign's strategy of working with G8 and other global governance organizations claiming it would prove detrimental to the overall cause of poverty eradication (Nash 2008).

Bono has become the best known face of the African anti-poverty campaign, meeting with no less than the Pope, President Bush, former British Prime Minister Blair and even touring Africa with the then US Treasury Secretary, Paul O'Neill, in 2002 as he campaigned for debt relief and increased aid to the continent (Street 2004: 438). As a *USA Today* article proclaimed, 'in the world of A-list celebrities, most roads leads to Bono' (Freydkin 2006). To plan the Make Poverty History campaign in 2005, Bono relied on the organizational and business acumen of Sir George Geldof (Cooper 2008: 59). The 'Live 8' concerts, the flagship event of the Make Poverty History campaign brought together 100 artists for concerts in eleven cities around the world, and the key event in Hyde Park was telecast to about two billion people. Sirs Paul McCartney and Elton John, Coldplay, Madonna and Mariah Carey were part of the star line-up. Other events included a TV movie, *The Girl in the Café*, broadcast on 'BBC1' and 'HBO', marches and demonstrations.

As stated earlier, the purpose of the campaign was to change the terms of the debate on Africa from charity to justice as signalled by a march on 6 July 2005 called the Long Walk to Justice. The discourse on the African crisis that this campaign sought to alter has been largely defined by development agencies, particularly the World Bank and IMF. Below are broad strokes of that discourse.

The Global Economic Development Paradigm

During colonial times, European metropoles designed their own development policies for the territories they governed. With the decolonization of most of the Third World, Rostow's modernization theory took centrestage as outlined in his well-known text, *The Stages of Economic Growth: A Non-communist Manifesto* (1960). According to it, nations would go through three stages of development – traditional, precapitalist (take off) and maturity – signified by industrialization, prosperity and mass consumption.

The focus was on individual nations, using certain policy measures, to approach the success enjoyed by industrialized nations. The World Bank and IMF were given the mandate to help streamline these economies under one system of global capitalism realized through the spread of liberal market policies throughout the world. This is sometimes referred to as the Washington Consensus – the World Bank, IMF and the US Treasury Department consensus on development policies for the Third World (Sumner 2004: 1403). It is both a paradigm and an era that dominated the 1980s and 1990s.

As Gillian Hart (2001) observes, in the early 1990s, the common wisdom of the Washington Consensus was seemingly unassailable. After the 1997 Asian crisis, however, and the admission even by the World Bank that the Asian Tigers' growth[3] had been facilitated by state intervention, not just market forces, and that the deregulation of capital markets had something to do with the crash, cracks began to appear in the edifice of neo-liberal orthodoxy represented by the consensus (Hart 2001: 652). Battered with criticism from all sides, the World Bank launched the Comprehensive Development Framework (CDF) under Wolfensohn's presidency in 1999 (Hart 2001: 653). While the World Bank and IMF have disavowed the Washington consensus, Smith observes that neo-liberalism may have adopted a human face due to criticism and protests, but the heart remains unchanged (Smith 2006: 13).

Despite the prevalence of the neo-liberal globalization outlook, all discursive power does not reside in the dominant; the subjects do engage in forms of resistance (Escobar 1995: 11). Hence, development discourse is not 'hermetically sealed' or resistant to challenge by counter discourses (Crush 1995: 20). For that reason, social movements on a global scale and other non-state political actors, such as celebrity activists, have attempted to reorient world opinion on issues of development. In the case of Make Poverty History Campaign, this change on the rhetoric of Africa from charity to justice was to be accomplished largely through the media, by large-scale events designed to attract media attention.

The Media Discourse

The media are one of the important social agents transmitting ideas and messages about the world. In Gaye Tuchman's view, they are an important social institution because of their ability to impart public character to events (Tuchman 1978: 3). While news reports are not the only factor shaping the public's understanding of the world, they do play a significant role (Tuchman 1978: 4). According to MacDonald though, the media, at best, only partially generate ideas and societal values since they have to contend with others striving to control public discourse, including politicians, advertisers, lobby groups and so forth (Macdonald

2003: 2). But when it comes to issues where the public have no other form of reference, the media become powerful opinion formers and shapers (Tuchman 1978: 2; van Dijk 2008: 58). The media's access to public discourse gives them enormous power and control over public debate (van Dijk 2008: 14). Furthermore, the prestige press influences elite classes who wield power in global economic and political arenas. To understand the contours of this discourse, this study employed Critical Discourse Analysis (CDA) as a theoretical and methodological approach.

From a discourse analysis perspective,

> discourse refers to a group of statements which structure the way a thing is thought, and the way we act on the basis of that thinking. In other words, discourse is a particular knowledge about the world which shapes how the world is understood and how things are done in it. (Rose 2001: 136)

Media discourse has to do with patterns, features and schemas that emerge from media texts (MacDonald 2003: 2). While discourses compete and jostle for dominance, some are more dominant than others because of their location – statements coming from people endowed with authority will have more impact than those of people from a subordinate social position (Rose 2001: 137–8).

Critical media scholars have dispensed with the idea that the media simply reflect reality. Instead, the idea gaining currency is that the media play a constructive role in social reality. As a result, there is no single, unchanging universal meaning; 'meaning is *constructed by a system of representation*' (Hall 1997: 21, original emphasis). Knowledge produced by certain discourses interact with the distribution and exercise of power, defines how certain things are thought about and how identities are constructed within society. Class, gender, race and other cultural identities are predicated, to some degree, on public discourse emanating from journalists, scholars, politicians, writers and others operating in the public sphere (van Dijk 2008: vii). Critical discourse studies examine the role of the media discourse in perpetuating or resisting unequal power relations, exploring how media discourse 'may have an effect on resisting or reinforcing relationships of dominance, discrimination and exploitation' (Richardson 2007: 113).

Media discourses play a crucial role in international relations. Smith notes that 'international relations, global development, and popular media discourses on Africa often have produced, formed and performed the continent, especially with respect to the so-called 'Black Africa' or Sub-Saharan Africa, as a tragedy' (Smith 2006: 3). She argues that the continued use of words like 'tragedy' to describe the African crisis, while they may evoke solidarity and sympathy, such feelings are insufficient to cause the wide-ranging structural changes needed to change the situation in the continent (Smith 2006: 3).

Andreasson further states that discourse on African development is usually a reductive repetition predicated on 'Africa's fundamental inadequacies' (Andreasson 2005: 973) while Mayer observes that the western representation of Africa is messy – it is neither a linear ordering of progressive representation or constant deterioration, reflecting multiple forces and counter-forces in operation from colonization to globalization (Mayer 2002: 17). Since development is the central discourse on Africa in globalization, social campaigns provide the lens to analyse how it functions within global media.

There is of course no assumed direct cause-and-effect relationship between media discourse and audience interpretation. Discourse is processed through a complex web of conditions that influence individual reading, including personal history and experiences, goals and objectives of reading, social position and so forth (van Dijk 2008: 22). Nevertheless, van Dijk contends that by selecting what comprises news, picking headlines, choosing particular sources over others, placement and so forth, the media play a role in the creation and reproduction of social structures (van Dijk 2008: 35). Similarly, Tuchman states that 'the news net imposes order on the social world because it enables news events to occur at some location but not others' (Tuchman 1978: 23). Nonetheless, because discourse is not determinative, meaning happens in the negotiation between text and audience, so the role of discourse analysis is to outline the framework through which such a negotiation might take place (MacDonald 2003:3).

The Make Poverty History campaign was a global media event when the media had an opportunity to convert occurrences into news events. The following section outlines how two competing discourses about Africa were treated in the news media as an example of how media discourses function. The rhetoric of the anti-poverty lobby, led by celebrities, tried to counter commonly held perceptions regarding the African crisis as represented by the neo-liberal globalization discourse about African development by employing a moral discourse. This is a common global social justice movement strategy because

> framing poverty as a global and a moral problem focuses our attention on political economy processes of poverty production and perpetuation while bringing stronger and better informed criticisms against dominant development theories and pro-globalization arguments. (St Clair 2006: 147)

The Make Poverty History Case Study

The Make Poverty History campaign was a year-long campaign in the UK but also in other parts of the world. On their part, celebrities gave dozens of media interviews and participated in activities such as music concerts and rallies, as was outlined earlier, in support of the campaign. These activities were designed to put pressure on the 2005 G8 summit to make serious commitments to deal with African poverty. The British premier at the time, Tony Blair, as G8 Chair, aligned himself to the celebrity campaigners' position given that it mirrored his agenda for the 2005 summit – African poverty and climate change.

Since Tony Blair was hosting the 2005 G8 summit, it follows that the British media followed this story keenly. I therefore looked at newspaper reports by two major British newspapers, the broadsheets *Financial Times* (FT) and *The Times* (of London), to examine how the media crafted each side of the debate on the African development crisis. *The Times* is a national English newspaper, part of the Rupert Murdoch dynasty, published by the News Corporation Group. *The Times* is one of the quality papers in Britain and tends to subscribe to conservative positions (Carvalho 2005: 2). It is a national daily with a circulation of 615, 000 (World Association of Newspapers 2008: 886). The *Financial Times,* from London, covers international business and financial events (Durham 2007: 58). It has international editions in nine sites and is a powerful voice in global finance as was evidenced by its influence, for example, in the Asian crisis of 1997 (Durham 2007: 58). It has a circulation of 449,000 (World Association of Newspapers 2008: 886). Since the G8 meeting was in July, as were the 'Live 8' concerts, I examined the reports in these publications between June and July 2005. From Lexis-Nexis, I retrieved 30 articles from the *Financial Times* (FT) and 50 from *The Times* and I adopted Critical Discourse Analysis (CDA) in analysing them. Van Dijk (2008) states there is no method specific to critical discourse studies, but researches employ whatever methods seem to fit the objectives of a particular study. CDA is a close textual reading of broad understandings regarding social phenomena, in this case, the problem of Africa's underdevelopment. In other words, I examined ways in which these papers constructed the debate regarding African underdevelopment to establish what common sense understandings were used in the media to analyse causes and solutions to Africa's abject poverty.

Given their conservative political leanings, coverage by these papers did not differ significantly in their framing of the issues, except that *The Times* wrote more stories on the issue than the *Financial Times*. In constructing their discourse on the African crisis, the two papers drew from a variety of sources including the leaders of G8 nations, international financial institutions reports, activist groups, individuals and celebrity campaigners.

Overall, the discourse on African poverty – its causes and proposed solutions – from these publications legitimized the position of international governance institutions and rich countries, which touted the neo-liberalization approach as the pathway to development. The celebrity campaigner's attempt to recast the debate in moral terms was disparaged. The contours of this discourse that emerged from these two papers had three clear outlines.

- First, a framing of these problems as an ideological divide between the 'left and the right' of the political spectrum.
- Second, a discounting of the moral discourse employed by celebrity campaigners who attempted to historicize the development project from a global perspective by linking Africa's woes to the international economic system.
- And third, framing of aspects of trade justice in terms similar to those of the campaigners resulting in some level of convergence between the two competing discourses.

Media coverage of the anti-poverty debate revolved around the causes and solutions to the African crisis, with reference to three key issues: debt cancellation, aid and trade justice. Both papers broadly covered the arguments concerning the African crisis as advanced by celebrity and global justice campaigners, calling for the cancellation of African debt, increased aid, and improved terms of trade since according to this view, conditions in the global economy had contributed to these problems. The media characterized these arguments as the political 'left' position. The converse position advanced by international governance institutions such as the World Bank, which called for more trade liberalization in Africa as the pathway to economic development, was characterized as the political 'right'. Thus, there was a degree of polarization of perspectives in the media coverage of these issues.

The Make Poverty History campaign, and the Blair administration, couched their argument for supporting Africa's cause in moral terms. As chief campaigner, Bob Geldof declared, in a 14 June *Times* article, during the G8 summit, he 'hoped for tough public debate on what is clearly the greatest political problem of our time', which he described as the remorseless 'pornography of poverty that is paraded across our television screen every night' (Geldof 2005: 19). Hilary Benn, Britain's International Development Secretary, told the *Financial Times* on 2 July that dealing with global poverty 'is the great moral challenge of our generation' (Newman 2005: 6).

Continuing on the same theme, a 1 June *Times* article reported that Sir Bob Geldof pointed out that the purpose of Live 8 was 'not for charity but for political justice'(Sherwin 2005: 4). Talking about his romantic comedy, *The Girl in the Café*, written to articulate the African issue, Richard Curtis, another key campaigner, said his role and those of other celebrity activists was 'to keep the simple moral fact in the politicians' minds' according to *The Times* of 18 June (Sweeting 2005: 38). Africa had improved, Curtis argued, on the basis of the reduced number of wars to a third of what it used to be a decade ago; further, more countries had adopted democratic changes but poverty had not ended, so more and better aid was required (Sweeting 2005: 38).

Geldof continued this moral discourse by laying the blame for Africa's woes on the West. A *Times* news report on 8 June 2005, reported that 'Geldof's rhetoric [was] that the capitalist West has, through a combination of greed and selfishness, failed the people of Africa' (Linklater 2005: 19). The *Financial Times* reported that Geldof attacked 'the injustice of western trade policies' and blamed the white West for many of Africa's historical problems ranging from poverty to cattle disease (Shrimsley 2005: 15). He then asked people to act – 'I believe you can change the condition of the most put-down and beaten-down people on this planet' as reported by the *Financial Times* on 30 June (2005: 15). As these reports indicate, Geldof tried to recast the issue of African poverty in broader terms and to redefine it as an issue of justice, arguing that it was incumbent on the rich segments of the world to help Africa in the interests of justice. He attempted to draw a connexion between the wealth of the rich nations and Africa's underdevelopment. On their part, the media discounted this position and provided a different narrative to explain the dire conditions in the continent.

The news articles in these two publications objected to heavy moralizing by Geldof and Brown. While a *Financial Times* article of 6 July expressed agreement that there was a moral imperative 'to help' (Wolf 2005: 21), Gordon Brown's emphasis on debt forgiveness and more generous aid was considered short-sighted according to a report in *The Times* 4 July (Lea 2005: 44). Another *Times* report on 1 June charged Geldof with 'arm-twisting, cajoling and moral blackmail' (Sherwin 2005: 4). All in all, the campaigners were accused of being motivated 'by misplaced morality and condescending post-colonial guilt' according to an opinion article in *Times* 4 July (Lea 2005: 44). The press reports called for a hard-headed unsentimental evaluation of Africa's woes. In addition, these reports refuted charges by Geldof and other campaigners that the rich nations were culpable in the suffering of the Third World. For example, a *Times* article on 8 July stated 'to some extent, it is assumed, our standard of living is built at the expense of Africa and the poorer parts of Asia and of Latin America. They could not be more wrong' (Searjeant 2005: 59).

The thorny issue of debt relief received a lot of attention with divergent views on the issue dominating coverage. For example, in a *Times* report of 14 June, the anti-poverty campaigners called for the cancellation of outstanding debt owed by African countries and argued that the money should never have been given out in the first place, and therefore the West had a moral obligation to write off the debt (2005: 17). The campaigners maintained that these debts were odious and should not be paid because the loans were given to dictators in a bygone era. The debt cancellation rationale was 'that Africa has become more democratic, and that a new generation of leaders should not have to suffer the burden of crippling debts incurred by their predecessors' according to *The Times* 4 June (2005: 23). The anti-poverty campaigners were quoted as expressing dissatisfaction with the provisions for debt relief that catered to only a few countries, with debt relief measures that would not take effect until 2010. According to a *Times* article of 9 June, they called for urgent debt relief for 62 countries (Beeston 2005: 40). The G8 had approved relief for eighteen countries.

On the other side of the debate, these publications advanced the argument that debt relief could bolster undemocratic governments if not well administered. While no one quibbled with the necessity of debt forgiveness, the necessity for conditions of good governance and transparency was stressed in the *Financial Times,* 6 July (Wolf 2005: 21). Also, some of the articles expressed concern that debt relief would let Africa's kleptomaniac leaders 'off the hook' (*Times* 14 June 2005: 17). Geldof and his compatriots were accused of being unappreciative of the steps undertaken by G8 countries to forgive debt in eighteen of the poorest African countries. The media presented the tension between the Africa campaigners' position, which stressed the urgency of aid relief, and the economic liberalism perspective, which stressed the need for internal reform within Africa as a precondition for debt relief. While Geldof and other campaigners attempted to link Africa's woes to external conditions, many texts laid the blame on internal conditions, blaming African leaders for the situation their countries found themselves in. By giving short thrift to historical and structural dimensions of Africa's woes, the media narrowed the possibilities of a wide-ranging debate on Africa's problems beyond a few policy issues related to economic growth.

The same position held true on the role of aid in African development. Again, the media presented two polarized positions. The celebrity anti-poverty campaigners and their collaborators in the social justice movement demanded a dramatic increase in aid to Africa to facilitate meaningful change. They wanted rich countries to double the aid, which they felt was just a trickle. Anna MacDonald, of Oxfam urged the Group of eight for an 'ambitious agreement' that would mark a significantly larger aid package to provide debt relief so the poorest countries could provide basic social services to their populations according to a report in *The Times* on 9 June (Beeston 2005: 40). They complained that the amounts proposed by G8 were miniscule and only accounted for 10 per cent of the aid required (Beeston 2005:40). Besides, only $10 –20 of the billion Gleneagles agreement would be new money and the increase would not be realized until 2010, a five-year wait according to the *Financial Times* on 9 July (Beattie 2005: 8).

On the other side of this argument, several articles claimed that Africa had benefited from more aid per capita than any other region in the world, and that more money, unless under the most stringent conditions, was not warranted. Reports stated that Africa was beneficiary to 'vast sums of money' according to *The Times* of 2 July (2005: 23). *The Times* of 7 July stated that Africa was gearing to receive 'a tsunami of fresh money is in the aid pipeline'(Hoffman 2005a, 2005b: 46) from the G8, and had 'received more foreign aid in real terms than the Marshall Plan' according to *The Times* of 8 June (Linklater 2005: 19). Concern was expressed that huge sums of money to be given to Africa would result in Dutch disease – artificially inflated values of a nation's currency. A lot more newsprint was dedicated to describing the failures of aid due to mismanagement and corruption as well as creating dependency. This contrasted with claims by the campaigners that the money provided had been minimal. The media presentation of the debate in a polarized manner narrowed the possibilities of envisioning a middle ground on the role of development aid and debt relief.

However, when it came to trade reform, there was a degree of convergence between the campaigners' rhetoric and media discourse. Geldof urged western nations to 'get rid of the nauseating protectionism and subsidies that cause people to suffer in Africa' when he wrote an article in *The Times* of 14 June (Geldof 2005: 19). Similarly, articles in both papers decried the unfairness of farm subsidies given to US and European farmers, which made products from the Third World less competitive. For example, *The Times* of 4 July 2005, labelled European subsidies to farmers 'immoral practices' that together with kleptomaniac leadership in Africa, served to entrench poverty.

Despite the convergence in this instance, the campaigners' argument was undermined to some degree by the pejorative terms used to characterize them.

Teun van Dijk notes, power elites have means to control counter discourses through censorship, branding non-conformists as communists, terrorists, enemies of freedom etc to take these ideas out of circulation (van Dijk 2008: 37). By branding Geldof 'mad', 'licensed fool', 'bully', 'demagogue', and elements of the anti-poverty advocates as 'violent anti-capitalists', 'frustrated extremists' and 'wreckers' (Linklater 2005: 10; Lister 2005: 8), their position was further delegitimized. We are invited to see Geldof as unstable and therefore not to rely on his judgment or assessment of the social problems he is articulating. Further, the media presented the campaign as Blair's and Geldof's personal crusades rather than an issue of global importance.

Conclusion

As we have seen, the media reported widely on the differing positions held by celebrity campaigners and their collaborators from the global justice movement, and those held by international governance institutions and other leading agencies i.e. the 'left' and 'right' positions. These reports showed a wide disparity between these two perspectives on the issues of debt relief and aid, but a confluence of opinion in some aspects of the trade debate, with both positions acknowledging that trade distortions in agricultural products are caused by subsidies given to European and US farmers.

Can celebrities change our view of the world? Is there truth to Geldof's claim that 'we have helped to define the terms of debate for these times'? (Geldof 2005: 19). Clearly, by their visibility, celebrity campaigners raised the stakes in this debate during the 2005 G8 summit. But judging this as a debate contest, we may conclude they lost out. After all, media reports poked holes in the celebrity campaigners' assessment and recommendations regarding the causes and solutions to Africa's grinding poverty.

But it is not that simple. Not all their messages were filtered through the media; through their concerts and campaign website, they had opportunities to interact directly with the public. Hence, by an examination of the media discourse, we cannot account for what the public perceptions may have been following the campaign, which would have been a very interesting study.

While they may not have changed the debate in the media, the campaigners scored some major points. They raised Africa's profile in the international arena. African problems are normally discussed in local rather than global terms even in a global public sphere. However, due to the campaign, the debate expanded to consider issues beyond African misrule and corruption. As Andreasson rightly observes

> insisting on epistemological decentralizations in this way, i.e. broadening the scope of ideas being taken seriously in debates about development, means that we could make possible a re-evaluation of how we think about Africa, about modernity, about development. (Andreasson 2005: 983)

And even though the press was unwilling to explore systemic causes of poverty, the celebrities' rhetoric forced a discussion on this issue, even though it amounted to the media counteracting the campaigners' claims that wealthy nations were culpable in the suffering of poor nations. It is not that the celebrities' campaign was unproblematic however, as it did not question the premise of the one-size-fits-all development paradigm; it just sought to improve African inclusion in the global system.

In sum, while the preponderance of the media discourse centred on African failure to create modern economic and political institutions, there was acknowledgement of systemic structural issues affecting Africa's development. Thus, views that have been peripheral moved a little closer to the centre even as they encountered resistance. While the neo-liberal position was ultimately legitimated in the media discourse, the global justice position made headway in the international public sphere, especially given that the two publications under discussion are politically conservative.

It is not that what celebrity campaigners had to say was particularly new – global civil society groups have been making the same arguments for years. But celebrities had the visibility and media access to put their points across, extending the contours of the debate on Third World poverty in the global arena. Celebrities may not alter the perspectives but they muddied up the waters, so that what was once a clear consensus on Africa is not so apparent, and this may have raised possibilities for a broader, historically informed debate on Africa. The major achievement of the campaign was probably deepening the fissures in the neo-liberal edifice.

References

Andreasson, S. (2005), 'Orientalism and African Development Studies: The "reductive repetition" Motif in Theories of African Underdevelopment', *Third World Quarterly*, 26:6, pp. 971–986.

'Art and ideas column', *Financial Times*, 30 June 2005, p. 15, Available at: http://www.lexisnexis.com:80/us/lnacademic/results/docview/docvie…isb=22_T4989517665&treeMax=true&treeWidth=0&csi=293847&docNo=189. Accessed 31 October 2008.

Beattie, A. (2005), 'Campaigners divided on aid promises for Africa Anti-Poverty Initiative', *Financial Times*, 9 July, p. 8, http://www.lexisnexis.com.proxy.lib.siu.edu/us/lnacademic/search/homesubmitForm.do. Accessed 31 October 2008.

Beeston, R. (2005), 'Why the West's billions may end up in the wrong hands', *Times*, 9 June, p. 40, Available at: http://www.lexisnexis.com:80/us/lnacademic/results/docview/docvie […] cisb=22_T4989517665&treeMax=true&treeWidth=0&csi=10939&docNo=228. Accessed 31 October 2008.

Bird, S. and Rumbelow, H. (2005), 'I'll drop farming subsidies if EU does the same, says Bush', *Times*, 4 July, p. 6, Available at: http://www.lexisnexis.com:80/us/lnacademic/results/docview/docvie…cisb=22_T4989517665&treeMax=true&treeWidth=0&csi=10939&docNo=168.Accessed 31 October 2008.

Carvalho, A. (2005), 'Representing the Politics of the Greenhouse Effect: Discursive Strategies in the British Media', *Critical Discourse Studies*, 2:1, pp. 1–29.

Cooper, A. F. (2008), *Celebrity Diplomacy*, Boulder: Paradigm.

Crush, J. (1995), 'Introduction: Imagining Development', in J. Crush (ed.), *Power of Development*, London: Routledge, pp. 1–23.

Durham, F., D. (2007), 'Framing the state in globalization: The *Financial Times* coverage of the 1997 Thai currency crisis', *Critical Studies in Media Communication* 24: 1, pp. 57–76.

Escobar, A. (1995), *Encountering Development: The Making and Unmaking of the Third World*, New Jersey: Princeton University Press.

Freydkin, D. (2006), 'Celebrity Activists Put Star Power to Good Use: They Bring Prestige Press To a Myriad Causes, Charities', *USA Today*, [Internet] 23 June, Available at: http://www.usatoday.com/life/people/2006-06-22-celeb-charities-main_x.htm. Accessed 24 December 2007.

Geldof, B. (2005), 'Don't blink: The world is tilting on its axis', *Times*, 14 June, p. 19. Available at: http://www.lexisnexis.com:80/us/lnacademic/results/docview/docvie…cisb=22_T4989517665&treeMax=true&treeWidth=0&csi=10939&docNo=215. Accessed 31 October 2008.

Gitlin, T. (2003), *The Whole World is Watching: Mass Media in the Making and the Unmaking of the New Left*, Berkeley: University of California Press.

Hall, S. (1997), 'The Work of Representation', in S. Hall (ed.), *Representation: Cultural Representations and Signifying Practices*, London: Sage, pp. 13–74.

Hart, G. (2001), 'Development critiques in the 1990s: *Culs de sac* and Promising Paths', *Progress in Human Geography*, 25:4, pp. 649–658.

Hoffman, K. (2005a), 'Aid community cannot make poverty history', *Times*, 7 July, p. 46, Available at: http://www.lexisnexis.com:80/us/lnacademic/results/docview/docvie...cisb=22_T4989517665&treeMax=true&treeWidth=0&csi=10939&docNo=158. Accessed 31 October 2008.

—— (2005b), 'Lack of investment is the real tragedy in Africa', *Financial Times*, 10 June, p. 19, Available at: http://www.lexisnexis.com:80/us/lnacademic/results/docview/docvie...isb=22_T4989517665&treeMax=true&treeWidth=0&csi=293847&docNo=223. Accessed 31 October 2008.

Lea, R. (2005), 'Saving the world means more than just Africa', *Times*, 4 July, p. 44, Available at: http://www.lexisnexis.com:80/us/lnacademic/results/docview/docvie...cisb=22_T4989517665&treeMax=true&treeWidth=0&csi=10939&docNo=170. Accessed 31 October 2008.

Linklater, M. (2005), 'Bob Geldof's brazen appeal to popular outrage won't make poverty history', *Times*, 8 June, p. 19, Available at: http://www.lexisnexis.com:80/us/lnacademic/results/docview/docvie...cisb=22_T4989517665&treeMax=true&treeWidth=0&csi=10939&docNo=229. Accessed 31 October 2008.

Lister, D. (2005), 'Edinburgh braced for violence as anarchist come flooding in', *Times*, 4 July p. 8, Available at: http://www.lexisnexis.com:80/us/lnacademic/results/docview/docvie...cisb=22_T4989517665&treeMax=true&treeWidth=0&csi=10939&docNo=171. Accessed 31 October 2008.

Macdonald, M. (2003), *Exploring Media Discourse*, London: Arnold.

Marshall, P. D. (1997), *Celebrity and Power: Fame in Contemporary Culture*, Minneapolis: University of Minnesota Press.

Mayer, R. (2002), *Artificial Africas: Colonial Images in the Times of Globalization*, New Hampshire: University Press of New England.

Nash, K. (2008), 'Global Citizenship as Show Business: The Cultural Politics of Make Poverty History', *Media, Culture & Society*, 30:2, pp. 167–181.

Newman, C. (2005), 'Rich nations "must avoid climate disaster" Group of Eight Summit', *Financial Times*, 2 July, p. 6, Available at http://www.lexisnexis.com:80/us/lnacademic/results/docview/docvie...isb=22_T4989517665&treeMax=true&treeWidth=0&csi=293847&docNo=174. Accessed 31 October 2008.

'Out of debt', *Times*, 14 June 2005, p. 17, Available at: http://www.lexisnexis.com:80/us/lnacademic/results/docview/docvie...&cisb=22_T4989399445&treeMax=true&treeWidth=0&csi=10939&docNo=13. Accessed 31 October 2008.

Pompper, D. (2003), 'Probing Symbiotic Relationships: Celebrities, Mass Media, and Global Justice', in A. Opel and D. Pompper (eds), *Representing Resistance: Media, Civil Disobedience, and the Global Justice Movement*, Westport, Connecticut: Praeger Publishers, pp. 149–169.

Richardson, J. E. (2007), *Analysing Newspapers: An Approach from Critical Discourse Analysis*, New York: Palgrave Macmillan.

'Rock the world', *Times*, 4 June 2005, p. 23, Available at: http://www.lexisnexis.com:80/us/lnacademic/results/docview/docvie...cisb=22_T4989517665&treeMax=true&treeWidth=0&csi=10939&docNo=236. Accessed 31 October 2008.

Rose, G. (2001), *Visual Methodologies: An Introduction to the Interpretation of Visual Materials*, London: Sage Publications.

Searjeant, G. (2005), 'Only the rich West can save the poor', *Times*, 8 July, p. 59, Available at: http://www.lexisnexis.com:80/us/lnacademic/results/docview/docvie...cisb=22_T4989517665&treeMax=true&treeWidth=0&csi=10939&docNo=153. Accessed 31 October 2008.

Sherwin, A. (2005), 'Geldof goes global for new Live 8 crusade to save Africa', *Times*, 1 June, p. 4, Available at: http://www.lexisnexis.com:80/us/lnacademic/results/docview/docvie...cisb=22_T4989517665&treeMax=true&treeWidth=0&csi=10939&docNo=242. Accessed 31 October 2008.

Shrimsley, R. (2005), 'A self-indulgent wading, deep into the shallows of spiritual belief', *Financial Times*, 24 June, p. 15, Available at: http://www.lexisnexis.com:80/us/lnacademic/results/docview/docvie...isb=22_T4989517665&treeMax=true&treeWidth=0&csi=293847&docNo=203. Accessed 31 October 2008.

Smith, M. S. (2006), 'Discourses on development: Beyond the "African Tragedy"', in M. S. Smith (ed.), *Beyond the 'African Tragedy': Discourses on Development and the Global Economy*, Hampshire: Ashgate, pp. 1–22.

St Clair, A. (2006), 'Global Poverty: Development Ethics Meets Global Justice', *Globalizations*, 3:2, pp. 139–158.

Street, J. (2002), 'Bob, Bono and Tony B: The Popular Artist as Politician', *Media, Culture & Society*, 24, pp. 433–441.

—— (2004), 'Celebrity Politicians: Popular Culture and Political Representation', *British Journal of Politics and International Relations*, 4:6, pp. 435–452.

Sumner, A. (2006), 'In Search of a the Post-Washington (Dis)consensus: The "Missing" Content of PRSPS', *Third World Quarterly*, 27:8, pp. 1401–1412.

Sutcliffe, B. (1999), 'The Place of Development in Theories of Imperialism and Globalization', in R. Munck and D. O'Hearn (eds), *Critical Development Theory: Contributions to a New Paradigm*, London: Zed, pp. 135–154.

Sweeting, A. (2005), 'Making comedy history', *Times*, 18 June, p. 38, Available at: http://www.lexisnexis.com:80/us/lnacademic/results/docview/docvie...cisb=22_T4989517665&treeMax=true&treeWidth=0&csi=10939&docNo=208. Accessed 31 October 2008.

'The better tune', *Times*, 4 July 2005, p. 17, Available at: http://www.lexisnexis.com:80/us/lnacademic/results/docview/docvie...cisb=22_T4989517665&treeMax=true&treeWidth=0&csi=10939&docNo=169. Accessed 31 October 2008.

Thérien, J. (1999), 'Beyond the North-South divide: The Two Tales of World Poverty', *Third World Quarterly*, 20:4, pp. 723–742.

Tuchman, G. (1978), *Making News: A Study in the Construction of Reality*, New York: Free Press.

Van Dijk, T. (2008), *Discourse and Power*, New York: Palgrave, Macmillan.

West, D. M. and John, O. (2003), *Celebrity Politics*, New Jersey: Prentice Hall.

'When the music stops', *Times*, 2 July 2005, p. 23, Available at: http://www.lexisnexis.com:80/us/lnacademic/results/docview/docvie...cisb=22_T4989517665&treeMax=true&treeWidth=0&csi=10939&docNo=180. Accessed 31 October 2008.

Wolf, M. (2005), 'Aid will not make poverty history – but it is worth trying', *Financial Times*, 6 July, p. 21, Available at: http://www.lexisnexis.com:80/us/lnacademic/results/docview/docvie...isb=22_T4989517665&treeMax=true&treeWidth=0&csi=293847&docNo=159. Accessed 31 October 2008.

World Association of Newspapers (2008), *World Press Trends 2008*, Paris: World Association of Newspapers/ZenithOptimedia.

Notes

1. Bono: TED Prize wish: Join my call to action on Africa, Viewed on 19 March 2009 http://www.youtube.com/watch?v=1VOlXwhp00Y&feature=channel
2. Yahoo movies, '2008's Highest-Paid Actresses', 5 December 2008, viewed on 8 December 2008, http://movies.yahoo.com/photos/collections/gallery/1300/2008s-highestpaid-actresses/fp#info
3. South Korea, Taiwan, Singapore, Hong Kong, Thailand, Indonesia, The Philippines and Malaysia. CRS Report: The 1997 Asian Financial Crisis. Available at: http://www.fas.org/man/crs/crs-asia2.htm [Accessed 12 February 2010].

Chapter 13

Fame and Symbolic Value in Celebrity Activism and Diplomacy

George Pleios

Introduction

The history of fame runs parallel to the history of western civilization, according to Giles (2000: 12–14), who views fame (or how well known and recognizable an individual is) in a historical context. Starting off from Giles' essential differentiation between fame in pre-modern and modern societies – while concurrently taking into account how culture is perceived (and made) through different socio-historical periods – I would argue that *celebrity diplomacy and activism* can be seen as the diplomatic activity of the people who are famous for being famous in late modernity.

Bearing that in mind, in this chapter I examine celebrity diplomacy and celebrity activism as a synthesis of politics and spectacle in the field of foreign relations emanating from adding symbolic value to a wide range of activities and products. More specifically, at first I analyse celebrity diplomacy and activism from the perspective of political economy and mass communication theory; this is followed by the distinction between cultural, social, economic, and political celebrity diplomacy and activism. My main contention in this chapter is that the activities of celebrities are not only a synthesis of both celebrity diplomacy/activism and public diplomacy, but are also shifting from the cultural to the political field, which leads to the celebretization of diplomacy itself.

Celebrities as the Personification of Symbolic Value

The phenomenon of the people-who-are-known-for-being-known has been prevalent ever since antiquity. Homer, Caesar and Alexander the Great, Jesus Christ, Charlemagne, Colombo, the great intellectuals, artists, religious and political leaders belong to this social group (Giles 2000: 12–14). Even though this phenomenon seems diachronic, the characteristics that attribute fame to someone vary through time. Famous people are not just '[...] people who are charismatic and appealing' (Ferris 2007: 371–384), but people who possess those attributes considered supreme within a specific socio-cultural frame. Thus, Klapp's distinction between individuals that are distinguished for their achievements/ heroism and those who have fame and reputation thanks to their media visibility is not just a logical differentiation, but also a historical one (1949).

What brings fame along depends on two interconnected factors: the first has to do with culture in different historical eras, while the second with the significance of the media in social life. Taking cue from Raymond Williams' cultural theory approach, we can distinguish between three periods in the evolution of culture: (1) in traditional societies, (2) in modern societies up to the nineteenth century and (3) during the twentieth century (1960: introduction). In traditional societies, culture was perceived as the training of man. At its core lies the ancient ideal of nobility and goodness (*kalokagathia*). During early modernity, culture is perceived as a set of achievements in areas like science, technology, education, etc or as the total sum of these cultural forms (Tylor 1920). Finally, in the twentieth century, culture was perceived as a way of life (Williams 1960: xiv; Demertzis 1989: 22–23).

Glorified (or well-known) people that belonged to the first category were Achilles, Alexander the Great and great philosophers among others (Garland 2005). The same tradition continued with Christ and the Saints (Orth 2004), up to Loyola and Luther (Rojek 2001: 51–100). In modernity, fame was acquired primarily by those who were distinguished for their achievements in a certain cultural form. Hence from the fifteenth to the nineteenth century, individuals like Gutenberg and Watt, Hegel and Marx, Goethe and Beethoven, were portrayed in or connected to artworks, and thus acquired fame (Braudy 1997). In the twentieth century, a paradigm shift changed what made someone well known: the epic virtues of the past have been gradually replaced by the coarse and trivial attributes of mass culture heroes (Orth 2004).

In the nineteenth century people gained fame thanks to their presence in the press (Carter 2006). As a result, the tradition of appointing famous writers, athletes, media stars of the likes of Washington Irving, Art Linkletter, Alva Myrdal, Georgios Seferis, Lawrence Durrell, António Egas Moniz and Octavio Paz as conventional diplomats was formed. This tradition is probably the most important forerunner of modern celebrity diplomacy, though it differs from it due to two reasons – the kind of famous people, cultural activity and the nature of their engagement in diplomatic action: first, individuals such as those mentioned above were not celebrities usually (in the modern sense of the term); second, they were appointed as conventional diplomats. For this reason, they have been evaluated in their role as diplomats by the standards of traditional diplomacy. This tradition can be described as *diplomacy of the famous*.

Both famous people's *diplomacy* (like those in early twentieth and nineteenth centuries) and present-day celebrity *diplomacy* are distinct from famous people's and celebrities' *activism* (activism of artists and intelligentsia in early modernity and the activism of media and entertainment celebrities in late modernity, respectively): in the latter case, the case of *diplomacy*, famous people or celebrities are acting in the name of official political structures likes ministries, governmental organizations, UN etc, whereas in the former, the case of *activism*, such a connection is not necessary. Famous or celebrity *activism* is usually exercised in the name or is promoted by social movements and pressure groups (Edward and McCarthy 2004; Clemens and Minkof 2004; Gamson and Wolfsfeld 1993).

With the development of mass culture in the twentieth century, publicity protagonists become gradually the stars of the day. The famous people of the nineteenth century were replaced by actors, directors, authors and composers (Morin 1992: 238). If the development of the print media (Thompson 1995) is the most important cultural change in the transition from tradition to modernity, a similar change in the transition to late modernity is the emergence of screen (iconistic) media and radio (Pleios 2001, Chapters 3–4). While the spread of print media is due to the economic and social power of the bourgeoisie and the emergence of the public sphere (Habermas 1989), the dominance of electronic, especially screen media is associated with major economic, social and cultural changes in the twentieth century. As the study of mass culture and television has shown (Baudrillard 1975; Dunn 1986), although screen media have many origins, their cultural dominance is tightly connected to the increasing economic, social and cultural role of consumption in modern societies. Television, for example, was rapidly developed in late 1940s, 1950s and 1960s, thanks to advertising (in the US) (Dominick 1990: 180, 256), which attempted to attract the widening income of working and middle classes (Leiss et al. 2005), which resulted from corporate wage practices (Davis 1991, Chapter 2) or/and thanks to governmental subsidies (in Europe) as a part of widening consumption that resulted from state wage and social policies.

A significant part of the interplay between mass culture and mass consumption can be explained by the changes that took place in the commodity structure in late modernity. In terms of political economy, the most important value of a commodity now is its symbolic value, namely its attribute to be an indispensable carrier of a certain and specific modern or high modern way of life, which facilitates its exchange, and thus its production and consumption (Baudrillard 1975; Pleios 2001, Chapter 3). In this perspective, the symbolic value of commodities makes them able to symbolize in material, not only in cognitive terms, desirable social identities – within the particular frame of social relations. Therefore, the consumption and appropriation of the commodities' symbolic value can generate or promote an imaginary social or cultural mobility. And this is a main reason for the production and circulation of commodities with high symbolic value (or simply commodities – symbols). Thus, all social institutions and practices, which produce the symbolic value of commodities (like media, public relations and advertising agencies, a great part of educational institutions etc, in short information industries – Webster 1994: 10–18) become central in the process of social structuration.

The mass media, mainly the screen or moving image media, as well as the advertising industries, the public relations agencies, in short the entire sector of promotional culture (Wernick 1991) is taking part in the process of adding symbolic value to the commodities. But beyond that, the semiotic structure of the symbolic value itself is similar to the semiotic structure of the screen media text – they both are 'pictures' in Arnheim's understanding of the term. According to Arnheim (1969, Chapters 8, 12, 13,) 'pictures' are the images '[…] to the extent to which they portray things located at a lower level of abstractness than they are themselves […] Abstractness is a means by which the picture interprets what it portrays' (Arnheim 1969: 137). Thus, the screen or iconistic or moving image media texts do not describe (represent) the real world but a more abstract view of this world. In the same manner, the symbolic value of commodities – symbols (like 'beauty', 'power', 'desirableness', 'virtue, and so on) added through the media and promotion culture, is more abstract than the commodities themselves and their use value.

Hence, thanks to the symbolic value, added by the iconistic and other media, commodities can transfer or generate in their consumers' (and spectators at the same time) heads, accepted by the social systems and desirable by the individuals' social identities. In this sense, the consumption of iconistic or moving image texts and culture can stimulate or maintain the individuals' engagement in the intensive labour process and consequent social activities because their output can fulfill individuals' personal development and seeking of social/ cultural mobility. Therefore the media, mainly the iconistic ones, adding symbolic value to commodities, can contribute in a unique way to the maintenance of a societal system set up for the production, circulation and consumption of commodities – symbols (Pleios 2001). Despite national circumstances or contextual factors, this is probably the main reason why modern celebrities emerge mainly from the showbiz and the media (Bonner et al. 1999; Giles 2000: 3).

In this context, celebrities are elites who live in high visibility and they are the objects of collective gossip, the channels of which are the mass media (Alberoni 1972; Pringle 2004; Cashmore 2006, Chapter 4). Beyond these attributes, celebrities have two more characteristics as iconistic media personae that make them able or even effective in adding symbolic value to their own off-media activities: first they personify those desirable values that are being added in the products advertised by them, competing parties, sport teams etc in iconistic media. Through personification, celebrityhood helps reproduce consumerism and the economic and social system as well (Cashmore 2006: 269). Thus, personification not only makes the symbolic values hidden in commodities or symbols visible, but also gives them power in many societal fields. In this sense, behind the non-institutional power that exercises celebrities in social movements, diplomacy, protection of the environment, religion, politics, economy and so on, we must see the institutional power of celebrity culture in the societal system.

Given this argument, celebrities' work can be considered as an 'achievement', which is a prerequisite within the context of (late) modern economy and society. Thus, from a socio-economic perspective, modern celebrities are more important than they appear to be, although they are not known for any other achievement than their media image (Boorstin 1980; Braudy 1997). Showbiz 'heroes' become gradually a significant social force able to exercise influence on issues outside the world of showbiz (Ellis 2007). This is well known to advertisers and propagandists as for several decades celebrities have been used to promote relevant goals – for example, testimonial technique in propaganda or advertisement campaigns (Jowett and O' Donnell 1992: 232).

Although such a statement was valid through the twentieth century mass culture, it has become more applicable in modern *media democracies*. This happens because, unavoidably, politics are now represented in a more theatrical and personalized way (Meyer and Hinchman 2002; Corner 2000). This results from the combination of marketing with politics (Street 2003: 441) – something that was initially considered a social pathology. As a result, actors, journalists and TV stars become more often protagonists in politics and vice versa (Ronald Reagan, Arnold Schwarzenegger in the United States, Melina Mercouri in Greece), despite the kind of culture they represent (e.g. high/low, Hollywood/Bollywood), which is another question from the 'spectacle' point of view. Media celebrities become protagonists not only in the sphere of domestic politics (Meyer and Hinchman 2002, Chapter 4; Street 2004), but also in the foreign affairs and international relations area.

Thus, the value of celebrity diplomacy and activism and of celebrities themselves in dealing with various social and political problems across the globe is not contained in the utilitarian ('use value') dimension of their actions. Namely, it does not consist of their own abilities in terms of traditional diplomacy; neither of their diplomatic efforts in the settlement of international issues, unlike traditional diplomats who may not share fame in the way celebrities do. Moreover, it is not contained in the meanings that celebrity diplomats may have as symbols (of peace, cooperation, social protest etc).

The celebrity's ability lies in the fact that the meaning of a media star as a symbol is transferred to his/her status as a diplomatic agent and vice versa. Deliberation in finding a solution to a problem, and its implementation, takes place according to the media persona's values, norms and meanings, not according to political values, which means that diplomatic issues are handled and are being resolved in mass communication terms. Under these circumstances, celebrities like Bono and Jolie are not just supporters of, or fighters against, diplomats and political leaders who seek to settle international issues. They are not any more *enthusiastic amateurs* (Cooper 2007), like in the past – like Jane Fonda, Victor Jara, Vanessa Redgrave etc. Celebrities have become protagonists themselves in the diplomatic arena or *master manipulators* (Cooper 2007).

Thus, the symbolic value of celebrity diplomats/activists, drawing from their public/media image (Ellis 2007; Collins 2008), consists of setting (or shifting) a certain issue (humanitarian, political, etc.), as well as the identities and relationships between people who are involved in this issue, from a specific social, political and cultural framework/field to another. This new framework/field, on the one hand, seems acceptable to the parties involved, particularly to those that have a negative power relations balance; on the other hand, it is in line with the values of those that have a positive balance in the power relations system. Therefore, if consensus is a key social function of the media system (Hermann and Chomsky 1988), such a consensus is achieved (and) through celebrity diplomacy and activism (or sought) also in the area of international relations.

From this perspective, celebrity diplomacy/activism is similar to persuasion or public relations, since celebrities place their fame in the service of international of national institutions, organizations etc – what Cooper (2007) calls *entrapment*. Although it seems that the celebrity aspect obscures the diplomacy/activism aspect, what often is taking place is just the opposite: celebrity diplomacy and celebrity activism are processes of cultural and ideological transformation of international issues to a consensus in favour of those who belong to the strong pole in the world and/or national power relations system. It is true, as Alex de Waal (2008) points out, that a '[…] celebrity […] acts as a bridge between a (western) audience and a faraway tragedy'. But at the same time this tragedy is set up by the rules of the (western) spectacle and/or political 'game' (Kellner 2010). Thus, by the media influence that exercises celebrities, issues of social inequality or political or economic oppression become 'humanitarian disasters', 'water crises', 'misunderstanding crises' etc. (Minear and Smith 2007; Cottle and Nolan 2008). But humanitarian disasters are not self-generated as such. Starving in Biafra or dying in Darfur or Kosovo etc is primarily a matter of politics and balance of power (de Waal 2005; Morris 1999; Hansen and Aronson 1995; Mamdani 2009). Humanitarian disasters are one of the many consequences of that.

From Entertainment to Political Celebrity Diplomacy and Activism

Following the above analysis, we can distinguish two types of well-known or public persons (Marshall 1997: part I) and two types of political activity exerted by them. Well-known people can be divided into (1) famous people and (2) celebrities. Famous people are individuals known because of their achievements in various fields of economy, culture and society (early modernity). Celebrities, according to Giles (2000: 3), are known for the fame that they acquire by their presence in the media and other forms of entertainment (late modernity).

On the other hand, the political activity of well-known people (as well as of those who are not known) in the field of international relations can be divided into (1) activism and (2) diplomatic activity. In the first case, known people are being involved mainly as supporters and therefore as propagandists of political persons, parties, movements etc – like the artists and intellectuals against hunger, absolutist regimes in various countries or the wars in Vietnam, Iraq etc (Vallely 2009). In the second case, known people (famous or celebrities) undertake action by appointment on behalf of an organization, state or movement in order to promote an issue of international interest – like Hepburn, Belafonte, Bono, Jolie etc have done (see Table 1).

In this sense, there are famous activists and diplomats, as well as celebrity activists and diplomats. Although all mentioned forms of famous/celebrity activism/diplomacy have been developed during the nineteenth and twentieth century, as I have already argued, famous activism (or FA in Table 1) is more typical of early modernity, whereas celebrity diplomacy (or CD in Table 1) emerges from the convergence of spectacle and politics in late modernity. Thus, this classification also has a historical dimension where political activity is shifting from activism to diplomacy and the type of known people is moving from fame to celebrity.

Therefore, when celebrities got involved in handling controversial issues in early modern conditions, though they may not have had a clear ideological or political orientation, they tended to be dealt with in a suspicious or hostile way.

In this perspective, the following case can serve as an enlightening example. Theodorakis along with other Greek and Turkish artists (e.g. the Turkish singer Zulfu. Livaneli) have

Table 1: Categories of socio-political activity and of known/visible people.

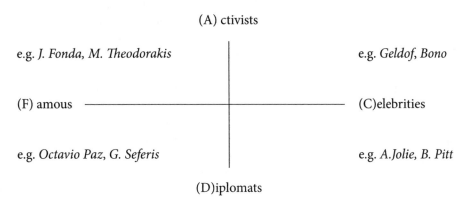

(A) ctivists

e.g. *J. Fonda, M. Theodorakis*   e.g. *Geldof, Bono*

(F) amous   (C)elebrities

e.g. *Octavio Paz, G. Seferis*   e.g. *A.Jolie, B. Pitt*

(D)iplomats

been working really hard for rapprochement between Greek and Turkish citizens for more than two decades through the establishment of Greek–Turkish friendship committees and artistic events. Although their efforts met initially with a lot of criticism in both countries, the artists were established as significant 'peace makers' on the civil society level. But when in May 1997 a joint concert was organized in the Green Line in Cyprus, bringing together the hugely popular media stars Greek singer Sakis Rouvas and the Turkish Burak, the reactions of civil society were quite different. This initiative was negatively portrayed by the Greek media, public opinion and various organizations. Moreover, a counter-concert was organized resulting in violent incidents. The differences in civil society's reactions can be explained, as already mentioned, by relating the kind of famous people's cultural activity and the nature of their engagement in diplomatic action in each case. Theodorakis, Livaneli and the others are not celebrities in the modern sense of the term; neither are they diplomats. They exercise activism, so typical for early modern conditions, which characterize Greece and Cyprus to a great extent (Tsoukalas 1996; Sevastakis 2004). On the contrary, Rouvas and Burak are typical celebrities in today's terms. Thus, the conflict between the type of famous people's diplomatic activity on one hand and the type of socio-cultural frame on the other, leads to suspiciousness and rejection and does not favour celebrity diplomacy or even celebrity activism.

The convergence of entertainment and diplomacy seems to be an important reason for challenging the role of celebrities as diplomats by both sides of the political spectrum and by both artists and diplomats, while this is not the case for activists (Vallely 2009). What I want to stress here is that beyond the criticism exercised (Vallely 2009; Kellner 2010), more celebrity activists become accepted as celebrity diplomats. Certainly, this is related to the kind of issues these celebrities get involved with (for example, humanitarian disasters). In other words, behind the acceptance of celebrity diplomats within the domain of formal politics (for example, the meeting of George Clooney with American President

Barak Obama on February 2009 to discuss the Darfur crisis), the presence of celebrity diplomats in international relations proliferates (Johnson 2009 – usually not due to their diplomatic qualifications. In this perspective what is also interesting in contemporary media democracies is that celebrities being involved in international relations issues originate not only from the 'narrow circle' of entertainment, but also involve '[…] intellectuals and other high-profile individuals' (Falt 2009).

Celebrity diplomacy, as already stated, derives from adding symbolic value in diplomatic activities in a mediatized world. Celebrities from entertainment perhaps are the most appropriate persons for this, but they are not the only ones. Since adding symbolic value in diplomacy becomes a necessity in our mediatized world, a wide range of such personas, regardless of their field of origin, can be (celebrity) diplomats. What we call celebrity diplomacy and celebrity activism is just the most visible option, but not the only one, of a wider process of celebretization of diplomacy. Thus, actually, celebrity diplomats originate from a wider spectre of societal fields.

From a sociological point of view, this is an essential criterion for their classification. We can distinguish four main categories of celebrity diplomats and activists:

1. Those that come from the 'marriage' of *spectacle* and *politics* (Lees-Marshment 2001) or politainment (Meyer and Hinchman 2002; Bennett 2003, Chapter 1; Edelman 1988). They are the ones that Street (2003) calls 'celebrity politicians' – the politicians who are overexposed in the media. They act more like diplomats rather than activists. In fact, a continuously growing part of politicians belong to this category of celebrity politicians, because politics is increasingly being conducted by theatrical means (Meyer and Hinchman 2002). There are three sub-categories within this group: (i) former *politicians* (prime ministers, presidents etc.) like Tony Blair, Al Gore, Michael Gorbachev, Richard Holbrook etc; (ii) former *militaries* (generals, higher officers etc.) like Colin Powell and (iii) former *diplomats* (former ambassadors, heads of diplomatic missions etc.) like Edvard Shevardnadze.

2. Those that come from *art, entertainment and culture* (musicians, actors, academics, religious officials, athletes etc.) like Bono, George Clooney, Bob Geldof, Angelina Jolie etc. They are more activists than diplomats. Their diplomatic activity is not included in 'highly centralized diplomacy' (Kellner 2010); neither does it become their main, among all, activity: they possibly follow to some extent the established tradition of their predecessors, as was formed during the long period of early modernity.

3. Representatives of various *social organizations* (leaders of social movements, trade unions etc.) like Gloria Steinem (the famous US activist, journalist and feminist), Juan Somavia (the Director General of the International Labour Organization), Mother Teresa (Greene 2004) etc. They are activists and diplomats at the same time. On the one hand, they act on a rationale of social movements, while on the other, they are 'players' within the frame of the established political and financial system. This is so because in most western (at least) countries that have accepted to a varying degree the corporatist principles, such

social organizations taking part to some extent in policy-making or at least often have discussions with officials (Panitch 1977; Smith 2006).

4. Executives of *economic organizations* (corporate leaders, national and international financial organizations, banks, industries etc.), like Bill Gates, George Soros, Muhammad Yunus (the founder of Grameen Bank or the poor's bank) etc. They are activists and diplomats at the same time. This is so, for the same reasons as in the case of representatives of social organizations, but mostly because of the significance of the markets and economic actors in contemporary societal systems as well as at an international relations level (Slater and Tonkiss 2001).

The expansion of the fields of origin of celebrity diplomats does not recant Cooper's (2007) discrimination between occasional (*glamorous enthusiasts*) and systematic celebrity activists (those who, like Bono, get involved systematically and for a longer time in favour of a specific issue); instead it confirms it. In this sense, the appointment of former politicians as either official or unofficial diplomats for the settlement of regional or international issues (like Tony Blair's appointment as a mediator for the Palestinian issue) is not owed solely to their political jurisdiction. It appears that it owes much to their television image as celebrity politicians:

> From the UN's Goodwill ambassadors to the employment of Ambassador Holbrooke as a Balkan trouble-shooter, diplomats have realized the power of public relations both to publicize the issues and legitimize their causes. (Finn 2000: 2)

Conclusions

The expansion of celebrity diplomacy and activism is not only a logical process but also a historical one. It contributes to the transformation of the whole spectrum of diplomatic relations and activities with a high symbolic media value, especially with regard to international problems. Celebrities that come from entertainment, as well as political, social and economic media celebrities, are concerned with grand, medium and small-scale problems in international relations, raising global awareness by speaking both to state leaders and public opinion through the media. In this sense, diplomacy is being reconstructed by the media logic, undergoing a celebretization process, with celebrities from culture, art and especially entertainment standing as the locomotive of this process.

If politicians–celebrity diplomats appeal mostly to nation or world leaders, things are different for cinema and TV stars. Whereas stars seek encounters with political leaders (like Clooney with Obama), they appeal at the same time to the wider public, without which they could not claim any negotiating power. If politicians–celebrity diplomats use political and/or other concessions and exercise various forms of pressure to achieve the convergence of different views, artists as celebrity diplomats implement sentimental influence. When artists meet with political leaders, they manage the effect of their influence on the wider publics and seek to exercise similar influence to the leaders as well. In particular, the more celebrity diplomats and activists come from the media and entertainment (e.g. A. Jolie), the less diplomatic jurisdiction they appear to have (Cooper 2009) – the opposite seems to be an exception (e.g. Sydney Poitier, who since 1997 has been the Bahamian ambassador to Japan). This has to do with the aspect of celebrity diplomacy they get involved with. On the contrary, the more celebrity diplomats are related to politics, the more diplomatic qualifications they have, and therefore the closer they get to political leaders. On the contrary, the more they come from entertainment, they either directly or indirectly appeal to the public, encouraging self dealing with the problems and exercising pressure to the leaders.

References

Alberoni, F. (1972), 'The Powerless Elite: Theory and Sociological Research on the Phenomenon of Stars', in D. McQuail (ed.), *Sociology of Mass Communication*, Baltimore: Penguin.

Arnheim, R. (1969), *Visual Thinking*, Berkeley: University of California Press.

Baudrillard, J. (1975), *The Mirror of Production*, St. Louis: Telos Press.

—— (1998), *The Consumer Society: Myths and Structures*, London: Sage.

Bennett, L. (2003), *News. The Politics of Illusion*, 5th ed., New York: Longman.

Boorstin, J. D. (1980), *The Image: A Guide to Pseudoevents in America*, New York: Athenaeum.

Bonner, F., Farley, R., Marshall, D. and Turner, G. (1999), 'Celebrity and the media', *Australian Journal of Communication*, 26:1, pp. 55–70.

Braudy, L. (1997), *The Frenzy of Renown: Fame and its History*, New York, NY: Vintage Books.

Carter, J. (2006), 'The nineteenth-century press and the development of the artist-celebrity', GLS Final Project, http://ir.lib.sfu.ca/retrieve/3749/etd2397.pdf. Accessed 19 September 2009.

Cashmore, E. (2006), *Celebrity Culture*, London: Routledge.

Clemens, E. and Minkoff, D. (2004), 'Beyond the Iron Law: Rethinking the Place of Organizations in Social Movement Research', in D. Snow, S. Soule and H. Kriest (eds), *The Blackwell Companion to Social Movements*, Oxford: Blackwell.

Collins, S. (2008), 'Making the Most out of 15 Minutes Reality TV's Dispensable Celebrity', *Television & New Media*, 9 (2), pp. 87–110.

Cooper, A. (2007), *Celebrity Diplomacy*, Boulder: Paradigm Publishers.

Cooper, A. F. (2009), 'The A-List of Celebrity Diplomacy: Bono and Sir Bob as Serious International Actors', http://www.allacademic.com/meta/p311771_index.html. Accessed 26 September 2009.

Corner, J. (2000), 'Mediated persona and political culture: dimensions of structure and process', *European Journal of Cultural Studies*, 3:3, pp. 389–405.

Cottle, S. and Nolan, D. (2008), 'Global Humanitarianism and the Changing Aid-Media Field', *Journalism Studies*, 8:6, pp. 862–878.

Davis, M. (1991), *Prisoners of the American Dream: Politics and Economy in the history of the U.S. Working Class*, London & New York: Verso.

Demertzis, N. (1989), *Culture, Modernity, Political Culture*, Athens: Papazisis (in Greek).

de Waal, A. (2005), 'Briefing: Darfur, Sudan: Prospects for peace', *African Affairs*, 104:414, pp. 127–130.

—— (2008), 'The Humanitarian Carnival: A Celebrity Vogue', *World Affairs*, in http://www.worldaffairsjournal.org/articles/2008-Fall/full-DeWaal.html. Accessed 14 July 2010.

Dominick, J. (1990), *The Dynamics of Mass Communication*, New York: McGraw Hill.

Dunn, R. (1986), 'Television, consumption and the commodity form', *Theory, Culture and Society*, 3:1, p. XXX.

Edelman, M. (1988), *Political Spectacle*, Chicago: Chicago University Press.

Edwards, B. and McCarthy, J. (2004), 'Resources and Social Movement Mobilization', in D. Snow, S. Soule and H. Kriest (eds), *The Blackwell Companion to Social Movements*, Oxford: Blackwell.

Ellis, J. (2007), 'Stars as a Cinematic Phenomenon', in S. Redmont and S. Holmes, (eds), *Stardom and Celebrity. A Reader*, London: Sage.

Falt, E. (2009), 'How Insiders View the Issues Facing Celebrity Diplomacy', http://www.un.int/wcm/webdav/site/creative/shared/documents/CCOI_Speech_Annenberg.pdf. Accessed 22 September 2009.

Ferris, K. O. (2007), 'The Sociology of Celebrity', *Sociology Compass*, 1:1, pp. 371–384.

Finn, E. (2000), 'International relations in a changing world: a new Diplomacy?', International Affairs, 5:2, in http://www.sam.gov.tr/perceptions/Volume5/June-August2000/VolumeVN2EdwardFinn.pdf. Accessed 11 July 2010.

Gamson, W. and Wolfsfeld, G. (1993), 'Movements and media as interacting systems', *Annals of the American Academy of Political and Social Science*, 528 (Citizens, Protest, and Democracy), pp. 114–125.

Garland, R. (2005), 'Celebrity in the Ancient World', *History Today*, 55, p. XXX.

Giles, D. (2000), *Illusions of Immortality*, London: Macmillan Press.

Greene, M. (2004), *Mother Teresa: A Biography*, Westport, Connecticut: Greenwood Press.

Habermas, J. (1989), *The Structural Transformation of the Public Sphere*, London: Polity Press.

Hansen, A. and Aronson, D. (1995), '*The Politics of Mercy' (review)*. Reviewed work(s): *1988. Surrender or Starve: The Wars behind the Famine* by Robert D. Kaplan *1990. American Policy and African Famine: The Nigeria-Biafra War, 1966–70* by Joseph E Thompson, *Canadian Journal of African Studies / Revue Canadienne des Études Africaines*, 29:3, pp. 498–505.

Hermann, E. and Chomsky, N. (1988), *Manufacturing Consent*, New York: Pantheon Books.

Johnson, T. (2009), 'The evolution of celebrity diplomacy', http://www.politico.com/news/stories/0309/20489.html. Accessed 22 September 2009.

Jowett, G. S. and O' Donnell, V. (1995), *Propaganda and Persuasion*, Newbury Park: Sage.

Kellner, D. (2010), 'Celebrity diplomacy, spectacle and Barack Obama', *Celebrity Studies*, 1:1, p. 121–123.

Klapp, E. O. (1949), 'Hero Worship in America', *American Sociological Review*, 14 (1) pp. 53–62.

Lees-Marshment, J. (2001), 'The Marriage of Politics and Marketing', *Political Studies*, 49:4, pp. 692–713.

Leiss, W., Kline, S., Jhally, S. and Botterill, J. (2005), *Social Communication in Advertising. Consumption in the Mediated marketplace*, London: Routledge.

Leonard, M., Stead, C. and Smewing, C. (2002), *Public Diplomacy*, London: The Foreign Policy Centre.

Mamdani, M. (2009), *Saviors and Survivors: Darfur, Politics, and the War on Terror*, Boston: Pantheon Books.

Marshall, D. (1997), *Celebrity and Power*, Minneapolis: University of Minnesota Press.

Meyer, T. with Hinchman, L. (2002), *Media Democracy: How the Media Colonize Politics*, Cambridge: Polity Press.

Minear, L. and Smith, H. (eds) (2007), *Humanitarian Diplomacy: Practitioners and their Craft*, New York: United Nations University Press.

Morin, E. (1992), 'The Spirit of Times', in Th. Adorno et al. (eds), *The Media Culture*, Athens: Alexandreia (in Greek).

Morris, N. (1999), 'UNHCR and Kosovo: a personal view from within UNHCR', *Forced Migration Review*, vol. 5, pp. 14–17.

Orth, M. (2004), *The Importance of Being Famous: Behind the Scenes of the Celebrity-Industrial Complex*, New York: H. Holt.

Panitch, L. (1977), 'The Development of Corporatism in Liberal Democracies', *Comparative Political Studies*, vol 10, pp. 61–90.

Pleios, G. (2001), *The Discourse of Image. Ideology and Politics*, Athens: Papazisis (in Greek).

Pringle, H. (2004), *Celebrity Sells*, Chichester, West Sussex: Wiley John & Sons.

Rojek, C. (2001), *Celebrity*, London: Reaktion Books.

Ross, C. (2002), 'Public Diplomacy comes of Age', *The Washington Quarterly*, 25:2, pp. 75–83.

Sevastakis, N. (2004), *Mundane Country: Aspects of Public Space and Antinomies of Values in Contemporary Greece*, Athens: Savalas (in Greek).

Slater, D. and Tonkiss, F. (2001), *Market Society: Markets and Modern Social Theory*, Cambridge: Blackwell.

Smith, M. (2006), 'Pluralism, Reformed Pluralism and Neopluralism: the Role of Pressure Groups in Policy-Making', *Political Studies*, 32:2, pp. 302–322.

Street, J. 2004. 'Celebrity Politicians: Popular Culture and Political Representation', *British Journal of Politics and International Relations*, 6, (4), pp. 435–452.

Thompson, J. (1995), *The Media and Modernity*, Cambridge: Polity Press.

Tsoukalas, K. (1996), 'Tradition and Modernity', in K. Tsoukalas (ed.), *Journey to Discourse and History*: Texts 1969–1996, Athens: Plethron (in Greek).

Tylor, E. (1920), *Primitive Culture*, New York: J.P. Putnam's Sons.

Vallely, P. (2009), 'From A-lister to Aid worker: Does celebrity diplomacy really work?", http://www.independent.co.uk/news/people/profiles/from-alister-to-aid-worker-does-celebrity-diplomacy-really-work-1365946.html. Accessed 11 September 2009.

Webster, F. (1994), *Theories of Information Society*, London: Routledge.

Wernick, A. (1991), *Promotional Culture: Advertising, Ideology and Symbolic Expression*, London: Sage.

Williams, R. (1960), *Culture and Society 1780–1950*, New York Garden City: Anchor Books.

Chapter 14

Celebrity Culture and Postcolonial Relations within the Portuguese
Media Landscape: The Case of Catarina Furtado

Ana Jorge

Introduction: Sailing south

This chapter looks at the work of the United Nations (UN) Portuguese Goodwill Ambassador Catarina Furtado, for the Portuguese-speaking countries, pointing out the possibilities of celebrity activism within the context of postcolonial relations and the country's semi-peripheral character. The chapter starts by setting the Portuguese historical and geopolitical context, and goes on to analysing how Catarina Furtado is a central element in the emergence of celebrity culture within the national media landscape, also revealing the ways in which her personal and media narratives are intricate with her activism. We then address a particular campaign promoted by Furtado to help Guinea-Bissau and highlight the ways in which she is placed at the centre of the agency, and conclude about the implications this kind of celebrity activism has on the Portuguese postcolonial culture context.

In the fifteenth century, Portuguese sailors launched into the sea seeking new sources of raw materials, giving 'new worlds to the world' – Camões, the epic Portuguese poet, wrote this in the following century. This small southern European country was far from the centre of the continent, but reinvented the geographies of the modern world. However, Portugal was not able to promote sustainable development from colonial exploitation: while, in the seventeenth century, it considered its colonies to be primitive, the other European countries still looked down on Portugal as being primitive itself (Santos 2002). It was that 'semi-peripheral impotency' (Santos 1994: 13), rather than a colonial supremacy, which helps explain both why Portugal inaugurated the Discoveries and was the last country to return from the colonialist adventure, in the 1970s, after the other European powers.

In fact, the dictatorship regime between 1928 and 1974 tried to distance the country from the Second World War and, in the decades after it, to resist international pressure, particularly from the UN, for decolonization, presenting an image of an integrating colonialism that was not racist and instead promoted assimilation, symbolized by the *mulattos*, *mestizos* and *crioulos*[1]. In the 1950s, while other European powers were in the process of decolonization, the Portuguese regime promoted the emigration of rural Portuguese from the metropolis to the 'overseas provinces', the regime's alternative label for 'colonies' (Pinto 2005). When, in 1961, nationalist movements in Angola, Mozambique and Guinea-Bissau announced independence, the regime declared war on them, which would only end with the regime's downfall, in 1974. The sudden process of decolonization and Portugal's inability to support the former colonies in the international community left them open to the disputes of the Cold War, plunging them into long civil wars (Santos 1994).

The breakout from decades of the country's isolationism because of the dictatorship was marked by the adhesion to the European Economic Community in 1985. Establishing bilateral relations with former colonies, though, was not as straightforward, and was built around a common cultural feature, regarded as important cultural capital in the face of globalization: language. It was not until 1996 that the Community of Portuguese Language Countries (CPLP) was established, comprising the African countries Angola, Cape Verde, Guinea-Bissau, Mozambique, San Tome and Prince (which form the African Countries of Portuguese Official Language – PALOP, in the Portuguese abbreviation), Brazil and (since 2002) East-Timor. The CPLP is still gaining maturity around its project of political-diplomatic, economical, social, cultural, juridical and technical-scientific cooperation (Pinto 2005), and does not exclude other regional cooperation (for instance, Mozambique joined the British Commonwealth as a result of its proximity with South Africa) and multilateral relations (through the UN, the World Bank, the Organization for Economic Cooperation and Development and the European Union), with Portugal having hosted, during the Portuguese European Presidency, the European Union–African Summit in November 2007.

The geopolitical position of Portugal, in the semi-periphery – on the edge of Europe, yet near and historically connected with the South – has a parallel in its development, directly linked to and sustained by European Union membership, though, at the same time, characterized by features of underdevelopment: corruption, parallel economies and deepening inequalities (Santos 1993). This reading has implications for Portugal's relations with developing countries, for consistent domestic development is not yet accomplished, while the country is characterized by a weak civil society and NGO culture as a result of its dictatorial past. We will now explore the ways in which celebrity activism is constructed within this postcolonial and semi-peripheral context.

Glamorous Diplomacy

Although deeply committed to the cultural industries, celebrities hold a special form of cultural power that cannot be reduced to economic power, as they represent individual success (Marshall 1997), in such a way that one can argue that they 'do not so much represent their own individuality as symbolize the cultural and social meaning we attach to individuality' (Lumby 1999: 115). If the articulation of public and private spheres under the guise of celebrities is constitutive of their persona (Dyer 2005), some authors have interpreted celebrity discourse as a possibility to give public attention to issues formerly considered as private (Marshall 1997; Lumby 1999), whereas others note that it reduces the types of representation, especially of women, more likely to be portrayed as celebrities highlighting their personal life, relationships and lifestyle over their professional career (Gledhill 2000; McRobbie 2009).

Celebrities' capacity to communicate public issues has been taken further, whether as agents in their own name or representing other organizations (Street 1997; Thrall et al. 2008). Notably, the UN's communication strategy comprises the systematic deployment of famous personalities, mainly from the North. This strategy was implemented by the first UN Secretary-General coming from Africa, Kofi Annan and was inspired by previous experiences in communicating development issues through well-known individuals in the entertainment industry, as well as by the legacy of Princess Diana and her awareness-raising of landmines in Angola. Celebrities, Annan felt, would help make the UN's agenda more humane and personal, bridging the gap between institutional policies and society. However, Annan's vision for celebrity advocacy, in which the agenda would be set by the elites, who mobilize citizens to exert pressure over governments, is very much a northern, specifically Northern American, vision (Alleyne 2005), as we will try to argue.

In Portugal, celebrity Catarina Furtado was chosen by the United Nations as a Goodwill Ambassador due to her public visibility and opinions regarding women's rights. In 1999, her campaign with the Family Planning Association (APF), the Portuguese partner of the UN Population Fund (UNFPA),[2] seemed a trial for her official nomination as Goodwill Ambassador in 2001. Furtado's geographical plan of action, determined centrally by the UNFPA, is that of a *lusophone*, in Portuguese-speaking countries, particularly the African countries (known as PALOP, as mentioned above), comprising about 230 million people. In that first year, she promoted a trip to Mozambique, with the Population and Development Parliamentary Commission and APF, to raise awareness among the government and local populations of HIV/AIDS. Covered by the Portuguese society magazine *Lux*, the broadcast station *SIC*, in which she worked at the time, and also by the local media, the trip targeted elites and the wider population in Mozambique and at home, where there is a significant Mozambican immigrant community.

Her nomination as UNFPA's Goodwill Ambassador seemed to be the culmination of the great visibility she had attained through the 1990s. Catarina Furtado was then, and still is, referred to as 'Portugal's sweetheart' and is the daughter of a well-known journalist, Joaquim Furtado, who broke the news of the reinstatement of democracy in 1974. After receiving an education in dancing, Catarina went on to study journalism and, at the age of twenty, she presented the music chart show in the public broadcasting television network, *RTP*. She is well known, nevertheless, for her association with the overwhelming success of the early days of commercial television: she presented the hugely popular *Chuva de Estrelas/ Falling Stars* (*SIC*, 1993), an international format in which the lay public acted out songs by popular artists. This show, along with others, marked the appearance of a new era in the Portuguese television landscape, which until then was a state monopoly. Popular magazines were launching several new 'famous' faces, placing Furtado at the centre of media attention. By the beginning of the 1990s, more than fifteen years after the revolution, the country was not only a European Union member, but it was also characterized by a growing consumer culture, a buzzing media sector – and Catarina Furtado positioned herself, in her own words, as 'the pioneer of a new generation of communicators' (Fialho 2008).

Her celebrity status was built, first and foremost, by the diversity of her career, as television presenter and an actress in television, theatre and cinema, as she states: 'often people ask me: "what job should I write down?" Some days I say "presenter", others I say "actress"' (Ribeiro 2006). Moreover, she builds a consistent link between her private life and her career and public acting as a Goodwill Ambassador. On the one hand, Catarina's activism is shown as a natural consequence of her education ('I've learnt with my mother to be solidary' – Amante 2001) and her previously established public personality (Anonymous 2009c), while, on the other hand, also adding to her sensitivity: 'Do you know 'I was someone before and now I am someone else?' That's exactly it' (Gato 2007). Therefore, she uses this argument to fight the criticism inherent to celebrity activism (Cooper 2008), as an opportunity for image creation and spin control to the benefit of celebrities rather than the actual cause ('I am not moved by that [criticism], nor am I deterred by it' (Fialho 2008), trying to legitimize her actions and distance herself from opportunist motives, as 'others may do' (Anonymous 2008a). However, in showing her activism and personality as feeding off each other to build a serious persona, she portrays her action as a continuation of her femininity and motherhood, as someone who by essence takes care of others (Macdonald 1995) and does not contribute to a more political framing of the actions.

Furthermore, her activism also helps Catarina Furtado to reclaim a serious television career. When, in 2003, she left the commercial television network she was associated with during the 1990s, for the public broadcasting television network, *RTP*, Catarina sought to distance herself from commercial television and regain credibility as a serious television persona and, crucially, to work on projects where entertainment is used to serve the causes for the common good. Although she hosted, with great ratings, a music academy in a reality show format, *Operação Triunfo/Operation Triumph*, she tried to claim distance from that type of television and position herself in a sphere of 'good entertainment', which brings leisure and education together on the public broadcasting channel, as opposed to a commercial one: 'entertainment, when it is good, is a public service' (Fialho 2008). Besides presenting galas for organizations dealing with disabled children (2004), the elderly (2008) or immigrant communities (2008), it is her activist projects that allow Furtado to distinguish her television work. At a national level, she promoted shows that have stemmed from her action with the UNFPA and the APF, focusing on promoting sexual education and family planning and raising awareness of excluded communities (Delimbeuf 2005): *Hip Hop Pobreza Stop/Hip Hop Stop Poverty* (2008), a show where young people reflected on social exclusion and poverty through rap and graffiti, and *Este é o Meu Bairro-Cova da Moura/This is my Neighbourhood – Cova da Moura* (2008) a series of film documentaries set in one of the country's most excluded, destitute and criminalized immigrant neighbourhoods.

However, it is her action in the Portuguese-speaking countries that has brought her more attention and where her activism is most evident, usually through campaigns where she raises funds for specific projects, visits those countries to distribute the funds, while also documenting the event in order to raise awareness back home (in the same context that Angelina Jolie did with 'MTV' or Bob Geldof with the 'BBC' – Cooper 2008). Catarina Furtado's fund-raising is outrightly emotional: 'when you appeal to people's good hearts, they help' (Sala 2008; Anonymous 2009c), and, although she tries to 'protect these people's dignity', exploiting the suffering of others is necessary to get people to help (Fialho 2008). She is placed at the centre of the agency, using the media to overcome funding difficulties in Portugal: 'I have a tiny power that gave [*sic*] me confidence to put my ideas forward, although I have barely any money. It is not paid work, in Portugal it is difficult to get support, but I struggle to get things done' (Ribeiro 2006). The media are deeply committed at every stage of her activist strategy, which she defends as being complemented with rationality and accountability, publicly showing her campaigns on television, through the international public broadcasting channels (*RTPÁfrica* and *RTPInternacional*) and secondary media: 'I show what was done and where the money was spent, and this is the only way that makes sense because we know there is a lot of corruption' (Sala 2008). Part of this emotional discourse relies on the glorification of the missionaries and voluntary workers (Littler 2008) in PALOP countries, in the documentaries *Príncipes do Nada/Princes of Nothing* (2005–2006), but also Catarina's image of personal sacrifice as she talks about the degree of personal risk she undertook when travelling to these countries during her pregnancy (Martins 2006).

While Catarina Furtado relies on her private life to help her build part of her professional and public image, trying to construct proximity and familiarity as a television personality (Langer in Marshall 2006; see also Reeves 1988), she evokes that intimacy rather than showing it off to the audience in her effort to establish her serious persona: she talks about privacy and family, but does not appear with them in public. When the magazines showed the intermingling of her work and personal life after she performed as an actress in a television series in 2004 with actor João Reis, who she married the following year, 'in a very secret ceremony' (Curião 2005), she justified: 'the audience was never used to seeing me at home or in my car, in private moments. If I never did that, why should I let them in my own wedding?' (Martins 2006). Again, although she gave out several interviews and did photo shoots on both her pregnancies in women's glossy magazines (Anonymous 2006; Martins 2006; Ribeiro 2006; Gato 2007), and often speaks about marriage and motherhood, she seems self-conscious about protecting her children from media exposure: 'I grew up live,[3] but I always knew that I would be poorer if I showed my affections. [...] Now that I have children, I preserve their identities because I do not know if they will [...] question my decision to expose them. My father never did that to me' (Gato 2007). Furtado shows and hides her private life at the same time, arguing that she does it as part of her activist role: 'I only show my work, and it makes sense that I say more so that people can know me better and know what I think about such an ill-fitting world' (Alegria 2009). Career, fame, family, motherhood and activism seem to be mixed together *naturally* when she worked on television during her pregnancy and promoted breastfeeding as part of her campaign for maternal and children's health (Anonymous 2007b), a UNFPA cause, without falling prey to what she saw as the easy fame of showing her children off.

In fact, this strategy is a consequence of Catarina Furtado's high ranking in the national celebrity hierarchy: although she is a synthesis of the development of a national celebrity culture that revolves around television, her reservation towards appearing in more commercial events or exposing her children helps to set her apart from 'new celebrities' or 'celetoids' (Turner 2006). Unlike those ephemeral celebrities who, because of a more saturated media exposure, exert little power to negotiate with the various media (Turner et al. 2000), she claims: 'I need magazines generally when I have a new show and need to promote it' (Fialho 2008). Furthermore, as we already argued, her Goodwill Ambassador status reinforces her celebrity dimension and allows her to consolidate her television work with programmes that bring information and entertainment together. Her activist dimension as a UNFPA Goodwill Ambassador together with the constructed visibility of her private life serve a common project of building up a reputation about a sensitive, well-educated media persona, who talks about her emotions to the extent that they are linked to her career and public life, a frame that, to her mind, contributes to raise the quality level of television production and of the national celebrity culture.

In a growing national celebrity culture, at the heart of which Catarina Furtado is placed, there is an increasing tendency to promote causes and solidarity initiatives, trying to remedy the multiple signs of domestic underdevelopment we mentioned above. In this seemingly daily and small initiatives we can read a contamination from the discourses of globally dominant celebrity cultures, such as North American and British, to the intermediate cultures such as the Portuguese, impressing solidarity and activism as an 'obligation' that ultimately leads to a saturation and trivialization of these practices (Thrall et al. 2008). The vicious effect is that it is not just public organizations that need to be associated with celebrities to benefit from their visibility, but it is more and more celebrities that associate with more or less staged solidarity actions to help them build their own celebrity narratives and legitimize their stardom, contributing to showing them less as authentic and more as calculated actions.

Dancing for a Good Cause

The campaign for Guinea-Bissau promoted by Catarina Furtado reveals, we believe, not only her *modus operandi* but also the limitations of this type of action and discourse for development aid.

In 2006, Catarina Furtado was again at the centre of the national celebrity culture when she hosted the *Dança Comigo/Dance with Me*, adapting *Strictly Come Dancing*, the BBC celebrity version of *Come Dancing* in the Portuguese public broadcasting television network, where the audience witnessed yet another facet of celebrity spectacle as famous contestants were invited to dance with professional dancers. Although dismissive about commercial television, she regards this as 'one of those perfect formats where mass entertainment can be linked with quality' (Freixo 2008a). Yet again, her private life and public activism came together as she not only presented the programme during her pregnancy, as we have mentioned, but also used motherhood to help raise awareness for UNFPA's mission when in

December 2006, the *RTP* ran a Sunday telethon of twelve hours of *Dança Comigo Especial por uma Boa Causa/Dance with Me-Special Edition for a Good Cause.*

In the UNFPA fund-raising show, dance rehearsals and performances of invited celebrities, professional musicians and dancers were used to hook audience attention and augment donations. There was a great contrast between the aid development cause, which the show was appealing to and Catarina Furtado's luxurious dresses and gala image, as were the contrasting tones during the show, as the hosts and the audience rejoiced at each single announcement of raised funds, only to then go back to a serious and responsible tone to appeal for donations. This proved to be an effective way to make the audience empathize with the cause, raising an important sum of €253,000 and resulting in a personal moment of triumph for Furtado while concurrently attributing this success to the 'solidarity of the Portuguese people'.

This media campaign took on a political and institutional wrapping when the Secretary of Foreign Affairs and Cooperation, João Gomes Cravinho, decided to double the amount of donations made by the audience through the Portuguese Aid and Development Institute (IPAD). He later hosted the delivery ceremony of the funds to the UNFPA's Executive Director, Thoraya Ahmed Obaid, when the latter visited Portugal in May 2007, celebrating 'the greatest ever donation made by the Portuguese citizens to UNFPA' and putting Catarina Furtado in an agency role, as the funds were announced to 'be spent on a single project in a Lusophone country, to be selected jointly by the UNFPA, Ms Furtado and the Secretary of State' (Anonymous 2007a). This political sponsoring of the campaign was signalled again in the media event of the announcement of the documentary of the campaign, also hosted by the Foreign Affairs Ministry and the CPLP, without, however, removing any of Catarina Furtado's stardom in the project ('Catarina helps mothers in Guinea' – Bueno 2009; Anonymous 2009b).

The funds collected by the television show and the governmental agency were transformed into the project 'Help reduce maternal and neonatal mortality in Oio and Gabu', in Guinea-Bissau, the last country on the United Nations' Human Development Index. In the Portuguese overseas policy, Guinea-Bissau was a colony used for manual labour and exports, with no investment in infra-structure and scarce European immigration (Silva 1997). The ethnical diversity (30 tribes) and the economic condition and underdevelopment (dependent on farming and fishing) do not contribute to political stability. In 2008, there were more than 22,000 immigrants from Guinea-Bissau in Portugal, though the actual number of illegal migrants might be higher, and there are now many second- and third-generation immigrants, by now Portuguese citizens (Pinto 2005).

The more 'serious' media coverage focused on Guinea-Bissau's women and children, be it on the Portuguese voluntary workers in Africa (Anonymous 2008c) or on Guinea-Bissau as the poorest country in the Development Index (Rico and Fonseca 2008; Anonymous 2008d), where Catarina Furtado and her campaign as such are not mentioned. Whereas few media (Ferreira 2008) followed the official UNFPA press release, reporting that, 'dressed in jeans and a t-shirt, one of Portugal's best-known actresses and television personalities laid down the first construction brick of a maternity surgical unit in this dusty town in eastern Guinea-Bissau' [Gabu] (Anonymous 2009a), most of the media coverage was centred on the celebrity of Furtado herself. Prior to the trip, the choice to spend the funds in Guinea-Bissau was leaked to the press, in interviews (Anonymous 2008e) or through rumours that Catarina could meet with Angelina Jolie, or Brad Pitt representing her (Delimbeuf 2008). The fact that the meeting never actually materialized (Galamas 2008) seems a minor detail, one less photo-opportunity that does not change the fact that Catarina Furtado has, on a national scale, a role that brings her to the sphere of global celebrities (Delimbeuf 2005; Amante 2001). In fact, Furtado's participation in this global sphere of celebrity activism and her narrative imbrication of pregnancy/motherhood, marriage, career and activism discourses, similar to Jolie's, bring journalists to take the comparison further and ask Catarina if she is planning to adopt a child on one of her trips to developing countries (Fialho 2008; Anonymous 2008e).

Her persona is at the centre of the news stories on the campaign also when some stories anticipated her personal risks and sacrifices ('Catarina faces cholera outbreak' – Anonymous 2008f; 'The presenter will visit places without water or electricity' – Bajouco 2008), but also in more staged visibility: before and after the trip, she posed for a photo shoot for the society magazine *Caras*, linking her motherhood experience, professional career and activism together again, as she promoted her television work and action as Goodwill Ambassador as two sides of the same coin: it seems to be yet another opportunity given by *RTP* to 'run programs where I'm allowed to speak for those who cannot' and to bring together 'my television work and my role as the UNFPA's Ambassador' (Freixo 2008a).

In the midst of this media coverage centred on her celebrity status rather than the cause she was campaigning for (Cooper 2008), the complexity of Guinea-Bissau's situation goes amiss. The documentary aired on the Portuguese public station on the campaign, *Dar Vida Sem Morrer/Give Birth without Dying* (Freitas 2009), tried to portray the reality of the maternal and neonatal condition in that African country through a combination of an emotional discourse, running through cases of sick children and women to interviews with doctors, nurses and humanitarians, and a rational line, presenting underdevelopment indicators. Through personal cases of death and disease, but also stories of human triumph against adversity, she tries to call public attention to infrastructural problems while praising the medics who work 'day and night', sometimes not even earning their minimal wages. Furtado shows human suffering in the documentary as part of her declared strategy to raise awareness and mobilize the audience, while also attempting to bring down the causes of maternal mortality in Guinea-Bissau: the Health Minister, Eugénia Araújo, in her interview, talks about a cultural background of forced and teenage marriages, polygamy, female genital mutilation and illiteracy as the cause of the problem.

However, with a very high rate of illiteracy (around 80 per cent), most lay people Catarina Furtado interacts with in Guinea-Bissau do not speak Portuguese, hence the need to employ interpreters. Furthermore, Catarina is not recognizable to the local population, as most of them do not have electricity, let alone television. Furthermore, there is a great gap between herself, as the rich, happy, successful, northern celebrity she is to Guinea-Bissau's people, and the poor and sick people in the South she encounters. Celebrity value is cultural, based on a notion of western individualism that establishes distinctions and recognitions (Marshall 1997), but it is not as relevant in other cultural systems, where societal status is based on tribal power, such as happens in Guinea-Bissau. The lack of recognition of Catarina Furtado's celebrity, both for practical reasons of no access to television and cultural reasons of the value attributed to the individual, makes the action a spectacle to the home audience rather than an actual awareness campaign in Guinea-Bissau. And to the home audience, Catarina invites the audience to think how fortunate they are being in a (semi-) developed country and better off, when she says she values her privileged position more after returning from the developing countries (Freixo 2008b). The mismatch between the celebrity discourse and the legitimacy to campaign for developing countries, even if with a common history, reveals the frailty of the cultural basis on which UN's agency attributed the regional mandate to Catarina Furtado. The cultural root of celebrity discourse is taken for granted in UN's strategy of activism while its universality is debatable, being mostly a western value connected to individualism (Marshall 1997) and in societies where close solidarity is nearly non-existent, unlike tribal societies.

Overall, then, media exposure of the campaign remains focused on Catarina Furtado's persona, rather than the predicament of Guinea-Bissau, especially regarding women and children, through celebrity media, magazines and popular newspapers, creating an emotional discourse mostly targeted at women, where motherhood and the maternal situation is treated more as personal than a public issue, through a discourse of rights and addressing public policies for health, motherhood and reproduction. Rather, the audience is presented the contrast between Catarina Furtado's image of planned, happy, safe motherhood and the maternal conditions in Guinea-Bissau. Indeed, the natural link that is built between Furtado's motherhood experience, her sensitivity and her activism is signalled in the title of the biography about her living by the UNFPA's motto, *Catarina Furtado – Porque Cada Pessoa Conta/Because everyone counts* (Anonymous 2009c). The Goodwill Ambassador's role is presented as a natural corollary of Catarina's narrative and works to construct her celebrity story, not in an ephemeral, flitting way, but deeply rooted in her previous and subsequent persona, bridging together public, professional and personal spheres.

On the other hand, the political support to Furtado's campaign contributes to maintaining her discourse at the personal level. Because she built the project in partnership with the Portuguese cooperation agency, no confrontation with the aid to development is made, at least publically, and the structural issues around the relationship between Portugal and its former colonies affecting development are not debated. In fact, it seems that this very incapacity of the Portuguese state to support its former colonies is consistent with the decision to be associated with an action started out in television by Furtado. That this very campaign has been framed as a success of 'the solidarity of the Portuguese' and Catarina Furtado's own initiative shows how the former metropolis is incapable of providing development aid to its colonies and is increasingly dependent on media visibility to put the message across. The media power of celebrity culture seems to compensate for the deficit in political power and a poorly mobilized civil society, and lends visibility to the campaigns built on emotional campaigns, trading off legitimacy for a greater appeal to the audiences. Furtado collaborates with the government as well as NGOs, celebrating their role in aid, while she claims that her role is to give them visibility to mobilize civil society and to lobby politicians in Portugal and in developing countries to improve maternal and infant conditions. It is greatly debatable, however, whether her agency as a visibility lender could be relevant and significant in such a weakly mobilized society, let alone change the structures (Cooper 2008).

In fact, only a few days after *Dar Vida Sem Morrer/Giving Birth without Dying* documentary was aired, in early March 2009, Guinea-Bissau found itself in a new crisis after the Head General Tagmé Na Waié and President 'Nino' Vieira were killed, in what seemed to be related to its condition as a narco-state, between South America and Europe (Booth 2009). Portugal's diplomatic help, through CPLP, to the country in yet another crisis proved insufficient, but there was no public debate calling for greater intervention, and Catarina Furtado did not promote that either, as she is used to talking through celebrity media and not mainstream news media. Catarina Furtado's 'tiny power', as she claims (Ribeiro 2006), gives her authority to try to mobilize consciences and get funding, but she does not act outside her mandate and no responsibility is drawn from her action since she is not elected (Alberoni in Marshall 2006) and she does not speak for a constituency. The limits of her agency are set by herself, building media narratives of small problems affordable solutions–success, claiming the personal success for the campaigns. Whereas Bob Geldof and Bono were criticized by other NGOs and movements in Davos 2007 for reducing development aid to smaller, more manageable, goals, and setting an agenda that is not universal and with a questionable legitimacy, Catarina Furtado's agenda goes unquestioned.

Conclusions

In this chapter I have tried to show how Catarina Furtado's action on behalf of the Portuguese-speaking, underdeveloped countries under the UNFPA Goodwill Ambassador role consolidates her activism and is constructed as both deriving from and contributing to her celebrity persona. The imbrication of personal, professional and activist spheres of action, as well as the limited sphere of action constructed for the celebrity activist under the UN's mandate, accentuates Furtado's agency and protagonism. Besides being placed at the centre of activism, as a consequence of the celebrity diplomacy model envisioned by the UN, her UNFPA mandate and the political institutions' support make her activism one of consensus rather than one of confrontation (Cooper 2008). Unlike the United States of America and the United Kingdom, where celebrity activism could be said to fit in a more liberal conception of the state, in Portugal, celebrity activism can rather be seen as a sign of its intermediate development and the state's incapacity to tackle development issues and its colonial past. Everything seems to depend on the state in this southern European country, yet the state is not capable of offering remedies for all problems, while civil society is not developed enough to compensate for that. If that helps to create the scenario where Catarina Furtado's role as UNFPA's Goodwill Ambassador stresses her agency, her lack of independence from the UN, the state and civil society does not allow for greater confrontation and promotion of the public debate around the responsibility towards former colonies as developing countries.

Moreover, I hope to have demonstrated how the UN's strategy of communicating through celebrities is not universally replicable. There is neither an undifferentiated South nor North, and that is not sufficiently recognized by the cultural–regional mandates: the specific condition of Portugal as semi-peripheral and postcolonial culture has particular implications on the ways in which celebrity activism is developed. The cultural basis of celebrity is mostly from western, democratic and urban societies, where the media play a very important role in contemporary culture (Marshall 1997; Turner et al. 2000), and if its recognition may not happen in developing countries for the cultural distance between the celebrity's origin and destiny of the campaign, its legitimacy for the home audience is largely questionable as well, as their privileged status in society does not allow them to claim representativeness, and the extent to which it is a calculated effort of visibility or an authentic gesture resonates when more and more celebrities engage in pseudo-activism.

In effect, as Furtado pays attention to and adapts strategies of other global celebrity activists and ambassadors, such as Angelina Jolie and Bob Geldof, her work as a Goodwill Ambassador exerts influence over the national celebrity culture, with more and more initiatives in which celebrities associate with greater or smaller public causes, yet with no parallel to her role supported by the UNFPA. In this expansion of celebrity culture that, with growing media importance, increasingly calls upon personalities to convey more and more private and public discourses (Marshall 2006), Catarina Furtado is set apart from the 'new', i.e. commercial, celebrities in a media field she herself helped create in Portugal, through 'good' and useful, public service entertainment, which the role as Ambassador helps to sustain, so that she is not just another celebrity, but a pivotal celebrity in the national media culture.

If celebrity discourse can give visibility to otherwise neglected issues, and do so outside traditional mainstream news media (Cooper 2008; Turner et al. 2000), contributing to bringing citizenship and political issues into the public discourse (Van Zoonen 2005), the framings and bias it imposes on the discourse also have to be accounted for. In these personalized and dramatized actions, in which celebrities lend their fame to raise awareness on 'noble' causes, chosen by them or others, the mobilization of citizens is framed as help to 'solidarity', to fellow citizens or people in developing countries. In this type of discourse, framed as sensitive and feminine (Macdonald 1995; McRobbie 2009), the causes and stakeholders are not confronted, the ways of thinking about how global inequality should be fought are replicated and the *pity* discourse, instead of a framing of the issues around *rights* and *justice*, tends to be perpetuated (Littler 2008). In other words, the emotional and casuistic framing of the aid campaigns is hardly capable of raising political debates around development that are connected with some of the cultural and historical bonds upon which the very UN Goodwill Ambassadors' strategy takes place. In the postcolonial and semi-peripheral setting of the Portuguese society, celebrity discourses around Catarina Furtado's activism as Goodwill Ambassador and its media resonance operate in cultural political circuits, as they contribute to accentuating the ways in which the national culture is influenced by the powers at the centre of the globe, such as the North American, how it envisages the fight to inequality and how it establishes its relations with its periphery.

Acknowledgements

The author wishes to thank the Portuguese Science and Technology Foundation for funding the Ph.D. research from which this chapter is part, and the Media and Journalism Research Centre (CIMJ/UNL) for bearing the English proofreading costs of this text.

References

Alegria, C. (2009), 'Catarina Furtado: "Gosto de me arranjar e já passei esse ritual à minha filha"' ['Catarina Furtado: "I like to tidy myself up and I've passed that ritual on to my daughter"'], *Caras*, 23 January. http://aeiou.caras.pt/. Accessed 30 January 2009.

Alleyne, M. D. (2005), 'The United Nations' Celebrity Diplomacy', *SAIS Review*, XXV:1, pp. 175–185.

Amante, P. (2001), 'Catarina Furtado: Embaixadora de Boa Vontade da ONU namora há cinco anos com João Gil' ['Catarina Furtado: UN Goodwill Ambassador has been dating João Gil for five years'], *Caras*, 10 November, without pages.

Anonymous (2006), 'Catarina Furtado', *Activa*, June, p. 1.

—— (2007a), 'Record-Breaking Donation from Portuguese Public', UNFPA, 23 May, http://www.unfpa.org/news/news.cfm?ID=980. Accessed 12 November 2008.

—— (2007b), 'Catarina Furtado: a mamã que dá de mamar' ['Catarina Furtado: the mother who breastfeeds'], *Sapo Fama*, 12 December, http://fama.sapo.pt/index.php?option=com_content&task=view&id=272&Itemid=68. Accessed 3 March 2009.

—— (2008a), 'Sexta à Noite', *RTP1*, (unknown day) January 2008.

—— (2008b), 'Catarina Furtado: Boas acções na Guiné' ['Catarina Furtado: Good actions in Guinea'], *Caras*, 26 July, without page.

—— (2008c), 'Eles viveram como voluntários em África' ['They lived as volunteer workers in Africa'], *TV Mais*, 25 July, pp. 50–54.

—— (2008d), 'Mundo Imperfeito' ['Imperfect World'], *SIC*, 16 September, 29 min, in sic.aeiou.pt. Accessed 28 March 2009.

—— (2008e), 'Nunca apresentaria um reality-show' ['I would never present a reality show'], *Diário de Notícias, Notícias TV*, 16 May, pp. 72–75.

—— (2008f), 'Catarina enfrenta surto de cólera' ['Catarina faces cholera outbreak'], *TV Guia*, 18 July, without page.

—— (2009a), 'Goodwill Ambassador Catarina Furtado Lays the Foundation for Improved Maternal Health in Guinea-Bissau', UNFPA, 25 July, http://www.unfpa.org/public/News/pid/1151. Accessed 12 November 2008.

—— (2009b), 'Catarina Furtado ajuda mães da Guiné-Bissau' ['Catarina Furtado helps Guinea-Bissau's mothers'], *Sapo Fama*, 18 February, http://fama.sapo.pt/index.php?option=com_content&task=view&id=3389&Itemid=20. Accessed 13 April 2009.

—— (2009c), 'Catarina Furtado – Porque Cada Pessoa Conta' ['Catarina Furtado – Because Everyone Counts'], *Biography Channel*, 25 February, 50 min.

Bajouco, M. (2008), 'Catarina voa para Bissau' ['Catarina flies to Bissau'], *Correio da Manhã*, 18 July, p. 42.

Booth, J. (2009), 'Guinea-Bissau factfile: drugs, guns and slaves', *Times Online*, 2 March, http://www.timesonline.co.uk/tol/news/world/africa/article5830742.ece. Accessed 3 March 2009.

Bueno, F. (2009), 'Catarina ajuda mães da Guiné' ['Catarina helps Guinea's mothers], *Correio da Manhã*, 18 February, in http://www.correiodamanha.pt/noticia.aspx?channelid=00000092-0000-0000-0000-000000000092&contentid=A7BE77FC-3D2E-4AF5-B878-77A57A561FDA. Accessed 3 March 2009.

Cooper, A. (2008), *Celebrity Diplomacy*, London: Paradigm Publishers.

Curião, C. (2005), 'Catarina 'fecha' casamento' ['Catarina 'closes down' wedding'], *Correio da Manhã*, 3 July, p. 60.

Delimbeuf, K. (2005), 'Por uma Boa Causa' ['For a Good Cause'], *Expresso/ Única*, 2 April, pp. 26–30.

—— (2008), 'Catarina vai estar com Brad Pitt' ['Catarina will meet Brad Pitt'], *Expresso/Única*, 7 June, p. 9.

Dyer, R. (2005), *Heavenly Bodies – Film Stars and Society*, London; New York, Routledge.

Ferreira, V. V. (2008), 'Dança com África' ['Dancing with Africa'], *Destak*, 31 July.

Fialho, J. (2008), 'As missões de Catarina' ['Catarina's missions'], *Sol/Tabu*, 27 September, pp. 1, 30–38.

Freitas, R. (2009), 'Dar Vida Sem Morrer' ['Give Birth without Dying'], *RTP1*, 26 February, 53 min.

Freixo, R. (2008a), 'A felicidade de Catarina Furtado como mulher, mãe e profissional' ['Catarina's happiness as a woman, a mother and a professional'], *Caras*, 19 July, without pages.

—— (2008b), 'Tenho aprendido muito com os meus filhos' ['I've been learning a lot with my children'], 27 September, pp. 1, without pages.

Galamas, M. (2008), 'Catarina Furtado esteve na Guiné em missão solidária' ['Catarina Furtado was in Guinea in a solidary mission'], *VIP*, 30 July, p. 28.

Gato, S. (2007), 'O papel principal' ['The main role'], *Elle*, October, pp. 1, 204–209.

Gledhill, C. (2000), 'Re-examining Stardom: Questions of Texts, Bodies and Performances', in C. Gledhill and L. Williams (eds), *Reinventing Film Studies*, London: Arnold, pp. 183–201.

Littler, J. (2008), '"I feel your pain": cosmopolitan charity and the public fashioning of the celebrity soul', *Social Semiotics*, 18:2, pp. 237–251.

Lumby, C. (1999), *Gotcha: Life in a Tabloid World*, Australia: Allen & Unwin.

Macdonald, M. (1995), *Representing Women: Myths of Femininity in the Popular Media*, London; New York: Hodder Arnold.

Marshall, P. D. (1997), *Celebrity and Power: Fame in Contemporary Culture*, Minneapolis; London: University of Minnesota Press.

Marshall, P. D. (Ed.) (2006), *The Celebrity Culture Reader*, New York; London: Routledge.

Martins, R. L. (2006), 'Princesa encantada' ['Princess charmed'], *Vogue*, May, pp. 1, 149–153.

McRobbie, A. (2009), *The Aftermath of Feminism*, London: Sage.

Pinto, J. F. (2005), *Do Império Colonial à Comunidade dos Países de Língua Portuguesa: Continuidades e Descontinuidades*, Lisboa: Ministério dos Negócios Estrangeiros.

Reeves, J. L. (1988), 'Television Stardom: A Ritual of Social Typification and Individualization', in J. W. Carey (ed.), *Media, Myths, and Narratives: Television and the Press*, Newbury Park, Beverly Hills, London, New Delhi: Sage, pp. 146–160.

Ribeiro, A. M. (2006), 'Deslumbrante! Catarina Furtado mais sedutora que nunca' ['Astonishing! Catarina Furtado more seductive than ever'], *Máxima*, December, pp. 1, 76–83.

Rico, C. and Fonseca, R. (2008), 'Um mundo imperfeito' ['An imperfect world'], *Visão*, 24 July, pp. 100–102.

Sala, A. (2008), 'António Sala entrevista Catarina Furtado' ['António Sala interviews Catarina Furtado'], *Rádio Renascença*, 16 January, 53 min. http://www.rr.pt/programasDetalhe.aspx?Conten tId=233048&AreaId=13&SubAreaId=123&ZoneId=. Accessed 13 April 2009.

Santos, B. S. (ed.) (1993), *Portugal: um Retrato Singular*, Oporto: Edições Afrontamento.

—— (1994), *Pela Mão de Alice: o Social e o Político na Pós-Modernidade*, Oporto: Edições Afrontamento.

—— (2002), 'Between Prospero and Caliban: Colonialism, Postcolonialism, and Inter-identity', *Luso-Brazilian Review*, 39:2, pp. 9–43.

Silva, A. D. (1997), *A Independência da Guiné-Bissau e a Descolonização Portuguesa*, Oporto: Edições Afrontamento.

Street, J. (1997), *Politics and popular culture*. Oxford, Polity.

Thrall, A. T., Lollio-Fakhreddine, J., Berent, J.. Donnelly, L.. Herrin, W., Paquette, Z., Wenglinski, R. and Wyatt, A. (2008), 'Star Power: Celebrity Advocacy and the Evolution of the Public Sphere', *The International Journal of Press/Politics*, 13:4, pp. 362–385.

Turner, G. (2006), 'The mass production of celebrity: "Celetoids", reality TV and the "demotic turn"', *International Journal of Cultural Studies*, 9:2, pp. 153–165.

Turner, G., Bonner, F. and Marshall, P. D. (2000), *Fame Games – The Production of Celebrity in Australia*, Cambridge: Cambridge University Press.

Van Zoonen, L. (2005), *Entertaining the Citizen: When Politics and Popular Culture Converge*, Oxford: Rowman & Littlefield Publishers, Inc.

Notes

1. *Mulattos* and *mestizos* are words that derive from Portuguese and Spanish colonialism, the former meaning the people born from one white and one black parent, and the latter, people born from one European parent and one American or Indian parent. *Crioulos* is a word derived from Portuguese colonialism, meaning the hybrid between the colonizer's and native languages. The three terms express the idea of hybridization of the colonizer's and colonized cultures.

2. The United Nations Population Fund (UNFPA) is an agency which promotes equal rights and opportunities, with a special focus on poverty, reproductive health, HIV/AIDS and gender equality.

3. Live as in television in real time.

Chapter 15

Big Dog Celebrity Activists: Barking up the Wrong Tree

Varihi Scott

Introduction

Successful celebrities are powerful communicators, often in the traditional sense of storytellers and almost always in the modern sense of public relations experts. Through activism, celebrities seek to change our world for the better but this chapter argues that the communications approaches used in traditional forms of celebrity activism in western societies actually reinforce the inequalities they set out to reduce. It goes on to discuss examples of celebrity activism that draw on a wider range of celebrities' skills, enabling impoverished and marginalized people to represent themselves, and so potentially change our understanding of how to improve our world.

The Problem: What Forms of Communication Create Change or 'who are you to speak for me'?

Discussing how the USA's poor are consistently portrayed negatively in the media and through the texts studied in formal education, bell hooks says that we must 'intervene in the existing system of representation' so that people experiencing poverty are credited with as much dignity and integrity as people in other classes in society (1994: 200).

Chambers argues that to change our understanding of the poor and transform abuses of power and wealth, academics that study the global poor should conduct a 'pedagogy of the non-oppressed' and include themselves in the process (2005: 194). Celebrity activists normally address the non-oppressed in the form of western audiences but to consider whether their form of pedagogy can lead to change, it is important to consider the methods they use.

Journalist, Ken Wiwa, said of the main 'Live8' concerts: 'The selection of musicians would not draw a crowd in Ouagadougou' (Cooper 2008: 111). Live8's organizers would argue that being big in Ouagadougou was not their goal, they were aiming to change minds in the more affluent parts of the world – though I wish to argue that by separating the means from the end, they limit their chances of achieving their goal.

The analytical perspective used here is communication for development, which supports poverty alleviation and challenges marginalization by focusing on communication, identity, representation and culture. A literature review informs a comparative analysis of traditional forms of celebrity activism, focusing on concerts, telethons and goodwill ambassadors.

This is followed by a discussion of how some celebrity-founded initiatives, which enable marginalized people to represent themselves, compare to more traditional methods. This comparison of communication activities working at opposite ends of society aims to highlight some of the problems of celebrity involvement in the humanitarian area of international politics, by using examples that will illustrate the extent to which these problems are being addressed or have been overcome.

Defining Celebrity Activism, Development and Communication for Development

Celebrity Activism

This term, encompassing many forms of celebrity involvement in social and political issues, is undergoing a period of expansion. In 2008, following Andrew Cooper, celebrity diplomacy was suggested as a new and more sophisticated form of activism by Huliaras and Tzifakis (2008), who identified clear changes between work done by previous generations of famous activists, and less involved celebrities, with the more professional approaches taken by the likes of Mia Farrow and the ubiquitous Bono. They suggest, for example, that the controversy-mired campaigning against the 2003 US invasion of Iraq by actors Sean Penn and George Clooney, no longer represents how today's activism is implemented. Cooper argues that the few celebrities who do exhibit behaviour recognizable as diplomatic, in the professional rather than colloquial sense, do so when they:

> combine the assertive individualism characteristic of the West with an appreciation of universal or cosmopolitan values. They abhor the use of violence. They engage in continuous dialogue, although not in a restrictive fashion, with multilateral forums such as the United Nations (UN) and Group of 8 (G8). They are eager to balance what can be considered 'megaphone diplomacy' with face-to-face engagement with official actors up to the level of chief executive, whether presidents or prime ministers. (2008: 2)

The necessity of a western sensibility is unexplained. However, it could be argued that Clooney's campaigning style for Darfur has moved towards diplomacy, as shown in his addressing the UN Security Council and meeting international heads of state including Barack Obama (Wagner 2009). Cooper's focus on interactions with specific fora is central to his definition. He reports an observer's comment on Bono's interactions with world leaders as 'guys with egos respond[ing] to other guys with egos' and goes on to say '[t]his mix of factors – a narcissistic affinity with popular celebrities and a big dog mentality – created the ideal atmosphere for advocacy' (2008: 43).

Philanthrocapitalism is another new word that has become attached to some forms of celebrity activism. Coined and elaborated on by journalist Matthew Bishop (Bishop 2007; Bishop and Green 2008, 2010) and simultaneously critiqued by Michael Edwards (2008, 2010), this word means using business principles to address social problems.

Bono's company, (RED), and celebrity-studded fora such as the Clinton Global Initiative are often cited as examples of philanthrocapitalism in action, while Edward's critiques of philanthrocapitalism's top-down approach echo many of the concerns mentioned later in this chapter regarding the post-democractic nature of 'Live Aid' and 'Live8'.

That the term celebrity activism might encompass activities ranging from the controversial to the deeply conservative might seem problematic; however, for this chapter the focus is simply on the communications approaches of the people involved.

Development

Many issues addressed by celebrity activists fall into the academic area of development studies within politics, geography or economics, and are dealt with in the industrial world by the international development branch of the non-profit sector. The term development is most often associated with economic development but is widely used to indicate foreign-sponsored activities in countries deemed to be lacking in infrastructure, amenities, civil society, recognition of rights and access to the means for creating and sustaining physical and social well being. Rist (2008: 4) argues that development is a preoccupation of rich countries because 'on the road to growth, no one can stop and wait for the slow movers'. He sees development as 'a system, which maintains and reinforces exclusion while claiming to eliminate it' (2008: 6), while the United Nations Development Program (UNDP)'s Human Development Reports define development as: 'the enlargement of people's choices' (Nederveen Pieterse 2001: 6). Chambers makes the yet more concise suggestion of 'good change' – however 'good' and 'change' are being interpreted at the time (2005: 186). It is assumed here that while the intentions of government and corporate bodies might more often equate with Rist's definition, Chambers' definition applies to the intentions of private individuals – even famous ones – that freely choose to get involved in transnational activism.

Communication for Development

Communication for development is both a tool used to tackle development issues, such as community radio projects to deal with community-based problems, and a means of articulating aspects of development projects and programmes, such as explaining and publicising an immunization initiative to families. It has been around since the 1950s and is made up of a wide range of approaches including social marketing, where marketing techniques are used to achieve socially beneficial behavioural change; health promotion and health education; entertainment education, which focuses on mass media-conveyed role models; face-to-face and peer-to-peer communication strategies; enabling communities to lobby mass media producers; and social mobilization, where communities are facilitated in defining a problem around which to attract strategic allies in order to address the problem (Hemer and Tufte 2005).

The following sections show that analysing celebrity activism from a communications-for-development perspective can shed new light on its potential effectiveness and identify some shared territory.

Concerts, Telethons and Goodwill Ambassadors

Waisbord (2005) has identified five ideas that are common to the theories and practices in communication for development. These five key ideas are the fostering of community empowerment; an integration of top-down and bottom-up approaches; the use of a toolkit of communication strategies; the use of personal communication with multimedia activities; and using approaches that take into consideration factors affecting the individual as well as their environment. This section discusses activism-based concerts, telethons and goodwill ambassadors in terms of Waisbord's five ideas.

Concerts

Concerts like 'Live8' do not empower their community of viewers: they give clear instructions on how to send in money or sign a petition and you can do as instructed or not. Celebrities boost audience size, demonstrate the credibility of the cause and organizers, and enable organizers to target certain demographics. By interspersing documentary film and celebrity statements between musical performances, serious issues are kept short enough to prevent the audience from switching off and multi-media merchandise enables viewers to keep a DVD of the event or buy the official book: in this sense a small range of multi-media products are available. Backstage interviews give an impression of personal communication but the community being communicated to never gets a chance to discuss options for how their money could be spent or meet the development people that will spend the money.

Hague et al. (2008) compare the 'Live Aid' and 'Live8' concerts with events organized by a 1970s and 1980s UK movement called Rock Against Racism (RAR). The RAR organizers chose musicians whose anti-racism stance was clear in their lyrics or line-up, and used the events to give upcoming anti-racist bands increased exposure alongside more established acts (Hague et al. 2008: 13). Bob Geldof, the force behind the 'Live Aid' and 'Live8' events, is shown, by contrast, stating that he does not want to give anyone a lesson in politics at his shows and that his performers are chosen purely for their commercial value (Hague et al. 2008: 9).

Denis Jackson of Family Health International, said the 1985 Live Aid concerts made the issues of famine, 'part of people's personal history. Everyone remembers where they were at the time even if the issues around delivery of the aid turned out to be more complex than they had realised' (Smith 2006). Vallely claims that the concerts were also influential for Tony Blair and Gordon Brown (2005) – both later to become UK prime ministers. A means of communication that moves people at all levels of society is surely a good thing. However, Hague, Street and Savigny see the 'Live Aid' and 'Live8' concerts as echoing post-democracy, which they describe as a condition in which, 'while the institutions of democracy exist, politics is actually conducted by unaccountable elites. [...] In such an order, the citizen is a passive bystander, witness only to politics as spectacle'. And that to allow the citizens to still feel as if they are participating, the elites copy the methods of the entertainment industry, and so, 'Politics becomes a variation on consumption, in which brands, images and celebrities become the key' (2008: 8). They argue that by selecting performers on the basis of their selling power, the main 'Live8' events (as opposed to the hastily put together 'Africa Calling' event that featured a wider range of musicians) were instruments of conservatism rather than of change because they reproduced existing values: 'Its politics emerge after the people (the demos), thereby foreclosing the possibility of constructing and reconstructing this people' (2008: 20). A report on how British television portrayed developing countries in 2005 backs this up, finding that 'Live8' did not change the already negative public perceptions about Africa and that for some it reinforced the impression that 'the developing world is a hopeless cause' (Smith et al. 2006: 6).

Once Bob Geldof responded to news footage of the 1984–85 famine in Ethiopia by gathering together some famous friends to record a song that would raise money from the public, which would then be used to send food to Ethiopia, many of us have accepted this as how the minority world public participates in development. Had he gathered together famous people to form human shields in the conflict areas that were blocking aid already there from getting through, or organized his famous friends to withhold payment of taxes until their governments acted, we might see the world a little differently. The point is not that these are better or less naïve responses; merely that what we appear to have come to accept as the obvious response is far from the only course of action available.

Commercially driven activism-based concerts, then, talk down to us, reinforce the status quo and we appear to have let them shrink our imaginations.

Telethons

Disability rights activist, Brown, points out that telethons create islands of need in a schedule of normality, thus denying that the recipients of the funds raised by the telethon are integral parts of society (2006). Devereux criticizes telethons for being *a*political because they allow the donors to assume positions of power by bestowing good, without asking them to challenge the forces that have led to such inequities in society, or indeed without challenging the donors' role in contributing to these inequities (1996). PANOS, a pioneer in producing media products with those who the products represent, says: 'the process of producing information (such as who produces it, who owns it) is often as important as the information itself'.[2] So far we are not in a position to find out whether, if the producers, directors and presenters of telethons were members of the groups for whom funds were being raised, they would choose to merely ask for sympathy and ad hoc sums of money.[3]

Red Nose Day, organized by Comic Relief, is the UK's nationwide biennial telethon for development. DFID (2000) and Woods (2005) consider that it addresses the criticisms levelled at telethons while continuing to develop ever more diverse ways of engendering public awareness and participation, although DFID (2000) says that in practice it deals too simplistically with serious issues.

Quoting George W. Bush, the author Dambissa Moyo says, 'we need to be careful of the soft bigotry of low expectations' (The GOOD 100, 2010); if low expectations are the reason for over-simplification then the media coverage of Moyo's 2009 book, *Dead Aid* provides an interesting counter. Between February and June 2009, this book on aid economics, written by a hitherto unknown Zambian economist, was featured in newspapers, radio and television shows across Europe, Africa, North America and Australasia,[4] and sparked what has been termed 'the aid debate' (Wooten 2010) that spread through social media, indicating that at least some members of the telethon's target audience are prepared to engage with more complex material.

Comic Relief's connections and popularity in the British entertainment and media industries give it unparalleled resources and its roadshows, documentaries, new media campaigns and production of materials for schools[5] mean that it works hard to take its messages to wherever its audience finds most convenient. One problem with this degree of audience penetration is that the images and messages Comic Relief creates about the people it seeks to help are much more widely available than those from other sources: directors from poor countries do not get their films broadcast in the same western primetime slots as telethons and community groups rarely have press officers to get their stories circulated in foreign newspapers – we see the marginalized and impoverished through Comic Relief's eyes.

From a smaller development organization's point of view, Comic Relief distributes its funds among a wide range of organizations that could not afford such lavish fundraising activities (Vallely 2007); if the organization does not qualify for funding from Comic Relief, there are other funders, but if it wants to communicate a different view of development then it is up against a considerable Goliath.

In 'Comic Relief: The Fool's Guide' a retrospective of 21 years of Red Nose Days,[6] many contributors repeated how innovative the telethon was with comedy but none mentioned innovations in development. The viewer is never told why some organizations and types of development projects receive funding and others not. The millennium development goals have been mentioned but not the debate around their selection and means of pursuit. Comic Relief's grant application material[7] shows that the organization keeps up with development trends but the fact that there are different ways of doing development is never presented to the telethon viewer, so again the viewing community is not empowered by its participation.

Comic Relief was founded in 1985 by British film director and screenwriter, Richard Curtis. Senior Comic Relief staff led the Make Poverty History[8] campaign in 2005, which was the UK and Ireland's version of the ONE campaign. The ONE website[9] identifies Bono as a co-founder. This means that most celebrity diplomacy in the Anglo-sphere has close links with either Richard Curtis's or Bono's organizations or both.[10] Actor Matt Damon describes 'listening and learning trips' conducted by Bono's organizations, where celebrities travel to Africa for a short course in development problems and solutions (Johnson 2007). The concept of providing training is perhaps to be welcomed but this breadth of influence reinforces the problem of homogenization.

Dieter and Kumar are concerned about the large-scale plans of Bono's organizations and the role played in them by economist Jeffrey Sachs, who they claim is advocating a 'Big Push' of aid for Africa that is akin to the much criticized development policies of the 1950s and 1960s (2008: 261). However, the concern here is less with competing development ideologies and more that one successful but small group of people have allowed themselves to create something of a monopoly. Perhaps surprisingly, Geldof raises a similar point in Adams: 'The only thing I am certain of, is that we are always wrong. Otherwise this thing would have been resolved. But then everyone else is wrong too' (Adams 2009) and goes on to say that he hates the 'empire-building' of DATA[11] and would prefer a smaller, more dynamic organization.

Red Nose Day telethons, then, are not concerned with communication for development: you are in their target audience if you are considered smart enough to have disposable income; however, you are not considered smart enough to understand the behind-the-scenes theories and decisions. If you are a small development organization with a different story to tell, you have a gigantic opponent in getting your voice heard. Like concerts, telethons use the appearance of mass public participation to concentrate power in the hands of a small elite who actually act.

Goodwill Ambassadors

As a form of celebrity activism, goodwill ambassadorship is as varied as the ambassadors involved. Goodwill ambassadors' activities include visiting members of the groups with which the ambassador's organization works; fronting press conferences; talking with politicians and business leaders; giving motivational and awareness-raising talks, and participating in fundraising events. The toolkit of communications strategies deployed can include serving as advocates, publicists, mediators, motivators, fund-raisers, facilitators, networkers and educators. Some ambassadors focus on one or a few of these roles but others might use them all.

One of the criticisms Edwards makes against philanthrocapitalism and its market-based attempts at social transformation is that, 'systemic change involves social movements, politics and the state, which these experiments generally ignore' (2008: 37). I have discussed the marketing-based problems with concerts and telethons, and their illusory creation of social movements but goodwill ambassadors might be different in that some do talk directly with politicians and legislative bodies on political matters.

Bowman-Johnston (2007), Smith (2007), Darnton (2005), James (2006), and Tenove (2006), cover the perils of employing goodwill ambassadors wherein accountability is a recurring theme. Africa Action, a USA-based group that chose not to join the ONE campaign (Bowman-Johnson 2007), cites concerns about the readiness of famous 'representatives' to make concessions. Cooper points out that celebrity diplomats, unlike their professional counterparts, not only lack formal training but also 'cannot easily claim that they speak for a constituency, whether defined as a cause or a people' (2008: 2). There is no mechanism for the goodwill ambassador to be disciplined or dismissed by the poor that they represent; they only lose their position if the people listening to them stop listening. Many parallels of mandate and the need to mobilize people can be drawn between Edwards' and Fowler's description of non-governmental development organizations (NGDOs) and the documented work of goodwill ambassadors, including perceived political bias when NGDOs – and by extension their ambassadors – receive a large proportion of their funding from governments (Fowler 2002).

Adding to concerns of unaccountability and partiality, Huliaras and Tzifakis argue that celebrities' ability to influence is overstated (2008) and Kumi Naidoo, a life-long activist who worked alongside Bono at the 2005 G8 summit in Scotland, concurs

Having access does not mean you have any influence; in fact, having access can sometimes reduce your influence. You think that because a powerful government official says roughly what you want to hear, you have made progress, but then at the first opportunity they make a U-turn or lower the bar. (Moss 2009)

For a person experiencing hardship, a visit from a goodwill ambassador might result in a positive change in that being recognized as a person and listened to is important for everyone but this is a *precursor* to empowerment, not empowerment itself. Siobhan Redmond, who has worked with CARE for over ten years, says that as an actress, all she is really qualified to do is listen as carefully as she can and then tell the stories of the people she has met.[12] Musician and UNICEF ambassador, Angelique Kidjo, incorporates practical advice when she goes to villages and discusses what people can do to help themselves (BBC Tyne 2007). Actor Don Cheadle's book about activism for Darfur (Cheadle and Prendergast 2007) tells you a lot about the work and thoughts of an activist while Angelina Jolie's diaries (Jolie 2003) of her early days as an ambassador for UNHCR often include accounts of the people she meets, in their own words. Both the books convey credibility-building first-hand knowledge and considerably more detail and subtlety than is possible in film clips during telethons or speeches at concerts; these are not face-to-face communications but they are quite personal nonetheless. In Redmond, Kidjo, Cheadle and Jolie's cases, if the poor could choose whether they wanted these people as their champions and what they would like them to do then this would be much more of a bottom-up communications approach.

So far, therefore, goodwill ambassadorship offers some potential for communication that creates change but probably not political change. Ambassadors' work uses a wide range of strategies and depends on mixing personal with multi-media activities. Their organizational affiliations might place obstacles in their path and if their fame fades they will be replaced; however, if you get the chance to talk with one, your words could be relayed to world leaders, though you are unlikely to hear about it.

Among the findings here then are that big concerts and telethons use large amounts of star power to limited effect, which is not necessitated by the medium but is the choice of the organizers. Further, the methods used and power wielded by the concert and telethon organizers discussed, form a wall that prevents people in need of help from communicating directly with those who are keen to help, while goodwill ambassadors are among the few able to pass through that wall.

Celebrity-led Alternatives

Louverture Films

When asked by *Oprah* Magazine what you should do to change the world, actor Danny Glover said: 'use your artistry' (Ensler 2008). Dickenson describes him as 'progressive Hollywood aristocracy' (Dickenson 2006: xi) indicating both the duration and extent of his activism. In 2005, Glover and former UN consultant, Joslyn Barnes founded Louverture

Films (Davidson 2008), which raises money to make films that tell less widely known stories of Africans and Africa's diaspora, prioritizes working with majority world film-makers and hires and trains cast and crew from communities of colour within the USA. Louverture provides work for established African directors and actors, supplies new material to African film audiences around the world, and works in Africa and the USA to increase the capacity of Africa's many national film-making industries through education and apprenticeship opportunities, alternative models of financing and alternative distribution strategies.[13]

Louverture is all about integrating top-down and bottom-up approaches: by providing training and strategically using location selection to provide income and employment, it assists people at the very bottom of the global film industry. By then also using its position as a US film company to get round some of the restrictions placed on foreign film companies seeking access to the US market, it enables the marginalized to tell their own stories, in their own way, to an audience usually denied access to those voices.

Louverture's toolkit of communication strategies includes advocacy, community media, inter-personal communication and multimedia activities. Glover's fame probably attracts a wider western audience to the films and his long-standing experience of activism combined with Barnes' familiarity with the development industry mean they have a considerable amount of insight to offer the people they are training and the organizations they are helping to network. This range of talent enables them to use approaches that work for the diverse nature of their communities, the individuals in those communities and those communities' environments.

FilmAid International
Responding to the 1999 conflict in Kosovo, actor Julia Ormond and producer Caroline Baron took films and screening equipment to refugee camps to provide some light relief to children and families. Their rapid intervention was supported and encouraged by relief and development organizations including Doctors of the World, UNICEF, IRC and the UNHCR. They formed FilmAid International, which now works in many refugee camps using the choice of films screened to provide practical information on health issues, tackle sensitive issues such as conflict resolution and domestic violence, enable a broader view of the outside world, particularly important for children brought up in the camps, and encourage people to plan positive futures for themselves. FilmAid sources appropriate material, where possible, in local languages, oversees the creation and running of makeshift cinemas by refugees, facilitates discussions after screenings of the educational material, produces videos with refugees to address specific local issues arising in camps, and teaches basic camera and editing techniques to young adults to enable them to create their own films with which to communicate with their fellow refugees.[14]

In allowing residents to select what they view, prioritizing material depicting their native culture and/or in their own language, and teaching how to use the medium for their own purposes, FilmAid goes a long way towards empowering its community. Also, providing training and employment opportunities not only eases camp life but potentially broadens the refugees' opportunities for employment and societal integration when they leave, giving them some very practical power with which to improve their lives.

FilmAid's camp advisory committees represent the camp demographics, are used to guide programmes, pre-screen all material and relay community feedback. However, details of the feedback mechanism are not clear. Integration of top-down and bottom-up approaches is clear, though, in the use of a level of film analysis to tackle residents' problems and then the teaching of film-making so that residents can use the medium to explore their own interests and concerns in their own way.

Like Louverture, FilmAid's toolkit of communication strategies includes advocacy methods and community media, and its peer-to-peer activities are strong examples of combining personal communication with multimedia activities.

In using approaches that take into consideration factors affecting the individual as well as their environment, FilmAid's location within refugee camps makes it ideally targeted. The medium of film is also more accessible to those who have sustained injuries to sight or hearing, while overcoming problems of literacy and third party mediation.

Social Networking, Sitcoms and Exposing Human Rights Abuses

Between the post-democratic concerts and telethons, the varied goodwill ambassadors and the storytelling-centred Louverture and FilmAid, are many more famous entertainers and their organizations trying new ways of making the world a better place. This section briefly outlines three that take very different approaches to enabling marginalized people to represent themselves.

1. Kevin Bacon's Sixdegrees.org initiative, run in association with US-based NGO Network for Good,[15] enables users to create 'badges' for their chosen charities. The badges are placed on social networking sites and blogs, and explain why the user supports the charity. Space for text and a photo is small, though you can add a video link. Celebrity badges are featured, presumably for attention-grabbing and credibility-lending reasons; however, the striking thing is that no differentiation is made between people raising money for a charity they support, and people raising money for a charity they receive support from. Beneficiaries of charities have as much scope to represent themselves as funders have to describe why they support the charities that they do.

2. Celebrities play only a small part in the Rwanda Cinema Center. The Center is run by a group of Rwandan film-makers and includes a touring film festival called Hillywood, which takes films made by Rwandan directors and producers, in the local language, out to smaller towns and screens them on large inflatable screens. Many people in the Rwandan film industry gained their expertise through working on foreign films and television programmes about the 1994 genocide but as global attention moved on, so did that source of income and employment. However, it has left behind a pragmatic optimism about the

new skills: actor Kennedy Mazimpaka is quoted as saying 'Right now we need anything that can develop Rwanda. So why not a film industry?' (Hughes 2007). Aside from the film festival, the Center also works on training young people to make films about their own issues, an audio-visual testimonies archive, and in partnership with the University of California, Los Angeles (UCLA), a project specializing in comedy film-making. In support of this project are cast and crew from the US sitcom *Everybody Loves Raymond*, and the show's creator and one of its stars also serve on the RCC's board of advisors.[16] This is a good example of celebrities meeting a need defined by those they are helping, rather than imposing their version of help irrespective of need.

3. The musician Peter Gabriel is an exceptional celebrity activist who is rarely referenced as such. In 1980 he co-founded WOMAD,[17] the World of Music, Arts and Dance festival, which gives a western stage to musicians from all countries, particularly Africa and Asia. WOMAD now has regular festivals in several countries. Gabriel's record label, Real World Records,[18] gives WOMAD performers a chance to access markets that would normally be beyond their reach. After having the idea, along with businessman Richard Branson, for the group of global leaders known as The Elders[19] – and so arguably using big dog style powers of influence – Gabriel went on, in 1992, to co-found WITNESS.[20] Gabriel is known for experimental film-making as well as music, and WITNESS is a human rights NGO that provides cameras and training on how to use them, to human rights groups around the world. The organization's website shows the films created and a site called 'the hub' is an online community where anyone with an e-mail address can upload their films and access the tools and support to campaign against human rights abuses. In each of these instances, Gabriel uses what he has learned as a performer to build three very different types of 'stages' for other people.

Conclusion

The concerts and telethons organized by Comic Relief and ONE get the public and politicians talking about issues that they might otherwise ignore and they raise an enormous amount of money. However, these organizations talk down to their audience, reinforce the idea of the well-intentioned westerner fixing the world's problems and their sheer size and influence mean that if someone else has a better idea for doing what they do, we might never hear about it. Goodwill ambassadors are changing the world one conversation at a time but their effectiveness is determined as much by their own skills as the roles they are requested or permitted to perform.

Louverture, FilmAid, Sixdegrees.org, the Rwanda Cinema Centre, WITNESS and WOMAD all show what can be done when celebrities use their professional skills rather than their star power: they do, as hook suggests, and change the system of representation. It is hard to imagine the civil rights movement making the progress it has done if most of its leaders were white, or that feminism would have got far if women were only glimpsed during male-fronted fund-raisers. Change happens when we allow ourselves to hear and get to know new people and new points of view. World-class entertainers know how to get our attention and how to tell a story. They can harness those skills to help people silenced by extreme poverty, injustice, or made invisible in a globalized world, speak for themselves. There are numerous ways of giving the silenced a means of getting the rest of us to hear and understand them, and doing so is an essential part of what we regard as progress.

References

Adams, T. (2009), 'Our man in Africa', http://www.guardian.co.uk/politics/2008/may/11/development. africa. Accessed 18 January 2009.

BBC Tyne (2007), 'Angelique Kidjo: exclusive interview', http://www.bbc.co.uk/tyne/content/articles/ 2006/11/01/kidjo_interview_feature.shtml?page=1. Accessed 6 April 2007.

Bishop, M. (2007), 'What is philanthrocapitalism?', *Alliance*, March, 2007.

Bishop, M. and Green, M. (2008), *Philanthrocapitalism: How the Rich Can Save the World*, London: Bloomsbury Press.

—— (2010), *The Road from Ruin: How to Revive Capitalism and Put America Back on Top*, New York: Crown Publishing Group.

Bowman-Johnston, K. (2007), 'Celebrity Activists', *Sojourners Magazine*, <http://www.sojo.net/>. Accessed 9 January 2007.

Brown, S. E. (2006), 'The Truth About Telethons', http://www.dimenet.com/disculture/archive. php?mode=N&id=17. Accessed 9 February 2006.

Chambers, R. (2005), *Ideas for Development*, London: Earthscan.

Cheadle, D. and Prendergast, J. (2007), *Not on our Watch. The Mission to end Genocide in Darfur and Beyond*, New York: Hyperion.

Cooper, A. F. (2008), *Celebrity Diplomacy,* USA: Paradigm Publishers.

Darnton, A. (2005), 'Public Development Awareness in the UK', *BOND Networker* (Electronic version), September 2005.

Davidson, J. R. C. (2008), 'A Conversation with Danny Glover and Joslyn Barnes', *World Literature Today*, 82: 2, pp. 24–30.

Devereux, E. (1996), 'Good causes, God's poor and telethon television', *Media Culture & Society*, 18:1, pp. 47–68.

DFID (2000), *Viewing The World. A study of British television coverage of developing countries*, London: Department for International Development.

Dickenson, B. (2006), *Hollywood's New Radicalism. War, Globalisation and the Movies from Regan to George W. Bush*, London: I.B. Tauris.

Dieter, H. and Kumar, R. (2008), 'The Downside of Celebrity Diplomacy: The Neglected Complexity of Development', *Global Governance*, 14:3, pp. 259–64.

Edwards, M. (2008), *Just Another Emperor? The Myths and Realities of Philanthrocapitalism*, New York: Demos and The Young Foundation.

—— (2010), *Small Change: Why Business Won't Save the World*, San Francisco: Berrett-Koehler.

Ensler, E. (2008), 'A Million Ways to Save the World', *Oprah Magazine,* April 2008, p. 79.

Fowler, A. (2002), 'NGO futures – beyond Aid: NGDO Values and the Fourth Position', in M. Edwards and A. Fowler (eds), *The Earthscan reader on NGO Management*, London: Earthscan.

Hague, S., Street, J. and Savigny, H. (2008), 'The Voice of the People? Musicians as Political Actors', *Cultural Politics*, 4:1, pp. 5–24.

Hemer, O. and Tufte, T. (eds), *Media and Glocal Change. Rethinking Communication for Development*, Buenos Aires and Göteborg: CLACSO and Nordicom.

hooks, b. (1994), *Outlaw Culture. Resisting Representations*, Abingdon: Routledge.

Hughes, A. (2007), 'Rwandans flock to "Hillywood" films', http://www.bbc.co.uk//go/pr/fr/-/2/hi/africa/6530227.stm. Accessed 6 April 2007.

Huliaras, A. and Tzifakis, N. (2008), 'The Dynamics of Celebrity Activism: Mia Farrow and the "Genocide Olympics" Campaign', *Karamanlis Working Papers in Hellenic and European Studies*, No. 7. The Fletcher School of Law and Diplomacy, Medford, Massachusetts, July 2008.

James, C. (2006), 'Megastars Out To Save The World: those halos can tarnish in an instant', *The New York Times*, 13 November 2006.

Johnson, B. D. (2007), 'Matt Damon talks to Brian D. Johnson about celebrities rescuing Africa, Harper's betrayal, and actors in the White House', *Maclean's*, 12 October 2007.

Jolie, A. (2003), *Notes from my Travels. Visits with Refugees in Africa, Cambodia, Pakistan, and Ecuador*, New York: Pocket Books.

Moss, S. (2009), 'Kumi Naidoo: "History teaches us that the only time you move forward is when decent people put their lives on the line"', http://www.guardian.co.uk/environment/2009/nov/30/kumi-naidoo-greenpeace-copenhagen. Accessed 31 November 2009.

Moyo, D. (2009), *Dead Aid. Why Aid is Not Working and How There is Another Way for Africa*, London: Allen Lane.

Nederveen Pieterse, J. (2001), *Development Theory. Deconstructions/Reconstructions*, London: Sage.

Rist, G. (2008), *The History of Development. From Western origins to global faith*, 3rd ed., London: Zed Books.

Smith, A. (2006), 'All in a good cause?', http://www.guardian.co.uk/theobserver/2002/jan/27/life1.lifemagazine2. Accessed 18 January 2006.

Smith, L. (2007), 'Star Quality', http://www.ncvo-vol.org.uk/vsmagazine/features/?id=1877. Accessed 27 March 2007.

Smith, J., Edge, L. and Morris, V. (2006), '*Reflecting the Real World?: How British TV portrayed developing countries in 2005*', London: the International Broadcasting Trust.

Tenove, C. (2006), 'Stars Above Africa', *The Walrus Magazine*, 11 December 2006.

The GOOD 100 (2010), 'Dambissa Moyo', http://www.good.is/post/the-good-100-dambisa-moyo/. Accessed 10 January 2010.

Traub, J. (2008), 'The Celebrity Solution', <http://www.nytimes.com/2008/03/09/magazine/09CELEBRITY-t.html?_r=1&pagewanted=all>. Accessed 10 March 2008.

Vallely, P. (2005), *Hello World. Live8 The Official Book*, London: Century.

—— (2007), 'The Big Question: Is Comic Relief Worth Supporting – or is it past its sell-by date?', *The Independent*, 16 March 2007.

Wagner, A. (2009), 'Board Member George Clooney Meets With US Pres Obama And VP Biden', <http://notonourwatchproject.org/features/13>. Accessed 30 February 2009.

Waisbord, S. (2005), 'Five Key Ideas: Coincidences and Challenges in Development Communication', in O. Hemer and T. Tufte (eds), *Media and Glocal Change. Rethinking Communication for Development*, Buenos Aires and Göteborg: CLACSO and Nordicom, pp. 77–91.

Woods, M. (2005), 'Comic Relief Review 2002—2004', *Comic Relief*, London.

Wooten, K. Y. (2010), 'The Sachs-Moyo-Easterly Aid Debate: An Activist's Perspective', <http://www.huffingtonpost.com/kristi-york-wooten/the-sachs-moyo-easterly-a_b_210473.html>. Accessed 10 January 2010.

Notes

1. In the UK, the expression barking up the wrong tree comes from a dog chasing a cat or squirrel. The creature being pursued climbs a tree and escapes through adjacent plants or buildings but the dog, unaware, remains barking up at the tree, keenly focused in the wrong place. Big dog, comes from Cooper's observations about Bono mixing with political leaders (2008: 43).
2. www.panos.org/network/mission.asp.
3. This chapter was in the final stages of editing as the Hope For Haiti Now telethon was being organized by George Clooney, with Haitian musician Wyclef Jean as co-presenter.
4. From correspondence with marketing department of publisher.
5. At time of writing, the most recent account of Comic Relief's media coverage available on its website is for 2005–2006 http://www.comicrelief.com.
6. Broadcast 3 February 2009 BBC1 10.35pm.
7. http:www.comicrelief.com/apply_for_a_grant.
8. http://www.makepovertyhistory.org.
9. http://www.one.org.
10. For example, Comic Relief's financial statement for 2007 states that 362 artists participated in its 2007 Red Nose Day campaign, retrieved 1 February 2009, http://www.comicrelief.com/files/cr09/files/imce/charity_projects2006-2007.pdf, while the 'Live 8' concerts, listed on the ONE website as a previous campaign, featured more than 1000 musicians, retrieved 1 February 2009 http://www.one.org/c/international/pastcampaign/1041/.
11. Now part of ONE.
12. Unpublished interview with the author, May 2007.
13. www.louverturefilms.com.
14. http://www.filmaid.org.
15. http://www.sixdegrees.org.
16. http://www.rwandacinemacenter.org.
17. http://womad.org.
18. http://www.realworldrecords.com.
19. http://www.theelders.org.
20. http://www.witness.org.

Conclusion

Making Sense of Transnational Celebrity Activism: Causes, Methods and Consequences

Liza Tsaliki, Christos Frangonikolopoulos and Asteris Huliaras

S ince the beginning of the millennium much discussion and debate have taken place on the increasing role of celebrity activism in global politics, and the aim of this book has been to contribute to this debate and take it further. Celebrity activism, however, is not a new phenomenon. As Michael, Cynthia and Rachel Stohl underline in their chapter, celebrity activism has been a powerful and commonplace phenomenon since the nineteenth century.

However, it seems that in the last three decades we have witnessed a qualitative change. Asteris Huliaras and Nikolaos Tzifakis (Chapter 1) argue that the current scale of celebrity activism is unprecedented. Mark Wheeler (chapter 2) agrees with this claim and makes a useful distinction between the *conforming* celebrity activist of the 1950s, 1960s and 1970s, and the *transformative* celebrity activist after the 1980s. In the first case, celebrities acted as 'good international citizens' and concentrated only in developing ad hoc, inter-personal relationships with UN officers. In the second case, celebrity activities became characterized by a widening of their roles, taking an active interest in global politics, becoming central players on a wide variety of political issues such as aid, conflict, human rights and development.[1]

This is a reality that cannot be dismissed in foreign policy, global politics and international communication. We need, therefore, in conclusion of this book, to outline and examine the *causes* that explain the rise and increasing influence of celebrity activists. In so doing, it is also necessary to examine the *methods* they are using in drawing attention to global issues, as well as the *consequences* the projection and lobbying of these issues have on international politics. This will be done not only by highlighting the arguments raised by the authors of this collective work, but also by linking their findings to the relevant academic discussion.

Numerous explanations have been offered to explain the rise and role of celebrity activists in international politics. Celebrity activism, it is often argued (Sabbato et al. 2000), is a way for stars to remain in the news in periods when they have no new movie or CD to promote. This is clear in Ana Jorge's (Chapter 14), where it is clearly shown how personal and media narratives intricate with the activism of celebrities. In fact, and as shown by Littler (2008), public displays of support for the 'afflicted' of the world, can be a way for celebrity activists to raise their profile above the commercial world, and in so doing, construct a personality of compassion and altruism.

These are significant explanations for this, although other factors are also at work (Street 2002). Changes and shifts in the global information ecosystem (Compton and Comor 2007), the way in which citizens, especially in the developed world, consume and receive information through the spread of 'soft news' (Babcock and Whitehouse 2005), as well as the rise of global information networks (Rai and Cottle 2007; Cottle and Rai 2008), have created a spectacle culture (Kellner 2010) that allows celebrities to use their status and access to the media as an instrument to push their issues or agendas. In particular, the diversification of global media networks and satellite technologies provide worldwide distribution of entertainment and political content. As Castells (2007: 246–248) would argue, the diffusion of the Internet and mobile communication, facilitates the development of 'mass self-communication' that connects the local and the global. The communication system of the industrial society was centred on the mass media, characterized by the mass distribution of one-to-many messages. The communication foundation of the contemporary world is the global web of horizontal communication networks that include the multimodal exchange of interactive messages from many to many. This is not denying that the media space is not shaped by governments and global business conglomerates. But at the same, it would be wrong to neglect the role the media play in creating a global platform for transnational activists and movements. By mobilizing and communicating through the Internet and acting on the mainstream media system, particularly by creating events that send powerful images and messages, celebrity activists induce a debate on the hows, whys and whats of global political and social issues (O'Brien and Szeman 2003).

This development, when combined with the 'democratization' of foreign policy, as Michael, Cynthia and Rachel Stohl argue in Chapter 11, not only allows celebrities to act as transnational lobbyists/activists, but also facilitates openness, discourse and information dissemination on issues of global concern. In a world characterized by the failure of the nation state to stand up to an increasing number of transnational threats, there is a shift from focusing mainly on states, statesmen and other political leaders. This, according to Huliaras and Tzifakis in Chapter 1, has opened up the field of international relations and global politics to other actors and other types of activity (Alleyne 2005), which mainly rely on the *social power* of individuals and NGOs (van Ham 2010). Social power, defined as the ability to set standards, create norms and values that are deemed legitimate and desirable, without resorting to state-centric power and coercion, is a central part of contemporary global politics.

Celebrity activists, therefore, should not be undervalued or dismissed. Where governments and traditional international organizations face a myriad of challenges of legitimacy and efficiency, celebrity activists are blurring and questioning the traditional barriers of the diplomatic state-centric establishment in the contemporary era of globalization (Cooper 2007a). Although the concept of globalization is so broad and diverse that it is difficult to effectively define or generalize it, we could define it as a 'set of processes that bring people and places together' (Harris 1993: 757). Contact between people, places and organizations has become more frequent, more sustained, and encompasses a wider variety of activities. Indeed, not everything or everyone is globalized; yet the global networks that structure the planet affect everything and everyone (Castells 2008: 81). These include global financial markets, global production and distribution of goods and services, international trade, global movement of immigrants and refugees, global networks of science and technology, global media and global cultural industries.

In addition, according to Beck (2006), the critical issues conditioning everyday life for people and their governments in every country are largely shaped by globally interdependent processes that move beyond the realm of ostensibly sovereign state territories and produce new forms of political solidarity and understanding of international cooperation. The increasing difficulty of nation states in confronting and managing the processes of globalization encourages governments to associate with each other, building an intense network of international institutions and supranational organizations. There is not a single world state, but a system of global governance in which states are increasingly hemmed in by a set of agreements, treaties and rules of a transnational character (Held and McGrew 2007). This increasing sense of mutual interdependence, combined with the advances in the media, has shifted the interests and values of societies from the *national* to the *global* domain,[2] giving shape to a *global public sphere* in which information and knowledge, political values, ethics and lifestyles are exchanged, and are becoming increasingly autonomous from nation state contexts (Volkmer 2003).

In this context, celebrity activists, as Nash (2008) has shown, operate within the framework of *globalism*, cultivating the potential for shifting the concerns of politics away from traditional struggles of sovereignty towards issues of mutual concern. Celebrities provide and represent *cosmopolitanism* to audiences, constructing the identity of global citizenship and solidarity, and questioning the dominant national orientation of politics. In that direction, celebrities rely on their power resources, scope of influence, soft power and charismatic authority (Pease and Brewer 2008; Ferris 2007; Brown et al. 2003; Fraser and Brown 2002; Elliot 1998). In addition, they have also developed significant tools for persuading and strategically framing issues, allowing them to leverage their value and build broad political coalitions (Busby 2007; Barratt 2005). Not only do they use the power and attraction of the media, but they have also facilitated the formation, as Cooper argues (2007b: 128–129), of 'sustainable hybrid networks' through which celebrities dramatize the need to do something and corporate celebrities provide the material resources. As Mark Wheeler stresses in Chapter 2, celebrity activists have introduced new forms of political engagement, which indicate a transformation of high politics with a more populist approach to citizenship and global politics.[3] In fact, and as shown in Chapter 5 by Henk Huijser and Jinna Tay on the 'Elders', celebrities are successful in developing a two-level communication and lobbying approach, connecting not only with the political and economical elites, but also with citizens and audiences. This is an approach beyond the capabilities of politicians and other state officials as they are limited by the logic and boundaries of traditional politics and nation states.

This reality allows celebrity activists to:

1. Act as a *bridge* between a (western) audience and a 'faraway' tragedy. A celebrity, as de Waal (2008) argues, is the focus for empathy, an emotional interpreter, telling the story and explaining the problem with just sufficient cues for the audience to supply the sadness and the anger.

2. *Complement* the work of NGOs and global civil society, enhancing their work and strengthening their agendas. As Virgil Hawkins illustrates in Chapter 4 this is clear in the 'Save Darfur Coalition'. Indicative is also the work of Nicholas Cage with Amnesty International, as examined and analysed in Chapter 11 of Michael, Cynthia and Rachel Stohl. In fact, one may even argue as Dorothy Njoroge does in Chapter 12 on the 'Make Poverty History' Campaign, that celebrity activists are part of a much wider global social justice movement made up of grassroots organizations, NGOs and global activist publics. Celebrities, she suggests, possess substantial personal wealth and contribute financially to movements they support, use their media skills as spokespersons for their causes and have a network of contacts they can employ to give access to movements to elites in the political and financial sectors. In addition, continues Njoroge, it is not that what celebrity campaigners have to say is particularly new – global civil society groups have been making the same arguments for years. However, celebrities, have the visibility and media access to put their points across, extending the contours of the debate on global problems in the global arena. Celebrities may not alter perspectives but they muddy the waters. As her chapter on Bono and the Poverty Campaign indicate, while the preponderance of the British media's neo-liberal discourse centred on African 'failure' to create modern economic and political institutions, there was acknowledgement of systemic structural issues affecting Africa's development. Thus, views that have been peripheral moved a little closer to the centre even as they encountered resistance.

3. Develop new models of *visionary leadership*, especially, as Huddart (2005) argues, through the 'non-confrontational' reordering of political and economic forces in the service of global goals. An excellent example in this direction is provided with Bob Geldof and Live Aid, as it not only illustrates the ability of the popular pop artist to initiate global action through the juxtaposition of structures and processes from the music industry to the aid context, but also the skilful linking of the affect generated by popular music with that generated by famine imagery to trigger philanthropic activity among consumers of popular music (Westley 1991). Indicative in this direction is also the launching of Product Red in 2006, a brand licensed to partner companies such as American Express, Apple, Starbucks, Converse, Motorola, Gap, Emporio Armani, Hallmark, Microsoft and Dell. It is an initiative that was begun by the U2 front man Bono and Bobby Shriver of DATA to raise money for the Global Fund to fight AIDS, Tuberculosis and Malaria. Each partner company creates a product with the Product Red logo. In return for the opportunity to increase its own revenue through the Product Red products it sells, a percentage of the profit is given to the Global Fund (Richey and Ponte 2008).

It is clear, therefore, that celebrity activists can achieve imaginative coalition building and exercise significant *discursive power* by setting global issues and problems on the agenda, influencing the terms of discussion, crystallizing possible alternatives and stimulating a global debate. In so doing, however, they find it extremely difficult to exert influence and impact upon the final decisions (decisional power). As Mark Wheeler notes in Chapter 2, celebrities may be critical of many regimes and the role of the United Nations itself. This, as he argues,

> may, in part, be reflective of a certain naivety in understanding the processes of political diplomacy. Further, it may be seen to indicate how a gulf exists between celebrity and political expectations in which popular political 'narratives' uncomfortably clash with the realist policies which have defined international power.

In Chapter 7, Evanthis Hatzivassileiou and Georgios Kazamias also point out that celebrities may be successful in dealing with humanitarian crises, but not with highly contested political issues and protracted conflicts. Regardless of their commitment to a cause, celebrities do not seem to accurately understand the aims of the actors that they want to bring closer in resolving a conflict. It is also difficult for them to be 'integrated' in a consistent foreign policy, as not only do they have to encounter the mistrust of the professionals, but also the inflamed public opinions when proposing conflict resolution initiatives. Celebrity activism, then,

> has become more pragmatic recently in the sense that it avoids getting involved in controversial issues and it demonstrates greater restraint in its demands and manifestations. More importantly, celebrities have learned that they have greater political leverage when they enter into coalitions and develop activities within larger networks. (Houliaras and Tzifakis, Chapter 1)

All this has led to criticisms that while celebrity power may bring public attention to global issues, it is limited in affecting real change (Hoijer 2004; Jamieson 2005). This reality becomes all the more important when considering the dependency of celebrity activists with contemporary commercialized media logic (Cottle and Nolan 2007; Popkin 2006; Franks 2004; Clifford 2002). In particular, analysts have talked of '*charitainment*', doubting the 'authority' given to celebrity activists who have little, if any, training, experience or study in grave humanitarian and development problems (Hume 2006a). In Chapter 8, Varihi Scott talks about *philanthrocapitalism*, stressing that concerts and telethons use large amounts of celebrity-star power to limited effect. This, it is argued, is not necessitated by the medium but by the choice of the organisers, as the methods that are used prevent people in need of help from communicating directly with those who are keen to help.[4]

Riina Yrjola points out in Chapter 9 that the

> discourses on Bono and Geldof not only shed light on the different ways in which political agency is distributed and allowed among different subjects, but also are informative of a broader construction of North-South world relations [...] As the ideals of cosmopolitan humanitarian individuals – altruistic, self-sacrificing, apolitical world-citizens – they are described to be on a historical 'crusade' and 'mission' to promote equality and

empathy for African [...] These discourses not only frame humanitarianism specifically as a western activity, but also through them Africa emerges as an unwordly continent void of intelligence, will or capability to take care of itself [...] In Geldof's and Bono's humanitarian discourses, saving Africa through western humanitarian aid became an act of justice, fairness and intelligence [...] In these discourses, the West was articulated as an actor who did not have any economic, strategic or political interests in Africa [...] As a consequence, celebrity criticism turns, almost paradoxically, into a call for increasing western action in Africa. By repeating the old narratives from the western past in the African context – the heroic actions of the British and Americans ending WW2 and taking action against the Holocaust – Africa became framed as a specifically western destiny and calling [...]. As a result, these celebrity discourses rather end up repeating and maintaining western authority over Africa, than radically opening up new ways for Africa to be or become.

Nowhere to be seen or heard in these celebrated humanitarian stories are any accounts of African refugees who arrive at European shores alive, only to be taken into refugee camps before they are expedited back (Iweala 2007; Hume 2006b; O'Neil 2006a; O' Neil 2006b).

Discouraging is also the finding that celebrity activists might be more interested in constructing their own image than the causes they take up, and that activism is more a question of egoistic branding than an altruistic attempt of doing something good. As argued by Virgil Hawkins in Chapter 4, a major factor in celebrity choice of which conflict to take up is whether or not the conflict can be 'sold' to target audiences. The severity of the problem itself is, at best, a secondary concern. Media-savvy celebrities, argues Hawkins,

[...] are surely aware of what will sell and what won't, and may well choose to focus their attention accordingly. Both the media and its consumers (the general public) are more likely to be receptive to a simple and sensational plot in which there is an 'obvious' terrible injustice to be countered. Such a situation makes advocacy work much more effective: the plot is easier to understand, the message easier to deliver, and a reaction easier to generate. Furthermore, celebrities do not usually attempt to pluck conflicts from obscurity and bring them to the fore. Most conflicts that celebrities choose to target are those already on the media and public agendas – in fact it is often because of media coverage that they learn about the conflicts they choose to focus on. They essentially take up a cause that is already known and established, attempting to give a boost to existing attention and outrage.

In fact, as Michael, Cynthia and Rachel Stohl have shown in Chapter 11, although Nicholas Cage may publicly state that he wants deeper involvement with the arms control issue, in reality, either because he is not that interested or he is too busy with other work and interests, he only gets involved intermittently. As they argue, while Amnesty International reports that Cage expressed a sincere interest in going on an Amnesty mission to Africa to support the Control Arms campaign or the child soldier issue on two occasions, they were unable to schedule the mission. Cage also expressed interest in maintaining involvement. Cage indicated that he wanted to do more [...] before moving on to his next film. However, while several attempts were made to keep Cage involved with Amnesty International work, for example by inviting him to go on a AI mission to Africa, doing media work on a launch of a report that Cage himself funded, or engaging in face to face lobbying with U.S. congressional staff, Cage's professional filming commitments appear to have prevented any further public involvement with the organization. Thus, although Amnesty International worked with Cage and Cage's agent, as well as distributor Lion's Gate, to help AI with promotional work, nothing further developed.

One problem with this reality, argues Hawkins, is that the attention generated generally ends up being focused on the celebrity him/herself, with the issue to which the celebrity is trying to draw attention, remaining in the background. Celebrity concerts or films, then, provide a 'frame' for news stories that keep the celebrity activist in the spotlight, Michael, Cynthia and Rachel Stohl continue. In fact, when arms dealer Viktor Bout was arrested in Thailand, the arrest was framed by many news agencies in terms of the film character in *Lord of War* and references to Nicolas Cage having portrayed the arms dealer. Although the film continues to appear in government and international organizations documents as a reference point for the issue of arms sales, ironically little media attention has been given to Bout's successful attempts to avoid extradition to the United States to face arms trafficking charges.

Celebrity activists, therefore, often end up acting in contradictory ways as they try to influence the media agenda (Lester 2006). Raising and setting global issues and problems on the agenda is not the same thing as solving them. In fact, celebrity action can become part of the problem, not of the solution. As noted above, they cultivate negative stereotypes of people in need. In addition, and as shown by Hawkins' chapter, celebrity activists, while being aware of their contribution to a brief rise in media coverage in select circumstances, they are also aware they will not have a detectable impact on long-term coverage or general public awareness.[5]

Given the private ownership/monopoly of mainstream media, but also the infotainment conventions that filter what counts as information and news, the media are often too passive and weak to establish the contours of alternative debate and controversy. In addition, the news routine and a reporting system of assigning reporters to governmental institutions, the national parliaments and the international institutions, encourage journalists to be overtly dependent on official sources and thus manage the debate about global problems on terms that often favour the elites over celebrity activists. As a result, the predominant news framing is usually negative. Thus, despite the growing 'sympathy' for celebrity activists, the media is very far from articulating a position that will set the foundation for more equitable structures of global governance, and more democratic and popular policies on the resolution of global problems (Bennett et al. 2004).

In fact, one could argue, as Hawkins did back in 2002, that the focus on the direct influence the media may have on their audiences and on governments *obscures* a far greater impact media coverage has on conflicts and global problems. This impact stems from the fact that there exists a major *imbalance* in the media coverage of conflicts in the world today. Media coverage of the pre- and post-violent phases of conflicts is negligible, and despite the proliferation of news and current affairs on global television channels, most conflicts in the world suffer from an almost complete 'media blackout'. In order to delineate these from other crises receiving a higher share of coverage, they are often characterized as 'forgotten'. This not only signifies a pronounced inequality and irregularity in media attention and public awareness, but also that crises are severely ignored, neglected and suppressed.

This is best exemplified in the coverage of the African continent. Indicative are the results of Hawkin's (2002) comprehensive study on Western media sources ('CNN World News', 'BBC World News', *Yomiuri, New York Times, Le Monde*). Undertaken in 2000, the study found that the least covered continent was Africa, making up between just 1.9 per cent and 9.3 per cent of the total coverage. In addition, all media sources that were studied devoted a disproportionately large amount of coverage to a single conflict with a relatively low level of death and humanitarian suffering. Conflicts with massive death tolls, refugee numbers and related humanitarian problems were ignored. Conflict in Africa, for example, which has been, in the post Cold War period, responsible for up to 90 per cent of the world's total dead, suffered from almost complete media neglect. Coverage of the massive war in Congo, which caused over one million deaths in 2000, was almost insignificant, at best being covered as the eighth most covered conflict (*New York Times*). Other major conflicts, including those in Angola and Sudan, were completely ignored by the media. Neither of these conflicts was able to enter the top fifteen most covered conflicts in any of these media sources. The conflict in Africa that received the most coverage was Sierra Leone, which still failed to reach a level higher than the fifth most covered conflict ('BBC').

Bearing the above in mind, one could argue (Marks and Fisher 2002) that the media, by inspiring the masses to take up popular causes, deploy celebrities as chief vehicles for the simulation of political consent and the buttressing of the existing political order.[6] Essential to this strategy is a 'politics of distraction' (Weiskel 2005) and the making of the world's conflicts and global problems less relevant politically. This becomes all the more important when considering, as Couldry and Markham (2007) do, that those who follow celebrity culture are the least engaged in politics and less likely to involve themselves in discussion or action on global problems. In fact, as Baum (2002, 2005) and Franks (2006) have shown and rightly argued, due to selective coverage by the entertainment-oriented 'soft news' media, many individuals are exposed to information and images about conflicts and humanitarian disasters, as an incidental by-product of seeking entertainment.

Thus, and drawing upon the work of Boltanski (1999), we would argue that we live in a culture that is dominated by a *politics of pity* rather than the *politics of justice*. In line with this thought, celebrity activists, it could be stressed, expose distant problems and play a basic role in giving publicity to human suffering, in fostering a collective humanitarian global compassion and challenging audiences to include strangers in their moral conscience. But their approach is full of ambiguities and dangers. The connection between 'us' – *the fortunate* and the 'victims' – *the sufferers*, occurs mainly through the visual images and narratives of celebrity activists. Images can be very good at connecting our emotions with the plight of others. However, although the identification may be *intense*, it is also *shallow*. The spectacle culture of celebrity activists makes it impossible to provide in-depth and extensive information. They make audiences feel for a particular victim, without, however, understanding why or how he/she has become a victim. Under the avalanche of live and visual images there is no time for analysing events, and pity is used as a discursive mode to mediate between celebrity and suffering. Audiences visualize rather than engage with the real political questions of cause, effect and social justice.

As a consequence, and as Holleufer rightly argues (1996: 611), the failure to provide any kind of interpretation or insight ends up making an appalling stereotype seem natural, that of humanity divided into two groups treated unequally by fate: on the one hand all those who are suffering, and on the other hand, all those who are not. The 'more fortunate among us derive a sense of security from being shown an evil that only effects others, and to which humanitarian assistance, which soothes our conscience, is the providential solution'. Thus, even though the fortunate can become aware of the suffering of the unfortunate (Tester 2004: 191), awareness is not due to the political power of the unfortunate; rather it is entirely connected to the ability of the international news producers and the work of celebrity activists. Whereas in politics distance can be overcome through mobilization and platforms, with celebrity activists it is overcome through mediation. Consequently, the possibility of a sense of obligation on the part of the fortunate non-sufferers towards the unfortunate sufferers is entirely contingent and intensely mediated.

It is, therefore, of no surprise that we have yet to see an initiative of celebrity activism that embraces a participatory approach and lets the people who are supposed to benefit from development, humanitarian and conflict resolution actions set their own priorities and define their own understanding of development. In fact, and as Graham Finlay reminds us in Chapter 10, the majority of celebrity activism is individually controlled, unaccountable for and strongly identified with one celebrity's personality and brand. However, as he argues, we

can imagine an approach to celebrity activism that embraces participatory development and lets the people who are supposed to benefit from development and humanitarian actions set their own priorities and define their own understanding of development [...] Celebrities are effective because of whatever aspect of their lives resonates with a wide public. Often this depends on the force of their personalities and the strength of their convictions, forcefully expressed. Nevertheless, if those convictions include a strong commitment to democracy and to seeing poor people as people, as agents capable of deciding how to live their own lives, then the power of celebrity can be effectively harnessed to more complex development projects. After all, the international media will pay as much attention to Madonna sitting down in dialogue with the beneficiaries of Raising Malawi as it will to her writing cheques for orphans' education or for her adoption of individual African children [...] Celebrity activism is increasingly important to the global dialogue about issues of humanitarian assistance, development and human rights. More and more, the work of prominent people like Madonna on such causes shapes ordinary people's understanding of their own relationship to the global poor [...] This is a responsibility that many celebrity activists acknowledge [...] This responsibility is not simply to do something, but to do it in the right way, in a way that respects legal and democratic processes, and the agency of the people you are trying to help.

According to Boltanski (1999: 191), celebrity activists need to show 'people not only in the passivity of their suffering, but also in the action they take to escape and confront it'. Knowledge about people in conflict, crisis and poverty must be produced with the input of those people (Magubane 2007; Van Home 2008). They need to be both at the centre of production of knowledge and culture. There is need, says Varihi Scott in Chapter 15, of developing alternative communication celebrity-led initiatives that challenge and change existing systems of representation, identity and culture. Change, it is argued,

happens when we allow ourselves to hear and get to know new people and new points of view. World-class entertainers know how to get our attention and how to tell a story. They can harness those skills to help people silenced by extreme poverty, injustice, or made invisible in a globalized world, speak for themselves. There are numerous ways of giving the silenced a means of getting the rest of us to hear and understand them, and doing so is an essential part of what we regard as progress.

In addition, contends Roy Crovel in Chapter 6, we need to have a broader understanding of what constitutes a celebrity. Hollywood and pop stars are definitely celebrities, but many of the effects of celebrity activism can also be observed in activism by other and less famous individuals. Novelists, artists and academics can act as celebrities reaching and mobilizing support and action in groups with significant cultural capital in their respective audiences. Working together, several such celebrities could potentially have a significant influence over political events. As illustrated by Crovel, this type of activism was effective in reducing the general level of violence and abuse of human rights in Chiapas. The list of celebrities engaged in Chiapas, he argues,

makes a few points clear: First, the typical celebrity engaged in Chiapas was not the typical Hollywood-celebrity. While internationally famous, they appealed first and foremost to a specific audience, not the general public. The activities of these celebrities must be understood and analyzed in close connection with the networks of global activists. Second, these celebrities did not have to worry about their image or reputation. For most of them solidarity with the indigenous population of Mexico was not very different from other political activities they had been engaged in. Saramago and Garcia Marquez, for instance, both had long histories of involvement with political and social movements, often taking sides on controversial issues. In contrast to Hollywood-activists, they did not have to worry about the next role or what the audience might think. Because of their long standing involvement with social issues, it is difficult to accuse them of embracing the cause in order to 'remain celebrities' or of self serving image building. These celebrities have more in common with 1960s celebrities who embraced controversial issues like the fight against the Vietnam War and the struggle for equal rights in the US. Their engagement in Chiapas seems to be rooted in conviction rather than in public relations [...] Third, their activism was something more than just supporting the Zapatistas. In fact, many of these activists have criticised the Zapatistas and would feel uncomfortable with being grouped together under the umbrella 'solidarity activists'. While many of their articles could fairly be described as supporting the general goals of the Zapatistas, these celebrity authors are clearly out to be active participants in a global dialogue, presenting their own analysis and points of views, even when these are divergent from the views of the Zapatistas.

Global problems defy the degree of simplification demanded by commercialized media discourses and celebrity activities. Therefore, and following Sue Tait in Chapter 8,

publics must be interpellated in ways that transform a cause, which is subject to both fashion and commodification, into meaningful and constructive action. The formation of witnessing publics requires facilitating a sense of empowerment to act towards the prevention of atrocity, which requires being able to imagine how history can be prevented from reoccurring. It requires being able to imagine collective response as a possibility, and as a possibility that will change the conditions that have produced suffering.

The 'bystanders', the audiences of western societies, as Michael Stohl pointed out in 1987, not only have (1) to notice that something is happening, but also have (2) to interpret global events, (3) to decide they have a responsibility, (4) to decide what form of action to take and (5) to decide how to implement that action. Thus, if public attention is instrumental in bringing change in global politics, then celebrity activists are not doing their job properly. It is very difficult for 'bystanders' to move through these five steps. While celebrity activism has the potential to create awareness, raise much-needed funds and drive 'political action', this potential is at the same time firmly wedded into and limited by the contemporary politics of entertainment and media consumption. Publics have difficulty in moving from the role of the uninformed and uninvolved citizens, to 'aware bystanders'. This must be healed by redressing the balance between the current priorities of a spectacle culture and a competitive driven media market, and the need to properly inform and engage publics.

References

Alleyne, M. (2005), '"The United Nations" Celebrity Diplomacy', *SAIS Review*, 25:1, pp. 175–185.

Andersson, J. (2007), *Pop Culture Icons as Agents of Change? The Roles and Functions of Celebrity Activists in Peace and Development Related Global Issues*, Växjö Universitet, School of Social Sciences, Peace and Development Studies, Växjö, Sweden.

Archibugi, Daniel (2008), *The Global Commonwealth of Citizens: Towards Cosmopolitan Democracy*, Princeton: Princeton University Press.

Babcock, W. and Whitehouse, V. (2005), 'Celebrity as a Postmodern phenomenon, Ethical Crisis for Democracy and Media Nightmare', *Journal of Mass Media Ethics*, 20:2 and 3, pp. 176–191.

Barratt, B. (2005), 'Speaking with a louder voice: International human rights and Celebrity Activism', *Paper Presented at the Annual Meeting of the International Studies Association*, March 2005.

Baum, Matthew (2002), 'Sex, lies and war: how soft news brings foreign policy to the inattentive public', *American Political Science Review*, 96:1, pp. 91–109.

—— (2005), 'Soft News and Foreign Policy: How expanding the audience changes the policies', *Japanese Journal of Political Science*, 8:1, pp. 115–145.

Beck, Ulrich (2006), *Power in the Global Age*, Cambridge: Polity Press.

Bennett, L. et al. (2004), 'Managing the Public Sphere: Journalistic Construction of the Great Globalization Debate', *Journal of Communication*, 54:3, pp. 437–455.

Bjorn, H. and Oden, B. (eds) (2002), *Global Governance in the 21st century: Alternative Perspectives on World Order*, Almkvist & Wiksell International, Gothenburg.

Beardsworth, Richard (2008), 'Cosmopolitanism and Realism: Towards a theoretical convergence?', *Millennium: Journal of International Studies*, 37:1, pp. 69–96.

Boltanski, L. (1999), *Distant Suffering: Morality, Media and Politics*, Cambridge: Cambridge University Press.

Brown, W., Basil, M. and Bocarnea, M. (2003), 'Social Influence of an international celebrity: responses to the death of Princess Diana', *Journal of Communication*, 53:4, pp. 587–605.

Busby, W. J. (2007), 'Bono made Jesse Helms cry: Jubilee 2000, Debt Relief and moral action in international politics', *International Studies Quarterly*, 51:2, pp. 247–267.

Castells, M. (2007), 'Communication, Power and Counter-power in the Network Society', *International Journal of Communication*, 1:1, pp. 238–266.

—— (2008), 'The New Public Sphere: Global Civil Society, Communication Networks and Global Governance', *ANNALS, American Academy of Political and Social Science*, 616:1, pp. 78–93.

Clifford, B. (2002), 'Merchants of Morality', *Foreign Policy*, March–April, pp. 36–44.

Compton, J. and Comor, E. (2007), 'The Integrated News Spectacle, Live 8 and the Annihilation of Time', *Canadian Journal of Communication*, 32:1, pp. 29–53.

Cooper, A. (2007a), 'Celebrity Diplomacy and the G8: Bono and Bob as Legitimate International Actors', Canada, CIGI Working Paper No.29.

—— (2007b), 'Beyond Hollywood and the Boardroom: Celebrity Diplomacy', *Politics & Diplomacy*, 125, Summer/Fall 2007, pp. 125–132.

Cottle, S. and Nolan, D. (2007), 'Global humanitarianism and the changing aid media field: "everybody was dying for footage"', *Journalism Studies*, 8:6, pp. 862–880.

Cottle, S. and Rai, M. (2008), 'Global 24/7 news providers: Emissaries of global dominance or global public sphere?', *Global Media and Communication*, 4:2, pp. 157–181.

Couldry, N. and Markham, T. (2007), 'Celebrity Culture and Public Connection: Bridge or Chasm?', *International Journal for Cultural Studies*, 10:4, pp. 403–421.

De Waal, A. (2008), 'Humanitarian carnival: Celebrity vogue', *World Affairs Journal*, International Relations and Security Network, http://www.isn.ethz.ch. Accessed 13 July 2010.

Elliot, A. (1998), 'Celebrity and Political Psychology: Remembering Lennon', *Political Psychology*, 19:4, pp. 833–853.

Fain, S. (2008), 'Celebrities, Poverty and the Mediapolis: A Case Study of the ONE Campaign', *Paper Presented at the London School of Economics Media and Humanity Conference*, September 2008.

Ferris, K. (2007), 'The Sociology of Celebrity', *Social Compass*, 1:1, pp. 377–384.

Franks, S. (2004), 'The World on the Box: International Issues in News and Factual Programmes', *The Political Quarterly*, 75:4, pp. 423–428.

—— (2006), 'Lacking a Clear Narrative: Foreign Policy Reporting after the Cold War', *The Political Quarterly*, 76:1, pp. 91–101.

Fraser, B. and Brown, W. (2002), 'Media, Celebrities and Social Influence: Identification with Elvis Presley', *Mass Communication and Society*, 5:2, pp. 183–206.

Harris, R. G. (1993), 'Globalization: Trade and Income', *Canadian Journal of Economics*, 26:4, pp. 755–776.

Hawkins, V. (2002), 'The Other Side of the CNN Factor: the media and conflict', *Journalism Studies*, 3:2, pp. 225–240.

Held, David and McGrew, Antony (eds) (2007), *Globalization Theory: Approaches and Controversy*, Cambridge: Polity Press.

Hoijer, B. (2004), 'The discourse of global compassion: the audience and media reporting of human suffering', *Media, Culture and Society*, 26:4, pp. 513–531.

Holleufer, G. (1996), 'Images of Humanitarian Crises: Ethical Implications', *International Review of the Red Cross*, 315:36, pp. 609–613.

Huddart, S. (2005), '"Do we need another hero? Understanding celebrities" roles in advancing social causes', Canada: McGill University, McConnell Program for National Voluntary Sector Leaders.

Hume, M. (2006a), 'When celebrities rule the earth', published on spiked-online.com 24 October 2006, spiked-online.com/index.php/…/1978/. Accessed 17 June 2010.

—— (2006b), 'Why is Madonna treating Africa like a little orphan that needs adopting?', published on *Times*, timesonline.co.uk/…/article599854.ec. Accessed 13 October 2006.

Iweala, U. (2007), 'Stop trying to 'save' Africa', published on *the Washington Post*, washingtonpost.com/…/AR200707130/. Accessed 15 July 2007.

Jamieson, D. (2005), 'Duty to the distant: Aid, assistance and intervention in the developing world', *Journal of Ethics*, 9:1, pp. 150–170.

Kellner, D. (2010), 'Celebrity diplomacy, spectacle and Barack Obama', *Celebrity Studies*, 1:1, pp. 121–123.

Lester, L. (2006), 'Lost in the wilderness? Celebrity, Protest and the News', *Journalism Studies*, 7:6, pp. 907–921.

Linklater, A. (1998), *The Transformation of Political Community: Ethical Foundations of the post-Westphalian Era*, Cambridge: Polity Press.

Littler, J. (2008), 'I feel your pain: cosmopolitan charity and the public fashioning of the celebrity soul', *Social Semiotics*, 18:2, pp. 237–251.

Magubane, Z. (2007), 'Brand the beloved country: Africa in celebrity culture post 09/11', *CODESPRIA Bulletin*, Nos. 1 & 2, pp. 4–9.

Marks, M. and Fisher Z. (2002), 'The King's New Bodies: Simulating consent in the age of Celebrity', *New Political Science*, 24:3, pp. 371–394.

Meyer, D. (1995), 'The challenge of cultural elites: Celebrities and social movements', *Sociological Inquiry*, 65:2, pp. 181–206.

Nash, K. (2008), 'Global citizenship as show business: the cultural politics of Make Poverty History', *Media, Culture and Society*, 30:2, pp. 167–181.

O'Brien, S. and Szeman, I. (eds) (2003), 'Content Providers of the World Unite! The Cultural Politics of Globalization', McMaster University, Institute on Globalization and the Human Condition.

O'Neil, B. (2006a), 'The Hollywood Actor's Burden', published on spiked-online.com, spiked-online. com/index.php/site/.../54/. Accessed 4 May 2006.

—— (2006b), 'Brad, Angelina and the rise of "celebrity colonialism"', published on spiked-online.com, spiked-online.com/index.php/site/.../327/. Accessed 30 May 2006.

Pease, A. and Brewer, P. (2008), 'The Oprah Factor: The effects of celebrity endorsement in a Presidential primary campaign', *The International Journal of Press/Politics*, 13:4, pp. 386–400.

Popkin, S. (2006), 'Changing Media, Changing Politics', *Perspectives on Politics*, 4:2, pp. 327–341.

Rai, M. and Cottle, S. (2007), 'Global Mediations: On the changing ecology of satellite television news', *Global Media and Communication*, 3:1, pp. 51–78.

Richey, A. L. and Ponte, S. (2008), 'Better Red than Dead? Celebrities, consumption and international aid', *Third World Quarterly*, 29:4, pp. 711–729.

Sabbato, L., Stempel, M. and Lichter, R. (2000), *Peep Show: Media and Politics in an Age of Scandal*, Lanham: Rowman & Littlefield.

Stohl, M. (1987), 'Outside a Small Circle of Friends: States, Genoside, Mass Killing and the Role of Bystanders', *Journal of Peace Research*, 24:2, pp. 151–166.

Street, J. (2002), 'Bob, Bono and Tony B: the popular artist as politician', *Media Culture and Society*, 24:4, pp. 433–441.

—— (2004), 'Celebrity Politicians: Popular Culture and Political Representation', *BJPIR*, 6:4, pp. 435–452.

Tester, K. (2004), 'September 11, 2001: Sociological Reflections', in C. Paterson and A. Sreberny (eds), *International News in the twenty-first century*, Eastleigh: John Libbey Publishing.

Thrall, A. Tr. et al. (2008), 'Star Power: Celebrity Advocacy and the Evolution of the Public Sphere', *The International Journal of Press Politics*, 13:4, pp. 362–385.

Van Ham, P. (2010), *Social Power in International Relations*, London: Routledge.

Van Home, C. (2008), 'African Aid: Beyond Celebrity Platitudes', C2C E-Journal: Canada's Journal of Ideas, http://www.c2cjournal.ca/public/article/31. Accessed 15 September 2010.

Volkmer, I. (2003), 'The Global Network Society and the Global Public Sphere', *Development*, 46:1, pp. 9–16.

Waller, M. and Linklater, A. (eds) (2003), *Political Loyalty and the Nation State*, London: Routledge.

Weiskel, Timothy (2005), 'From sidekick to sideshow: Celebrity, entertainment and the politics of distraction', *American Behavioural Scientist*, 49:3, pp. 393–409.

Westley, Frances (1991), 'Bob Geldof and Live Aid: The Affective Side of Global Social Innovation', *Human Relations*, 44:10, pp. 1011–1036.

Notes

1. For similar distinctions, see Huddart (2005: 30–40) and Andersson (2007: 10–21).
2. New perspectives identified variously as 'global governance' (Bjorn and Oden 2002) and 'cosmopolitan democracy' (Archibugi 2008), point to the development of solutions outside the power-broking and conventional state-centric structures of the realist framework (Beardsworth 2008). Not only is the structure of the international system more complex than that suggested by the pattern of interactions between separate states, but global politics never took place among

closed political communities. States have always been *open social systems* with significant domestic and foreign inputs and outputs. This is all the more true today in our highly interconnected and interdependent world (Waller and Linklater 2003; Linklater 1998). Within such a political framework, the designation of policies and strategies cannot be based on myopic national interests and considerations, but should be collectively organized in order to cater for global solutions to global problems that affect the globe as a whole. The *logic of consequences* has dominated explanations in international politics quite justifiably. International actors seek to maximize their security, economic advantage, welfare and other fundamental goals, and in so doing, pursue controversial and conflictual politics. However, an increasing number of actions can no longer be understood under that prism. The fundamental changes that the international system has been undergoing necessitate an increasing adherence to norms, principles and moral values. The *logic of appropriateness*, thus, becomes a crucial prism through which to account for peaceful, negotiated solutions in progressively more parts of the world than in the recent past. The emphasis has turned from specific *inter-state conflicts* (although in a number of cases these remain highly contested issues) to *global public problems and goods*. For example, how are we to ensure that all citizens breathe clean air? How can we ensure that the world remains free from nuclear attacks? The need to secure such public goods forces international actors to follow global norms. The organization of global solutions, then, is not so much driven by the logic of consequences, but by that of appropriateness. People and individuals feel that action *should* be taken so that fundamental human rights are not endangered. That is not a naïve objective, but a logical attempt by which the narrow state-centric dialogue on global issues could be extended to include others whose concern was no less demanding of recognition.

3. For a similar argument, see Street (2004).
4. For a similar argument see Fain (2008).
5. For a similar argument see Thrall et al. (2008).
6. For a similar argument see Meyer (1995).

Notes on Contributors

Annika Bergman-Rosamond (Ph.D.) is Senior Researcher at the Danish Institute for International Studies in Copenhagen. Her research focuses on Nordic internationalism, international theory (with an emphasis upon cosmopolitanism), the English School and social constructivism. Her book, *Non-Great Powers in International Politics: The English School and Nordic Internationalism*, will be published by Routledge in 2011. Together with Mark Phythian she is the editor of the book *War, Ethics and Justice: New Perspectives on a Post-9/11 World*, to be published by Routledge in 2011.

Graham Finlay is a lecturer in political theory and human rights in the School of Politics and International Relations, University College Dublin. He has published a number of articles on the history of political thought, migration, development and development education. In 2006–2007, he was the weekly Los Angeles celebrity correspondent for *Moncrieff*, a nationally broadcast Irish radio show. This article was finished while he was the 2009–2010 Ginny and Robert Loughlin Founder's Circle Member in the School of Social Sciences at the Institute for Advanced Study, Princeton, and he is tremendously grateful to both the Loughlins and to the Institute for their very generous support.

Christos A. Frangonikolopoulos is Assistant Professor of International Relations at the School of Journalism and Mass Communications, Aristotle University of Thessaloniki. He also teaches at the Greek Open University. In the past, he has worked as a diplomatic newspaper correspondent (Ependitis, 1995–2003) and was an advisor to the Greek Parliament (1997–2003). In 2004–05 he also worked for ET3/ public television, and was responsible for the research and presentation of ten (10) hourly documentaries on Greek Civil Society. He was born in South Africa in 1965, studied Politics and Government (BA Honours) and International Relations (PhD) at the University of Kent at Canterbury (England). In Greece, he is the author of the book *The Global Role of Non-Governmental Organizations* (I. Sideris, 2007) and co-author of the following books: *Greek Media and Foreign Policy* (I. Sideris, 2011), *An Introduction to Cosmopolitan Democracy* (I. Sideris, 2010), *The Resolution of International Conflicts* (I. Sideris 1994). He is also editor of *Media and Society in Greece* (I. Sideris, 2005) and co-editor of: *Functions and Roles of Greek Foreign Policy* (I. Sideris 1994). His current research interests include Media and Foreign Policy in Greece, Public and Cultural Diplomacy, and Celebrity Diplomacy.

Evanthis Hatzivassiliou (b. 1966), received his B.A. from the University of Thessaloniki, and his M.A. and Ph.D. from the International History Department of the LSE (in 1989 and 1992, respectively). He is associate professor of contemporary history at the University of Athens. His main areas of research include the issue of Cyprus and Greek foreign policy in the twentieth century.

Virgil Hawkins is Assistant Professor at the Global Collaboration Center, Osaka University, Japan. His primary research interest is in the response to foreign conflict (particularly the lack thereof) by key actors in the world, including policy-makers, the media, the public and academia. He is also author of *Stealth Conflicts: How the World's Worst Violence is Ignored* (Ashgate 2008).

Henk Huijser is a researcher in the Public Memory Research Centre and a lecturer in the Learning and Teaching Support Unit at the University of Southern Queensland.

Asteris Huliaras is Professor of Comparative Politics in the Department of Political Science and International Relations at the University of Peloponnese. He specializes in African politics and development cooperation. His articles have been published in *African Affairs, European Foreign Affairs Review, Geopolitics, International Journal, Mediterranean Quarterly, The Journal of Balkan and Near Eastern Studies, The Journal of Contemporary African Studies, The Journal of Modern African Studies, The Journal of North African Studies, Orbis* and *Survival.*

Ana Jorge is a Communication Sciences PhD student in New University of Lisbon, with a research fellowship, has a masters in Sociology of Communication and has worked as a press agent. She has participated in projects concerning women's representation in the press and lifestyle magazines, and is currently working on the European network EU Kids Online and a Portuguese-American project on digital inclusion and integration.

George Kazamias, (b. 1964), received his B.A. from the University of Thessaloniki and his Ph.D. from the University of Bradford, UK. He is Associate Professor of European History in the Department of History and Archaeology, University of Cyprus. His research interests include the relations of Greece with Britain and the US in the twentieth century, post-independence history of Cyprus, oral history and the hellenic diaspora.

Roy Krøvel is Associate Professor of Journalism at Faculty of Journalism, Library and Information Science, Oslo University College, Norway. He holds a Ph.D. in history and is also a civil engineer. Books published include *Svart hvitt i farger*, Spartacus: Oslo 1997; *Ryggsekkjournalister og informasjonskrigere*, Spartacus: Oslo 1999; *En velsignet forbannelse,*

Tapir: Trondheim 2003; *Fra gerilja til globale solidaritetsnettverk i Chiapas, Mexico*, NTNU: Trondheim 2006.

Dorothy W. Njoroge recently completed her Ph. D in Mass Communication and Media Arts at Southern Illinois University Carbondale and is currently a visiting lecturer at Culver-Stockton College in Missouri. A native of Kenya, she previously taught at Daystar University in Kenya. She has also worked in a non-profit organization in East and Central Africa and is interested in the issues of social justice, human development and media discourse.

George Pleios, Ph.D. in Sociology of Culture and the Mass Media, is Associate Professor and Director of the Social Research in the Mass Media Lab at the Department of Communication and Mass Media, University of Athens. He has authored three books and edited another four. He is widely published in Greek and foreign reviews and collective books, and has been primary investigator in more than seventeen research projects. His research interests focus on the relationship between the mass media and society.

Varihi Scott is the founder of Good Ness Communications, an independent company that helps people apply communications for development approaches to marketing and communications areas of international development. In a fifteen-year career, she has worked in community-based organizations, large and small NGOs and on communications and corporate social responsibility in the private sector.

Cynthia Stohl is Professor of Communication at the University of California, Santa Barbara. The author of over 90 articles and an award winning book, *Organizational Communication: Connectedness in Action*, her work focuses on communication network structures and processes as they are manifest in collaborative activity. In both 2007 and 2008, Professor Stohl received the International Communication Association's Outstanding Article Award. Based upon research supported by the National Science Foundation, her book co-authored with Bruce Bimber and Andrew Flanagin, *Interacting and Engaging: Collective Action in Contemporary Organizations*, will soon be published by Cambridge University Press. At present Professor Stohl is co-investigator on a New Zealand Marsden Foundation grant studying new media and the global social justice movement in Aotearoa/New Zealand.

Michael Stohl is Professor in the Department of Communication at the University of California, Santa Barbara and the author, editor or coeditor of thirteen books and more than 100 scholarly articles and book chapters. His research and teaching focus on political and organizational communication and global relations with special reference to political violence, terrorism and human rights. He was a member of the Search for Common Ground sponsored United States-Soviet Union Task Force on International Terrorism, which met in Moscow and Santa Monica in January and September 1989. In 2005, he was an invited expert at the Club of Madrid International Summit on Democracy, Terrorism and Security.

In 2008, his article, co-authored with Cynthia Stohl, 'Networks of Terror', published in *Communication Theory* in May 2007 was awarded Outstanding Article of the Year by the International Communication Association.

Rachel Stohl is an associate fellow at Chatham House, London based in Washington, D.C. She has served as a consultant to the United Nations Group of Governmental Experts on the United Nations Conventional Arms Register and to the UN Group of Governmental Experts on the Arms Trade Treaty. Rachel was a senior analyst at the Center for Defense Information in Washington, D.C. from 1998 to 2009. She has also served as a Scoville Fellow at the British American Security Information Council in D.C., worked at the United Nations Center for Disarmament Affairs in New York and has also been a consultant for Oxfam America, Oxfam Great Britain and the Small Arms Survey. She is co-author of two books, *The International Arms Trade* (Polity Press 2009) and *The Beginners Guide to the Small Arms Trade* (Oneworld Publishing 2009) and has appeared in numerous documentaries, including *Making a Killing: Inside the International Arms Trade*, available on the DVD of the feature film *Lord of War*.

Sue Tait has most recently published articles about imagery of death in *The International Journal of Cultural Studies, Critical Studies in Media Communication*, and *Science and Culture*. She has written about the domestication of cosmetic surgery for Feminist media studies, and is currently researching the role of media in processes of bearing witness to suffering.

Jinna Tay is an Australian Research Council research fellow in the Centre for Critical and Cultural Studies at the University of Queensland whose most recent project is 'Television Studies after TV: Understanding television in the Post-Broadcast Era' (published by?), co-edited with Professor Graeme Turner.

Liza Tsaliki is a Lecturer at the Faculty of Communication and Mass Media at the National and Kapodistrian University of Athens. After having been awarded her Ph.D. on the role of Greek television on the construction of national identity from the University of Sussex, she taught at the University of Sunderland between 1996–2000; she then moved to the Radboud University of Nijmegen in the Netherlands to research the digital civil society across the European Union as a Marie Curie Post Doctoral Fellow (2000-2002). She is currently a Visiting Senior Fellow at the London School of Economics on the EU-funded project *EU Kids Online*, and the commentaries editor for the *International Journal of Media and Cultural Politics*. Current projects include co-editing three volumes on the culture of pornography (with Katherine Sarikakis).

Nikolaos Tzifakis is Lecturer of International Relations in the Department of Political Science and International Relations of the University of Peloponnese. He has taught as

Visiting Lecturer in the Department of Political Science of the University of Crete, the School of Humanities of the Hellenic Open University and the Department of Geography of the Harokopion University of Athens. He has research interests in contemporary developments in the Balkans, EU external policies and International Relations theory. His recent publications include, *Inter Alia*, articles in *Ethnopolitics, European Foreign Affairs Review, Global Society, International Journal, Journal of Political and Military Sociology, Journal of Southern Europe and the Balkans*, and *Perspectives*.

Mark Wheeler specializes in political communication, celebrity and political engagement; globalization and the mass/multi media; the politics and culture of Hollywood; the representation of political issues in US popular culture and European Television Policy. His numerous publications include *Politics and the Mass Media* (Oxford: Blackwells 1997); *European Television Industries* (co-authored with Jeanette Steemers and Petros Iosifidis, London: British Film Institute 2005); *Hollywood: Politics and Society*, (London: British Film Institute 2006).

Riina Yrjölä is a Ph.D. candidate in political science at University of Jyväskylä, Finland where she is currently completing her dissertation on the contemporary celebrity politicians' imaginaries on Africa. She has affiliations to two on-going Finnish Academy funded projects: 'Politics and Arts' (University of Jyväskylä) and 'Ethics, Politics and Emergencies – Humanitarian Frame for Co-option and Collaboration in World Politics' (University of Tampere). Her research interests include the aesthetics of celebrity humanitarianism, 'postcolonialism', critical humanitarianism and the global politics of humanity.